THE LOEB CLASSICAL LIBRARY

LIVY

VI

BOOKS XXIII—XXV

355

LIVY

WITH AN ENGLISH TRANSLATION

IN FOURTEEN VOLUMES

VI

BOOKS XXIII—XXV

TRANSLATED BY
FRANK GARDNER MOORE
PROFESSOR EMERITUS IN COLUMBIA UNIVERSITY

CAMBRIDGE, MASSACHUSETTS
HARVARD UNIVERSITY PRESS
LONDON
WILLIAM HEINEMANN LTD
MCMLXXXIV

American ISBN 0-674-99392-6
British ISBN 0 434 99355 7

First printed 1940
Reprinted 1952, 1958, 1966, 1984

Printed in Great Britain

CONTENTS

	PAGE
TRANSLATOR'S PREFACE	vii
THE MANUSCRIPTS	ix
BOOK XXIII	1
SUMMARY OF BOOK XXIII	171
BOOK XXIV	173
SUMMARY OF BOOK XXIV	337
BOOK XXV	339
SUMMARY OF BOOK XXV	503
APPENDIX: THE TOPOGRAPHY OF SYRACUSE	505
INDEX OF NAMES	511
MAPS AND PLANS—	
1. CENTRAL ITALY	*At end*
2. SOUTH ITALY AND SICILY	"
3. SYRACUSE	"
4. TARENTUM	"
5. SPAIN	"

TRANSLATOR'S PREFACE

This volume furnishes one span of a bridge ultimately to connect the Vth (1929) with the IXth (1935), that is, to link book XXII, the last of those translated by Professor Foster, with book XXXI, where the late Professor Sage began his work upon the Fourth Decade. In these three books (XXIII–XXV) are covered the years 216–212 B.C., including the consequences of disaster at Cannae, also Capua taken, Syracuse besieged for two years and finally captured, and the successes of Publius and Gnaeus Scipio in Spain, until they were separately overwhelmed by numbers.

For works dealing with this period of the Second Punic War the reader is referred to the *Cambridge Ancient History*, Vol. VIII, and the bibliographies for its chapters ii–iv, pp. 721 ff. Lists so recent and so generally accessible make it unnecessary to insert here a bibliography, to supplement those already contained in Vols. V (pp. xiii ff.) and IX (p. xv ff.). A recent work of Professor Fabricius, of Copenhagen, correcting current errors in the topography of Syracuse, is discussed in the Appendix.

The text here offered represents careful and oft-repeated consideration of its many problems. Obligations to a long line of previous editors, including Madvig, Weissenborn, H. J. Müller, Riemann, are gratefully acknowledged. In particular every student of Livy is now constantly aware of his great indebtedness to the labours of the late Professors Walters and

Conway, whose Oxford text edition reached a third volume in 1928 (books XXI–XXV). Every citation of the Puteanus made by them has been verified for the present volume by collation of the facsimile published by the Bibliothèque Nationale, with corrections in a very few instances.

Limited space for critical notes on so small a page obviously forbade the inclusion of the mass of interesting conjectures, often of recent date, especially many of the plausible *supplementa* suggested by Conway or Walters, where a short line (14–22 letters) may have been omitted in *P* or its archetype; also such emendations as Professor G. H. Hirst's *aries* for *acies* in XXIII. xvi. 12 (p. 54; *Classical Review* XXV, 109), or Professor E. H. Warmington's suggestion that in XXV. xxxvii. 11 (p. 480) *ad arma* may originally have been directly followed by *ad portas*, which in the MSS. and in our text follows the second *discurrunt*, suspiciously repeated and hence, he thinks, to be omitted (as also *ac*, which may have been inserted later before *velut*).

The translator is indebted to the publishers of the *Cambridge Ancient History* for permission to use three maps from Vol. VIII, with such alterations as were deemed necessary. The map of Syracuse is based upon a large Italian sheet (Catania, 1931), with important additions and radical changes due chiefly to the map of the Danish historian Fabricius mentioned above.

It may be added that this translation was begun, as it happened, at Syracuse, with the passages in XXIV and XXV dealing with the siege and capture of the city, and that such an opportunity was due to a second visit after an interval of forty years.

THE MANUSCRIPTS[1]

P = codex Puteanus, Paris, Bibliothèque Nationale 5730, 5th century.
C = Colbertinus, Paris, do. 5731, 10th century (or 9th).
R = Romanus, Vatican Library, 9th century.
M = Mediceus, Florence, Laurentian Library, 10th century.
B = Bambergensis, Bamberg, 10th century (or 11th).
D = Cantabrigiensis, Trinity College, Cambridge, 12th century.
A = Agennensis, British Museum, 13th century.
N = Laurentianus Notatus, Florence, 13th century (rarely cited).
F = Fragmenta Monacensia (two), Munich, 11th century.[2]
x = inferior MS. or MSS., 14th or 15th century (for P^x, A^x, etc., see below).
y = late correction in a MS. (*e.g.*, A^y).
z = early editor or commentator.

From *P* all the rest of the MSS. of XXI–XXV are directly or indirectly descended. In the critical notes corrections presumed to be by the original scribe are

[1] For details consult the Oxford text of Walters and Conway, vol. III, 1928. The best MS. of the Epitomes is the Nazarianus, Heidelberg, 9th century.

[2] A few chapters of XXIII only, beginning at xxxii. 11 and xlvii. 1.

marked P^1, by later hands, P^2, P^3, etc., corrections which cannot be so listed (mainly erasures), P^x; and so for the other MSS. Arabic numbers in parenthesis indicate three or more MSS., as follows:

(1) *CRMDA* (with *B* from XXIV. vii. 8, and so for each of the numbers below [1]).
(2) *CRMD* (3) *CRMA* (4) *CRM* (5) *CRDA*
(6) *CRD* (7) *CMDA* (8) *CMD* (9) *CMA*
(10) *RMDA* (11) *RMD* (12) *RMA* (13) *RDA*
(14) *MDA*

[1] Unless *B* is separately mentioned.

LIVY

FROM THE FOUNDING OF THE CITY

BOOK XXIII

I. After the battle of Cannae and the capture and plunder of the camps, Hannibal had moved at once out of Apulia into Samnium, being invited into the land of the Hirpini by Statius Trebius, who promised that he would turn over Compsa to him. Trebius was a Compsan of high rank among his people, but opposed by the party of the Mopsii, a family made powerful by the favour of the Romans. After the news of the battle of Cannae, and when the coming of Hannibal had been made known by utterances of Trebius, since the Mopsii had left the city, it was handed over to the Carthaginians without resistance and a garrison admitted. There Hannibal left all his booty and the baggage, divided his army, and ordered Mago either to take over such cities of that region as were deserting the Romans or to compel them to desert in case they refused. He himself made his way through the Campanian region to the Lower Sea,[1] intending to attack Neapolis, that he might have a seaport. On entering the territory of the B.C. 216

[1] *I.e.* the Tuscan Sea; cf. xxxviii. 1.

A.U.C. 538 intravit, Numidas partim in insidiis—et pleraeque
cavae sunt viae sinusque occulti—quacumque apte
poterat disposuit, alios prae se actam praedam ex
7 agris ostentantis obequitare portis iussit. In quos,
quia nec multi et incompositi videbantur, cum turma
equitum erupisset, ab cedentibus consulto tracta in
8 insidias circumventa est; nec evasisset quisquam,
ni mare propinquum et haud procul litore naves,
piscatoriae pleraeque, conspectae peritis nandi
9 dedissent effugium. Aliquot tamen eo proelio
nobiles iuvenes capti caesique, inter quos et Hegeas,
praefectus equitum, intemperantius cedentes secutus
10 cecidit. Ab urbe oppugnanda Poenum absterruere
conspecta moenia haudquaquam prompta oppugnanti.

II. Inde Capuam flectit iter luxuriantem longa
felicitate atque indulgentia fortunae, maxime tamen
inter corrupta omnia licentia plebis sine modo liber-
2 tatem exercentis. Senatum et sibi et plebi obnoxium
Pacuvius Calavius fecerat, nobilis idem ac popularis
3 homo, ceterum malis artibus nanctus opes. Is cum
eo forte anno quo res male gesta ad Trasumennum est
in summo magistratu esset, iam diu infestam senatui
plebem ratus per occasionem novandi res magnum
ausuram facinus ut, si in ea loca Hannibal cum victore exercitu venisset, trucidato senatu traderet

[1] He was called *medix tuticus*; cf. xxxv. 13. For the defeat of Flaminius at the Trasumennus cf. XXII. iv ff.

Neapolitans, he stationed some of the Numidians in ambush, wherever he conveniently could (and most of the roads are deep-cut and the turnings concealed). Other Numidians he ordered to ride up to the gates, making a display of the booty they were driving along before them from the farms. Against these men, because they seemed to be few in number and disorganized, a troop of cavalry made a sally, but being drawn into the ambush by the enemy's purposely retreating, it was overpowered. And not a man would have escaped if the proximity of the sea and the sight of vessels, chiefly of fishermen, not far from the shore had not given those who could swim a way of escape. However a number of young nobles were captured or slain in that battle, among them Hegeas, a cavalry commander, who fell as he rashly pursued the retreating. From besieging the city the Carthaginian was deterred by the sight of walls such as by no means invited an attacker. B.C. 216

II. Hannibal then directed his march to Capua, which was pampered by its long-continued prosperity and the favour of fortune, but, along with the general corruption, especially from the licence of the common people, who enjoyed an unlimited freedom. As for the senate, Pacuvius Calavius, a noble who was at the same time of the people's party, but had gained his influence by base arts, had made it subservient both to himself and to the common people. He, being in their highest office,[1] as is happened, in the year of the defeat at Lake Trasumennus, thought that the commons, long hostile to the senate, would use the opportunity of a revolution and dare to commit a great crime, namely, if Hannibal should come into the region with his victorious army, they would slay

A.U.C. 38

4 Capuam Poenis, inprobus homo sed non ad extremum
perditus, cum mallet incolumi quam eversa re
publica dominari, nullam autem incolumem esse
orbatam publico consilio crederet, rationem iniit
qua et senatum servaret et obnoxium sibi ac plebi
5 faceret. Vocato senatu cum sibi defectionis ab
Romanis consilium placiturum nullo modo, nisi
6 necessarium fuisset, praefatus esset, quippe qui
liberos ex Appii Claudii filia haberet filiamque
7 Romam nuptum M. Livio dedisset; ceterum maiorem
multo rem magisque timendam instare; non enim
per defectionem ad tollendum ex civitate senatum
plebem spectare, sed per caedem senatus vacuam
rem publicam tradere Hannibali ac Poenis velle;
8 eo se periculo posse liberare eos, si permittant sibi
et certaminum in re publica obliti credant,—cum
9 omnes victi metu permitterent, "Claudam" inquit
"in curia vos et, tamquam et ipse cogitati facinoris
particeps, adprobando consilia quibus nequiquam
adversarer, viam saluti vestrae inveniam. In hoc
10 fidem, quam voltis ipsi, accipite." Fide data
egressus claudi curiam iubet, praesidiumque in
vestibulo relinquit, ne quis adire curiam iniussu suo
neve inde egredi possit.

III. Tum vocato ad contionem populo "Quod saepe" inquit "optastis, Campani, ut supplicii sumendi vobis ex improbo ac detestabili senatu

the senators and hand over Capua to the Carthaginians. A bad man, but not utterly abandoned, he preferred to dominate a state still intact rather than one that had been wrecked, yet believed that none was intact if deprived of its deliberative body. He accordingly entered upon a scheme to save the senate and at the same time to make it submissive to himself and to the commons. Summoning the senate he began by saying that, unless it should prove necessary, a plan to revolt from the Romans would by no means have his approval, since he had children by a daughter of Appius Claudius and had given a daughter in marriage to Marcus Livius at Rome. But, he went on to say, something much more serious and more to be dreaded was impending; for the common people were not aiming to rid the state of the senate by a revolt, but by the massacre of the senate wished to hand over the republic, left helpless, to Hannibal and the Carthaginians. From that danger he could free them if they should leave it to him, and, forgetting civil conflicts, trust him. When, overcome by fear, they unanimously left matters to him, "I will shut you up," he said, "in the Senate House and, just as if I were myself a sharer in the crime intended, by approving plans which it would be vain for me to oppose, I will find a way to save you. For this accept a pledge, as you yourselves desire." Having given the pledge he went out, ordered the Senate House to be closed and left a guard before the entrance, that no one might be able to enter the Senate House or leave it without his order. B.C. 216

III. Then calling the people to an assembly he said: "You have often desired, Campanians, to have the power to exact punishment from a base and

A.U.C. 538

2 potestas esset, eam non per tumultum expugnantes domos singulorum, quas praesidiis clientium servorumque tuentur, cum summo vestro periculo, sed
3 tutam habetis ac liberam; clausos omnis in curia [1] accipite, solos, inermis. Nec quicquam raptim aut forte temere egeritis; de singulorum capite vobis ius sententiae dicendae faciam, ut quas quisque
4 meritus est poenas pendat; sed ante omnia ita vos irae indulgere oportet, ut potiorem ira salutem atque utilitatem vestram habeatis. Etenim hos, ut opinor, odistis senatores, non senatum omnino habere non
5 voltis; quippe aut rex, quod abominandum, aut, quod unum liberae civitatis consilium est, senatus habendus est. Itaque duae res simul agendae vobis sunt, ut et veterem senatum tollatis et novum
6 cooptetis. Citari singulos senatores iubebo de quorum capite vos consulam; quod de quoque censueritis fiet; sed prius in eius locum virum fortem ac strenuum novum senatorem cooptabitis
7 quam de noxio supplicium sumatur." Inde consedit et nominibus in urnam coniectis citari quod primum sorte nomen excidit ipsumque e curia produci iussit.
8 Ubi auditum est nomen, malum et inprobum pro se
9 quisque clamare et supplicio dignum. Tum Pacuvius "Video quae de hoc sententia sit; date igitur pro malo atque inprobo bonum senatorem et iustum."
10 Primo silentium erat inopia potioris subiciundi; deinde cum aliquis omissa verecundia quempiam

[1] curia *D? Madvig*: curiam *P*(3)*D*[2]*?*

odious senate. That power you have, not by riotously storming, with great danger to yourselves, the houses of individuals who defend them with garrisons of clients and slaves, but you have the power secure and unrestricted. As they are shut up there, every man of them, in the Senate House, seize them, left alone, unarmed! And do nothing in haste or at haphazard. I will give you the right to decide their fate in each separate case, so that each shall pay the penalty he has deserved. But above all things you should vent your wrath with due regard to the conviction that your safety and advantage are worth more than wrath. For it is these senators that you hate, I think; it is not your wish to have no senate at all. In fact you must either have a king—save the mark!—or else a senate, the only deliberative body in a free state. And so you have two things to do at the same time—to do away with the old senate, and to choose a new one. I will order the senators to be called one by one and will consult you as to their fate. Whatever is your opinion in each case shall be done, but before punishment is inflicted on the guilty one you will choose in his place a brave and active man as a new senator." He then sat down, and after the names had been placed in the urn, he ordered the first name drawn by lot to be called and the man himself to be led out of the Senate House. On hearing the name every man shouted his loudest, that he was a bad man and base and deserved punishment. Upon that Pacuvius said: "I see what your verdict is in this man's case; therefore in place of a bad man and base nominate a good and just senator." At first there was silence from their inability to suggest a better man. Then when someone, over- B.C. 216

A.U.C. 538 nominasset, multo maior extemplo clamor oriebatur,
11 cum alii negarent nosse, alii nunc probra nunc
humilitatem sordidamque inopiam et pudendae artis
12 aut quaestus genus obicerent. Hoc multo magis
in secundo ac tertio citato senatore est factum, ut
ipsius paenitere homines appareret, quem autem in
13 eius substituerent locum deesse, quia nec eosdem
nominari attinebat, nihil aliud quam ad audienda
probra nominatos, et multo humiliores obscurioresque
ceteri erant eis qui primi memoriae occurrerant.
14 Ita dilabi homines, notissimum quodque malum
maxime tolerabile dicentes esse iubentesque senatum ex custodia dimitti.

IV. Hoc modo Pacuvius cum obnoxium vitae beneficio senatum multo sibi magis quam plebi fecisset,
sine armis iam omnibus concedentibus dominabatur.
2 Hinc senatores omissa dignitatis libertatisque memoria plebem adulari;[1] salutare, benigne invitare,
3 apparatis accipere epulis, eas causas suscipere, ei
semper parti adesse, secundum eam litem iudices
dare quae magis popularis aptiorque in volgus
4 favori conciliando esset; iam vero nihil in senatu
agi[2] aliter quam si plebis ibi esset concilium. Prona
semper civitas in luxuriam non ingeniorum modo
vitio sed afluenti copia voluptatium et inlecebris
5 omnis amoenitatis maritimae terrestrisque, tum vero

[1] adulari *Salmasius* : advari *P* : adfari *P*²(1).
[2] agi *Madvig* : act *P*(4) : actum *C*ˣ*DA*.

---

[1] Capua, prospering by its varied industries established by the Etruscans, was already noted for its wealth and a luxury greater than that of Croton and Sybaris; Polybius VII. i. 1 and III. xci. 6; Cicero *Leg. Agr.* II. 95; cf. Strabo V. iv. 3.

coming his timidity, named a man, at once there was a much louder outcry, some saying they did not know him, others taunting him, now with shameful conduct, now with low rank and sordid poverty and the disreputable nature of his trade or business. All the more was this done in the case of the second and third senator called. So it was clear that people were dissatisfied with the man himself, but had no one to put in his place. For nothing was gained by once more naming the same men, who had been named only to be reviled. And the rest were much lower in rank and less known than those who first came to mind. Accordingly men slipped away, saying that the most familiar evil is the most endurable, and bidding Pacuvius release the senate from confinement. B.C. 216

IV. In this way Pacuvius, having made the senate much more subservient to himself than to the common people by saving their lives, ruled without arms, as all now gave way to him. Thereafter the senators, forgetting their rank and freedom, flattered the common people, greeted them, invited them graciously, entertained them at well appointed feasts; invariably undertook cases, appeared as counsel, or as jurors gave a verdict, only for that side which was the more popular and better suited to win favour with the populace. Moreover, nothing was done in the senate otherwise than if a meeting of the common people was being held there. The state had always been inclined to luxury,[1] not only from defects in character, but also from the abundant opportunity for indulgences and the beguilement of all the charms of sea and land. But at that time, thanks to the servility of the leading men and the

A.U.C. 538

ita obsequio principum et licentia plebei lascivire
6 ut nec libidini nec sumptibus modus esset. Ad
contemptum legum, magistratuum, senatus accessit
tum, post Cannensem cladem, ut, cuius aliqua verecundia erat, Romanum quoque spernerent imperium.
7 Id modo erat in mora ne extemplo deficerent, quod
conubium vetustum multas familias claras ac potentis
8 Romanis miscuerat, et [1] cum militarent aliquot [2] apud
Romanos, maximum vinculum erant trecenti equites,
nobilissimus quisque Campanorum, in praesidia Sicu-
larum urbium delecti ab Romanis ac missi. V. Horum
parentes cognatique aegre pervicerunt ut legati ad
consulem Romanum mitterentur.

Ii nondum Canusium profectum sed Venusiae cum
paucis ac semiermibus consulem invenerunt, quam
poterant [3] maxime miserabilem bonis sociis, superbis
atque infidelibus, ut erant Campani, spernendum.
2 Et auxit rerum suarum suique contemptum consul
3 nimis detegendo cladem nudandoque. Nam cum
legati aegre ferre senatum populumque Campanum
adversi quicquam evenisse Romanis nuntiassent
pollicerenturque omnia quae ad bellum opus essent,
4 "Morem magis" inquit "loquendi cum sociis ser-
vastis, Campani, iubentes quae opus essent ad bellum
imperare, quam convenienter ad praesentem for-
5 tunae nostrae statum locuti estis. Quid enim nobis

[1] et *Crévier* : et quod $P(2)A$ Conway[2].
[2] aliquot (aliquod) $P(2)A^2$: aliquando *Conway, placing* cum-*clause after* Campanorum.
[3] poterant $P(1)$: poterat *z*.

---

[1] As belonging to the most prominent families and dispersed among the cities of Sicily, they were in effect hostages.

licence of the common people, they were so unrestrained that no limit was set to passion or to expense. To their contempt for laws, the magistrates, the senate, there was now added, after the defeat at Cannae, their disparagement of the Roman power also, for which there used to be some respect. All that held them back from at once revolting was that the long-established right of intermarriage had united many distinguished and powerful families with the Romans, and that, although a considerable number were serving on the Roman side, the strongest bond was the three hundred horsemen, noblest of the Campanians, who had been chosen to garrison Sicilian cities by the Romans and sent thither.[1] V. Their parents and relatives with difficulty carried their point, that representatives should be sent to the Roman consul. B.C. 216

These men found the consul not yet departed for Canusium, but with a few half-armed men at Venusia,[2] exciting the utmost pity in good allies, but contempt in the haughty and faithless, such as were the Campanians. And the consul increased the contempt for his situation and for himself by needlessly uncovering and laying bare the disaster. For when the delegation had reported that the senate and the Campanian people were distressed that any reverse had befallen the Romans, and were promising everything that might be needed for the war, he said: "You, Campanians, have observed the customary manner of speaking to allies, in bidding me requisition whatever is needed for the war, rather than spoken conformably to the present state of our fortunes.

[2] Immediately after the battle of Cannae; XXII. xlix. 14; liv. 1 and 6.

A.U.C. 538

ad Cannas relictum est, ut, quasi[1] aliquid habeamus, id quod deest expleri ab sociis velimus? Pedites vobis imperemus, tamquam equites habeamus? Pecuniam deesse dicamus, tamquam ea tantum desit?
6 Nihil, ne quod suppleremus quidem, nobis reliquit fortuna. Legiones, equitatus, arma, signa, equi virique, pecunia, commeatus aut in acie aut binis postero die
7 amissis castris perierunt. Itaque non iuvetis nos in bello oportet, Campani, sed paene bellum pro nobis
8 suscipiatis. Veniat in mentem, ut trepidos quondam maiores vestros intra moenia compulsos, nec Samnitem modo hostem sed etiam Sidicinum paventis, receptos in fidem ad Saticulam defenderimus, coeptumque propter vos cum Samnitibus bellum per centum prope annos variante fortuna eventum
9 tulerimus. Adicite ad haec, quod foedus aequum deditis, quod leges vestras, quod ad extremum, id quod ante Cannensem certe cladem maximum fuit, civitatem nostram magnae parti vestrum dedimus
10 communicavimusque vobiscum. Itaque communem vos hanc cladem quae accepta est credere, Campani, oportet, communem patriam tuendam arbitrari esse.
11 Non cum Samnite aut Etrusco res est, ut quod a nobis ablatum sit in Italia tamen imperium maneat; Poenus hostis, ne Africae quidem indigena,[2] ab ultimis terrarum oris, freto Oceani Herculisque

[1] quasi A^y: quia $P(1)$.
[2] indigena $P(1)$: indigenam x Madvig.

---

[1] On the contrary, it was by aiding the Sidicinians against the Samnites that the Campanians became involved in the 1st Samnite War, 343 B.C.; VII. xxix.

For what has been left to us at Cannae, so that, as if B.C. 216
we had something, we may wish what is lacking to be made up by the allies? Are we to requisition infantry from you, as though we had cavalry? Are we to say that money is lacking, as if that alone were lacking? Nothing has fortune left us, even to supplement. Legions, cavalry, arms, standards, horses and men, money and supplies have vanished either in the battle or in the loss of two camps the next day. And so you, Campanians, have not to help us in war, but almost to undertake the war in our stead. Recall how, when your ancestors were once confined in alarm within their walls, dreading not only the Samnite enemy but also the Sidicinian,[1] we took them under our protection and defended them at Saticula. Also how with varying fortunes we endured for almost a hundred years[2] the war begun with the Samnites on your account. Add to this that upon your submission we gave you a fair treaty and your own laws, and finally—and before the disaster at Cannae this was certainly the greatest privilege—our citizenship to a large number of you and shared it with you. A share, then, Campanians, you should believe you have in this disaster which has befallen us, and should think that you must defend the country in which you have a share. Not with the Samnite or Etruscan is the struggle to have the power which has been wrested from us nevertheless remain in Italy. A Carthaginian enemy, not even of African origin, is dragging after him from the farthest limits of the world, from the strait of Ocean and the Pillars of Hercules, soldiers who

[2] Really seventy-one years. More rhetorical exaggeration in *propter vos*, and especially in the following sentence.

A.U.C. 538 columnis, expertem omnis iuris et condicionis et lin-
12 guae prope humanae militem trahit. Hunc natura et moribus inmitem ferumque insuper dux ipse efferavit pontibus ac molibus ex humanorum corporum strue faciendis et, quod proloqui etiam piget, vesci cor-
13 poribus humanis docendo. His infandis pastos epulis, quos contingere etiam nefas sit, videre atque habere dominos et ex Africa et a Carthagine iura petere et Italiam Numidarum ac Maurorum pati provinciam esse, cui non, genito modo in Italia,
14 detestabile sit? Pulchrum erit, Campani,[1] prolapsum clade Romanum imperium vestra fide, vestris viribus
15 retentum ac recuperatum esse. Triginta milia peditum, quattuor milia equitum arbitror ex Campania scribi posse; iam pecuniae adfatim est frumentique. Si parem fortunae vestrae fidem habetis, nec Hannibal se vicisse sentiet nec Romani victos esse."

VI. Ab[2] hac oratione consulis dimissis redeuntibusque domum legatis unus ex iis, Vibius Virrius, tempus venisse ait quo Campani non agrum solum ab Romanis quondam per iniuriam ademptum recupe-
2 rare, sed imperio etiam Italiae potiri possint; foedus enim cum Hannibale quibus velint legibus facturos; neque controversiam fore quin, cum ipse confecto bello Hannibal victor in Africam decedat exercitumque deportet, Italiae imperium Campanis relin-
3 quatur. Haec Virrio loquenti adsensi omnes ita

[1] Campani *z*: campanis *P*(1).
[2] ab *Gronovius*: *om.* *P*(1) *Conway*.

[1] So Polybius had said of Hannibal's polyglot troops, οἷς οὐ νόμος, οὐκ ἔθος, οὐ λόγος, κτλ., XI. xix. 4.

[2] Livy makes Varro repeat exaggerated statements about Hannibal; cf. Appian *Hann.* 28.

are unacquainted with any civilized laws and organization and, one may almost add, language too.[1] B.C. 216
Ruthless and barbarous by nature and custom, these men have been further barbarized by the general himself, in making bridges and embankments of piled up human bodies, and by teaching them—horrible even to relate—to feed upon the bodies of men.[2] To see and have as our masters men who fatten upon these unspeakable feasts, men whom it is a crime even to touch, and to get our law from Africa and Carthage, and to allow Italy to be a province of the Numidians and the Mauri—who, if merely born in Italy, would not find that abominable? It will be a glorious thing, Campanians, if the Roman power, brought low by disaster, shall have been maintained and restored by your loyalty and your resources. Thirty thousand foot-soldiers and four thousand horsemen can be enrolled from Campania, I believe. Moreover you have sufficient money and grain. If you have a loyalty to match your prosperity Hannibal will not be aware of his victory, nor the Romans of their defeat."

VI. After this speech of the consul the legates were dismissed, and on their way home Vibius Virrius, one of them, said the time had come when the Campanians could not only recover the territory formerly taken from them unjustly by the Romans, but could also gain authority over Italy. For they would make a treaty with Hannibal on their own terms. And there would be no doubt that, when Hannibal, upon the completion of the war, retired as victor to Africa and removed his army, authority over Italy would be left to the Campanians. Having agreed unanimously with these words of Virrius, they

A.U.C. 538 renuntiant legationem uti deletum omnibus videretur
4 nomen Romanum. Extemplo plebes ad defectionem ac pars maior senatus spectare; extracta tamen
5 auctoritatibus seniorum per paucos dies est res. Postremo vincit sententia plurium, ut iidem legati qui ad consulem Romanum ierant ad Hannibalem
6 mitterentur. Quo priusquam iretur certumque defectionis consilium esset, Romam legatos missos a Campanis in quibusdam annalibus invenio, postulantes ut alter consul Campanus fieret, si rem Ro-
7 manam adiuvari vellent; indignatione orta summoveri a curia iussos esse, missumque lictorem qui ex urbe educeret eos atque eo die manere extra finis
8 Romanos iuberet. Quia nimis compar Latinorum quondam postulatio erat, Coeliusque et alii id haud [1] sine causa praetermiserant [2] scriptores, ponere pro certo sum veritus.

VII. Legati ad Hannibalem venerunt pacemque cum eo his [3] condicionibus fecerunt, ne quis imperator magistratusve Poenorum ius ullum in civem Campanum haberet, neve civis Campanus invitus militaret
2 munusve faceret; ut suae leges, sui magistratus Capuae essent; ut trecentos ex Romanis captivis Poenus daret Campanis, quos ipsi elegissent, cum quibus equitum Campanorum, qui in Sicilia stipendia

[1] id haud *Aldus* : haud A^y : sit aut *P*(4) : ita ut $C^x DA$.
[2] praetermiserant *P*(1) : -miserint C^4; -missuri erant *Madvig*.
[3] his *z* : *om.* *P*(1).

---

[1] Not so to Calavius' son; viii. 3 and 11.
[2] Cicero mentions this demand of Capua; *Leg. Agr.* II. 95.

made such a report of their embassy that the Roman name seemed to all to have been blotted out.[1] At once the populace and most of the senate were aiming to revolt. But action was postponed for a few days by the weighty advice of the older men. Finally the view of the majority prevailed, that the same legates who had gone to the Roman consul should be sent to Hannibal. Before they went to him and before the plan to revolt was settled upon, I find in some of the annals that legates were sent to Rome by the Campanians with the demand that, if they wished them to aid the Roman state, one of the consuls should be a Campanian;[2] that resentment was aroused and the legates were ordered to be removed from the Senate House, and that a lictor was sent to lead them out of the city and bid them lodge that night outside of Roman territory. Because there was once a suspiciously similar demand made by the Latins,[3] and Coelius and other historians had not without reason omitted the matter, I have been afraid to set this down as established. B.C. 216

VII. The legates came to Hannibal and made an alliance with him on these terms: that no general or magistrate of the Carthaginians should have any authority over a Campanian citizen, and that no Campanian citizen should be a soldier or perform any service against his will; that Capua should have its own laws, its own magistrates; that the Carthaginian should give the Campanians three hundred of the Roman captives of their own choosing, with whom there should be an exchange of the Campanian

[3] That one of the consuls should be from Latium, 340 B.C., VIII. v. 5 and 7 (the threat of Manlius mentioned below, xxii. 7).

A.U.C. 538

3 facerent, permutatio fieret. Haec pacta; illa insuper quam quae pacta erant facinora Campani ediderunt: nam praefectos socium civisque Romanos alios, partim aliquo militiae munere occupatos, partim privatis negotiis inplicitos, plebs repente omnis conprehensos velut custodiae causa balneis includi iussit, ubi fervore atque aestu anima interclusa foedum in modum exspirarent.[1]

4 Ea ne fierent neu legatio mitteretur ad Poenum, summa ope Decius Magius, vir cui ad summam auctoritatem nihil praeter sanam civium mentem
5 defuit, restiterat. Ut vero praesidium mitti ab Hannibale audivit, Pyrrhi superbam dominationem miserabilemque Tarentinorum servitutem exempla referens, primo ne reciperetur praesidium palam
6 vociferatus est, deinde ut receptum aut eiceretur aut, si malum facinus quod a vetustissimis sociis consanguineisque defecissent forti ac memorabili facinore purgare vellent, ut interfecto Punico praesidio
7 restituerent Romanis se. Haec—nec enim occulta agebantur—cum relata Hannibali essent, primo misit qui vocarent Magium ad sese in castra; deinde, cum is ferociter negasset se iturum, nec enim Hannibali ius esse in civem Campanum, concitatus ira Poenus conprehendi hominem vinctumque adtrahi
8 ad sese iussit. Veritus deinde ne quid inter vim tumultus atque ex concitatione animorum inconsulti certaminis oreretur, ipse praemisso nuntio ad Marium Blossium, praetorem Campanum, postero

[1] ex(s)pirarent *P*(1): exspirarunt *Heusinger*.

horsemen who were serving in Sicily. Such were the terms. In addition to what was agreed upon the Campanians perpetrated these misdeeds: the populace suddenly seized prefects of the allies and other Roman citizens, some of them employed in a military duty, some engaged in private business, and with the pretence of guarding them ordered them all to be confined in the baths, that there they might die a terrible death, being suffocated by the extreme heat. B.C. 216

Such conduct and the sending of an embassy to the Carthaginian had been opposed to the utmost by Decius Magius, a man who lacked nothing for the attainment of the highest authority except sanity on the part of the citizens. But when he heard that a garrison was being sent by Hannibal, recalling the haughty rule of Pyrrhus and the wretched servitude of the Tarentines as warning examples, he at first openly protested that the garrison should not be admitted; then, after it had been admitted, either that it should be driven out, or, if they wished to atone for their evil action in having revolted from their oldest allies and men of the same blood by a brave and notable act, that they should slay the Punic garrison and return to their Roman allegiance. When this was reported to Hannibal (for it was not done in secret), he first sent men to summon Magius to him at the camp. Then when the latter replied with spirit that he would not go, for Hannibal had no authority over a Campanian citizen, the Carthaginian was enraged and ordered the man to be seized and brought before him in chains. Later, fearing that in the use of force some commotion, and in view of the excitement some unpremeditated conflict, might occur, he first sent word to Marius Blossius, the

A.U.C. 538 die se Capuae futurum, proficiscitur e castris cum
9 modico praesidio. Marius contione advocata edicit
ut frequentes cum coniugibus ac liberis obviam irent
Hannibali. Ab universis id non oboedienter modo
sed enixe, favore etiam volgi et studio visendi tot
iam victoriis clarum imperatorem, factum est.
10 Decius Magius nec obviam egressus est nec, quo
timorem aliquem ex conscientia significare posset,
privatim [1] se tenuit; in foro cum filio clientibusque
paucis otiose inambulavit trepidante tota civitate ad
11 excipiendum Poenum visendumque. Hannibal ingressus urbem senatum extemplo postulat, precanti-
busque inde primoribus Campanorum ne quid eo die
seriae rei gereret diemque ut [2] ipse adventu suo
12 festum laetus ac libens celebraret, quamquam
praeceps ingenio in iram erat, tamen, ne quid in
principio negaret, visenda urbe magnam partem diei
consumpsit.

VIII. Deversatus est apud Ninnios Celeres, Sthe-
nium Pacuviumque, inclitos nobilitate ac divitiis.
2 Eo Pacuvius Calavius, de quo ante dictum est, princeps factionis eius quae traxerat rem ad Poenos,
filium iuvenem adduxit abstractum a Deci Magi
3 latere, cum quo ferocissime pro Romana societate
adversus Punicum foedus steterat, nec eum aut
inclinata in partem alteram civitas aut patria maiestas
4 sententia depulerat. Huic tum pater iuveni Hanni-

[1] privatim $P(1)$: privato *Gronovius*.
[2] ut $P(1)$: et *Gruter*.

[1] Chapters ii–iv.

Campanian magistrate, that he would be in Capua the next day, and then he set out from the camp with a small escort. Marius, calling an assembly, ordered them to go out to meet Hannibal *en masse* with wives and children. This was done by all not only obediently but also eagerly, owing to the enthusiasm of the crowd as well and the desire to go and see a general already famous for so many victories. Decius Magius neither went out to meet him nor remained in seclusion, by doing which he might show some fear due to conscience. He strolled idly in the market-place with his son and a few clients, although the whole city was astir to welcome and to see the Carthaginian. Hannibal entered the city and at once demanded a session of the senate, and then when the leading Campanians begged him not to do any serious business that day, and that he should himself cheerfully and willingly honour the day gladdened by his coming, though he was naturally hot-tempered, still in order not to deny them anything at the start, he spent a large part of the day in seeing the city. B.C. 216

VIII. He lodged at the house of the Ninnii Celeres, the brothers Sthenius and Pacuvius, men distinguished for their rank and wealth. To that house Pacuvius Calavius, of whom mention has been made above,[1] leader of the party which had drawn the state to the side of the Carthaginians, came bringing his young son. He had got him away from the company of Decius Magius, with whom the son in the most confident spirit had stood up for the Roman alliance against a treaty with Carthage. And neither the decision of the state for the other side nor his father's high position had dislodged him from his opinion. Such was the young man to whom his father, rather

A.U.C. 538 balem deprecando magis quam purgando placavit,
victusque patris precibus lacrimisque etiam ad
5 cenam eum cum patre vocari iussit, cui convivio
neminem Campanum praeterquam hospites Vibel-
liumque Tauream, insignem bello virum, adhibiturus
6 erat. Epulari coeperunt de die, et convivium non
ex more Punico aut militari disciplina esse sed, ut
in civitate atque etiam domo diti ac [1] luxuriosa,[2]
7 omnibus voluptatium inlecebris instructum. Unus
nec dominorum invitatione nec ipsius interdum
Hannibalis Calavius filius perlici ad [3] vinum potuit,
ipse valetudinem excusans, patre animi quoque eius
8 haud mirabilem perturbationem causante. Solis
ferme occasu patrem Calavium ex convivio egressum
secutus filius, ubi in secretum—hortus erat posticis
9 aedium partibus—pervenerunt, " Consilium " inquit
" adfero, pater, quo non veniam solum peccati, quod
defecimus ad Hannibalem, impetraturi [4] ab Romanis,
sed in multo maiore dignitate et gratia simus Cam-
10 pani quam umquam fuimus futuri." [5] Cum mira-
bundus pater quidnam id esset consilii quaereret,
toga reiecta ab umero latus succinctum gladio nudat.
11 " Iam ego " inquit " sanguine Hannibalis sanciam
Romanum foedus. Te id prius scire volui, si forte
abesse, dum facinus patratur, malles."

IX. Quae ubi vidit audivitque senex, velut si iam
2 agendis quae audiebat interesset, amens metu "Per

[1] diti ac *Kreyssig* : divad *P*(1).

[2] luxuriosa *Gronovius* : variosa *P*(4).

[3] perlici ad *Heerwagen* : perhola *P* : perholla P^2(4).

[4] impetraturi A^y : impetravi *P* : impetrari P^2 ? (1) : impetremus A^y : impetrare possimus *x*.

[5] futuri *Madvig* : *om.* *P*(1).

by pleading than by excusing, reconciled Hannibal, B.C. 216
and he, prevailed upon by the father's prayers and tears, even ordered that the son should be invited with the father to a dinner at which he was to have the company of no Campanian except his hosts and Vibellius Taurea, a distinguished soldier. They began feasting by daylight, and the banquet was not according to Carthaginian custom or military regimen, but provided with all that tempts indulgence, as it was to be expected in a city, and a house as well, of wealth and luxury. Calavius the son was the only one who could not be prevailed upon to drink either by the invitation of the owners or even, now and then, of Hannibal. He himself pleaded ill health as an excuse, while his father alleged distress of mind also, at which one could not wonder. About sunset the son followed the elder Calavius coming out from the feast, and when they had reached a secluded spot—it was a garden in the rear of the house—he said: "I propose a plan, father, by which we may not only gain pardon from the Romans for our offence in having revolted to Hannibal, but as Campanians may be in a position of much greater respect and favour than we should ever have been otherwise." When the astonished father asked what that plan was, the son throwing his toga off his shoulder bared his side girt with a sword. "Presently," he said, "I will ratify a treaty with the Romans by the blood of Hannibal. I wished you to know that in advance, in case you should prefer not to be there when the deed is being done."

IX. When the old man saw and heard that, he was beside himself with fear, as if he were already present at the execution of the plan of which he was

A.U.C. 538 ego te" inquit, "fili, quaecumque iura liberos iungunt parentibus, precor quaesoque ne ante oculos patris
3 facere et pati omnia infanda velis. Paucae horae sunt intra quas iurantes per quidquid deorum est, dextrae dextras iungentes, fidem obstrinximus,—ut sacratas fide manus digressi a conloquio extemplo in
4 eum armaremus? Ab hospitali mensa surgis, ad quam tertius Campanorum adhibitus es ab Hannibale,—ut eam ipsam mensam cruentares hospitis sanguine? Hannibalem pater filio meo potui pla-
5 care, filium Hannibali non possum? Sed sit nihil sancti, non fides, non religio, non pietas; audeantur infanda, si non perniciem nobis cum scelere ferunt.
6 Unus adgressurus es Hannibalem? Quid illa turba tot liberorum servorumque? Quid in unum intenti omnium oculi? Quid tot dextrae? Torpescent in
7 amentia illa? Voltum ipsius Hannibalis, quem armati exercitus sustinere nequivere,[1] quem horret populus Romanus, tu sustinebis? Ut ab aliis[2]
8 auxilia desint, me ipsum ferire corpus meum opponentem pro corpore Hannibalis sustinebis? Atqui per meum pectus petendus ille tibi transfigendusque est. Sed hic te deterreri sine potius quam illic vinci; valeant preces apud te meae, sicut pro te
9 hodie valuerunt." Lacrimantem inde iuvenem cernens medium conplectitur atque osculo haerens non

[1] sustinere nequivere *Wölfflin* (nequeunt *Gronovius*): sustineren *P*: -em R^2M: -rent (6): -re M^2.

[2] ut ab aliis *Mayerhöfer*: italis *P*: talis P^1? (1): ut alia *Drakenborch*.

being told, and said: "I pray and implore you, my son, by all the rights which link children to their parents, not to do and suffer all that is unutterable before the eyes of your father. It is but a few hours since, with an oath by all the gods that exist and joining our right hands to his, we pledged our honour. Was it with the intention, as soon as we left the conference, to arm against him the hands hallowed by our plighted faith? From the hospitable board, to which you were invited by Hannibal with but two other Campanians, do you rise with the intention of staining that very board with the blood of a guest? Was I able as a father to reconcile Hannibal with my son, and can not reconcile my son with Hannibal? But assuming that there is nothing hallowed, no honour, no scruple, no filial devotion, dare to do unspeakable things, if they do not bring destruction to us as well as guilt. Single-handed will you attack Hannibal? What of that crowd, so many free men and slaves? What of all men's eyes fixed upon one man? What of so many sword-hands? Will they be paralysed in the moment of that mad deed? Will you withstand Hannibal's own countenance, which armed forces have been unable to withstand, which the Roman people dreads? Supposing that help from others is lacking, will you bring yourself to strike *me*, when I interpose my body in place of Hannibal's? And yet it is through my breast that you will have to attack him and run him through. But allow yourself to be dissuaded here, rather than overpowered there. Let my prayers prove effectual with you, as they have proved this day for you." Seeing the young man in tears he threw his arms about his waist, and repeatedly kissing him he did B.C. 216

A.U.C. 538 ante precibus abstitit quam pervicit ut gladium
10 poneret fidemque daret nihil facturum tale. Tum
iuvenis " Ego quidem " inquit " quam patriae debeo
pietatem exsolvam patri. Tuam doleo vicem, cui
11 ter proditae patriae sustinendum est crimen, semel
cum defectionem [1] inisti [2] ab Romanis, iterum cum
pacis cum Hannibale fuisti auctor, tertio hodie, cum
restituendae Romanis Capuae mora atque impedi-
12 mentum es. Tu, patria, ferrum, quo pro te armatus
hanc arcem hostium inii, quoniam parens extorquet,
13 recipe." Haec cum dixisset, gladium in publicum
trans maceriam horti abiecit et, quo minus res
suspecta esset, se ipse convivio reddidit.

X. Postero die senatus frequens datus Hannibali.
Ubi prima eius oratio perblanda ac benigna fuit, qua
gratias egit Campanis quod amicitiam suam Romanae
2 societati praeposuissent, et inter cetera magnifica
promissa pollicitus est [3] brevi caput Italiae omni
Capuam fore iuraque inde cum ceteris populis
3 Romanum etiam petiturum. Unum esse exsortem
Punicae amicitiae foederisque secum facti, quem
neque esse Campanum neque dici debere, Magium
Decium; eum postulare ut sibi dedatur ac se praesente de eo referatur senatusque consultum fiat.
4 Omnes in eam sententiam ierunt, quamquam magnae
parti et vir indignus ea calamitate et haud parvo initio

[1] defectionem D^x*Az*: defectione *P*(2)A^x: defectionis *x* *Gronovius*.

[2] inisti *z*: inissa *P*: missa P^2*?*: imissa *RM*: in(*or* im)missa *CM*[1] *? DA*.

[3] est *Weissenborn*: *om.* *P*(1).

not desist from entreaties until he had prevailed upon him to put down his sword and give his pledge that he would do no such crime. Then the young man said: "As for me, I will pay my father the debt of devotion which I owe to my country. For you I am sorry, for you will have to meet the charge of thrice betraying your country, once when you took part in the revolt from the Romans, a second time when you advised peace with Hannibal, a third time today when you are an obstacle and a hindrance to restoring Capua to the Romans. Do you, my country, take back the sword with which I had armed myself in your defence and entered this stronghold of the enemy; for my father wrests it from me." Having thus spoken, he threw the sword over the garden wall into a street, and, that his conduct might not be open to suspicion, himself returned to the banquet. B.C. 216

X. On the following day a full session of the senate was given to Hannibal. There his speech was at the outset very genial and kindly, thanking the Campanians for having preferred his friendship to a Roman alliance. And among his other magnificent assurances he promised them that Capua should soon be the capital of all Italy, and that from it the Roman people along with the rest of the nations should derive its law. He said that *one* man had no part in friendship with Carthage and the treaty made with himself, namely Magius Decius, a man who ought neither to be a Campanian nor to be so called; he demanded that the man be surrendered to him, and that in his own presence his case be brought up and a decree of the senate framed. All voted for that proposal, although it seemed to many of them that the man did not deserve that misfortune; also

A.U.C. 538
5 minui videbatur ius libertatis. Egressus curia in
templo magistratuum consedit conprehendique Decium Magium atque ante pedes destitutum causam
6 dicere iussit. Qui cum manente ferocia animi
negaret lege foederis id cogi posse, tum iniectae
catenae, ducique ante lictorem in castra est iussus.
7 Quoad capite aperto est ductus, contionabundus
incessit ad circumfusam undique multitudinem
vociferans: "Habetis libertatem, Campani, quam
petistis; foro medio, luce clara, videntibus vobis nulli
Campanorum secundus vinctus ad mortem rapior.
8 Quid violentius capta Capua fieret? Ite obviam
Hannibali, exornate urbem diemque adventus eius
consecrate, ut hunc triumphum de cive vestro spec-
tetis."

9 Haec vociferanti,[1] cum moveri volgus videretur,
obvolutum caput est, ociusque rapi extra portam
iussus. Ita in castra perducitur extemploque in-
10 positus in navem et Carthaginem missus, ne motu
aliquo Capuae ex indignitate rei orto senatum
quoque paeniteret dediti principis et, legatione missa
ad repetendum eum, aut negando rem quam primam
peterent offendendi sibi novi socii, aut tribuendo
habendus Capuae esset seditionis ac turbarum auctor.
11 Navem Cyrenas detulit tempestas, quae tum in
dicione regum erant. Ibi cum Magius ad statuam

[1] vociferanti *x* : -te *P*(1).

---

[1] *I.e.* of Egypt. Ptolemy IV Philopator was then reigning; XXIV. xxvi. 1.

that the right of liberty was being infringed by a first act that was not insignificant. Leaving the Senate House Hannibal took his seat on the tribune of the magistrates and ordered the arrest of Decius Magius, and that he be placed at his feet and make his defence. While with undaunted spirit Magius was saying that by the terms of the treaty he could not be compelled to do that, chains were put upon him and he was ordered to be led to the camp with a lictor following. So long as they led him with bare head, he kept haranguing as he went, shouting to the crowd all about him: "You have the freedom you wanted, Campanians. Through the middle of the market-place, in broad daylight, before your eyes, I, who am second to no one of the Campanians, am being hurried away in chains to my death. What deed of greater violence could be done if Capua had been taken? Go to meet Hannibal, decorate your city and make the day of his coming a holiday,—that you may witness this triumph over your fellow-citizen." B.C. 216

As he was thus shouting and the populace seemed to be aroused, his head was covered and they were ordered to drag him more swiftly outside the gate. Thus he was led into the camp, at once put on shipboard and consigned to Carthage, for fear, if there should be some outbreak at Capua in consequence of the shameful act, the senate also might regret having surrendered a leading man, and, when an embassy was sent to demand his return, Hannibal either must offend his new allies by refusing their first request, or by granting it be obliged to keep at Capua a fomenter of insurrection and riots. A storm carried the ship to Cyrenae, which was then subject to kings.[1] On fleeing for refuge to the statue of

A.U.C. 538 Ptolomaei regis confugisset, deportatus a custodibus
12 Alexandream ad Ptolomaeum, cum eum docuisset
contra ius foederis vinctum se ab Hannibale esse,
vinclis liberatur, permissumque ut rediret, seu Romam
13 seu Capuam mallet. Nec Magius Capuam sibi tutam
dicere et Romam eo tempore quo inter Romanos
Campanosque bellum sit transfugae magis quam
hospitis fore domicilium; nusquam malle quam in
regno eius vivere quem vindicem atque auctorem
habeat libertatis.

XI. Dum haec geruntur, Q. Fabius Pictor legatus
a Delphis Romam rediit responsumque ex scripto
recitavit. Divi divaeque in eo erant quibus
2 quoque modo supplicaretur; tum "Si ita faxitis,
Romani, vestrae res meliores facilioresque erunt,
magisque ex sententia res publica vestra vobis
procedet, victoriaque duelli populi Romani erit.
3 Pythio Apollini re publica vestra bene gesta servataque
e [1] lucris meritis donum mittitote deque praeda,
manubiis spoliisque honorem habetote; lasciviam a
4 vobis prohibetote." Haec ubi ex Graeco carmine
interpretata recitavit, tum dixit se oraculo egressum
extemplo iis omnibus divis rem divinam ture ac vino
5 fecisse; iussumque a templi antistite, sicut coronatus
laurea corona et oraculum adisset et rem divinam
fecisset, ita coronatum navem ascendere nec ante

[1] e *Crévier, Madvig*: de *Weissenborn*: *om. P*(1) *Walters.*

---

[1] He had been sent to Delphi after the battle of Cannae; XXII. lvii. 5. His history, written in Greek, was one of Livy's sources.

King Ptolemy there, Magius was carried under guard to Ptolemy at Alexandria. And having informed him that he had been bound by Hannibal contrary to his treaty rights, he was freed from his chains and allowed to return to Rome or to Capua, as he might prefer. Magius said that Capua was unsafe for him, and on the other hand, at a time when there was a war between the Romans and the Campanians, Rome would be the abode of a deserter rather than of a guest; that he had no wish to live elsewhere than in the land of a king in whom he found the giver and defender of his freedom. B.C. 216

XI. While these things were going on, Quintus Fabius Pictor[1] returned to Rome from his embassy to Delphi and read from a manuscript the response of the oracle. In it were indicated the gods and goddesses to whom offerings should be made, and in what manner. It continued: "If you do thus, Romans, your situation will be better and easier, and your state will go on more in accordance with your desire, and the Roman people will have the victory in the war. When you have successfully administered and preserved your state, from the gains made you shall send a gift to Pythian Apollo and do honour to him out of the booty, the profits and the spoils. You shall keep yourselves from exulting." After reading these words translated from the Greek verses, he went on to say that, on coming out of the oracle, he had at once made offerings to all those divinities with incense and wine; also that he had been bidden by the high-priest of the temple, just as he had come to the oracle and also conducted the rite while wearing a garland of laurel, so also to wear the garland when he boarded the ship, and not to lay

A.U.C. 538

6 deponere eam quam Romam pervenisset; se, quaecumque imperata sint, cum summa religione ac diligentia exsecutum coronam Romae in aram Apollinis deposuisse. Senatus decrevit ut eae res divinae supplicationesque primo quoque tempore cum cura fierent.

7 Dum haec Romae atque in Italia geruntur, nuntius victoriae ad Cannas Carthaginem venerat Mago Hamilcaris filiius, non ex ipsa acie a fratre missus sed retentus aliquot dies in recipiendis civitatibus
8 Bruttiorum, quae [1] deficiebant. Is, cum ei senatus datus esset, res gestas in Italia a fratre exponit: cum sex imperatoribus eum, quorum quattuor consules, duo dictator ac magister equitum fuerint, cum
9 sex consularibus exercitibus acie conflixisse; occidisse supra ducenta milia hostium, supra quinquaginta milia cepisse. Ex quattuor consulibus duos occidisse; ex duobus saucium alterum, alterum toto amisso exercitu vix cum quinquaginta hominibus
10 effugisse. Magistrum equitum, quae consularis potestas sit, fusum fugatum; dictatorem, quia se in aciem numquam commiserit, unicum haberi impera-
11 torem. Bruttios Apulosque, partem Samnitium ac Lucanorum defecisse ad Poenos. Capuam, quod

[1] quae A^2: quaeq. $P(1)$: Apulorum Lucanorumque quae *Conway* (*one line*).

---

[1] Livy possibly mentioned others besides the Bruttii. In i. 4 Mago is in Samnium for the same purpose.

[2] Five consuls had been defeated by Hannibal: Scipio (Ticinus), Sempronius (Trebia), Flaminius (Trasumennus) Paulus and Varro (Cannae). As Scipio was the wounded consul of § 9, it must be Sempronius who is here omitted. Yet elsewhere much is made of the battle of the Trebia (xviii. 7; xlv. 6). A copyist may have written *viimperatoribus* instead

it aside until he should reach Rome. Further, that he had carried out with the utmost scrupulosity and care all the instructions given him, and had then laid the wreath upon the altar of Apollo at Rome. The senate decreed that at the first opportunity those rites should be duly observed with prayers. B.C. 216

While these things were happening at Rome and in Italy, Mago, the son of Hamilcar, had come to Carthage to report the victory at Cannae. He had not been sent by his brother directly from the battle, but had been detained for some time in taking over the Bruttian states which were revolting.[1] Accorded a hearing in the senate, he set forth the achievements of his brother in Italy: that he had fought pitched battles with six high commanders, of whom four were consuls,[2] and two a dictator and a master of the horse,[3] in all with six consular armies; that he had slain over 200,000 of the enemy and captured over 50,000;[4] that of the four consuls he had slain two;[5] of the other two one had fled wounded,[6] the other with barely fifty men, after losing his entire army;[7] that the master of the horse, whose power is that of a consul, had been routed and put to flight; that the dictator was accounted an extraordinary general because he never ventured into battle-line; that the Bruttians and Apulians and some of the Samnites and Lucanians had revolted to the Carthaginians; that

of *viiimperatoribus*. That done, the change of *v* to *iv* (same line and § 9) would be an effort to make the figures tally.

[3] Fabius Maximus, the Cunctator, and Minucius Rufus. Both are included among the defeated generals in spite of what is said in regard to the dictator in § 10.

[4] Exaggerated figures in both cases.

[5] Flaminius and Aemilius Paulus.

[6] Scipio at the Ticinus. [7] Terentius Varro.

A.U.C. 538 caput non Campaniae modo sed post adflictam rem
Romanam Cannensi pugna Italiae sit, Hannibali se [1]
12 tradidisse. Pro his tantis totque victoriis verum
esse grates deis immortalibus agi haberique.

XII. Ad fidem deinde tam laetarum rerum effundi
in vestibulo curiae iussit anulos aureos, qui tantus
acervus fuit ut metientibus dimidium supra [2] tris
2 modios explesse sint quidam auctores; fama tenuit,
quae propior vero est, haud plus fuisse modio.
Adiecit deinde verbis, quo maioris cladis indicium
esset, neminem nisi equitem, atque eorum ipsorum
3 primores, id gerere insigne. Summa fuit orationis,
quo propius spem belli perficiendi sit, eo magis
omni ope iuvandum Hannibalem esse; procul enim
ab domo militiam esse, in media hostium terra;
4 magnam vim frumenti pecuniae absumi, et tot acies,
ut hostium exercitus delesse, ita victoris etiam copias
5 parte aliqua minuisse; mittendum igitur supplementum esse, mittendam in stipendium pecuniam
frumentumque tam bene meritis de nomine Punico
militibus.

6 Secundum haec dicta Magonis laetis omnibus
Himilco, vir factionis Barcinae, locum Hannonis incre-
pandi esse ratus, " Quid est, Hanno? " inquit, " etiam
nunc paenitet belli suscepti adversus Romanos?
7 Iube dedi Hannibalem; veta in tam prosperis rebus

[1] se M^4 (*after* sit *in* A^2) : *om.* P(1).

[2] supra *Madvig* (*rejecting* dimidium P(1)) : super PM^3(5).

Capua, which was the capital not only of Campania, B.C. 216
but, since the blow inflicted upon the Roman state by the battle of Cannae, of Italy also, had surrendered to Hannibal. For these victories, so many and so great, it was proper, he said, that gratitude be expressed and felt toward the immortal gods.

XII. Then in evidence of such successes he ordered the golden rings to be poured out at the entrance of the Senate House. And so great was the heap of them that, when measured, they filled, as some historians assert, three pecks and a half. The prevailing report, and nearer the truth, is that there was not more than one peck. Then, that it might be proof of a greater calamity, he added in explanation that no one but a knight, and even of the knights only those of the higher class, wore that token. The main point of his speech was that the nearer Hannibal came to realizing his hope of ending the war, the more necessary it was to help him by every means. For his campaigning was far from home, in the midst of the enemy's country. A large amount of grain and money was being consumed, he said, and though so many battles had destroyed the enemy's armies, still they had considerably diminished the forces of the victor as well. Therefore they must send reinforcements, they must send money to pay them and grain to soldiers who had deserved so well of the Carthaginian nation.

After these words of Mago, while all were rejoicing, Himilco, a man of the Barca party, thought it an opportunity to rebuke Hanno. "Tell me, Hanno," he said, "is it still to be regretted that we undertook a war against the Romans? Order the surrender of Hannibal! In the midst of such successes forbid the

A.U.C. 538 grates deis immortalibus agi; audiamus Romanum
8 senatorem in Carthaginiensium curia." Tum Hanno:
"Tacuissem hodie, patres conscripti, ne quid in
communi omnium gaudio minus laetum quod esset
9 vobis loquerer; nunc interroganti senatori paeniteatne [1] adhuc suscepti adversus Romanos belli, si
reticeam, aut superbus aut obnoxius videar, quorum
alterum est hominis alienae libertatis obliti, alterum
10 suae. Respondeam [2]" inquit "Himilconi, non desisse
paenitere me belli neque desiturum ante invictum
vestrum imperatorem incusare quam finitum aliqua tolerabili condicione bellum videro; nec mihi
pacis antiquae desiderium ulla alia res quam pax
11 nova finiet. Itaque ista quae modo Mago iactavit
Himilconi ceterisque Hannibalis satellitibus iam
laeta sunt: mihi possunt laeta esse, quia res bello
bene gestae, si volumus fortuna uti, pacem nobis
12 aequiorem dabunt; nam si praetermittimus hoc
tempus quo magis dare quam accipere possumus
videri pacem, vereor ne haec quoque laetitia luxuriet
13 nobis ac vana evadat. Quae tamen nunc quoque
qualis est? 'Occidi exercitus hostium; mittite
milites mihi.' Quid aliud rogares, si esses victus?
14 'Hostium cepi bina castra,' praedae videlicet plena
et commeatuum; 'frumentum et pecuniam date.'
Quid aliud, si spoliatus, si exutus castris esses,
15 peteres? Et ne omnia ipse mirer—mihi quoque

[1] paeniteatne *Alschefski*: paeniteat me *P*(1).
[2] respondeam P^2(5)M^1?: -ead *P*: -ebo *x*: -eo *Madvig* (*or* -ebo).

---

[1] As in the last years of the 1st Punic War.

rendering of thanks to the immortal gods! Let us B.C. 216 listen to a Roman senator in the Carthaginian Senate House." Thereupon Hanno said: "I should have remained silent to-day, members of the senate, for fear of saying something which in the universal rejoicing would bring less joy to you. As it is, when a senator asks me whether it is still a matter of regret that we entered upon a war against the Romans, if I were to remain silent I should be thought either haughty or subservient, of which the one marks a man forgetful of another's independence, the other a man who forgets his own. I should like to say in reply to Himilco," he said, "that I have not ceased to regret the war, and will not cease to accuse your invincible commander until I shall see the war ended on some sufferable terms; nor will anything else than a new peace end my longing for the old peace. And so those facts which Mago has just boastfully reported already give joy to Himilco and the other minions of Hannibal, and *may* give joy to me, since successes in war, if we are willing to make use of our good fortune, will give us a more favourable peace. I mean that if we let slip this moment, when we may be considered as giving, rather than receiving, a peace, I fear that this joy also of ours may run to excess and come to nothing.[1] But even now what is it worth? 'I have slain armies of the enemy. Send me soldiers!' What else would you ask for if you had been defeated? 'I have captured two camps of the enemy,' full of booty and supplies, of course. 'Give me grain and money!' What else would you beg if you had been despoiled, if you had lost your camp? And, not to have all the amazement to myself—for it is right and proper for me too, having

A.U.C. 538 enim, quoniam respondi Himilconi, interrogare ius fasque est—velim seu Himilco seu Mago respondeat, cum ad internecionem Romani imperii pugnatum ad Cannas sit constetque in defectione totam Italiam
16 esse, primum, ecquis Latini nominis populus defecerit ad nos, deinde, ecquis homo ex quinque et triginta
17 tribubus ad Hannibalem transfugerit?" Cum utrumque Mago negasset, "Hostium quidem ergo" inquit "adhuc nimis multum superest. Sed multitudo ea quid animorum quidve spei habeat scire velim." XIII. Cum id nescire Mago diceret, "Nihil facilius scitu est" inquit. "Ecquos legatos ad Hannibalem Romani miserunt de pace? Ecquam denique mentionem pacis Romae factam esse adla-
2 tum ad vos est?" Cum id quoque negasset, "Bellum igitur" inquit "tam integrum habemus quam habuimus qua die Hannibal in Italiam est transgressus.
3 Quam varia victoria priore Punico[1] bello fuerit plerique qui meminerimus supersumus. Numquam terra marique magis prosperae res nostrae visae sunt quam ante consules C. Lutatium et A. Postumium fuerunt:
4 Lutatio et Postumio consulibus devicti ad Aegatis insulas sumus. Quod si, id quod di omen avertant, nunc quoque fortuna aliquid variaverit, tum pacem speratis cum vincemur, quam nunc cum vincimus
5 dat nemo? Ego, si quis de pace consulet seu deferenda hostibus seu accipienda, habeo quid sententiae dicam; si de iis quae Mago postulat refertis,

[1] Punico *P*(1): bracketed *Gronovius*.

---

[1] "Roman War" would seem to us better suited to a speaker addressing Carthaginians. Livy here prefers the Roman standpoint.

[2] It was this defeat which brought the previous war to an end, 241 B.C.

answered Himilco, to turn questioner,—I should like B.C. 216
either Himilco or Mago to answer, in the first place, whether any state among the Latins has revolted to us, although the battle of Cannae meant the utter destruction of the Roman power, and it is known that all Italy is in revolt; in the second place, whether any man out of the thirty-five tribes has deserted to Hannibal." On Mago's negative answer to both Hanno said: "Accordingly there remains, to be sure, a very great number of the enemy. But what spirit, what hope that multitude has, I should like to know.' XIII. As Mago said he did not know, "Nothing is easier to know," said Hanno. "Have the Romans sent any emissaries to Hannibal suing for peace? Has it been reported to you that even any mention of peace has been made at Rome?" The answer to this also being negative, "Therefore," he said, "we have the war intact, as truly as we had on the day on which Hannibal crossed into Italy. How often victory shifted in the previous Punic War[1] very many of us are alive to remember. Never have our fortunes seemed more favourable on land and sea than they were before the consulship of Gaius Lutatius and Aulus Postumius. But in the consulship of Lutatius and Postumius we were utterly defeated off the Aegates Islands.[2] And if now also—may the gods avert the omen!—fortune shall shift to any extent, do you hope that at the time of our defeat we shall have a peace which no one gives us now when we are victorious? For myself, if some one is about to bring up the question either of offering peace to the enemy or of accepting it, I know what opinion to express. But if you are raising the question of Mago's demands, I do not think it to the

A.U.C. 538 nec victoribus mitti attinere puto et frustrantibus nos falsa atque inani spe[1] multo minus censeo mittenda esse."

6 Haud multos movit Hannonis oratio; nam et simultas cum familia Barcina leviorem auctorem faciebat et occupati animi praesenti laetitia nihil quo vanius fieret gaudium suum auribus admittebant, debellatumque mox fore, si adniti paulum voluissent,
7 rebantur. Itaque ingenti consensu fit senatus consultum ut Hannibali quattuor milia Numidarum in supplementum mitterentur et quadraginta elephanti
8 et argenti talenta . . . que[2] cum Magone in Hispaniam praemissus est ad conducenda viginti milia peditum, quattuor milia equitum, quibus exercitus qui in Italia quique in Hispania erant supplerentur.

XIV. Ceterum haec, ut in secundis rebus, segniter otioseque gesta; Romanos praeter insitam industriam
2 animis fortuna etiam cunctari prohibebat. Nam nec consul ulli rei quae per eum agenda esset deerat, et dictator M. Iunius Pera rebus divinis perfectis latoque, ut solet, ad populum ut equum escendere liceret, praeter duas urbanas legiones, quae principio anni a consulibus conscriptae fuerant, et servorum dilectum cohortesque ex agro Piceno et Gallico

[1] spe *Gronovius*: que *P*(8): quae *C*⁴*R*: *om. A.*

[2] *A lost numeral* (D?) *and a general's name* (Carthalo *Madvig*) *have been corrupted into* dictator(que) *P*(1).

---

[1] Infantry are not mentioned as to be sent from Carthage. Mercenaries were to be engaged in Spain and sent thence to Hannibal.

[2] In fact Mago is still at Carthage in xxxii. 5.

point to send those things to victors, and I think it much less necessary to send them to men who are deluding us with a hope unfounded and empty." B.C. 216

Not many were moved by Hanno's speech. For the feud with the Barca family made his advice less weighty, and then minds filled with the joy of the moment would not listen to anything which made their rejoicing less well-founded. And they thought that, if they were willing to add a little to their efforts, the war would soon be finished. Accordingly the senate with great unanimity decreed that four thousand Numidians should be sent to Hannibal as a reinforcement;[1] also forty elephants and . . . silver talents. And . . . was sent in advance to Spain with Mago,[2] for the purpose of hiring twenty thousand infantry and four thousand horse, to reinforce the armies that were in Italy and those in Spain.

XIV. But, as usual in prosperous times, these measures were carried out without spirit and in leisurely fashion, while the Romans, in addition to their inborn activity, were prevented by misfortune also from delaying. That is, the consul was not found wanting in anything which it was his to do, and the dictator, Marcus Junius Pera, after performing the religious rites, proposed to the people according to custom a bill allowing him to be mounted.[3] And then, in addition to the two city legions which had been enrolled by the consuls at the beginning of the year, and the levy of slaves, also the cohorts raised from the Picene and Gallic districts, he stooped

[3] The dictator, as commander of the infantry, was by tradition unmounted. Special permission could be obtained from the people, as here, or from the senate, as Plutarch has it in *Fabius* iv.

A.U.C. 538 collectas, ad ultimum prope desperatae rei publicae
3 auxilium, cum honesta utilibus cedunt, descendit
edixitque qui capitalem fraudem ausi quique pecuniae [1] iudicati in vinculis essent, qui eorum apud
se milites fierent, eos noxa pecuniaque sese exsolvi
4 iussurum. Ea sex milia hominum Gallicis spoliis,
quae triumpho C. Flamini tralata erant, armavit,
itaque cum viginti quinque milibus armatorum ab
urbe proficiscitur.

5 Hannibal Capua recepta cum iterum Neapolitano-
rum animos partim spe, partim metu nequiquam
temptasset, in agrum Nolanum exercitum traducit,
6 ut non hostiliter statim, quia non desperabat voluntariam deditionem, ita, si morarentur spem, nihil
eorum quae pati aut timere possent praetermissurus.
7 Senatus ac maxime primores eius in societate Romana cum fide perstare; plebs novarum, ut solet,
rerum atque Hannibalis tota esse metumque agro-
rum populationis et patienda in obsidione multa
gravia indignaque proponere animo; neque auctores
8 defectionis deerant. Itaque ubi senatum metus
cepit, si propalam tenderent, resisti multitudini
concitatae non posse, secunda simulando [2] dilationem
9 mali inveniunt. Placere enim sibi defectionem ad
Hannibalem simulant; quibus autem condicionibus
in foedus amicitiamque novam transeant, parum
10 constare. Ita spatio sumpto legatos propere ad
praetorem Romanum Marcellum Claudium, qui

[1] pecuniae *z*: pecunia *P*(1).

[2] secunda simulando *CM*[7]: secunda simulanda simulando *P*(12); obsecundando *Gronovius*.

---

[1] He triumphed over the Gauls in the Po valley in 223 B.C.

to that last defence of a state almost despaired of, when honour yields to necessity: namely, he issued an edict that, if any men who had committed a capital offence, or were in chains as judgment debtors, should become soldiers under him, he would order their release from punishment or debt. Six thousand such men he armed with Gallic spoils which had been carried in the triumph of Gaius Flaminius,[1] and thus set out from the city with twenty-five thousand armed men. B.C. 216

Hannibal, after gaining possession of Capua and vainly trying, partly by hope, partly by fear, to work for the second time upon the feelings of the Neapolitans, led his army over into the territory of Nola. Though this was not at first with hostile intent, since he did not despair of a voluntary surrender, still he was ready, if they baulked his hope, to omit none of the things which they might suffer or fear to suffer. The senate and especially its leading members stood loyally by the alliance with Rome. But the common people, as usual, were all for a change of government and for Hannibal; and they called to mind the fear of devastation of their lands and the many hardships and indignities they must suffer in case of a siege. And men were not lacking to propose revolt. Accordingly the senators, now obsessed by the fear that, if they should move openly, there could be no resisting the excited crowd, found a way to postpone the evil by pretending agreement. For they pretend that they favour revolt to Hannibal, but that there is no agreement as to the terms on which they may go over to a new alliance and friendship. Thus gaining time, they send emissaries in haste to the Roman praetor, Marcellus Claudius, who

A.U.C. 538 Casilini cum exercitu erat, mittunt docentque
quanto in discrimine sit Nolana res: agrum Hannibalis esse et Poenorum, urbem extemplo futuram ni
11 subveniatur; concedendo plebei senatum ubi velint
defecturos se, ne deficere praefestinarent effecisse.
12 Marcellus conlaudatis Nolanis eadem simulatione
extrahi rem in suum adventum iussit; interim celari
quae secum acta essent spemque omnem auxilii
13 Romani. Ipse a Casilino Caiatiam petit atque inde
Volturno amni traiecto per [1] agrum Saticulanum
Trebianumque super Suessulam per montis Nolam
pervenit.

XV. Sub adventum praetoris Romani Poenus
agro Nolano excessit et ad mare proxime Neapolim
descendit, cupidus maritimi oppidi potiundi, quo
2 cursus navibus tutus ex Africa esset. Ceterum
postquam Neapolim a praefecto Romano teneri
accepit—M. Iunius Silanus erat, ab ipsis Neapoli-
tanis accitus—, Neapoli quoque, sicut Nola, omissa
3 petit Nuceriam. Eam cum aliquamdiu circumse-
disset, saepe vi saepe sollicitandis nequiquam nunc
plebe, nunc principibus, fame demum in deditionem
accepit, pactus ut inermes cum singulis abirent
4 vestimentis. Deinde ut qui a principio mitis omnibus
Italicis praeter Romanos videri vellet, praemia atque
honores qui remanserint [2] ac militare secum voluis-

[1] per *Otto*: perque *P*(1).
[2] remanserint *x*: remanserant *PC*[1](10).

---

[1] Marcellus had been sent to Canusium directly after the battle of Cannae to take command (XXII. lvii. 1), and is now near Capua.

[2] This wide detour into mountain country was in order to avoid meeting Hannibal.

was at Casilinum[1] with his army, and inform him in what danger the Nolan state is placed; that its territory is in the hands of Hannibal and the Carthaginians, and that the city will be so at once, if help be not given; that the senate, by conceding to the common people that they would revolt whenever the people wished, had prevented their making haste to revolt. Marcellus, after warmly praising the men of Nola, bade them postpone matters by the same pretence until his arrival; in the meantime to conceal the dealings they had had with him and all hope of Roman aid. He himself went from Casilinum to Caiatia, and thence, after crossing the river Volturnus, made his way to Nola through the territory of Saticula and that of Trebia, above Suessula and through the mountains.[2] B.C. 216

XV. Upon the arrival of the Roman praetor the Carthaginian left the territory of Nola and came down to the sea near Neapolis, desiring to gain possession of a coast town to which ships might have a safe passage from Africa. But on learning that Neapolis was held by a Roman prefect—it was Marcus Junius Silanus, who had been called in by the Neapolitans themselves—he turned aside from Neapolis also, as he had from Nola, and made for Nuceria. He had besieged that city for some time, often attacking, often attempting in vain to win over the populace, and at another time the leading citizens, when at last by starving them he gained their surrender, stipulating that they leave unarmed and with one garment only. And then, as from the beginning he had wished to be thought merciful to all Italians except the Romans, he promised rewards and honours to any who remained and would serve under

A.U.C. 538

5 sent proposuit. Nec ea spe quemquam tenuit;
dilapsi omnes, quocumque hospitia aut fortuitus
animi impetus tulit, per Campaniae urbes, maxime
6 Nolam Neapolimque. Cum ferme triginta senatores,
ac forte primus quisque, Capuam petissent, exclusi
inde, quod portas Hannibali clausissent, Cumas se
contulerunt. Nuceriae praeda militi data est, urbs
direpta atque incensa.

7 Nolam Marcellus non sui magis fiducia praesidii
quam voluntate principum habebat; plebs timebatur
et ante omnis L. Bantius, quem conscientia temptatae
defectionis ac metus a praetore Romano nunc ad proditionem patriae, nunc, si ad id fortuna defuisset, ad
8 transfugiendum stimulabat. Erat iuvenis acer et
sociorum ea tempestate prope nobilissimus eques.
Seminecem eum ad Cannas in acervo caesorum
corporum inventum curatumque benigne etiam cum
9 donis Hannibal domum remiserat. Ob eius gratiam
meriti rem Nolanam in ius dicionemque dare voluerat
Poeno, anxiumque eum et sollicitum cura novandi
10 res praetor cernebat. Ceterum cum aut poena cohi-
bendus esset aut beneficio conciliandus, sibi adsump-
sisse quam hosti ademisse fortem ac strenuum maluit
11 socium, accitumque ad se benigne appellat: multos
eum invidos inter popularis habere inde existimatu
facile esse quod nemo civis Nolanus sibi indicaverit

him. And yet he did not hold anyone by that hope. B.C. 216
They all dispersed, wherever hospitality or impulse happened to carry them, among the cities of Campania, especially Nola and Neapolis. A group of some thirty senators, and as it chanced all the most prominent, came to Capua, and being refused admission because they had closed their gates to Hannibal, went to Cumae. At Nuceria the booty was given to the soldiers, the city sacked and burned.

As for Nola, Marcellus held it not more by confidence in his force than by the good-will of the leading citizens. He was apprehensive of the common people and above all of Lucius Bantius, who was impelled by the consciousness of an attempted revolt and by fear of the Roman praetor, now to betray his native city, now, if fortune should not favour him in that, to desert. He was a young man of spirit and at that time almost the best-known horseman among the allies. He had been found half-dead at Cannae in a pile of the slain; and Hannibal, after nursing him kindly, had sent him home, even adding gifts. Out of gratitude for that service Bantius had wished to put the state of Nola under the authority and rule of the Carthaginian. And the praetor saw that he was troubled and tormented by his desire for a revolution. But since he had either to be restrained by punishment or else won over by kindness, Marcellus preferred rather to gain for himself a brave and energetic ally than merely to take such a man away from the enemy, and summoning him addressed him kindly. It was easy, he said, to judge that he had among his countrymen many who envied him, and this from the fact that no citizen of Nola had told the speaker how many were his

A.U.C. 538 quam multa eius egregia facinora militaria essent;
12 sed qui in Romanis militaverit castris, non posse
obscuram eius virtutem esse. Multos sibi, qui cum
eo stipendia fecerint, referre qui vir esset ille, quaeque et quotiens pericula pro salute ac dignitate populi
13 Romani adisset, utique Cannensi proelio non prius
pugna abstiterit quam prope exsanguis ruina super-
incidentium virorum, equorum armorumque sit
14 oppressus. "Itaque macte virtute esto" inquit;
"apud me tibi omnis honos atque omne praemium
erit, et quo frequentior mecum fueris, senties eam
15 rem tibi dignitati atque emolumento esse." Laeto-
que iuveni promissis equum eximium dono dat,
bigatosque quingentos quaestorem numerare iubet;
lictoribus imperat ut eum se adire quotiens velit
patiantur. XVI. Hac comitate Marcelli ferocis
iuvenis animus adeo est mollitus ut nemo inde
sociorum rem Romanam fortius ac fidelius iuverit.

2 Cum Hannibal ad portas esset—Nolam enim
rursus a Nuceria movit castra—plebesque Nolana
3 de integro ad defectionem spectaret, Marcellus sub
adventum hostium intra muros se recepit, non castris
metuens sed ne prodendae urbis occasionem nimis
4 multis in eam inminentibus daret. Instrui deinde
utrimque acies coeptae, Romanorum pro moenibus
Nolae, Poenorum ante castra sua. Proelia hinc
parva inter urbem castraque et vario eventu fiebant,

---

1 These silver coins at that time bore the image of Diana (of Victory not long after) driving a two-horse chariot (*biga*).

brilliant feats of arms. But to a man who had served B.C. 216
in the Roman camp his bravery could not be unknown. Many who had been in the service with Bantius were telling the speaker what a man he was, and what dangers he had incurred for the safety and honour of the Roman people, and how often; also how at the battle of Cannae he had not ceased fighting until, almost lifeless, he had been overwhelmed by the mass of men, horses and arms that fell upon him. "And so," he said, "all honour to your courage! Under me you will have every advancement and every reward, and the more constantly you are with me, the more you will feel that it is a distinction and an advantage to you." The youth was delighted with the promises, and Marcellus gave him a fine horse and ordered the quaestor to pay him five hundred denarii.[1] The lictors were bidden to allow him access to the commander whenever he wished. XVI. By this kindliness on the part of Marcellus the high spirit of the young man was so tempered that thereafter none of the allies more bravely and loyally aided the Roman cause.

While Hannibal was at the gates—for he again moved his camp from Nuceria to Nola—and the common people of Nola were making fresh plans to revolt, Marcellus, upon the arrival of the enemy, withdrew within the walls, not fearing for his camp, but lest he give the great number who were impatient for it an opportunity to betray the city. Then on both sides they began to form their battle-lines, the Romans before the walls of Nola, the Carthaginians in front of their camp. Thereupon there were small engagements with varying results in the space between the city and the camp, since the commanders

A.U.C. 538 quia duces nec prohibere paucos temere provocantis[1]
5 nec dare signum universae pugnae volebant. In hac cotidiana duorum exercituum statione principes Nola-
6 norum nuntiant Marcello nocturna conloquia inter plebem ac Poenos fieri statutumque esse ut, cum Romana acies egressa portis foret,[2] inpedimenta eorum ac sarcinas diriperent, clauderent deinde portas murosque occuparent, ut potentes rerum suarum atque urbis Poenum inde pro Romano acciperent.
7 Haec ubi nuntiata Marcello sunt, conlaudatis senatoribus Nolanis, priusquam aliqui motus in urbe
8 oreretur, fortunam pugnae experiri statuit. Ad tris portas in hostes versas tripertito exercitum instruxit; inpedimenta subsequi iussit, calones lixasque et invalidos milites vallum ferre. Media porta robora legionum et Romanos equites, duabus circa portis novos milites levemque armaturam ac sociorum
9 equites statuit. Nolani muros portasque adire vetiti, subsidiaque destinata inpedimentis data, ne occupatis proelio legionibus in ea impetus fieret. Ita instructi intra portas stabant.

10 Hannibali sub signis, id quod per aliquot dies fecerat, ad multum diei in acie stanti primo miraculo esse quod nec exercitus Romanus porta egrederetur
11 nec armatus quisquam in muris esset. Ratus deinde

[1] provocantis *M*^{1}?*A*^{x}: procantis *PCR?M* : procursantis *Luchs.*

[2] foret *Gronovius* : iret *P*(1) : staret *Weissenborn.*

wished neither to forbid small numbers who rashly challenged the enemy, nor to give the signal for a general engagement. During this daily guard-duty of the two armies leading citizens of Nola reported to Marcellus that conferences between the common people and the Carthaginians were taking place by night; and that it had been settled that, when the Roman force should be outside the gates and in line, they would plunder their baggage-train and their packs, then close the gates and take possession of the walls, so that, having the control of their affairs and the city in their own hands, they would then admit the Carthaginian instead of the Roman. This being reported to Marcellus, he warmly praised the senators of Nola and resolved to try the fortune of battle before there should be any movement in the city. At the three gates facing the enemy he drew up his army in three sections. He ordered the baggage to bring up the rear, the camp-servants and sutlers and incapacitated soldiers to carry stakes. At the middle gate he posted the pick of the legionaries with the Roman cavalry, at the two gates to right and left the recruits, light-armed and cavalry of the allies. The men of Nola were forbidden to approach the walls and gates, and the forces to be used as reserves were assigned to the baggage, in order to prevent an attack upon it while the legions were fighting. In this formation they were standing inside the gates. B.C. 216

Hannibal, who remained in battle-line under the standards until late in the day, as he had done for several days, at first wondered that the Roman army did not come out of the gate and that there was not one armed man on the walls. Then, supposing

A.U.C. 538 prodita conloquia esse metuque resides factos, partem militum in castra remittit iussos propere adparatum omnem oppugnandae urbis in primam aciem adferre, satis fidens, si cunctantibus instaret, tumultum ali-
12 quem in urbe plebem moturam. Dum in sua quisque ministeria discursu trepidat ad prima signa succeditque ad muros acies, patefacta repente porta Marcellus signa canere clamoremque tolli ac pedites primum, deinde equites, quanto maximo possent impetu in
13 hostem erumpere iubet. Satis terroris tumultusque in aciem mediam intulerant, cum duabus circa portis P. Valerius Flaccus et C. Aurelius legati in cornua
14 hostium erupere. Addidere clamorem lixae calonesque et alia turba custodiae inpedimentorum adposita, ut paucitatem maxime spernentibus Poenis
15 ingentis repente exercitus speciem fecerit. Vix equidem ausim adfirmare, quod quidam auctores sunt, duo milia et octingentos hostium caesos non
16 plus quingentis Romanorum amissis; sed [1] sive tanta sive minor victoria fuit, ingens eo die res ac nescio an maxima illo bello gesta est: [2] non vinci enim ab Hannibale [3] difficilius fuit quam postea vincere.

XVII. Hannibal spe potiundae Nolae adempta cum Acerras recessisset, Marcellus extemplo clausis portis custodibusque dispositis, ne quis egrederetur,

[1] amissis; sed *Alschefski*: amisisset *PMD?R*^{x}: amisisse *CM*^{x}: amisisse sed *A*.

[2] est *Freinsheim*: sit *P*(1).

[3] *After* Hannibale *P*(1) *have* vincentibus (*with* tum *or* tunc *x*): vinci timentibus *Weissenborn, Conway*.

the conferences to have been betrayed, and that inaction was the result of fear, he sent part of his soldiers back to the camp, with orders to bring up in haste to the front line all the equipment for besieging the city. He was quite confident that, if he should press the hesitating, the common people would stir up some outbreak in the city. While they were scattering to their several duties and hastening to the first standards, and the line was advancing to the walls, the gate suddenly opened and Marcellus ordered the trumpets to be sounded and a shout raised; that infantry at first, and then cavalry should sally out against the enemy with all the dash possible. They had carried sufficient panic and confusion into the centre, when Publius Valerius Flaccus and Gaius Aurelius, his lieutenants, sallied out of the two gates on this side and that, to attack the enemy's wings. Sutlers and camp-servants raised another shout, as did the rest of the crowd stationed to guard the baggage so that the shouting gave the sudden impression of a very large army to the Carthaginians, who particularly despised their small numbers. I should hardly venture to assert, what some have affirmed, that 2800 of the enemy were slain, while not more than 500 of the Romans were lost. But whether the victory was on such a scale or less, a very great thing, I rather think the greatest in that war, was accomplished that day. For not to be defeated by Hannibal was a more difficult thing than it was later to defeat him. B.C. 216

XVII. Now that Hannibal had lost hope of gaining Nola and had retired to Acerrae, Marcellus at once closed the gates, stationed guards to prevent anyone from leaving, and carried on in the forum an

A.U.C. 538

quaestionem in foro de iis qui clam in conloquiis
2 hostium fuerant habuit. Supra septuaginta damnatos proditionis securi percussit bonaque eorum iussit
3 publica populi Romani esse, et summa rerum senatui tradita cum exercitu omni profectus supra Suessulam
4 castris positis consedit. Poenus Acerras primum ad voluntariam deditionem conatus perlicere, inde[1] postquam obstinatos videt, obsidere atque oppugnare
5 parat. Ceterum Acerranis plus animi quam virium erat; itaque desperata tutela urbis, ut circumvallari moenia viderunt, priusquam continuarentur hostium opera, per intermissa munimenta neglectasque
6 custodias silentio noctis dilapsi, per vias inviaque qua quemque aut consilium aut error tulit, in urbes Campaniae, quas satis certum erat non mutasse fidem, perfugerunt.

7 Hannibal Acerris direptis atque incensis, cum a Casilino[2] dictatorem Romanum legionesque novas acciri[3] nuntiassent, ne quid[4] tam propinquis hostium castris Capuae quoque moveretur,[5] exercitum ad
8 Casilinum ducit. Casilinum eo tempore quingenti Praenestini habebant cum paucis Romanis Latinique nominis, quos eodem audita Cannensis clades contu-
9 lerat. Hi, non confecto Praeneste ad diem dilectu, serius profecti domo cum Casilinum ante famam adversae pugnae venissent, et, aliis adgregantibus sese Romanis sociisque, profecti a Casilino cum satis

[1] inde *P*(1), *but after* obstinatos; *before* postquam *Walters.*
[2] Casilino A^2 *Valla*: Casino *P*(1).
[3] novas acciri A^y *Valla*: nimis accipi *P*(5)M^x: acciri *Walters.*
[4] ne quid *Lipsius*: ne quis *P*(1): ne quid novi *Walters.*
[5] moveretur *Gronovius*: ererecurrunt *P*: recurrunt P^2?(4): occurreret *Lipsius.*

investigation of those who had been in secret conferences with the enemy. Over seventy having been condemned as traitors, he beheaded them and ordered that their possessions should be public property of the Roman people. And setting out with his whole army, after turning over the government to the senate, he pitched camp and established himself above Suessula. The Carthaginian first tried to entice Acerrae into a voluntary surrender; then, seeing them steadfast, prepared to blockade and attack them. But the men of Acerrae had more courage than resources. Accordingly they gave up hope of defending the city, and when they saw that their walls were being encircled, before the enemy's works should be made continuous, they slipped away in the dead of night through the gaps in the earthworks and through neglected guard-posts. Making their way along the roads and where there were none, just as prudence or chance guided the wanderer, they fled for refuge to those cities of Campania of which it was known that they had not changed sides. B.C. 216

After plundering and burning Acerrae, when word had come from Casilinum that the Roman dictator and fresh legions were being summoned, Hannibal led his army to Casilinum, in order to prevent any uprising at Capua also, while the enemy's camp was so near. Casilinum was at that time held by five hundred Praenestines, with a few Romans and Latins, whom the news of the disaster at Cannae had brought thither. As the levy at Praeneste was not completed at the proper date, they had been late in setting out from home, and had reached Casilinum before the news of the defeat. And joined by others, Romans and allies, they set out from Casilinum and, as

A.U.C. 538 magno agmine irent, avertit eos retro Casilinum
10 nuntius Cannensis pugnae. Ibi cum dies aliquot,
suspecti Campanis timentesque, cavendis ac struendis
in vicem insidiis traduxissent, ut de Capuae defectione agi accipique Hannibalem satis pro certo
habuere, interfectis nocte oppidanis partem urbis,
quae cis Volturnum est—eo enim dividitur amni—
occupavere, idque praesidii Casilini habebant Ro
11 mani. Additur et Perusina cohors, homines quadringenti sexaginta, eodem nuntio quo Praenestini
12 paucos ante dies, Casilinum conpulsi. Et satis
ferme armatorum ad tam exigua moenia et flumine
altera parte cincta tuenda erat: penuria frumenti
nimium etiam ut videretur hominum efficiebat.

XVIII. Hannibal cum iam inde haud procul esset,
Gaetulos cum praefecto nomine Isalca praemittit ac
primo, si fiat conloquii copia, verbis benignis ad
portas aperiundas praesidiumque accipiendum perlicere iubet: si in pertinacia perstent, vi rem gerere
ac temptare si qua parte invadere urbem possit.
2 Ubi ad moenia adcessere, quia silentium erat, solitudo
visa; metuque concessum barbarus ratus moliri
3 portas et claustra refringere parat, cum patefactis
repente portis cohortes duae, ad id ipsum instructae
intus, ingenti cum tumultu erumpunt stragemque
4 hostium faciunt. Ita primis repulsis Maharbal cum

[1] The right (north) bank of the river.

they were proceeding in a fairly large column, the report of the battle of Cannae turned them back again to Casilinum. There, being suspected by the Campanians and apprehensive, they spent some days in alternately guarding against plots and hatching them. When credibly informed that the revolt of Capua and Hannibal's entry were being negotiated, they slew townspeople in the night and seized that part of the city which is on this side[1] of the Volturnus—for it is divided by that river; and this was the garrison the Romans had at Casilinum. It was joined by a cohort from Perusia, four hundred and sixty men, who had been driven to Casilinum by the same news as the Praenestines a few days before. And there were quite enough men to defend so small a walled city, bounded on one side by the river. But the lack of grain made it seem that there were even too many men. B.C. 216

XVIII. Hannibal, being now not far away, sent his Gaetulians ahead under a prefect named Isalcas. And he ordered him, if there should be an opportunity for a conference, at first by kind words to entice them to open the gates and admit a garrison; but if they persisted in their obstinacy, to use force and see if at some point he could make his way into the city. When they approached the walls, because of the stillness they thought them deserted. And the barbarian, supposing the garrison had withdrawn in alarm, was preparing to force the gates and break open the bars, when suddenly the gates were opened and the two cohorts, drawn up inside for that very purpose, sallied out with a mighty uproar, and wrought havoc among the enemy. The first troops being thus beaten back, Maharbal, who had been

A.U.C. 538

maiore robore virorum missus nec ipse eruptionem
5 cohortium sustinuit. Postremo Hannibal castris
ante ipsa moenia oppositis[1] parvam urbem parvumque praesidium summa vi atque omnibus copiis oppugnare parat, ac dum instat lacessitque, corona undique circumdatis moenibus, aliquot milites et promptissimum quemque e muro turribusque ictos
6 amisit. Semel ultro erumpentis agmine elephantorum opposito prope interclusit trepidosque conpulit in urbem satis multis ut ex tanta paucitate interfectis. Plures cecidissent ni nox proelio intervenisset.
7 Postero die omnium animi ad oppugnandum accenduntur, utique postquam corona aurea muralis proposita est, atque ipse dux castelli plano loco positi segnem oppugnationem Sagunti expugnatoribus exprobrabat, Cannarum Trasumennique et
8 Trebiae singulos admonens universosque. Inde vineae quoque coeptae agi cuniculique; nec ad varios conatus hostium aut vis ulla aut ars deerat
9 sociis Romanorum. Propugnacula adversus vineas statuere, transversis cuniculis hostium cuniculos excipere, et palam et clam coeptis obviam ire, donec pudor etiam Hannibalem ab incepto avertit, castrisque communitis ac praesidio modico inposito, ne omissa res videretur, in hiberna Capuam concessit.
10 Ibi partem maiorem hiemis exercitum in tectis

[1] oppositis *P*(1) : positis *x Madvig*.

---

[1] The elephants sent by order of the Carthaginian senate (xiii. 7) must have arrived. Of those he had brought from Spain only one reached Central Italy (XXII. ii. 10).

[2] Awarded to the first man to scale the wall of a city; Polybius VI. xxxix. 5; Livy XXVI. xlviii. 5; Gellius V. vi. 16 and 19.

[3] Cf. XXI. xv.

sent with a larger number of picked men, was likewise unable to withstand the sally of the cohorts. Finally Hannibal pitched his camp directly before the walls and prepared to assault the small city and small garrison with the greatest violence and with all his forces. And while he was pressing the attack, the walls being completely encircled by his men, he lost a considerable number, the most active at that, being hit by missiles from the wall and the towers. When they actually sallied out once, he almost cut off their retreat by sending a column of elephants[1] against them, and drove them in alarm into the city, after a good number, for so small a force, had been slain. More would have fallen if night had not interrupted the battle. On the next day all were fired to make the assault, especially after a mural crown of gold[2] was displayed to them, and the general himself kept making their spiritless attack upon a fort on level ground a reproach to the captors of Saguntum,[3] reminding them singly and collectively of Cannae and Trasumennus and Trebia. Then they began to push forward their sheds also and mines. And to meet the different attempts made by the enemy no kind of activity, no ingenuity, proved lacking to the allies of the Romans. They set up defences to meet the sheds; by transverse mines they intercepted the enemy's mines; they forestalled his attempts both visible and invisible, until shame helped to divert Hannibal from his undertaking. And after fortifying his camp and posting a small garrison, that the attempt might not appear to have been abandoned, he retired into winter-quarters at Capua. B.C. 216

There he kept under roofs for the greater part of

A.U.C. 538 habuit, adversus omnia humana mala saepe ac diu
11 duratum, bonis inexpertum atque insuetum. Itaque,
quos nulla mali vicerat vis, perdidere nimia bona ac
voluptates inmodicae, et eo inpensius quo avidius ex
12 insolentia in eas se merserant. Somnus enim et
vinum et epulae et scorta balineaque et otium con-
suetudine in dies blandius ita enervaverunt corpora
animosque ut magis deinde praeteritae victoriae eos
13 quam praesentes tutarentur vires, maiusque id
peccatum ducis apud peritos artium militarium
haberetur quam quod non ex Cannensi acie protinus
ad urbem Romanam duxisset; illa enim cunctatio
distulisse modo victoriam videri potuit, hic error
14 vires ademisse ad vincendum. Itaque hercule, velut
si cum alio exercitu a Capua exiret, nihil usquam
15 pristinae disciplinae tenuit. Nam et redierunt
plerique scortis inpliciti, et, ubi primum sub pellibus
haberi coepti sunt, viaque et alius militaris labor
excepit, tironum modo corporibus animisque deficie-
16 bant, et deinde per omne aestivorum tempus magna
pars sine commeatibus ab signis dilabebantur, neque
aliae latebrae quam Capua desertoribus erant.

XIX. Ceterum mitescente iam hieme educto ex
2 hibernis milite Casilinum redit, ubi, quamquam ab
oppugnatione cessatum erat, obsidio tamen continua

[1] For the effect of wintering at Capua cf. xlv. 4 (the famous epigram, as if from the lips of Marcellus), and *ib*. 6 (Hannibal's words, as Livy imagined them). Strabo confirms, Polybius denies (V. iv. 13; XI. xix. 3 respectively).

the winter troops that had been hardened long and repeatedly against all human hardships, but had no experience or familiarity with comforts. And so those whom no severe hardship had conquered were ruined by excess of comfort and immoderate pleasures and the more completely ruined the more eagerly they in their inexperience had plunged into them. For sleep and wine, and feasts and harlots, and baths and idleness, which habit made daily more seductive, so weakened their bodies and spirits that it was their past victories rather than their present strength which thereafter protected them; and this was regarded among the military experts as a more serious failure in their commander than that he had not led his men from the field of Cannae forthwith to the city of Rome. For that delay could be regarded as having merely retarded the victory, this mistake as having robbed him of the power to win. And so in fact, just as if he were setting out from Capua with a different army, not a trace of the old-time morale survived. For they came back most of them ensnared by harlots, and also as soon as they began to be quartered in tents, and the march and other tasks of the soldier followed, they would give out both in body and in spirit after the manner of recruits. And afterwards through the whole season of summer camps a great many kept slipping away from their standards without furloughs; and deserters had no hiding-places other than Capua.[1] B.C. 216

XIX. But when winter was now growing mild, Hannibal led his troops out of winter quarters and returned to Casilinum. There, although they had been making no more attacks, an uninterrupted

A.U.C. 538 oppidanos praesidiumque ad ultimum inopiae
3 adduxerat. Castris Romanis Ti. Sempronius praeerat dictatore auspiciorum repetendorum causa
4 profecto Romam. Marcellum et ipsum cupientem
ferre auxilium obsessis et Volturnus amnis inflatus
aquis et preces Nolanorum Acerranorumque tenebant, Campanos timentium si praesidium Romanum
5 abscessisset. Gracchus adsidens tantum Casilino,
quia praedictum erat dictatoris ne quid absente eo
rei gereret, nihil movebat, quamquam quae facile
omnem patientiam vincerent nuntiabantur a Casi-
6 lino: nam et praecipitasse se quosdam non tolerantes
famem constabat, et stare inermes in muris, nuda
7 corpora ad missilium telorum ictus praebentes. Ea
aegre patiens Gracchus, cum neque pugnam conserere
dictatoris iniussu auderet—pugnandum autem esse,
si palam frumentum inportaret, videbat—neque clam
8 inportandi spes esset, farre ex agris circa undique
convecto cum conplura dolia conplesset, nuntium ad
magistratum Casilinum misit ut exciperent dolia
9 quae amnis deferret. Insequenti nocte intentis
omnibus in flumen ac spem ab nuntio Romano factam
dolia medio missa amni defluxerunt; aequaliterque
10 inter omnes frumentum divisum. Id postero quoque
die ac tertio factum est; nocte et mittebantur et
11 perveniebant; eo custodias hostium fallebant. Im-
bribus deinde continuis citatior solito amnis transverso

---

[1] If the auspices were alleged to be defective, the commander returned to Rome to take them again; VIII. xxx. 2.

[2] The city had not been entirely destroyed (xvii. 7), and part of the population must have returned.

blockade had nevertheless brought townspeople B.C. 216 and garrison to extreme want. The Roman camp was commanded by Tiberius Sempronius, since the dictator had gone to Rome to take new auspices.[1] Marcellus, who was likewise eager to bring aid to the besieged, was held back both by a flood of the river Volturnus and by entreaties of the men of Nola and Acerrae,[2] who feared the Campanians if the Roman garrison should withdraw. Gracchus, merely remaining near Casilinum, because it was the dictator's order that he take no action in his absence, made no move, although facts which would easily pass all endurance were being reported from Casilinum. For it was established that some, unable to endure hunger, had thrown themselves from the wall, and that men stood unarmed on the walls exposing unprotected bodies to wounds from missile weapons. Gracchus, though indignant at this, did not dare to engage the enemy without the dictator's order, and saw that, if he should try openly to carry in grain, he must fight. As there was also no hope of carrying it in secretly, he filled many huge jars with spelt brought from the farms all around, and sent word to the magistrate at Casilinum that they should catch up the jars which the river was bringing down. In the following night, while all were intent upon the river and the hope aroused by the Roman messenger, the jars set adrift in midstream floated down, and the grain was evenly divided among them all. This was done the next day also and the third day. It was night when they were set adrift and when they arrived. In that way they escaped the notice of the enemy's guards. After that the stream, now swifter than usual because of incessant rains, forced

A.U.C. 538 vertice dolia impulit ad ripam quam hostes servabant. Ibi haerentia inter obnata ripis salicta conspiciuntur, nuntiatumque Hannibali est, et deinde intentiore custodia cautum ne quid falleret Volturno ad urbem
12 missum. Nuces tamen fusae ab Romanis castris, cum medio amni ad Casilinum defluerent, cratibus excipiebantur.

13 Postremo ad id ventum inopiae est ut lora detractasque scutis pelles, ubi fervida mollissent aqua, mandere conarentur nec muribus aliove animali abstinerent et omne herbarum radicumque genus
14 aggeribus infimis muri eruerent. Et cum hostes obarassent quidquid herbidi terreni extra murum erat, raporum semen iniecerunt, ut Hannibal "Eone usque dum ea nascuntur ad Casilinum sessurus sum?"
15 exclamaret; et qui nullam antea pactionem auribus admiserat, tum demum agi secum est passus de
16 redemptione liberorum capitum. Septunces auri in singulos pretium convenit. Fide accepta tradiderunt sese. Donec omne aurum persolutum est, in vinculis
17 habiti; tum remissi summa cum fide. Id verius est quam ab equite in abeuntis inmisso interfectos. Praenestini maxima pars fuere. Ex quingentis septuaginta qui in praesidio fuerunt minus[1] dimidium ferrum famesque absumpsit: ceteri incolumes Praeneste cum praetore suo M. Anicio—scriba is antea

[1] minus *P*(1): haud minus *x* *Madvig.*

---

[1] Hannibal had a chain across the river according to Frontinus *Strat.* III. xiv. 2.

[2] This was to impress Hannibal with their confidence that their supplies would hold out for months, and that they did not need the grass and herbs of which he had deprived them; Frontinus III. xv. 3; Strabo V. iv. 10.

the jars by a cross current to the bank guarded by the enemy. There, caught among the willows growing on the banks, they were seen and it was reported to Hannibal. And thereafter by a closer watch they saw to it that nothing sent down the Volturnus to the city should escape notice.[1] However nuts which were poured out from the Roman camp, as they floated down the middle of the river to Casilinum, were caught by wattled hurdles. B.C. 216

Finally they reached such a pitch of distress that they tried, after softening them by hot water, to chew thongs and the hides stripped off of shields; and they did not abstain from rats and other animals, and dug out every kind of plant and root from the bank beneath the wall. And when the enemy had ploughed up all the grassy ground outside the wall, the garrison sowed turnips,[2] so that Hannibal exclaimed "Am I to sit before Casilinum until those seeds come up?" And the man who had never before listened to any terms now at last allowed them to treat with him in regard to ransoming the free men. Seven-twelfths of a pound of gold was agreed upon as the price per man.[3] On receiving his promise they surrendered. They were kept in chains until all the gold was paid, then with strict regard for his promise they were released. This is the more correct version than that they were slain by a charge of cavalry as they departed. The majority were Praenestines. Of the five hundred and seventy who were in the garrison sword and starvation carried off less than half. The rest returned safe to Praeneste with their commander Marcus Anicius, who had

[3] Nearly four times the ransom demanded for an ally (200 denarii) after the battle of Cannae; XXII. lii. 2.

A.U.C. 538
18 fuerat—redierunt. Statua eius indicio fuit Praeneste
in foro statuta, loricata, amicta toga, velato capite,
cum titulo lamnae aeneae inscripto, M. Anicium pro
militibus qui Casilini in praesidio fuerint votum
solvisse. Idem titulus tribus signis in aede Fortunae
positis fuit subiectus. XX. Casilinum oppidum redditum Campanis est, firmatum septingentorum
militum de exercitu Hannibalis praesidio, ne, ubi
Poenus inde abscessisset, Romani oppugnarent.
2 Praenestinis militibus senatus Romanus duplex
stipendium et quinquennii militiae vacationem decrevit; civitate cum donarentur ob virtutem, non
3 mutaverunt. Perusinorum casus obscurior fama est,
quia nec ipsorum monumento ullo est inlustratus nec
decreto Romanorum.

4 Eodem tempore Petelinos, qui uni ex Bruttiis
manserant in amicitia Romana, non Carthaginienses
modo qui regionem obtinebant, sed Bruttii quoque
ceteri ob separata ab se consilia oppugnabant.
5 Quibus cum obsistere malis nequirent Petelini, legatos
Romam ad praesidium petendum miserunt. Quorum
preces lacrimaeque—in questus enim flebiles, cum
sibimet ipsi consulere iussi sunt, sese in vestibulo
curiae profuderunt—ingentem misericordiam patri-
6 bus ac populo moverunt; consultique iterum a
M. Aemilio praetore patres circumspectis omnibus

---

[1] *I.e.* they did not accept.

[2] Petelia, not far north of Croton, was an exception to the statement that all the Bruttians had gone over to the Carthaginians; XXII. lxi. 12.

[3] Probably elected in place of Postumius, who fell in Gaul (xxiv. 11).

formerly been a clerk. As evidence there formerly stood in the forum of Praeneste a statue of the man, wearing a cuirass and draped in a toga, with his head covered. It had an inscription on a bronze plate, stating that Marcus Anicius had paid his vow on behalf of the soldiers who were in the garrison at Casilinum. The same inscription was placed beneath three images of gods set up in the Temple of Fortune. XX. The town of Casilinum was restored to the Campanians and defended by a garrison of seven hundred men from the army of Hannibal, that the Romans might not attack it when the Carthaginian should withdraw. To the Praenestine soldiers the Roman senate voted double pay and exemption from service for five years. Though rewarded for their courage with the gift of Roman citizenship, they made no change.[1] As to the fate of the Perusians the report is less clear, since no light has been thrown upon it either by any record of their own or by a decree of the Romans. B.C. 216

At the same time the Petelini,[2] who alone among the Bruttians had remained in the friendship of Rome, were being attacked not only by the Carthaginians, who were holding the region, but also by the rest of the Bruttians for not making common cause with them. Unable to withstand these dangers, the Petelini sent legates to Rome to ask for a garrison. The prayers of the legates and their tears—for when ordered to shift for themselves they gave way to tearful complaints before the entrance of the Senate House—stirred great compassion among senators and people. And when consulted a second time by Marcus Aemilius, a praetor,[3] the senators, after surveying all the resources of the empire, were

A.U.C. 538 imperii viribus fateri coacti nihil iam longinquis
sociis in se praesidii esse, redire domum fideque ad
ultimum expleta consulere sibimet ipsos in reliquum
7 pro[1] praesenti fortuna iusserunt. Haec postquam
renuntiata legatio Petelinis est, tantus repente
maeror pavorque senatum eorum cepit ut pars pro-
fugiendi qua quisque posset ac deserendae urbis
8 auctores essent, pars, quando deserti a veteribus
sociis essent, adiungendi se ceteris Bruttiis ac per eos
9 dedendi Hannibali. Vicit tamen ea pars quae nihil
raptim nec temere agendum consulendumque de
10 integro censuit. Relata postero die per minorem
trepidationem re tenuerunt optimates ut convectis
omnibus ex agris urbem ac muros firmarent.

XXI. Per idem fere tempus litterae ex Sicilia
2 Sardiniaque Romam allatae. Priores ex Sicilia T.
Otacilii propraetoris in senatu recitatae sunt:
P. Furium praetorem cum classe ex Africa Lilybaeum venisse; ipsum graviter saucium in discrimine
ultimo vitae esse; militi ac navalibus sociis neque
stipendium neque frumentum ad diem dari neque
3 unde detur esse; magnopere suadere ut quam
primum ea mittantur, sibique, si ita videatur, ex
4 novis praetoribus successorem mittant. Eademque
ferme de stipendio frumentoque ab A. Cornelio Mammula propraetore ex Sardinia scripta. Responsum

[1] pro *Madvig*: in *z*: *om.* *P*(1).

---

[1] The siege lasted eleven months, and at the last they were subsisting on hides, bark, twigs, etc.; xxx. 1 ff.; Polybius VII. i. 3.

compelled to admit that they themselves no longer had any means to protect distant allies. They ordered them to return home, and having fulfilled their obligation to the last, to shift for themselves for the future as best the situation permitted. When this outcome of the embassy was reported at Petelia, such dejection and fear unexpectedly seized their senate that some proposed to flee, each taking any possible road, and to abandon the city, while others, since they had been deserted by their old allies, proposed to join the rest of the Bruttians and through them to surrender to Hannibal. But those who thought nothing should be done hastily or rashly, and that they should deliberate again, prevailed. When the matter was brought up in less excitement the following day, the optimates carried their point, that they should bring in everything from the farms and strengthen the city and the walls.[1] B.C. 216

XXI. About the same time letters from Sicily and Sardinia were brought to Rome. First to be read in the senate were those from Sicily and Titus Otacilius, the propraetor, reporting that Publius Furius, the praetor, had come with his fleet from Africa to Lilybaeum; that Furius himself had been seriously wounded and his life was in the utmost danger; that neither pay nor grain was being furnished to the soldiers and the crews at the proper date, and they had no means of doing so; that he strongly urged that both be sent as soon as possible, and that they send a successor chosen, if they saw fit, from the number of the new praetors. Much the same facts in regard to pay and grain were reported from Sardinia by Aulus Cornelius Mammula, the propraetor. To each the reply was that there

A.U.C. 538 utrique non esse unde mitteretur, iussique ipsi
5 classibus atque exercitibus suis consulere. T. Otacilius ad unicum subsidium populi Romani, Hieronem,
legatos cum misisset, in stipendium quanti argenti
6 opus fuit et sex mensum frumentum accepit; Cornelio
in Sardinia civitates sociae benigne contulerunt. Et
Romae quoque propter penuriam argenti triumviri
mensarii rogatione M. Minuci tribuni plebis facti,
L. Aemilius Papus, qui consul censorque fuerat, et
M. Atilius Regulus, qui bis consul fuerat, et L.
7 Scribonius Libo, qui tum tribunus plebis erat. Et
duumviri creati M. et C. Atilii aedem Concordiae,
quam L. Manlius praetor voverat, dedicaverunt; et
tres pontifices creati, Q. Caecilius Metellus et Q.
Fabius Maximus et Q. Fulvius Flaccus, in locum P.
Scantini demortui et L. Aemili Pauli consulis et
Q. Aeli Paeti, qui ceciderant pugna Cannensi.

XXII. Cum cetera quae continuis cladibus fortuna
minuerat, quantum consiliis humanis adsequi po-
2 terant, patres explessent, tandem se quoque et
solitudinem curiae paucitatemque convenientium ad
3 publicum consilium respexerunt. Neque enim post
L. Aemilium et C. Flaminium censores senatus lectus
fuerat, cum tantum senatorum adversae pugnae, ad

[1] Hiero II had ruled Syracuse 270–215 B.C.; a faithful ally of the Romans from 263 to his death. For his sympathy and aid, including the gift of a golden Victory, after the battle of the Trasumennus, cf. XXII. xxxvii.

[2] In the citadel, begun in 217 B.C.; XXII. xxxiii. 7 f.

was nothing on hand to send, and they were ordered to provide for their own fleets and armies. Titus Otacilius sent legates to Hiero, the mainstay of the Roman people,[1] and received what money was needed for pay, and grain for six months. In Sardinia the allied states made generous contributions to Cornelius. And at Rome besides, on account of the lack of money, three bank-commissioners were named in accordance with a bill of Marcus Minucius, a tribune of the plebs, namely, Lucius Aemilius Papus, who had been consul and censor, and Marcus Atilius Regulus, who had been consul twice, and Lucius Scribonius Libo, who was at that time a tribune of the plebs. And Marcus Atilius and Gaius Atilius, elected duumvirs, dedicated a temple of Concord,[2] which Lucius Manlius had vowed in his praetorship. And three pontiffs, Quintus Caecilius Metellus and Quintus Fabius Maximus and Quintus Fulvius Flaccus, were elected[3] in place of Publius Scantinius, deceased, and of Lucius Aemilius Paulus, the consul, and Quintus Aelius Paetus, both of whom had fallen in the battle of Cannae. B.C. 216

XXII. After making good, in so far as they could accomplish it by human wisdom, the other losses fortune had caused by a series of disasters, the fathers at last had regard for themselves as well and for the desolate Senate House and the small number that came to the council of state. For since the censorship of Lucius Aemilius and Gaius Flaminius the list of the senate had not been revised, although the defeats and in addition the fate of individuals

[3] *I.e.* by the college of pontiffs. Fabius is the Delayer, dictator in 217 B.C. Fulvius was consul twice before this war, and twice again during the war, 212 and 209.

A.U.C. 538
hoc sui quemque casus per quinquennium absump-
4 sissent. Cum de ea re M. Aemilius praetor, dictatore
post Casilinum amissum profecto iam [1] ad exercitum,
exposcentibus cunctis rettulisset, tum Sp. Carvilius,
cum longa oratione non patrum [2] solum inopiam sed
paucitatem etiam civium ex quibus in patres legeren-
5 tur conquestus esset, explendi senatus causa et
iungendi artius Latini nominis cum populo Romano
magnopere se suadere dixit ut ex singulis populis
Latinorum binis senatoribus, quibus [3] patres Romani
censuissent, civitas daretur atque inde in [4] demor-
6 tuorum locum in senatum legerentur. Eam sententiam haud aequioribus animis quam ipsorum quon-
7 dam postulatum Latinorum patres audierunt; et
cum fremitus indignantium tota curia esset, et praecipue T. Manlius esse etiam nunc eius stirpis virum
diceret ex qua quondam in Capitolio consul minatus
esset quem Latinum in curia vidisset eum sua manu
8 se interfecturum, Q. Fabius Maximus numquam rei
ullius alieniore tempore mentionem factam in senatu
dicit quam inter tam suspensos sociorum animos
incertamque fidem id iactum quod insuper sollici-
9 taret eos. Eam unius hominis temerariam vocem
silentio omnium exstinguendam esse et, si quid
umquam arcani sanctive ad silendum in curia fuerit,

[1] iam A^y *Valla*: tam *P*(1): tandem *Luchs*: *om.* xC^x.
[2] patrum *H. J. Müller* (*this order*): senatus *x*: senatorum *Weissenborn*: eam *Harant*: *om. P*(1).
[3] quibus *J. H. Voss*: quos A^y: si *x*: *om. P*(1).
[4] inde in *x Frigell*: in *P*(1): ei in *Madvig*.

[1] Cf. above, vi. 8 and note.

had in the five years carried off so large a number of senators. Marcus Aemilius, the praetor, raised that question, as all demanded that he should, since the dictator had already gone to the army after the loss of Casilinum. Thereupon Spurius Carvilius, after complaining in a long speech, not of the lack of senators only, but also of the small number of citizens from whom men might be chosen into the senate, said that for the sake of recruiting the senate and of linking the Latins more closely with the Roman people, he strongly urged that citizenship be bestowed upon two senators from each of the Latin states, to be selected by the Roman fathers; and that from this number men be chosen into the senate in place of the deceased members. The fathers gave no more favourable hearing to this proposal than they had given to a former demand of the Latins themselves.[1] There was a murmur of indignation everywhere in the hall, and in particular Titus Manlius said that there still lived a man of the family to which belonged the consul who on the Capitol had once threatened that he would slay with his own hand any Latin he should see in the Senate House.[2] Upon that Quintus Fabius Maximus said that never had anything been mentioned in the senate at a more unfavourable moment than this had been broached, in the midst of such unsettled feeling and wavering loyalty among the allies, only to stir them up the more; that that rash utterance of a single man should be drowned by silence on the part of them all; and that, if there was ever any hallowed secret to be left unmentioned B.C. 216

[2] The threat was recorded in VIII. v. 7. The present Manlius had opposed ransoming the captives at Cannae; XXII. lx. 5 ff.

A.U.C. 538 id omnium maxime tegendum, occulendum, oblivis-
cendum, pro non dicto[1] habendum esse. Ita eius
rei oppressa mentio est.
10 Dictatorem, qui censor ante fuisset vetustissi-
musque ex iis qui viverent censoriis esset, creari
placuit qui senatum legeret, accirique C. Terentium
11 consulem ad dictatorem dicendum iusserunt. Qui ex
Apulia relicto ibi praesidio cum magnis itineribus
Romam redisset, nocte proxima, ut mos erat, M.
Fabium Buteonem ex senatus consulto sine magistro
equitum dictatorem in sex menses dixit. XXIII. Is
ubi cum lictoribus in rostra escendit, neque duos
dictatores tempore uno, quod numquam antea factum
2 esset, probare se dixit, neque dictatorem sine magistro equitum, nec censoriam vim uni permissam et
eidem iterum, nec dictatori, nisi rei gerendae causa
3 creato, in sex menses datum imperium. Quae in-
moderata forsan[2] tempus ac necessitas fecerit, iis
se modum impositurum: nam neque senatu quemquam moturum ex iis quos C. Flaminius L. Aemilius
4 censores in senatum legissent; transcribi tantum
recitarique eos iussurum, ne penes unum hominem
iudicium arbitriumque de fama ac moribus senatoris
fuerit; et ita in demortuorum locum sublecturum ut
ordo ordini, non homo homini praelatus videretur.
5 Recitato vetere senatu, inde primos in demortuorum
locum legit qui post L. Aemilium C. Flaminium cen-

[1] non dicto *M⁷A* : dicto *P*(11) : indicto *Alschefski*.
[2] forsan *Madvig* : fors *P*(1).

---

[1] *I.e.* Varro, defeated at Cannae.
[2] Minucius, master of the horse, had finally been given by the people equal authority with Fabius, but that did not make him legally a dictator; XXII. xxvi. 7; xxvii. 3.

in the senate, this above all others must be covered, concealed, forgotten, considered unsaid. So mention of the matter was suppressed. B.C. 216

It was decided that as dictator, to draw up the list of the senate, a man should be appointed who had previously been censor and was senior to all the other living ex-censors. And they ordered that Gaius Terentius,[1] the consul, be summoned that he might name a dictator. He returned to Rome by long stages from Apulia, leaving a garrison there; and that night, as was the custom, in accordance with the decree of the senate he named Marcus Fabius Buteo dictator for six months without master of the horse. XXIII. Fabius mounted the Rostra with his lictors and said that he did not approve of two dictators at the same time, an unprecedented thing,[2] nor of a dictator without master of the horse, nor of conferring a censor's power upon one man, and in fact to the same man a second time, nor of giving the full military authority for six months to a dictator not appointed for the conduct of affairs. He said that he would set a limit to such possible irregularities as the crisis and necessity had occasioned. For he would not eject from the senate any of those whom Gaius Flaminius and Lucius Aemilius as censors had chosen into the senate, but would order their names merely to be copied and read out, that judgment and decision in regard to the reputation and character of a senator might not rest with one man. And in place of the deceased he would make his choice in such a way that rank should obviously have been preferred to rank, not man to man. After reading the list of the old senate, he chose in place of the deceased first those who since the censorship of Lucius Aemilius

A.U.C. 538 sores curulem magistratum cepissent necdum in senatum lecti essent, ut quisque eorum primus creatus
6 erat; tum legit, qui aediles, tribuni plebis, quaestoresve fuerant; tum ex iis qui magistratus non[1] cepissent, qui spolia ex hoste fixa domi haberent aut
7 civicam coronam accepissent. Ita centum septuaginta septem cum ingenti adprobatione hominum in senatum lectis, extemplo se magistratu abdicavit privatusque de rostris descendit lictoribus abire
8 iussis, turbaeque se inmiscuit privatas agentium res, tempus hoc sedulo terens, ne deducendi sui causa populum de foro abduceret. Neque tamen elanguit cura hominum ea mora, frequentesque eum domum
9 deduxerunt. Consul nocte insequenti ad exercitum redit non facto certiore senatu, ne comitiorum causa in urbe retineretur.

XXIV. Postero die consultus a M. Pomponio praetore senatus decrevit dictatori scribendum uti, si e re publica censeret esse, ad consules subrogandos veniret
2 cum magistro equitum et praetore M. Marcello, ut ex iis praesentibus noscere patres possent quo statu res publica esset, consiliaque ex rebus caperent. Qui acciti erant, omnes venerunt relictis legatis qui
3 legionibus praeessent. Dictator de se pauca ac

[1] non *Sigonius*: *om.* *P*(1): non ⟨magistratus⟩ *Conway*: minores ⟨magistratus⟩ *Stroth.*

---

[1] In 220 B.C.; *Periocha* 20.
[2] Pending the revision of the list by the censors, once in five years in the normal course of things.

and Gaius Flaminius [1] had held a curule office and had not yet been chosen into the senate,[2] in each case in the order of his election. Then he chose those who had been aediles,[3] tribunes of the people or quaestors; then, from the number of those who had not held offices, the men who had spoils of the enemy affixed to their houses or had received the civic wreath.[4] Having thus chosen a hundred and seventy-seven into the senate with great approval, he at once abdicated his office and came down from the Rostra a private citizen, after ordering his lictors to leave him. And he mingled with the crowd of those engaged in private business, deliberately killing time, in order not to draw the people away from the forum for the purpose of escorting him. Yet men's attention was not relaxed by that delay, and so in large numbers they escorted him home. The consul returned that night to the army without informing the senate, for fear of being detained in the city to conduct the elections. B.C. 216

XXIV. On the next day the senate, presided over by Marcus Pomponius, the praetor, decreed that the dictator should be informed by letter that, if he thought it to the public interest, he should come with the master of the horse and the praetor, Marcus Marcellus, for the election of consuls, in order that from them in person the fathers could learn what was the condition of the state and make their plans in accordance with the facts. All of those summoned came, leaving their lieutenants to command the legions. The dictator spoke briefly and

[3] *I.e.* plebeian aediles.

[4] The reward of a soldier who had saved the life of a fellow-citizen.

A.U.C. 538 modice locutus in magistrum equitum Ti. Sempronium Gracchum magnam partem gloriae vertit, comitiaque edixit, quibus L. Postumius tertium absens, qui tum Galliam provinciam obtinebat, et Ti. Sempronius Gracchus, qui tum magister equitum et aedilis curulis
4 erat, consules creantur. Praetores inde creati M. Valerius Laevinus iterum, Ap. Claudius Pulcher,
5 Q. Fulvius Flaccus, Q. Mucius Scaevola. Dictator creatis magistratibus Teanum in hiberna ad exercitum redit relicto magistro equitum Romae, qui, cum post paucos dies magistratum initurus esset, de exercitibus scribendis conparandisque in annum patres consuleret.

Cum eae res maxime agerentur, nova clades nuntiata, aliam super aliam cumulante in eum annum fortuna, L. Postumium consulem designatum in
7 Gallia ipsum atque exercitum deletos. Silva erat vasta—Litanam Galli vocabant—qua exercitum traducturus erat. Eius silvae dextra laevaque circa viam Galli arbores ita inciderunt ut inmotae starent,
8 momento levi inpulsae occiderent. Legiones duas Romanas habebat Postumius, sociumque ab supero mari tantum conscripserat ut viginti quinque milia
9 armatorum in agros hostium induxerit. Galli oram extremae silvae cum circumsedissent, ubi intravit

[1] What were the special achievements of M. Junius Pera we are not told. Probably "glory" is only conventional for "credit." The consul is absent with the army.

[2] The northernmost town in Campania was Teanum Sidicinum, an important road centre in a strong position.

modestly of himself, and then diverted a large share B.C. 216
of the glory[1] to the master of the horse, Tiberius Sempronius Gracchus; and he ordered the elections at which these consuls were named: Lucius Postumius for the third time, then absent with Gaul as his sphere of action, and Tiberius Sempronius Gracchus, who was at that time master of the horse and curule aedile. Then the following men were elected as praetors: Marcus Valerius Laevinus for the second time, Appius Claudius Pulcher, Quintus Fulvius Flaccus, Quintus Mucius Scaevola. The dictator, after the election of magistrates, returned to the army and the winter quarters at Teanum,[2] leaving the master of the horse at Rome, in order that he, inasmuch as he was to enter upon office a few days later, might advise with the fathers in regard to enrolling and providing armies for the year.

Just as these measures were being taken, a fresh disaster was reported—for fortune was piling one upon another for that year—namely, that the consul designate, Lucius Postumius, had perished, himself and his army, in Gaul. There was a huge forest,[3] called Litana by the Gauls, by way of which he was about to lead his army. In that forest the Gauls hacked the trees to right and left of the road in such a way that, if not disturbed, they stood, but fell if pushed slightly. Postumius had two Roman legions, and had enlisted from the coast of the Upper Sea[4] such numbers of allies that he led twenty-five thousand armed men into the enemy's territory. The Gauls had surrounded the very edge of the forest,

[3] Near Mutina (Modena), and northwest of Bononia (Bologna).

[4] Cf. xxxviii. 1; contrast i. 5.

A.U.C. 538 agmen saltum, tum extremas arborum succisarum impellunt. Quae alia in aliam, instabilem per se ac male haerentem, incidentes ancipiti strage arma, viros, equos obruerunt, ut vix decem homines effu-
10 gerent. Nam cum exanimati plerique essent arborum truncis fragmentisque ramorum, ceteram multitudinem inopinato malo trepidam Galli saltum omnem armati circumsedentes interfecerunt, paucis e tanto numero captis, qui pontem fluminis petentes,
11 obsesso ante ab hostibus ponte, interclusi sunt. Ibi Postumius omni vi ne caperetur dimicans occubuit. Spolia corporis caputque praecisum ducis Boii ovantes templo quod sanctissimum est apud eos
12 intulere. Purgato inde capite, ut mos iis est, calvam auro caelavere, idque sacrum vas iis erat quo sollemnibus libarent poculumque idem sacerdotibus[1]
13 esset ac templi antistitibus. Praeda quoque haud minor Gallis quam victoria fuit; nam etsi magna pars animalium strage silvae oppressa erat, tamen ceterae res, quia nihil dissipatum fuga est, stratae per omnem iacentis agminis ordinem inventae sunt.

XXV. Hac nuntiata clade cum per dies multos in tanto pavore fuisset civitas ut tabernis clausis velut

[1] sacerdotibus *Alschefski*: sacerdotis *P*(1): sacerdoti *x Sigonius*.

---

[1] The particular spot chosen for the trap. Although *saltus* often = *silva*, the hacking of trees must have been confined to some stretch of the road offering special advantages to the enemy, and near the point where the road emerged into open country. Cf. xxxiii. 8.

[2] Here also it is difficult to believe that *saltus* is used as another word for "forest," since the whole *silva vasta* (§ 7) could hardly be surrounded by the Gauls. Cf. Frontinus I. vi. 4.

and when the column entered a defile[1] they pushed against the outermost of the trees that had been hacked near the ground. As these fell, each upon the next tree, which was in itself unsteady and had only a slight hold, piling up from both sides they overwhelmed arms, men and horses, so that hardly ten men escaped. For after very many had been killed by tree-trunks and broken branches, and the rest of the troops were alarmed by the unforeseen calamity, the Gauls under arms, surrounding the whole defile[2] slew them, while but few out of so many were captured,—the men who were making their way to a bridge over a river, but were cut off, since the bridge had by that time been occupied by the enemy. There Postumius fell fighting with all his might to avoid capture. Spoils taken from his body and the severed head of the general were carried in triumph by the Boians to the temple which is most revered in their land. Then after cleaning the head they adorned the skull with gold according to their custom. And it served them as a sacred vessel from which to pour libations at festivals and at the same time as a drinking cup for the priests and keepers of the temple. The booty also meant no less to the Gauls than the victory. For although a large part of the cattle had been crushed by fallen trees, still everything else was found strewn the whole length of the column of the slain, since nothing was scattered by flight. B.C. 216

XXV. When this disaster was reported, the city was for many days in such alarm that, in view of the stillness, like that of night, produced

Even in 43 B.C. there were still remnants of forest along the Aemilian Way; *ib.* II. v. 39.

A.U.C. 538 nocturna solitudine per urbem acta senatus aedilibus
2 negotium daret ut urbem circumirent aperirique tabernas et maestitiae publicae speciem urbi demi iuberent, tum Ti. Sempronius senatum habuit
3 consolatusque patres est, et adhortatus ne qui Cannensi ruinae non succubuissent ad minores calami-
4 tates animos summitterent. Quod ad Carthaginienses hostes Hannibalemque attineret, prospera modo essent, sicut speraret, futura, Gallicum bellum et omitti tuto et differri posse, ultionemque eam fraudis in deorum ac populi Romani potestate fore. De hoste Poeno exercitibusque, per quos id bellum
5 gereretur, consultandum atque agitandum. Ipse primum quid peditum equitumque, quid civium, quid sociorum in exercitu esset dictatoris, disseruit; tum Marcellus suarum copiarum summam exposuit.
6 Quid in Apulia cum C. Terentio consule esset a peritis quaesitum est; nec unde[1] consulares exercitus satis firmi ad tantum bellum efficerentur inibatur ratio. Itaque Galliam, quamquam stimulabat iusta ira, omitti eo anno placuit. Exercitus dictatoris con-
7 suli decretus est. De exercitu M. Marcelli, qui eorum ex fuga Cannensi essent, in Siciliam eos traduci atque ibi militare donec in Italia bellum esset
8 placuit; eodem ex dictatoris legionibus reici militem minimi quemque roboris, nullo praestituto militiae tempore nisi quod stipendiorum legitimorum esset.

[1] nec unde *Gronovius*: necundo *P*: ne secundo P^2R^x(14): nec secundo *C*: nec unde duo *Madvig*.

---

[1] This he did as *magister equitum*. His consulship would begin at the Ides of March; xxx. 17.

throughout the city by the closing of the shops, the senate charged the aediles with the duty of going about the city and ordering that shops be opened and the appearance of public mourning removed from the city. And then Tiberius Sempronius held a session of the senate;[1] and he comforted the fathers, and urged that men who had not given way to the catastrophe at Cannae should not lose heart in the face of lesser disasters. So far as concerned the Carthaginian enemy and Hannibal, he said that, if only coming events should prove favourable, as he hoped, a Gallic war could be both safely neglected and postponed, and punishment for that treachery would be in the power of the gods and of the Roman people. It was in regard to the Carthaginian enemy and the armies with which to carry on that war that they must deliberate and debate. He himself first stated what number of infantry and cavalry, of citizens and allies, were in the dictator's army. Then Marcellus set forth the total of his forces. As to what troops were in Apulia with the consul Gaius Terentius, those who knew were questioned; and no method of making up consular armies strong enough for so great a war was found. And so, although righteous indignation goaded them, it was decided that Gaul should be left out of account that year. The dictator's army was assigned to the consul. As for the army of Marcus Marcellus, it was voted that those of them who were survivors of the rout at Cannae should be transported to Sicily and serve there so long as there should be war in Italy; also that from the dictator's legions all the least efficient soldiers should be sent away to the same province, with no definite term of service except that of the campaigns B.C. 216

A.U.C. 538

9 Duae legiones urbanae alteri consuli, qui in locum L.
Postumi suffectus esset, decretae sunt, eumque, cum
primum salvis auspiciis posset, creari placuit;
10 legiones praeterea duas primo quoque tempore ex
Sicilia acciri, atque inde consulem, cui legiones
urbanae evenissent, militum sumere quantum opus
esset; C. Terentio consuli propagari [1] in annum
imperium, neque de eo exercitu quem ad praesidium
Apuliae haberet quicquam minui.

XXVI. Dum haec in Italia geruntur apparanturque.
nihilo segnius in Hispania bellum erat, sed ad eam
2 diem magis prosperum Romanis. P. et Cn. Scipionibus inter se partitis copias, ut Gnaeus terra, Publius
navibus rem gereret, Hasdrubal Poenorum imperator,
neutri parti virium satis fidens, procul ab hoste intervallo ac locis tutus tenebat se, quoad multum ac diu
obtestanti quattuor milia peditum et quingenti [2]
3 equites in supplementum missi ex Africa sunt. Tum
refecta tandem spe castra propius hostem movit,
classemque et ipse instrui pararique iubet ad insulas
4 maritimamque oram tutandam. In ipso impetu mo-
vendarum de integro rerum perculit eum praefec-
torum navium transitio, qui post classem ad Hiberum
per pavorem desertam graviter increpiti numquam

[1] propagari *P*(1): prorogari *A*ˣ*Madvig*.

[2] et quingenti (*i.e.* D) A^2z: et *P*(4): et mille *Alschefski* (*the numeral* ∞ *is often omitted in P*).

---

[1] The usual word would be *prorogari*. But Cicero has *provinciae propagator*, *Att.* VIII. iii. 3, and uses the verb in the sense of "prolong" in *Cat.* iii. 26; so Suetonius *Aug.* 23.

[2] *I.e.* than in Italy.

[3] As voted by the Carthaginian senate, xiii. 7.

[4] Cf. XXII. xix. 11 f. Their desertion now consisted in going over to native tribes which sided with the Romans,

fixed by law. The two city legions were assigned to the other consul, to be elected in place of Lucius Postumius; and it was voted that he be elected as soon as possible with due regard to the auspices; further, that two legions be summoned as soon as might be from Sicily, and that from them the consul to whom the city legions fell should take as many soldiers as he needed; also that the command of Gaius Terentius, the consul, should be extended[1] for one year and no reduction made in the army which he had for the defence of Apulia. B.C. 216

XXVI. During these operations and these preparations in Italy the war in Spain was no less active, but up to that time more successful[2] for the Romans. Publius and Gnaeus Scipio had divided the forces between them, so that Gnaeus should carry on the war on land, Publius with the fleet; and Hasdrubal, commander-in-chief of the Carthaginians, since he could not fully depend upon either arm of his forces, remained far from the enemy, being protected by distance and position, until, in answer to pleas urgent and long-continued, four thousand infantry and five hundred cavalry were sent from Africa to reinforce him.[3] Then, with hopes at last renewed, he moved his camp nearer to the enemy, and he too ordered that a fleet should be built and equipped, in order to protect the islands and the sea-coast. In the very flush of renewed operations he met a blow in the desertion of the commanders of his ships, who, being severely reprimanded after their abandonment of the fleet at the Hiberus in their fright,[4] had never

especially to the Tartesii (Turdetani), on the lower Baetis (Guadalquivir).

A.U.C. 538 deinde satis fidi aut duci aut Carthaginiensium rebus
5 fuerant. Fecerant hi transfugae motum in Tartesiorum gente, desciverantque iis auctoribus urbes
aliquot; una etiam ab ipsis vi capta fuerat.
6 In eam gentem versum ab Romanis bellum est,
infestoque exercitu Hasdrubal ingressus agrum
hostium pro captae ante dies paucos urbis moenibus
Chalbum, nobilem Tartesiorum ducem, cum valido
exercitu castris se tenentem, adgredi statuit.
7 Praemissa igitur levi armatura quae eliceret hostis ad
certamen, equitum partem ad populandum per agros
8 passim dimisit et [1] ut palantis exciperent. Simul et
ad castra tumultus erat et per agros fugaque et
caedes; deinde undique diversis itineribus cum in
castra se recepissent, adeo repente decessit animis
pavor ut non ad munimenta modo defendenda satis
animorum esset sed etiam ad lacessendum proelio
9 hostem. Erumpunt igitur agmine e castris tripu-
diantes more suo, repentinaque eorum audacia
terrorem hosti paulo ante ultro lacessenti incussit.
10 Itaque et ipse Hasdrubal in collem satis arduum,
flumine etiam obiecto tutum,[2] copias subducit et
praemissam levem armaturam equitesque palatos
eodem recipit, nec aut colli aut flumini satis fidens,
11 castra vallo permunit. In hoc alterno pavore certamina aliquot sunt contracta; nec Numida Hispano

[1] et *Heusinger*: *om.* *P*(1).

[2] tutum *Heerwagen*: tum *P*(1), *with* tutum *before* flumine.

since been entirely loyal either to the general or to the cause of Carthage. These deserters had made trouble in the tribe of the Tartesii, and at their instigation a number of cities had rebelled. One city had even been stormed by them. B.C. 216

It was against this tribe that the war was now diverted from the Romans, and Hasdrubal, having entered the territory of the enemy with a hostile army, resolved to attack a noble in command of the Tartesii, Chalbus, who with a strong army was keeping to his camp before the walls of a city captured a few days before. Therefore Hasdrubal, sending the light-armed in advance, to draw out the enemy to battle, scattered part of his cavalry over the farms to ravage them and to capture stragglers. There was confusion at the camp and at the same time flight and slaughter in the country around. Then, after they had made their way from all sides back to the camp by different roads, fear was so suddenly banished from their hearts that they had sufficient spirit not only to defend the fortifications but also to attack the enemy. Accordingly they sallied out of the camp in a column, dancing, as is their custom; and their sudden boldness inspired alarm in the enemy, who a little before had been the aggressor. And so Hasdrubal likewise led his forces up a very steep hill, further defended by a river in front. Also he got back the light-armed who had been sent ahead and the scattered cavalry to the same position. Unable to put sufficient confidence in either the hill or the river, he strongly fortified his camp with an earthwork. While fear was shifting thus from one side to the other, a number of engagements took place, and the Numidian horseman was no match for the

A.U.C. 538 eques par fuit nec iaculator Maurus caetrato, velocitate pari, robore animi viriumque aliquantum praestanti.

XXVII. Postquam neque elicere Poenum ad certamen obversati castris poterant neque castrorum
2 oppugnatio facilis erat, urbem Ascuam, quo finis hostium ingrediens Hasdrubal frumentum commeatusque alios convexerat, vi capiunt omnique circa agro potiuntur; nec iam aut in agmine aut in castris
3 ullo imperio contineri. Quam ubi neglegentiam ex re, ut fit, bene gesta oriri senserat Hasdrubal, cohortatus milites ut palatos sine signis hostes adgrederentur, degressus colle pergit ire acie instructa ad castra.
4 Quem ut adesse tumultuose nuntii refugientes [1] ex speculis stationibusque attulere, ad arma conclama-
5 tum est. Ut quisque arma ceperat, sine imperio, sine signo, incompositi, inordinati in proelium ruunt. Iam primi conseruerant manus, cum alii catervatim
6 currerent, alii nondum e castris exissent. Tamen primo ipsa audacia terruere hostem; deinde rari in confertos inlati, cum paucitas parum tuta esset, respicere alii alios et undique pulsi coire in orbem,
7 et dum corpora [2] corporibus applicant armaque armis iungunt, in artum conpulsi, cum vix movendis armis satis spatii esset, corona hostium cincti ad

[1] nuntii refugientes A^2z : nuntiares fugientes *PC?*(11) (*with* nuntiare *M*[1]*?A*).
[2] corpora *x* : *om.* *P*(1).

Spaniard, nor the Moorish dart-thrower for the man with the wicker shield, the Spaniard in both cases being an equal in speed and quite superior in spirit and strength. B.C. 216

XXVII. After the Tartesii had repeatedly failed to draw the Carthaginian out to battle by facing his camp, and it was also not easy to assault the camp, they took by storm the city of Ascua, to which Hasdrubal, on entering the land of the enemy, had brought grain and other supplies; and they gained possession of all the country around. And they could no longer be restrained by any authority either on the march or in camp. Hasdrubal, perceiving that this carelessness came, as usually happens, from success, exhorted his soldiers to attack the enemy while dispersed and in no formation, and coming down from the hill he proceeded to their camp in battle order. When his approach was reported by messengers fleeing wildly from the watch-towers and guard-posts, they shouted "To arms!" Snatching up arms, each man for himself, without commanders, without orders, in no units or formations, they dashed into battle. Already the first men had engaged, while some charged in separate masses and others had not yet left the camp. Nevertheless they at first frightened the enemy by sheer audacity. Then, as stragglers advancing against dense ranks, finding no safety in small numbers, they looked to one another for help; and, beaten back from every side, they formed a circle. And as they crowded bodies against bodies and touched arms to arms, they were forced into close quarters. Having hardly room enough to move their weapons, they were encircled by the enemy, and the slaughter continued until late in the

A.U.C. 538
8 multum diei caeduntur; exigua pars eruptione facta
silvas ac montis petit. Parique terrore et castra
sunt deserta et universa gens postero die in deditionem venit.
9 Nec diu in pacto[1] mansit; nam subinde ab Carthagine allatum est ut Hasdrubal primo quoque tempore
in Italiam exercitum duceret, quae volgata res per
Hispaniam omnium ferme animos ad Romanos avertit.
10 Itaque Hasdrubal extemplo litteras Carthaginem
mittit, indicans quanto fama profectionis suae damno
fuisset; si vero inde pergeret, priusquam Hiberum
11 transiret Romanorum Hispaniam fore; nam praeterquam quod nec praesidium nec ducem haberet
quem relinqueret pro se, eos imperatores esse
Romanos quibus vix aequis viribus resisti possit.[2]
12 Itaque si ulla Hispaniae cura esset, successorem sibi
cum valido exercitu mitterent; cui ut[3] omnia
prospere evenirent, non tamen otiosam provinciam
fore.

XXVIII. Eae litterae quamquam primo admodum
moverunt senatum, tamen, quia Italiae cura prior
potiorque erat, nihil de Hasdrubale neque de copiis
2 eius mutatum est; Himilco cum exercitu iusto et
aucta classe ad retinendam terra marique ac tuen-
3 dam Hispaniam est missus. Qui ut pedestris
navalisque copias traiecit, castris communitis navibus-
que subductis et vallo circumdatis, cum equitibus
delectis ipse, quantum maxime adcelerare poterat,

[1] pacto *Stroth*: pacato *P*(1).
[2] possit *P*(1) *Walters*: posset *Forchhammer*, *Madvig*.
[3] ut *Gronovius*: si *A*[2]: *om.* *P*(1).

---

[1] Evidently exaggerated, as in xxix. 16 and xxxii. 6. A prosperous city near the Hiberus is mentioned in xxviii. 10 as still loyal to the Carthaginians.

day. A very small part of them sallied out and made B.C. 216
for the woods and the mountains. In no less alarm the camp was abandoned, and on the next day the whole tribe surrendered.

Yet not for long did the tribe abide by the agreement. For soon came the order from Carthage that Hasdrubal should at the first opportunity lead his army into Italy. And the spreading of this news throughout Spain made nearly all incline to the side of the Romans.[1] Accordingly Hasdrubal at once sent a letter to Carthage, showing what a loss the mere report of his departure had caused; that if he were actually to leave the country, Spain would belong to the Romans before he should cross the Hiberus.[2] For besides the lack of both an army and a general to leave in his place, so able were the Roman generals that they could scarcely be resisted if the forces were evenly matched. And so, if they had any regard for Spain, they should send him a successor with a strong army. Even if all should go well, that man would still find it no peaceful province.

XXVIII. Though this letter at first greatly stirred the senate, nevertheless, since concern for Italy was older and stronger, no change was made either in regard to Hasdrubal or to his forces. But Himilco was sent with a complete army and an enlarged fleet to hold and defend Spain by land and sea. After transporting his land and naval forces, Himilco fortified a camp, beached his ships and surrounded them with an earthwork. Then he himself with picked horsemen, making his way with all possible speed, and with equal alertness through the

[2] The Ebro was the treaty boundary; XXI. ii. 7.

A.U.C. 538

per dubios infestosque populos iuxta intentus ad
4 Hasdrubalem pervenit. Cum decreta senatus man-
dataque exposuisset atque edoctus esset [1] ipse in
vicem quem ad modum tractandum bellum in
Hispania foret, retro in sua castra redit [2] nulla re
quam celeritate tutior, quod undique abierat ante-
5 quam consentirent. Hasdrubal priusquam moveret
castra pecunias imperat populis omnibus suae
dicionis, satis gnarus Hannibalem transitus quosdam
6 pretio mercatum nec auxilia Gallica aliter quam
conducta habuisse; inopem tantum iter ingressum
vix penetraturum ad Alpis fuisse. Pecuniis igitur
raptim exactis ad Hiberum descendit.

7 Decreta Carthaginiensium et Hasdrubalis iter ubi
ad Romanos sunt perlata, omnibus omissis rebus
ambo duces iunctis copiis ire obviam coeptis atque
8 obsistere parant, rati, si Hannibali, vix per se ipsi
tolerando Italiae hosti, Hasdrubal dux atque Hispaniensis exercitus esset iunctus, illum finem Ro-
9 mani imperii fore. His anxii curis ad Hiberum
contrahunt copias, et transito amne cum diu con-
sultassent utrum castra castris conferrent an satis [3]
haberent sociis Carthaginiensium oppugnandis mo-
10 rari ab itinere proposito hostem, urbem a propinquo
flumine Hiberam appellatam, opulentissimam ea
11 tempestate regionis eius, oppugnare parant. Quod
ubi sensit Hasdrubal, pro ope ferenda sociis pergit
ire ipse ad urbem deditam nuper in fidem Romanorum

[1] edoctus esset A^{v} *Valla*: edocuisset P^{2}?(1): -uisse *P*.
[2] redit *P*: rediit P^{3}(1).
[3] an satis A^{v} *Valla*: antis *PR*: an iis *C*: tantis (14).

wavering and the hostile tribes, reached Hasdrubal. B.C. 216
After setting forth the decrees and instructions of the senate, and being himself informed in turn how the war in Spain must be conducted, he went back to his own camp, being protected by his quickness more than anything else, since he had left each place before the enemy could agree upon action. Hasdrubal, before breaking camp, exacted money from all the tribes under his rule, knowing well that Hannibal had repeatedly bought the right of passage, and that he had Gallic auxiliaries only by hiring them; but that if he had set out on so long a march without funds, he would scarcely have made his way to the Alps. Therefore he exacted money in haste and came down to the Hiberus.

When news of the decrees of the Carthaginians and Hasdrubal's expedition reached the Roman commanders, both dropped everything, and uniting their forces prepared to meet and resist his efforts, thinking that if Hannibal, who was himself an enemy Italy could scarcely endure, should be joined by Hasdrubal as a general and by an army from Spain, that would be the end of the Roman power. Troubled by these apprehensions, they concentrated their troops at the Hiberus, crossed the river, and after protracted deliberation, whether to pitch camp near that of the enemy or to be satisfied with keeping him from his projected march by attacking allies of the Carthaginians, they prepared to attack a city which had its name Hibera from the river near by, the richest city of the region at that time. On learning this Hasdrubal, instead of bringing aid to his allies, proceeded likewise to attack a city which had recently surrendered to the Romans. Thus the siege

A.U.C. 538

12 oppugnandam. Ita iam coepta obsidio omissa ab Romanis est et in ipsum Hasdrubalem versum bellum.

XXIX. Quinque milium intervallo castra distantia habuere paucos dies, nec sine levibus proeliis nec ut
2 in aciem exirent; tandem uno eodemque die velut ex composito utrimque signum pugnae propositum est atque omnibus copiis in campum descensum.
3 Triplex stetit Romana acies: velitum pars inter antesignanos locata, pars post signa accepta; equites
4 cornua cinxere. Hasdrubal mediam aciem Hispanis firmat; in cornibus, dextro Poenos locat, laevo Afros mercennariorumque auxilia; equitum Numidas Poenorum peditibus, ceteros Afris pro cornibus apponit.
5 Nec omnes Numidae in dextro locati cornu, sed quibus desultorum in modum binos trahentibus equos inter acerrimam saepe pugnam in recentem equum ex fesso armatis transultare mos erat; tanta velocitas ipsis tamque docile equorum genus est.
6 Cum hoc modo instructi starent, imperatorum utriusque partis haud ferme dispares spes erant; nam ne multum [1] quidem aut numero aut genere militum [2] hi aut illi praestabant; militibus longe
7 dispar animus erat. Romanis enim, quamquam procul a patria pugnarent, facile persuaserant duces pro Italia atque urbe Romana eos pugnare; itaque, velut quibus reditus in patriam in [3] eo discrimine pugnae verteretur, obstinaverant animis vincere aut

[1] multum *P*(1): militum *Harant, Conway*: minimum *Koch*.
[2] militum *P*(3): multum *D Conway*.
[3] in *Madvig*: *om.* *P*(1).

---

[1] Cf. XXXV. xxviii. 8.

already begun was abandoned by the Romans and B.C. 216
the war directed against Hasdrubal himself.

XXIX. They had their camps five miles apart for a few days, not without skirmishes, but without drawing up lines of battle. Finally on one and the same day, as though by agreement, the signal for battle was raised on both sides and with all their forces they went down into the plain. The Roman line stood in triple ranks. Some of the light-armed were posted in the intervals between the maniples in advance of the standards, some placed behind the standards. Cavalry covered the wings. Hasdrubal made a strong centre of Spanish troops; on the right wing he placed Carthaginians, on the left Africans and mercenary auxiliaries. Of the cavalry he stationed the Numidians on the wing of the Carthaginian infantry, the rest on that of the Africans. And not all of his Numidians were placed on the right wing, but only those who, taking two horses apiece[1] after the manner of performers, had the custom of leaping armed from the tired horse to the fresh, often in the very heat of battle; such was the agility of the men, and so well-trained their breed of horses. While they were standing in this array, the hopes of the generals on the two sides were fairly balanced; for there was also not much superiority for the one army or the other either in the number or the type of its soldiers. But the spirit of the soldiers was far from being matched. For the Romans, although fighting far from their country, had been easily persuaded by their generals that they were fighting in defence of Italy and the city of Rome. And so, as men whose return to their native land would depend upon the issue of that battle, they had made up their

A.U.C. 538

8 mori. Minus pertinaces viros habebat altera acies;
nam maxima pars Hispani erant, qui vinci in Hispania
9 quam victores in Italiam trahi malebant. Primo
igitur concursu, cum vix pila coniecta essent, rettulit
pedem media acies, inferentibusque se magno impetu
10 Romanis vertit terga. Nihilo segnius in[1] cornibus
proelium fuit. Hinc Poenus, hinc Afer urguet, et
11 velut in circumventos proelio ancipiti pugnant; sed
cum in medium tota iam coisset Romana acies, satis
12 virium ad dimovenda hostium cornua habuit. Ita
duo diversa proelia erant. Utroque Romani, ut qui
pulsis iam ante mediis et numero et robore virorum
13 praestarent, haud dubie superant. Magna vis
hominum ibi occisa, et nisi Hispani vixdum conserto
proelio tam effuse fugissent, perpauci ex tota super-
14 fuissent acie. Equestris pugna nulla admodum fuit,
quia, simul inclinatam mediam aciem Mauri Numi-
daeque videre,[2] extemplo fuga effusa nuda cornua
15 elephantis quoque prae se actis deseruere. Hasdrubal usque ad ultimum eventum pugnae moratus e
media caede cum paucis effugit. Castra Romani
16 cepere atque diripuere. Ea pugna si qua dubia in
Hispania erant Romanis adiunxit, Hasdrubalique
non modo in Italiam traducendi exercitus sed ne
manendi quidem satis tuto in Hispania spes [3] reliqua

[1] in A^{1}: *om.* $P(1)$ *Frigell.*
[2] videre *Riemann, Luchs*: viderent P: viderunt $P^{3}(1)$.
[3] spes C^{4} *Gronovius*: spe $P(4)$: spem $M^{2}D$.

---

[1] As many as 25,000 according to Eutropius III. 11.

minds to win or die. The other battle-line had men less firmly resolved. For the majority were Spaniards, who preferred to be vanquished in Spain, rather than as victors to be dragged to Italy. Therefore at the first clash, when they had barely hurled their javelins, the centre fell back, and, as the Romans advanced with a great charge, retreated. On the wings, however, there was more spirited fighting. On the one hand the Carthaginians pressed them hard, on the other hand the Africans; and it was a double conflict against men presumed to have been surrounded. But, although the whole Roman line had by this time crowded into the centre, it had sufficient strength to force apart the wings of the enemy. Thus there were two battles in opposite directions. In both the Romans were unquestionably victorious, since, once the centre had been routed, they were superior both in the numbers and in the strength of their men. A great number of men [1] were slain there, and if the Spaniards had not fled in such confusion when the battle had scarcely begun, very few out of that entire line would have survived. The cavalry were not engaged at all, since, as soon as the Mauri and the Numidians saw the centre giving way, they at once abandoned the wings, exposed by their wild flight as they drove the elephants also before them. Hasdrubal, after waiting for the final outcome of the battle, escaped with a few men out of the midst of the slaughter. His camp the Romans captured and plundered. That battle brought to the Roman side all that still wavered in Spain, and Hasdrubal had left to him no hope, not only of leading his army over into Italy, but not even of remaining with any safety in Spain. When these facts were generally known B.C. 216

A.U.C. 538

17 erat.[1] Quae posteaquam litteris Scipionum Romae
volgata sunt, non tam victoria quam prohibito
Hasdrubalis in Italiam transitu laetabantur.

XXX. Dum haec in Hispania geruntur, Petelia
in Bruttiis aliquot post mensibus quam coepta oppugnari erat ab Himilcone praefecto Hannibalis expu-
2 gnata est. Multo sanguine ac volneribus ea Poenis
victoria stetit, nec ulla magis vis obsessos quam
3 fames expugnavit. Absumptis enim frugum ali-
mentis carnisque omnis generis quadrupedum suetae
insuetaeque,[2] postremo coriis herbisque et radicibus
4 et corticibus teneris strictisque foliis vixere, nec ante
quam vires ad standum in muris ferendaque arma
5 deerant expugnati sunt. Recepta Petelia Poenus
ad Consentiam copias traducit, quam minus pertina-
citer defensam intra paucos dies in deditionem
6 accepit. Isdem ferme diebus et Bruttiorum exercitus
Crotonem, Graecam urbem, circumsedit, opulentam
quondam armis virisque, tum iam adeo multis
magnisque cladibus adflictam ut omnis aetatis minus
7 duo milia civium superessent. Itaque urbe a
defensoribus vasta [3] facile potiti hostes sunt; arx
tantum retenta, in quam inter tumultum captae
8 urbis e media caede quidam effugere. Et Locrenses
descivere ad Bruttios Poenosque prodita multitudine
9 a principibus. Regini tantummodo regionis eius et
in fide erga Romanos et potestatis suae ad ultimum

[1] reliqua erat *Gronovius*: relinquerat *P*(11): reliquerat *CM*[3].

[2] insuetae *Fabri*: *om.* *P*(1).

[3] vasta *P*: vastata *P*[2](1).

---

[1] Hasdrubal's invasion of Italy was carried out nine years later to a fatal conclusion at the Metaurus, XXVII. xlix. 4.

[2] For the long siege of Petelia cf. the note on xx. 10.

at Rome through the letter of the Scipios, people B.C. 216
rejoiced, not so much over the victory, as that Hasdrubal's crossing into Italy had been prevented.[1]

XXX. While these things were going on in Spain, Petelia,[2] in the land of the Bruttii, was taken by Himilco, Hannibal's prefect, some months after the siege began. That victory cost the Carthaginians much blood and many wounds, and starvation[3] more than any assault overpowered the besieged. For after they had consumed their food-supply in cereals and flesh, the familiar and the unfamiliar, of four-footed beasts of every kind, they finally lived on hides and grasses and roots and tender bark and leaves stripped off. And they were not overpowered until they had no strength left to stand on the walls and bear arms. Having taken Petelia, the Carthaginian led his troops across to Consentia, and as it was less obstinately defended, he received its surrender within a few days. About the same time an army of the Bruttians also besieged Croton,[4] a Greek city formerly rich in arms and men, but even then so crushed by many great disasters that, including all ages, less than two thousand citizens remained. And so the enemy easily gained possession of the city bereft of its defenders. Only the citadel was still held, and to it some, in the uproar of a captured city, made their escape out of the midst of slaughter. And Locri went over to the Bruttians and Carthaginians, the populace having been betrayed by the leading men. Regium alone in that region remained loyal to the Romans and to the very last independent.

[3] Polybius also (VII. i. 3) gave such details as follow.

[4] The story of the siege and capture of Croton, on the Gulf of Tarentum, is told in some detail in XXIV. ii f.

A.U.C. 538

10 manserunt. In Siciliam quoque eadem inclinatio animorum pervenit, et ne domus quidem Hieronis
11 tota ab defectione abstinuit. Namque Gelo, maximus stirpis, contempta simul senectute patris simul post Cannensem cladem Romana societate ad Poenos
12 defecit, movissetque in Sicilia res, nisi mors adeo opportuna ut patrem quoque suspicione aspergeret, armantem eum multitudinem sollicitantemque socios
13 absumpsisset. Haec eo anno in Italia, in Africa, in Sicilia, in Hispania vario eventu acta.

Exitu anni Q. Fabius Maximus a senatu postulavit ut aedem Veneris Erycinae, quam dictator vovisset,
14 dedicare liceret. Senatus decrevit ut Ti. Sempronius consul designatus, cum primum [1] magistratum [2] inisset, ad populum ferret ut Q. Fabium duumvirum
15 esse iuberent aedis dedicandae causa. Et M. Aemilio Lepido, qui bis [3] consul augurque fuerat, filii tres, Lucius, Marcus, Quintus, ludos funebres per triduum et gladiatorum paria duo et viginti in
16 foro dederunt. Aediles curules C. Laetorius et Ti. Sempronius Gracchus, consul designatus, qui in aedilitate magister equitum fuerat, ludos Romanos
17 fecerunt, qui per triduum instaurati sunt. Plebei ludi aedilium M. Aurelii Cottae et M. Claudii Marcelli ter instaurati.

[1] primum *z* : *om.* *P*(1) *Madvig.*

[2] magistratum *xz* : honorem C^4x *Madvig* : ibo *P* : ibono $P^1?(3)$; bono *D*.

[3] qui bis $C^4M^1?DA^y$ *Valla* : quib. (quibus) *P*(3).

---

[1] Polybius makes him a model of filial devotion (VII. viii. 9). Coins prove that he was king with his father.

[2] This brief résumé covers the events narrated from XXII. xxxviii up to this point. An eventful year.

The same trend of feeling reached Sicily also, and even the house of Hiero did not hold aloof entirely from the revolt. For Gelo, the eldest son, scorning both the old age of his father and the Roman alliance since the disaster at Cannae, went over to the Carthaginians.[1] And he would have caused an uprising in Sicily, had not death, so timely as to besmirch even his father with suspicion, carried him off as he was arming the populace and trying to gain allies. Such were the checkered events of that year in Italy, in Africa, in Sicily, in Spain.[2] B.C. 216

At the end of the year Quintus Fabius Maximus requested of the senate that he be permitted to dedicate the Temple of Venus of Eryx[3] which he had vowed in his dictatorship. The senate decreed that Tiberius Sempronius, consul designate, as soon as he entered upon his office should propose to the people that they order that Quintus Fabius should be a duumvir for the purpose of dedicating the temple. And in honour of Marcus Aemilius Lepidus, who had been consul twice and augur, his three sons, Lucius, Marcus, Quintus, gave funeral games for three days and showed twenty-two pairs of gladiators in the Forum.[4] The curule aediles, Gaius Laetorius and Tiberius Sempronius Gracchus, consul designate, who in his aedileship had been master of the horse, celebrated the Roman Games, and on three of the days they were repeated. The Plebeian Games of the aediles, Marcus Aurelius Cotta and Marcus Claudius Marcellus, were repeated three times.

[3] Where the temple was we learn presently, xxxi. 9. Her chief temple was on the western headland of Sicily, Mt. Eryx.

[4] The earliest known example of a gladiatorial combat at Rome was in 264 B.C. That also was on the occasion of a funeral, and the gift of sons.

A.U.C. 539

Circumacto tertio anno Punici belli Ti. Sempronius consul idibus Martiis magistratum init.
18 Praetores Q. Fulvius Flaccus, qui antea consul
censorque fuerat, urbanam, M. Valerius Laevinus
peregrinam sortem in iuris dictione habuit; Ap.
Claudius Pulcher Siciliam, Q. Mucius Scaevola
19 Sardiniam sortiti sunt. M. Marcello pro consule
imperium esse populus iussit, quod post Cannensem
cladem unus Romanorum imperatorum in Italia
prospere rem gessisset.

XXXI. Senatus quo die primum est in Capitolio
consultus decrevit ut eo[1] anno duplex tributum
2 imperaretur, simplex confestim exigeretur, ex quo
stipendium praesens omnibus militibus daretur
3 praeterquam qui milites ad Cannas fuissent. De
exercitibus ita decreverunt ut duabus legionibus
urbanis Ti. Sempronius consul Cales ad conveniendum diem ediceret; inde eae legiones in castra
4 Claudiana supra Suessulam deducerentur. Quae
ibi legiones essent—erant autem Cannensis maxime
exercitus—eas Appius Claudius Pulcher praetor in
Siciliam traiceret, quaeque in Sicilia essent Romam
5 deportarentur. Ad exercitum cui ad conveniendum
Cales edicta dies erat, M. Claudius Marcellus missus,
isque iussus in castra Claudiana deducere urbanas
6 legiones. Ad veterem exercitum accipiendum de-
ducendumque inde in Siciliam Ti. Maecilius Croto
legatus ab Ap. Claudio est missus.
7 Taciti primo expectaverant homines uti consul

[1] eo C^x : quo eo *P*(5) : quod eo A^y : quo die eo *M*.

---

[1] In fact twice, 237 and 224 B.C.
[2] Named after Marcellus; cf. xvii. 3.

The third year of the Punic War being at an end, B.C. 215
Tiberius Sempronius entered upon office as consul on the Ides of March. Of the praetors Quintus Fulvius Flaccus, who had previously been consul[1] and censor, had by lot his assignment as judge between citizens, Marcus Valerius Laevinus had his as judge in the cases of strangers, while to Appius Claudius Pulcher Sicily was allotted, and Sardinia to Quintus Mucius Scaevola. That Marcus Marcellus should have full military authority as proconsul was ordered by the people, because he alone of the Roman commanders since the disaster at Cannae had met with success in Italy.

XXXI. The senate on the first day on which it was in session on the Capitol, decreed that a double tax should be imposed that year and the normal tax collected at once; that from it pay should be given in cash to all the soldiers except those who had been soldiers at Cannae. As for the armies, they decreed that Tiberius Sempronius, the consul, should set for the two city legions a date for mobilization at Cales; that these legions should be led thence to the Claudian Camp[2] above Suessula; that the legions already there—it was chiefly the army of Cannae—should be taken over into Sicily by Appius Claudius Pulcher, the praetor, and that those which were in Sicily should be brought to Rome. Marcus Claudius Marcellus was sent to the army for which a date of mobilization at Cales had been set; and he was ordered to conduct the city legions to the Claudian Camp. To take over the old army and conduct it thence to Sicily, Appius Claudius sent his lieutenant, Tiberius Maecilius Croto.

At first men had been waiting in silence for the

A.U.C. 539 comitia collegae creando haberet; deinde ubi ablegatum velut de industria M. Marcellum viderunt,
quem maxime consulem in eum annum ob egregie
in praetura res gestas creari volebant, fremitus in
8 curia ortus. Quod ubi sensit consul, " Utrumque "
inquit " e re publica fuit, patres conscripti, et M.
Claudium ad permutandos exercitus in Campaniam
proficisci et comitia non prius edici quam is inde
confecto quod mandatum est negotio revertisset, ut
vos consulem, quem tempus rei publicae postularet,
9 quem maxime voltis, haberetis." Ita de comitiis
donec rediit Marcellus silentium fuit. Interea
duumviri creati sunt Q. Fabius Maximus et T.
Otacilius Crassus aedibus dedicandis, Menti Otacilius, Fabius Veneri Erycinae; utraque in Capitolio
10 est, canali uno discretae. Et de trecentis equitibus
Campanis qui in Sicilia cum fide stipendiis emeritis
Romam venerant latum ad populum ut cives Romani
essent; item uti municipes Cumani essent pridie
quam populus Campanus a populo Romano defecisset.
11 Maxime ut hoc ferretur moverat quod quorum
hominum essent scire se ipsi negabant, vetere patria
relicta, in eam in quam redierant nondum adsciti.
12 Postquam Marcellus ab exercitu rediit, comitia
consuli uni [1] rogando in locum L. Postumii edicuntur.

[1] uni *P*(1): sub- *Madvig.*

---

[1] Exact situation of the temples is unknown; cf. xxxii. 20; XXII. ix. 10; x, 10.

[2] Mentioned in iv. 8 and vii. 2.

[3] The Roman citizenship which they had lost with the revolt of Capua was restored, while their municipal rights and privileges were transferred to loyal Cumae and made to antedate the Campanian secession.

consul to preside over an election for the naming of his colleague. Then, when they saw that Marcus Marcellus, whom they particularly desired to have elected consul for that year, on account of remarkable successes in his praetorship, had been sent away, apparently on purpose, murmurs began to be heard in the Senate House. Noting this the consul said: "Both acts were to the advantage of the state, fellow-senators, that Marcus Claudius should be sent to Campania to make the change of armies, and that the coming election should not be proclaimed until he, after accomplishing the task which was assigned him, should return thence, so that you might have the consul whom the critical situation in the state requires and whom you particularly desire." So until Marcellus returned, nothing was said about an election. Meanwhile Quintus Fabius Maximus and Titus Otacilius Crassus were made duumvirs for the dedication of temples, Otacilius for that of Mens, Fabius for that of Venus of Eryx. Both are on the Capitol,[1] separated by a single water-channel. And in regard to the three hundred Campanian knights[2] who, after loyally serving their terms in Sicily, had come to Rome, a bill was brought before the people that they should be Roman citizens; further, that they should be townsmen of Cumae from the day before that on which the Campanian people had revolted from the Roman people.[3] What had chiefly prompted the making of this proposal was that they said they did not themselves know with whom they belonged, having given up their old home-city, and not being enrolled as yet in the city to which they had returned. After Marcellus returned from the army, an election to name one consul in place of Lucius B.C. 215

A.U.C. 539

13 Creatur ingenti consensu Marcellus, qui extemplo
magistratum occiperet. Cui ineunti consulatum cum
tonuisset, vocati augures vitio creatum videri pro-
nuntiaverunt; volgoque patres ita fama ferebant,
quod tum primum duo plebeii consules facti essent,
14 id deis cordi non esse. In locum Marcelli, ubi is se
magistratu abdicavit, suffectus Q. Fabius Maximus
tertium.

15 Mare arsit eo anno; ad Sinuessam bos eculeum peperit; signa Lanuvii ad Iunonis Sospitae cruore manavere, lapidibusque circa id templum pluit. Ob quem imbrem novemdiale, ut adsolet, sacrum fuit, ceteraque prodigia cum cura expiata.

XXXII. Consules exercitus inter sese diviserunt.
Fabio exercitus Teani, cui M. Iunius dictator prae-
2 fuerat, evenit; Sempronio volones qui ibi erant[1] et
sociorum viginti quinque milia. M. Valerio praetori
legiones quae ex Sicilia redissent decretae; M. Claudius pro consule ad eum exercitum qui supra Suessulam Nolae praesideret missus; praetores in Siciliam
3 ac Sardiniam profecti. Consules edixerunt, quotiens
in senatum vocassent, uti senatores quibusque
in senatu dicere sententiam liceret ad portam

[1] qui ibi erant *Madvig*: que fierent *P*(1): qui fierent (forent) *x*.

---

[1] A very short list of portents and expiations, compared with those in XXI. lxii., XXII. i. and elsewhere.

[2] *I.e.* the slaves who, after the battle of Cannae, volunteered and were purchased by the state. By good service as soldiers they earned their freedom; xxxv. 6; XXII. lvii. 11; XXIV. x. 3; xiv. 4 f., etc.

Postumius was ordered by edict. With great unanimity Marcellus was elected, to assume office at once. Just as he was entering upon his consulship it thundered, and thereupon the augurs, being summoned, declared that there seemed to be a defect in his election. And the fathers widely circulated the statement that it did not meet the approval of the gods that two plebeians had then for the first time been elected consuls. In place of Marcellus, after he had abdicated, Quintus Fabius Maximus was substituted as consul for the third time. B.C. 215

The sea was aflame in the course of that year. At Sinuessa a cow gave birth to a colt. At the Temple of Juno Sospita at Lanuvium images of the gods dripped blood, and it rained stones around the temple—a shower on account of which there were ceremonies, as usual, for nine days. And the rest of the portents were duly expiated.[1]

XXXII. The consuls divided the armies between them. To Fabius fell the army at Teanum, formerly commanded by Marcus Junius, the dictator; to Sempronius the slave volunteers[2] who were at that place and twenty-five thousand of the allies. To Marcus Valerius, the praetor, were assigned the legions which had returned from Sicily. Marcus Claudius was sent as proconsul to the army which was above Suessula, in order to guard Nola. The praetors set out for Sicily and Sardinia. The consuls issued an edict that, whenever they might call a meeting of the senate, the senators and any who had the right to give an opinion in the senate[3] should assemble at the

[3] In the present case the persons meant can only be the newly-elected magistrates, since the list has just been revised, and none can be waiting for a new *lectio senatus*. Cf. xxiii. 5.

A.U.C. 539

4 Capenam convenirent. Praetores quorum iuris dictio
erat tribunalia ad Piscinam publicam posuerunt; eo
vadimonia fieri iusserunt, ibique eo anno ius dictum
est.

5 Interim Carthaginem, unde Mago, frater Hannibalis, duodecim milia peditum et mille[1] quingentos
equites, viginti elephantos, mille argenti talenta in
Italiam transmissurus erat cum praesidio sexaginta
6 navium longarum, nuntius adfertur in Hispania rem
male gestam omnesque ferme eius provinciae populos
7 ad Romanos defecisse. Erant, qui Magonem cum
classe ea copiisque omissa Italia in Hispaniam
averterent, cum Sardiniae recipiendae repentina
8 spes adfulsit: parvum ibi exercitum Romanum esse;
veterem praetorem inde A. Cornelium provinciae
9 peritum decedere, novum exspectari; ad hoc fessos
iam animos Sardorum esse diuturnitate imperii
Romani,[2] et proximo iis anno acerbe atque avare
imperatum; gravi tributo et conlatione iniqua
frumenti pressos; nihil deesse aliud quam aucto-
10 rem ad quem deficerent. Haec clandestina legatio
per principes missa erat, maxime eam rem moliente
Hampsicora, qui tum auctoritate atque opibus longe
11 primus erat. His nuntiis prope uno tempore turbati

[1] mille A^y *Aldus* : *om.* *P*(1).
[2] Romani *Luchs* : r *P*; *om.* P^2(1).

---

[1] By this gate in the "Servian Wall" the Via Appia left the city, near the east end of the Circus Maximus. Meeting probably in the nearby Temple of Honos, the senate could confer with returning generals outside the city.

[2] This swimming-pool of uncertain location was also outside the gate.

Porta Capena.[1] The praetors who had judicial duties B.C. 215
set up their tribunals at the Piscina Publica.[2] That place should be named—so they ordered—in recognizances,[3] and there justice was rendered that year.

Meanwhile Carthage, from which Mago,[4] Hannibal's brother, was on the point of transporting into Italy twelve thousand infantry and fifteen hundred cavalry, twenty elephants and a thousand talents of silver, with a convoy of sixty warships, received the news that in Spain operations had failed and nearly all the tribes in that province had revolted to the Romans. There were some who, neglecting Italy, were ready to divert Mago to Spain with that fleet and those forces, when there suddenly appeared a ray of hope of recovering Sardinia. It was reported that the Roman army there was small; that the old praetor, Aulus Cornelius, who was well acquainted with the province, was retiring, and a new praetor expected; further, that the Sardinians were now weary of the long continuance of Roman rule, and in the previous year had been ruled with harshness and greed; that they were burdened by a heavy tribute and an unfair requisition of grain; that nothing was lacking but a leader to whom they might go over. Such was the report of a secret embassy sent by the leading men at the special instigation of Hampsicora, who at that time was far above the rest in prestige and wealth. By such news they were almost at the

[3] The defendant was bound to give assurances (in one of the various forms prescribed by the praetor's edict) that he would appear on the day and at the place named—here at the Piscina instead of in the Forum.

[4] He had not yet gone to Spain, as was intended in xiii. 8.

A.U.C. 539 erectique Magonem cum classe sua copiisque in
12 Hispaniam mittunt, in Sardiniam Hasdrubalem deligunt ducem et tantum ferme copiarum quantum Magoni decernunt.
13 Et Romae consules transactis rebus quae in urbe
14 agendae erant movebant iam sese ad bellum. Ti. Sempronius militibus Sinuessam diem ad conveniendum edixit, et Q. Fabius, consulto prius senatu, ut frumenta omnes ex agris ante kal. Iunias primas in
15 urbes munitas conveherent; qui non invexisset eius se agrum populaturum, servos sub hasta venditurum, villas incensurum. Ne praetoribus quidem qui ad ius dicendum creati erant vacatio a belli administra-
16 tione data est. Valerium praetorem in Apuliam ire placuit ad exercitum a Terentio accipiendum; cum ex Sicilia legiones venissent, iis potissimum uti ad regionis eius praesidium, Terentianum exercitum
17 Tarentum [1] mitti cum aliquo legatorum; et viginti quinque naves datae quibus oram maritimam inter
18 Brundisium ac Tarentum tutari posset. Par navium numerus Q. Fulvio praetori urbano decretus ad
19 suburbana litora tutanda. C. Terentio proconsuli negotium datum ut in Piceno agro conquisitionem
20 militum haberet locisque iis praesidio esset. Et T. Otacilius Crassus, postquam aedem Mentis in Capitolio dedicavit, in Siciliam cum imperio qui classi praeesset missus.

[1] exercitum Tarentum *Madvig* : *om.* *P*(1)*F*.

---

[1] Either ripe or ripening, to be threshed in towns of such regions as were named in the order.

[2] In normal times short absences only from the city were permissible for the *urbanus* and the *peregrinus*.

same moment dejected and encouraged, and sent B.C. 215
Mago with his fleet and his forces to Spain. For Sardinia they chose Hasdrubal as general, and voted him about the same number of troops as to Mago.

And at Rome the consuls did what had to be done in the city, and were now bestirring themselves for the war. Tiberius Sempronius set his soldiers a date for mobilization at Sinuessa, and Quintus Fabius, after first consulting the senate, gave orders that all should bring their grain crops [1] from the farms into fortified cities before the next Kalends of June; that if any man should fail to do so, he would lay waste his farm, sell his slaves at auction and burn the farm buildings. Not even those praetors who had been appointed to administer justice [2] were granted exemption from the conduct of the war. It was decided that Valerius, the praetor, should go to Apulia, to take over the army from Terentius; that when the legions should arrive from Sicily, he should chiefly use these troops for the defence of that region; that Terentius' army should be sent to Tarentum under some one of the lieutenants. And twenty-five ships were given him, that with them he might be able to defend the coast between Brundisium and Tarentum. An equal number of ships was assigned by decree to Quintus Fulvius, the city praetor, for the defence of the shore near the city. Gaius Terentius as proconsul was given the task of conducting a levy of troops in the Picene territory and defending that region. And Titus Otacilius Crassus, after dedicating the Temple of Mens on the Capitol, was sent with full authority to Sicily, where he was to command the fleet.

A.U.C. 539

XXXIII. In hanc dimicationem duorum opulentissimorum in terris populorum omnes reges gentes-
2 que animos intenderant, inter quos Philippus Macedonum rex eo magis quod[1] propior Italiae ac mari
3 tantum Ionio discretus erat. Is ubi primum fama accepit Hannibalem Alpis transgressum, ut bello inter Romanum Poenumque orto laetatus erat, ita utrius populi mallet victoriam esse incertis adhuc
4 viribus fluctuatus animo fuerat. Postquam tertia iam pugna, tertia[2] victoria cum Poenis erat, ad fortunam inclinavit legatosque ad Hannibalem misit; qui vitantes portus Brundisinum Tarentinumque quia custodiis navium Romanarum tenebantur, ad Laciniae Iunonis templum in terram egressi sunt.
5 Inde per Apuliam petentes Capuam media in praesidia Romana inlati sunt deductique ad Valerium Laevinum praetorem, circa Luceriam castra haben-
6 tem. Ibi intrepide Xenophanes legationis princeps a Philippo rege se missum ait ad amicitiam societatemque iungendam cum populo Romano; mandata habere ad consules ac senatum populumque Ro-
7 manum. Praetor[3] inter defectiones veterum sociorum nova societate tam clari regis laetus admodum
8 hostes pro hospitibus comiter accepit; dat qui prosequantur, itinera cum cura demonstrent,[4] quae loca quosque saltus aut Romanus aut hostes teneant.
9 Xenophanes per praesidia Romana in Campaniam,

[1] quod *P*(1)*F*: quo *Aldus, Madvig*.
[2] tertia *M*¹*DAF*: tertiam *P*(4): tertium *Conway*.
[3] praetor *A*² *Muretus*: *om.* *P*(1)*F* (*i.e.* pr. *after* r.).
[4] demonstrent *P*(1)*F*: demonstrat *Gronovius* (*with* et *Luchs*).

XXXIII. To this conflict of the two richest peoples in the world all kings and nations had turned their attention, among them Philip, king of the Macedonians, all the more since he was nearer to Italy and separated from it only by the Ionian Sea. On first learning by report that Hannibal had crossed the Alps, although he had rejoiced at the outbreak of war between the Romans and the Carthaginians, still, as their resources were not yet known, he had wavered, uncertain which of the two peoples he wished to have the victory. Now that a third battle, a third victory, favoured the Carthaginians, he inclined to the side of success and sent ambassadors to Hannibal. These avoided the ports of Brundisium and Tarentum, because they were kept guarded by Roman ships, and landed at the Temple of Lacinian Juno.[1] Making their way thence toward Capua by way of Apulia, they encountered the centre of the Roman forces and were brought before Valerius Laevinus, the praetor, whose camp was near Luceria. There Xenophanes, the leader of the embassy, boldly said that he had been sent by King Philip to negotiate a friendly alliance with the Roman people; that he had communications for the consuls and for the senate and the Roman people. The praetor, who in the midst of the revolts of old allies was greatly delighted by a new alliance with so famous a king, hospitably received enemies as guests. He furnished men to escort them, to indicate the roads carefully, and what positions and what passes were held either by the Romans or by the enemy. Xenophanes made his way through the Roman forces into B.C. 215

[1] A famous temple on a promontory near Croton; cf. XXIV. iii. 3 ff.; XLII. iii. 2 ff.; Strabo VI. i. 11.

A.U.C. 539

inde qua proximum fuit in castra Hannibalis pervenit
foedusque cum eo atque amicitiam iungit legibus
10 his: ut Philippus rex quam maxima classe—ducentas
autem naves videbatur effecturus—in Italiam traiceret et vastaret maritimam oram, bellum pro parte
11 sua terra marique gereret; ubi debellatum esset,
Italia omnis cum ipsa urbe Roma Carthaginiensium
atque Hannibalis esset praedaque omnis Hannibali
12 cederet; perdomita Italia navigarent in Graeciam
bellumque cum quibus regi[1] placeret gererent[2];
quae civitates continentis quaeque insulae ad
Macedoniam vergunt, eae Philippi regnique eius
essent.

XXXIV. In has ferme leges inter Poenum ducem
2 legatosque Macedonum ictum foedus; missique cum
iis ad regis ipsius firmandam fidem legati, Gisgo et
Bostar et Mago, eodem, ad Iunonis Laciniae, ubi
3 navis occulta in statione erat, perveniunt. Inde
profecti cum altum tenerent, conspecti a[3] classe
Romana sunt quae praesidio erat Calabriae litoribus;
4 Valeriusque Flaccus cercuros ad persequendam retra-
hendamque navem cum misisset, primo fugere regii
conati; deinde, ubi celeritate vinci senserunt,
tradunt se Romanis et ad praefectum classis adducti,
5 cum quaereret qui et unde et quo tenderent cursum,
Xenophanes primo satis iam semel felix mendacium
struere, a Philippo se ad Romanos missum ad M.

[1] regi *Gronovius*: regibus *P*(1)*F*.

[2] placeret gererent *A*[2]: placerent *PC*[1]*RM*: placeret *CM*[1]*?DAF*.

[3] a *M*[1]*A*[x]: *om.* *P*(1).

Campania and thence by the shortest road to the camp of Hannibal, and arranged a treaty of friendship with him on the following terms: that King Philip with the largest possible fleet—and it was thought that he would make it two hundred ships—should cross to Italy and ravage the coast, and should carry on the war on land and sea with all his might; that after the war was over all Italy with the city of Rome itself should belong to the Carthaginians and Hannibal, and all the booty fall to Hannibal; that after the complete subjugation of Italy they should sail to Greece and wage war with such enemies as the king might choose; and that such states on the mainland and such islands as face Macedonia should belong to Philip and be a part of his kingdom. B.C. 215

XXXIV. On terms such as these a treaty was made between the Carthaginian general and the ambassadors of the Macedonians. And Gisgo and Bostar and Mago, who were sent with them as ambassadors, to reassure the king himself, reached the same place, the Temple of Juno Lacinia, where a ship lay in a hidden anchorage. Setting out thence and making for the open sea, they were sighted by the Roman fleet which was defending the coasts of Calabria. And Valerius Flaccus sent light craft to pursue the ship and bring her back; whereupon the king's ambassadors at first attempted to flee. Then, when they saw that they were being outstripped in speed, they surrendered to the Romans and were brought before the admiral of the fleet. When he asked who they were and whence, and whither they were bound, Xenophanes at first set up the false pretence which had been quite successful once before: that, being sent by Philip to the Romans, he had made his way

A.U.C. 539 Valerium, ad quem unum iter tutum fuerit, perve-
nisse, Campaniam superare nequisse, saeptam
6 hostium praesidiis. Deinde, ut Punicus cultus habi-
tusque suspectos legatos fecit Hannibalis inter-
7 rogatosque sermo prodidit, tum comitibus eorum
seductis ac metu territis, litterae quoque ab Hannibale ad Philippum inventae et pacta inter regem
8 Macedonum Poenumque ducem. Quibus satis cognitis optimum visum est captivos comitesque eorum
Romam ad senatum aut ad consules, ubicumque
9 essent, quam primum deportare. Ad id celerrimae
quinque naves delectae ac L. Valerius Antias, qui
praeesset, missus, eique mandatum ut in omnis
navis legatos separatim custodiendos divideret
daretque operam ne quod iis conloquium inter se
neve quae communicatio consilii esset.

10 Per idem tempus Romae cum A. Cornelius Mammula, ex Sardinia provincia decedens, rettulisset qui
status rerum in insula esset: bellum ac defectionem
11 omnis spectare; Q. Mucium, qui successisset sibi,
gravitate caeli aquarumque advenientem exceptum,
non tam in periculosum quam longum morbum
12 inplicitum, diu ad belli munia sustinenda inutilem
fore, exercitumque ibi ut satis firmum pacatae
provinciae praesidem esse, ita parum[1] bello quod
13 motum iri videretur, decreverunt patres ut Q.
Fulvius Flaccus quinque milia[2] peditum, quad-

[1] parum *P*(1)*F*: parvum M^2?A^y*x*: imparem *Madvig*: parum aptum *H. J. Müller*.

[2] quinque milia (= V̄) *z*: vel *PRMF* (cf. xxxvii. 13; xlvi. 4): vi C^4: mille DA^2.

to Marcus Valerius, the one man to whom there was a safe road; that he had been unable to get across Campania, which was blocked by the enemy's forces. Then, when Carthaginian dress and appearance cast suspicion on Hannibal's ambassadors, upon being questioned they were betrayed by their speech. Thereupon their attendants were led aside and frightened by threats; and a letter also from Hannibal to Philip was found, along with agreements between the king of the Macedonians and the Carthaginian general. So much being established, it seemed best to send the captured men and their attendants as soon as possible to the senate at Rome, or else to the consuls, wherever they might be. For that purpose five very swift ships were selected and Lucius Valerius Antias was sent to command them. And instructions were given him to distribute the ambassadors among all his ships, to be separately guarded; and he was to see to it that there should be no conversation among them or any interchange of plans. B.C. 215

About the same time at Rome Aulus Cornelius Mammula, on retiring from his province of Sardinia, reported what was the condition of affairs in the island: that all were aiming at war and rebellion; that Quintus Mucius, his successor, upon arriving was affected by the unwholesome climate and bad water, and having contracted an illness not so dangerous as protracted, would for a long time be useless for the performance of war duties; also that the army there, while strong enough to garrison a peaceful province, was not so for the war which seemed on the point of breaking out. The senate thereupon decreed that Quintus Fulvius Flaccus should enlist five thousand

A.U.C. 539 ringentos equites scriberet eamque legionem primo
quoque tempore in Sardiniam traiciendam curaret,
14 mitteretque cum imperio quem ipsi videretur, qui
15 rem gereret quoad Mucius convaluisset. Ad eam
rem missus est T. Manlius Torquatus, qui bis consul
et censor fuerat subegeratque in consulatu Sardos.
16 Sub idem fere tempus et a Carthagine in Sardiniam
classis missa duce Hasdrubale, cui Calvo cognomen
erat, foeda tempestate vexata ad Baliares insulas
17 deicitur, ibique—adeo non armamenta modo sed
etiam alvei navium quassati erant—subductae naves
dum reficiuntur aliquantum temporis triverunt.

XXXV. In Italia cum post Cannensem pugnam,
fractis partis alterius viribus, alterius mollitis animis,
2 segnius bellum esset, Campani per se adorti sunt
rem Cumanam suae dicionis facere, primo sollicitantes ut ab Romanis deficerent; ubi id parum
processit, dolum ad capiendos eos comparant.
3 Campanis omnibus statum sacrificium ad Hamas
erat.[1] Eo senatum Campanum venturum certiores
Cumanos fecerunt petieruntque ut et Cumanus eo
senatus veniret ad consultandum communiter, ut
eosdem uterque populus socios hostesque haberet;
4 praesidium ibi armatum se habituros, ne quid ab
Romano Poenove periculi esset. Cumani, quamquam suspecta fraus erat, nihil abnuere, ita tegi
fallax consilium posse rati.

[1] erat *Madvig* (*before* Campanis *Weissenborn*): *om.* *P*(1).

---

[1] In his first consulship, 235 B.C.; cf. xxii. 7.

[2] To the north-east of Cumae. An inscription gives some clue to its location.

[3] Their plan to aid the consul against the Campanians.

infantry and four hundred cavalry, and should see to it that that legion should be transported to Sardinia at the first opportunity; also that he should send whomever he thought best with full authority, to carry on the war until Mucius should recover. For that duty Titus Manlius Torquatus was sent, a man who had been consul twice and censor, and in his consulship had conquered the Sardinians.[1] About the same time a fleet which had been sent from Carthage also to Sardinia, under command of the Hasdrubal who was surnamed Calvus, was damaged by a terrible storm and driven to the Balearic Islands. And there the ships were beached, to such an extent had not only the rigging but also the hulls been injured; and while undergoing repairs they caused a considerable loss of time. B.C. 215

XXXV. In Italy, while the war was less active after the battle of Cannae, since the resources of one side had been broken and the spirit of the other sapped, the Campanians attempted without assistance to reduce the state of Cumae to subjection, at first tempting them to revolt from the Romans. When that failed, they contrived a ruse to entrap them. All the Campanians had a regular sacrifice at Hamae.[2] To it they informed the men of Cumae that the Campanian senate would come, and requested that the senate of Cumae should come thither to deliberate together, so that both peoples might have the same allies and enemies. They said they would have an armed guard there, lest there be any danger from the Roman or the Carthaginian. The Cumaeans, though they had suspected guile, made no objections, thinking that a ruse of their own[3] to outwit them could thus be concealed.

A.U.C. 539 5 Interim Ti. Sempronius consul Romanus Sinuessae,
quo ad conveniendum diem edixerat, exercitu
lustrato transgressus Volturnum flumen circa Liter-
6 num posuit castra. Ibi quia otiosa stativa erant,
crebro decurrere milites cogebat, ut tirones—ea
maxima pars volonum erant—adsuescerent signa
7 sequi et in acie agnoscere ordines suos. Inter quae
maxima erat cura duci, itaque legatis tribunisque
praeceperat, ne qua exprobratio cuiquam veteris
fortunae discordiam inter ordines sereret; vetus
miles tironi, liber voloni sese exaequari sineret;
8 omnis satis honestos generososque ducerent quibus
arma sua signaque populus Romanus commisisset;
quae fortuna coegisset ita fieri, eandem cogere
9 tueri factum. Ea non maiore cura praecepta ab
ducibus sunt quam a militibus observata, brevique
tanta concordia coaluerant omnium animi ut prope
in oblivionem veniret qua ex condicione quisque
esset miles factus.

10 Haec agenti Graccho legati Cumani nuntiarunt
quae a Campanis legatio paucos ante dies venisset
11 et quid iis ipsi respondissent: triduo post eum diem
festum esse; non senatum solum omnem ibi futurum
12 sed castra etiam et exercitum Campanum. Gracchus
iussis Cumanis omnia ex agris in urbem convehere

Meanwhile Tiberius Sempronius, the Roman consul, after reviewing his army at Sinuessa, at which place he had announced a date for mobilization, crossed the river Volturnus and pitched camp near Liternum. There, since the permanent camp lacked occupation, he required the soldiers to manœuvre frequently, that the recruits—they were most of the slave-volunteers—might learn to follow the standards and to recognize their own ranks in the battle-line. In this it was the commander's greatest care, and he had instructed the lieutenants and tribunes to the same effect, that no reproach of any man's previous lot should sow strife between the different classes of soldiers; that the old soldier should allow himself to be rated with the recruit, the freeman with the slave-volunteer; that they should consider all to whom the Roman people had entrusted its arms and standards as sufficiently honoured and well-born. He said that the same fortune which had compelled them to do so now compelled them to defend what had been done. These injunctions were not given with greater care by the commanders than that with which they were followed by the soldiers. And soon they were all united in a harmony so great that it was almost forgotten from what status each man had been made a soldier. B.C. 215

While Gracchus was thus employed, legates from Cumae reported to him on what mission an embassy had come a few days before from the Campanians, and what answer they had themselves given them; that the festival was to be three days later, and not only would the whole senate be there, but a camp also and a Campanian army. Gracchus, having ordered the Cumaeans to bring everything from the

A.U.C. 539 et manere intra muros, ipse pridie quam statum sacrificium Campanis esset Cumas movet castra.
13 Hamae inde tria milia passuum absunt. Iam Campani eo frequentes ex composito convenerant, nec procul inde in occulto Marius Alfius medix tuticus—is [1] summus magistratus erat Campanis—cum
14 quattuordecim milibus armatorum habebat castra, sacrificio adparando et inter id instruendae fraudi aliquanto intentior quam muniendis castris aut ulli
15 militari operi.[2] Nocturnum erat sacrum, ita ut ante
16 mediam noctem conpleretur. Huic Gracchus insidiandum tempori ratus, custodibus ad portas positis, ne quis enuntiare posset coepta, et ab decuma diei hora coactis militibus corpora curare somnoque
17 operam dare, ut primis tenebris convenire ad signum
18 possent, vigilia ferme prima tolli iussit signa, silentique profectus agmine cum ad Hamas media nocte pervenisset, castra Campana ut in pervigilio neglecta simul omnibus portis invadit; alios somno stratos, alios perpetrato sacro inermis redeuntis obtruncat.
19 Hominum eo tumultu nocturno caesa plus duo milia cum ipso duce Mario Alfio, capta . . . et [3] signa militaria quattuor et triginta.

[1] is *Fabri*: *om.* *P*(1).
[2] operi, *here* *P*(1) *add* triduum sacrificatum ad Hamas (*gloss on* § 11?)
[3] capta . . . et *Weissenborn*: capta est *PCR*: capta sunt *R*[1](14); capti * et *Madvig*.

---

[1] For this Oscan term cf. XXIV. xix. 2.

farms into the city and to remain inside the walls, B.C. 215 moved his own camp to Cumae the day before the Campanians had their regular sacrifice. Hamae is three miles distant. Already the Campanians in large numbers had gathered there according to agreement. And in concealment, not far from there, Marius Alfius, the *medix tuticus*,[1] that is, the chief magistrate of the Campanians, had his camp, with fourteen thousand armed men, he being decidedly more intent upon preparing the sacrifice and contriving treachery during the same than upon fortifying his camp or upon any task of the soldier. The sacrifice took place at night, but it was to be finished before midnight. Gracchus, thinking he must be in waiting for that moment, placed guards at the gates, that no one might be able to carry away news of his undertaking. And having assembled his soldiers as early as the tenth hour of the day, he ordered them to get themselves in condition and take care to sleep, so that, as soon as it was dark, they might come together at the signal; and at about the first watch he ordered that the standards be taken up. And setting out with a silent column, he reached Hamae at midnight and entered the Campanian camp by all its gates at once; for, as was to be expected in view of the vigil, it was carelessly guarded. Some they slew as they lay asleep, others as they were returning unarmed after the rite had been completed. More than two thousand men were slain in that affray by night, including Marius Alfius, the commander himself. Captured were . . . thousand men[2] and thirty-four military standards.

[2] The large number makes the correctness of *capta* (sc. *milia*) doubtful; cf. xxxvii. 11.

A.U.C. 539 XXXVI. Gracchus minus centum militum iactura
castris hostium potitus Cumas se propere recepit, ab
Hannibale metuens, qui super Capuam in Tifatis
2 habebat castra. Nec eum provida futuri fefellit
opinio. Nam simul Capuam ea clades est nuntiata,
ratus Hannibal ab re bene gesta insolenter laetum
exercitum tironum, magna ex parte servorum,
spoliantem victos praedasque agentem ad Hamas
3 se inventurum, citatum agmen praeter Capuam
rapit, obviosque ex fuga Campanorum dato praesidio
4 Capuam duci, saucios vehiculis portari iubet. Ipse
Hamis vacua ab hostibus castra nec quicquam praeter
recentis vestigia caedis strataque passim corpora
5 sociorum invenit. Auctores erant quidam ut protinus inde Cumas duceret urbemque oppugnaret.
6 Id quamquam haud modice Hannibal cupiebat, ut,
quia Neapolim non potuerat, Cumas saltem maritimam urbem haberet, tamen, quia praeter arma
nihil secum miles raptim acto agmine extulerat,
7 retro in castra super Tifata se recepit. Inde fatigatus
Campanorum precibus sequenti die cum omni
apparatu oppugnandae urbis Cumas redit, perpopu-
latoque agro Cumano mille passus ab urbe castra
8 locat, cum Gracchus magis verecundia in tali necessitate deserendi socios inplorantis fidem suam populi-
que Romani substitisset quam satis fidens exercitui.
9 Nec alter consul Fabius, qui ad Cales castra habebat,
Volturnum flumen traducere audebat exercitum,

XXXVI. Gracchus, having captured the camp of the enemy with the loss of less than a hundred soldiers, hastily withdrew to Cumae in fear of Hannibal, who had his camp on Mount Tifata above Capua. And he was not mistaken in his forecast. For as soon as the defeat was reported at Capua, Hannibal, thinking he would find the army of recruits, largely slaves, at Hamae gloating for once over a success, spoiling the defeated and driving off the booty, rushed his column with all speed past Capua, and ordered that those of the fleeing Campanians whom he met should be furnished with an escort and led to Capua, and the wounded carried on wagons. As for himself, he found at Hamae a camp deserted by the enemy, and nothing except the traces of recent slaughter and corpses of his allies scattered everywhere. Some advised him to lead his troops away forthwith to Cumae and to attack the city. Although Hannibal was very eager to do so, in order that he might have Cumae at least as a seaport, since he had been unable to gain one at Neapolis, nevertheless, as his soldiers in their rapidly moving column had brought out nothing but their arms with them, he withdrew again to his camp on Tifata. Moved by the importunities of the Campanians, he returned thence on the following day to Cumae with all the equipment for besieging the city, and after ravaging the territory of Cumae, pitched his camp a mile from the city. Meanwhile Gracchus, ashamed to desert allies in such straits and begging for his help and that of the Roman people, rather than because he had full confidence in his army, had remained there. Nor did the other consul, Fabius, who had his camp at Cales, venture to lead his army across the river Volturnus, being B.C. 215

A.U.C. 539 10 occupatus primo auspiciis repetendis, dein prodigiis
quae alia super alia nuntiabantur; expiantique ea
haud facile litari haruspices respondebant.

XXXVII. Eae causae cum Fabium tenerent, Sempronius in obsidione erat et iam operibus oppugna-
2 batur. Adversus ligneam ingentem admotam urbi
turrem aliam[1] ex ipso muro excitavit consul Romanus,
aliquanto altiorem, quia muro satis per se alto
3 subiectis validis sublicis pro solo usus erat. Inde
primum saxis sudibusque et ceteris missilibus
propugnatores moenia atque urbem tuebantur;
4 postremo, ubi promovendo adiunctam muro viderunt
turrem, facibus ardentibus plurimum simul ignem
5 coniecerunt. Quo incendio trepida armatorum multitudo cum de turre sese praecipitaret, eruptio ex
oppido simul duabus portis stationes hostium fudit
fugavitque in castra, ut eo die obsesso quam obsidenti
6 similior esset Poenus. Ad mille trecenti Carthaginiensium caesi et undesexaginta vivi capti, qui
circa muros et in stationibus solute ac neglegenter
agentes, cum nihil minus quam eruptionem timuis-
7 sent, ex inproviso oppressi fuerant. Gracchus, priusquam se hostes ab repentino pavore colligerent,
receptui signum dedit ac suos intra muros recepit.
8 Postero die Hannibal, laetum[2] secunda re consulem
iusto proelio ratus certaturum, aciem inter castra

[1] turrem aliam *Madvig*: aliam turrem *P*(1).

[2] laetum *Gronovius*: etum *P*(4): elatum *Aldus* (*after* re A^2x): tum P^3C^xD: cum *A*.

employed at first in taking new auspices and then with the portents which were being reported one after another. And as he was making expiation, the soothsayers kept repeating their opinion that it was not easy to obtain favourable omens. B.C. 215

XXXVII. While these reasons detained Fabius, Sempronius was blockaded and already beset by siege-works. As a defence against a great wooden tower which was moved up to the city, the Roman consul reared from the wall itself another tower considerably higher. For he had used the wall, which in itself was quite high, as a base, shoring it up with stout timbers. From that tower the defenders first held the wall and the city by hurling stones and stakes and every other missile. Finally, seeing that the enemy's tower had been pushed close against the wall, they hurled a vast amount of fire all at once from their blazing torches. While great numbers of armed men, alarmed by the fire, were leaping down from the tower, a sally out of two gates of the town at the same time routed the enemy's guards and sent them in flight to the camp, so that on that day the Carthaginian resembled a besieged army more than a besieger. About one thousand and three hundred were slain and fifty-nine captured alive of the Carthaginians, who were relaxing and idling along the walls and at guard-posts, and, having feared anything rather than a sally, had unexpectedly been overpowered. Gracchus, before the enemy could recover from their sudden fright, gave the signal for the recall and withdrew his men inside the walls. On the next day Hannibal, supposing that the consul, elated by success, would engage in a regular battle, drew up his line between the camp and the city.

A.U.C. 539

9 atque urbem instruxit; ceterum postquam neminem
moveri ab solita custodia urbis vidit nec committi
quicquam temerariae spei, ad Tifata redit infecta re.
10 Quibus diebus Cumae liberatae sunt obsidione,
iisdem diebus et in Lucanis ad Grumentum Ti.
Sempronius, cui Longo cognomen erat, cum Han-
11 none Poeno prospere pugnat. Supra duo milia
hominum occidit, et ducentos octoginta milites,[1]
signa militaria ad quadraginta unum cepit. Pulsus
finibus Lucanis Hanno retro in Bruttios sese recepit.
12 Et ex Hirpinis oppida tria, quae a populo Romano
defecerant, vi recepta per M. Valerium praetorem,
Vercellium, Vescellium, Sicilinum, et auctores defec-
13 tionis securi percussi. Supra quinque milia [2] captivorum sub hasta venierunt; praeda alia militi
concessa, exercitusque Luceriam reductus.

XXXVIII. Dum haec in Lucanis atque in Hirpinis
geruntur, quinque naves, quae Macedonum atque
Poenorum captos legatos Romam portabant, ab
supero mari ad inferum circumvectae prope omnem
2 Italiae oram, cum praeter Cumas velis ferrentur
neque hostium an sociorum essent satis sciretur,
3 Gracchus obviam ex classe sua naves misit. Cum
percunctando in vicem cognitum esset consulem Cumis
esse, naves Cumas adpulsae captivique ad consulem
4 deducti et litterae datae. Consul litteris Philippi
atque Hannibalis perlectis consignata omnia ad
senatum itinere terrestri misit, navibus devehi

[1] milites, *here* *P*(1) *add* amisit.
[2] quinque milia *Alschefski*: vel (*for* v̄) *P*(2); *cf.* xxxiv. 13.

---

[1] This Sempronius was consul with P. Scipio in 218 B.C., and defeated by Hannibal at the Trebia; XXI. vi. 3 and liv ff.

[2] *I.e.* from the Adriatic to the Mare Tuscum; cf. i. 5; xxiv. 8.

But on seeing that no one stirred from the usual defence of the city and that nothing was entrusted to a rash hope, he returned with nothing accomplished to Tifata. B.C. 215

At the same time that the siege of Cumae was raised, Tiberius Sempronius, surnamed Longus,[1] also fought successfully in Lucania, near Grumentum, with Hanno the Carthaginian. He slew above two thousand men, and captured two hundred and eighty soldiers and some forty-one military standards. Driven out of Lucanian territory, Hanno withdrew into the land of the Bruttians. And three towns of the Hirpini, Vercellium, Vescellium and Sicilinum, which had revolted from the Roman people, were forcibly recovered by Marcus Valerius, the praetor, and those who had advised revolt were beheaded. Over five thousand captives were sold at auction; the rest of the booty was given over to the soldiers, and the army led back to Luceria.

XXXVIII. While these things were going on in Lucania and among the Hirpini, the five ships which were carrying to Rome the captured ambassadors of the Macedonians and the Carthaginians cruised along nearly the whole coast of Italy from the Upper Sea to the Lower.[2] And when they were passing Cumae under sail, and it was uncertain whether they belonged to enemies or friends, Gracchus sent ships from his fleet to meet them. When in the course of questioning on both sides it was learned that the consul was at Cumae, the ships put in at Cumae and the prisoners were brought before the consul and the letters handed over to him. The consul, after reading the letters of Philip and Hannibal, sent everything under seal by land to the senate, and ordered the

A.U.C. 539

5 legatos iussit. Cum eodem fere die litterae legatique Romam venissent et percunctatione facta dicta cum scriptis congruerent, primo gravis cura patres incessit, cernentes quanta vix tolerantibus Punicum
6 bellum Macedonici belli moles instaret. Cui tamen adeo non succubuerunt ut extemplo agitaretur quem ad modum ultro inferendo bello averterent ab Italia
7 hostem. Captivis in vincula condi iussis comitibusque eorum sub hasta venditis, ad naves viginti quinque, quibus P. Valerius Flaccus praefectus praeerat,
8 viginti quinque[1] parari[2] alias decernunt. His comparatis deductisque et additis quinque navibus,
9 quae advexerant captivos legatos, triginta naves ab Ostia Tarentum profectae, iussusque P. Valerius militibus Varronianis, quibus L. Apustius legatus Tarenti praeerat, in naves inpositis quinquaginta quinque navium classe non tueri modo Italiae oram
10 sed explorare de Macedonico bello; si congruentia litteris legatorumque indiciis Philippi consilia essent, ut M. Valerium praetorem litteris certiorem faceret,
11 isque L. Apustio legato exercitui praeposito Tarentum ad classem profectus primo quoque tempore in Macedoniam transmitteret daretque operam ut
12 Philippum in regno contineret. Pecunia ad classem tuendam bellumque Macedonicum ea decreta est quae Ap. Claudio in Siciliam missa erat, ut redderetur

[1] quinque *Jac. Gronovius*: *om.* *P*(1).
[2] parari *M*² *Gronovius*: paratis *P*(1).

---

[1] The total should be fifty; the five which carried the captives are counted twice; cf. xxxiv. 9.

ambassadors to be carried on the ships. Letters B.C. 215 and ambassadors arrived at Rome on about the same day, and upon enquiry their words and the texts were in agreement. Thereupon the senators were at first gravely concerned, seeing how serious a war with Macedonia threatened, at a time when they could scarcely endure that with the Carthaginians. However, they were so far from giving way to that concern that they at once discussed how by actual aggressive warfare they might keep the enemy away from Italy. The prisoners were ordered put in chains, their attendants were sold at auction, and it was decreed that, in addition to the twenty-five ships which Publius Valerius Flaccus commanded as admiral, twenty-five others should be made ready. The latter being now ready and launched, with the addition of the five ships which had brought the ambassadors as captives, thirty ships sailed from Ostia for Tarentum. And Publius Valerius was ordered to put on board the soldiers who had been Varro's, and at Tarentum were commanded by Lucius Apustius, the lieutenant, and then with a fleet of fifty-five [1] ships not merely to defend the coast of Italy, but to get information in regard to the Macedonian war. If the designs of Philip should agree with the letters and with the statements of the ambassadors, then he was to inform Marcus Valerius, the praetor, by letter; and Valerius, after placing his lieutenant, Lucius Apustius, in command of the army, was to proceed to the fleet at Tarentum, and as soon as possible to cross into Macedonia and take steps to keep Philip within his kingdom. For the maintenance of the fleet and for the Macedonian war there was voted the money which had been sent to Appius Claudius in Sicily, to

A.U.C. 539 Hieroni regi; ea per L. Antistium legatum Tarentum
13 est devecta. Simul ab Hierone missa ducenta milia
modium tritici et hordei centum.

XXXIX. Dum haec Romani parant aguntque, ad
Philippum captiva navis una, ex iis quae Romam
missae erant, ex cursu refugit; inde scitum legatos
2 cum litteris captos. Itaque ignarus rex quae cum
Hannibale legatis suis convenissent quaeque legati
eius ad se adlaturi fuissent, legationem aliam cum
3 eisdem mandatis mittit. Legati ad Hannibalem
missi Heraclitus, cui Scotino cognomen erat,[1] et Crito
Boeotus et Sositheus Magnes. Hi prospere tulerunt
4 ac rettulerunt mandata; sed prius se aestas circum-
egit quam movere ac moliri quicquam rex posset:
tantum navis una capta cum legatis momenti fecit ad
dilationem imminentis Romanis belli.

5 Et circa Capuam, transgresso Volturnum Fabio
post expiata tandem prodigia, ambo consules rem
6 gerebant. Combulteriam et Trebulam et Austi-
culam urbes, quae ad Poenum defecerant, Fabius vi
cepit; praesidiaque in his Hannibalis Campanique
7 permulti capti. Et Nolae,[2] sicut priore anno, senatus
Romanorum, plebs Hannibalis erat, consiliaque

[1] cui . . . erat *spurious according to Gronovius.*
[2] et Nolae *P*(2)A^y : Nolae M^1.

---

[1] Pay for the soldiers had been lent by him in the previous year; cf. xxi. 5. His successor presently took the Carthaginian side; XXIV. vi f.

[2] Cf. xxxiv. 8 f.

[3] This term ("The Obscure") had been applied to the early philosopher of Ephesus of the same name, *ca.* 500 B.C. A pointless marginal note may have got into the text here, displacing the adjective of place which would be expected with this unknown Heraclitus.

be repaid to king Hiero.[1] This money was carried B.C. 215 to Tarentum by Lucius Antistius, the lieutenant. At the same time two hundred thousand pecks of wheat and a hundred thousand of barley were sent by Hiero.

XXXIX. While the Romans were engaged in these preparations and activities, the one captured ship escaped while under weigh from those which had been sent to Rome,[2] and returned to Philip. Thus it became known that the ambassadors had been captured with the letter. And so the king, not knowing what had been agreed upon between his ambassadors and Hannibal, and what message the latter's ambassadors were to have brought to him, sent another embassy with the same instructions. As ambassadors to Hannibal there were sent Heraclitus, surnamed Scotinus,[3] and Crito, the Boeotian, and Sositheus, of Magnesia. These succeeded in carrying and in bringing back instructions; but the summer was over before the king could make any active preparations. So effectual was the capture of a single ship and ambassadors in postponing a war which threatened the Romans.

Also in the vicinity of Capua both consuls were carrying on the war, now that Fabius, after finally making atonement for the prodigies,[4] had crossed the Volturnus. The cities of Combulteria and Trebula and Austicula, which had revolted to the Carthaginian, were forcibly taken by Fabius, and in them Hannibal's garrisons and very many Campanians were captured. And at Nola, just as in the previous year, the senate sided with the Romans, the common people with Hannibal, and secret plans were being formed for the

[4] Mentioned in xxxi. 15.

A.U.C. 539 occulta de caede principum et proditione urbis
8 inibantur. Quibus ne incepta procederent, inter Capuam castraque Hannibalis, quae in Tifatis erant, traducto exercitu Fabius super Suessulam in castris Claudianis consedit; inde M. Marcellum propraetorem cum iis copiis quas habebat Nolam in praesidium misit.

XL. Et in Sardinia res per T. Manlium praetorem administrari coeptae, quae omissae erant postquam Q. Mucius praetor gravi morbo est inplicitus.
2 Manlius navibus longis ad Carales subductis navalibusque sociis armatis, ut terra rem gereret, et a praetore exercitu accepto duo et viginti milia
3 peditum, mille ducentos equites confecit. Cum his equitum peditumque copiis profectus in agrum hostium haud procul ab Hampsicorae castris castra posuit. Hampsicora tum forte profectus erat in Pellitos Sardos ad iuventutem armandam, qua
4 copias augeret; filius nomine Hostus castris praeerat. Is adulescentia ferox temere proelio inito fusus fugatusque. Ad tria milia Sardorum eo proelio
5 caesa, octingenti ferme vivi capti; alius exercitus primo per agros silvasque fuga palatus, dein, quo ducem fugisse fama erat, ad urbem nomine Cornum,
6 caput eius regionis, confugit; debellatumque eo proelio in Sardinia esset, ni classis Punica cum duce

[1] Cf. xxxi. 3 and 5; xlvi. 9.

[2] Really proconsul; cf. xxx. 18; xxxii. 2; xlviii. 2.

[3] Acting in place of the regular praetor; cf. xxxiv. 15.

[4] Regularly called *socii navales*, from the time when seamen and oarsmen were allies, while the soldiers on board were Romans.

murder of the leading men and the betrayal of the city. That their undertaking should go no farther, Fabius led his army between Capua and the camp of Hannibal, which was on Tifata, and established himself above Suessula in the Claudian Camp.[1] From there he sent Marcus Marcellus, the propraetor,[2] with the forces which he had to Nola, to serve as a garrison. B.C. 215

XL. And in Sardinia under the direction of Titus Manlius, the praetor,[3] the operations which had been neglected ever since Quintus Mucius, the praetor, was attacked by a serious malady, were resumed. Manlius, after beaching his warships at Carales and arming their crews,[4] in order to wage war on land, and receiving an army from the praetor, made up a total of twenty-two thousand infantry and twelve hundred cavalry. With these cavalry and infantry forces he set out for the enemy's territory and pitched camp not far from the camp of Hampsicora. At that time Hampsicora, as it happened, had gone to the region of the Skin-clad Sardinians,[5] to arm their young men, in order to enlarge his forces. His son named Hostus was in command of the camp. He with the overconfidence of youth rashly went into battle, was routed and put to flight. About three thousand Sardinians were slain in that battle, some eight hundred taken alive. The rest of the army, at first wandering in flight through the farms and woods, then fled to the place to which it was reported that the commander had fled, a city named Cornus, the capital of that region. And the war in Sardinia would have been ended by that battle, had not the

[5] An earlier population living in the mountainous interior of the island and wearing goat-skins.

A.U.C. 539 Hasdrubale, quae tempestate deiecta ad Balearis erat,
7 in tempore ad spem rebellandi advenisset. Manlius
post famam adpulsae Punicae classis Carales se
recepit: ea occasio Hampsicorae data est Poeno se
8 iungendi. Hasdrubal, copiis in terram expositis et
classe remissa Carthaginem, duce Hampsicora ad
sociorum populi Romani agrum populandum profectus Carales perventurus erat, ni Manlius obvio
exercitu ab effusa eum populatione continuisset.
9 Primo castra castris modico intervallo sunt obiecta;
deinde per[1] procursationes levia certamina vario
eventu inita; postremo descensum in aciem. Signis
conlatis iusto proelio per quattuor horas pugnatum.
10 Diu pugnam ancipitem Poeni, Sardis facile vinci
adsuetis, fecerunt; postremo et ipsi, cum omnia
circa strage ac fuga Sardorum repleta essent, fusi;
11 ceterum terga dantes circumducto cornu quo pepu-
lerat Sardos inclusit Romanus. Caedes inde magis
12 quam pugna fuit. Duodecim milia hostium caesa,
Sardorum simul Poenorumque, ferme tria milia et
septingenti capti et signa militaria septem et viginti.

XLI. Ante omnia claram et memorabilem pugnam
fecit Hasdrubal imperator captus et Hanno et Mago,
2 nobiles Carthaginienses, Mago ex gente Barcina,
propinqua cognatione Hannibali iunctus, Hanno

[1] deinde per *Madvig*: deinceps *P*(1).

Carthaginian fleet commanded by Hasdrubal, which B.C. 215 had been carried by a storm to the Balearic Islands, arrived at the right moment to revive hopes for the rebellion. Manlius, when the arrival of the Punic fleet was reported, withdrew to Carales. By so doing he gave Hampsicora the opportunity to unite with the Carthaginian. Hasdrubal, after landing his forces and sending the fleet back to Carthage, set out with Hampsicora as his guide to lay waste the lands of allies of the Roman people. And he would have reached Carales, had not Manlius by confronting him with an army restrained him from his widespread devastation. At first camp faced camp at no great distance. Then charges led to skirmishes with varying results. Finally they went into line of battle. With standards against standards they fought a regular engagement for four hours. For a long time the Carthaginians made the issue uncertain, while the Sardinians were used to being easily defeated. Finally, when the slain and the fleeing Sardinians had covered the whole field, the Carthaginians also were routed. But when they tried to flee, the Roman general hemmed them in by a flank movement of the wing with which he had beaten back the Sardinians. It was a slaughter after that, rather than a battle. Twelve thousand of the enemy were slain, Sardinians and Carthaginians reckoned together. About three thousand seven hundred were captured, and twenty-seven military standards.

XLI. What more than all made it a famous and memorable battle was the capture of Hasdrubal, the commander, and Hanno and Mago, Carthaginian nobles, Mago being of the Barca family and nearly related to Hannibal, while Hanno had advised the

A.U.C. 539 auctor rebellionis Sardis bellique eius haud dubie
3 concitor. Nec Sardorum duces minus nobilem eam
pugnam cladibus suis fecerunt: nam et filius Hamp-
4 sicorae Hostus in acie cecidit, et Hampsicora cum
paucis equitibus fugiens, ut super adflictas res necem
quoque filii audivit, nocte, ne cuius interventus
5 coepta inpediret, mortem sibi conscivit. Ceteris
urbs Cornus eadem quae ante fugae receptaculum
fuit; quam Manlius victore exercitu adgressus intra
6 dies paucos recepit. Deinde aliae quoque civitates,
quae ad Hampsicoram Poenosque defecerant, obsidibus datis dediderunt sese; quibus stipendio
frumentoque imperato pro cuiusque aut viribus aut
7 delicto Carales exercitum reduxit. Ibi navibus longis
deductis inpositoque quem secum advexerat milite
Romam navigat Sardiniamque perdomitam nuntiat
patribus; et stipendium quaestoribus, frumentum
aedilibus, captivos Q. Fulvio praetori tradit.

8 Per idem tempus T. Otacilius praetor ab Lilybaeo
classi in Africam transvectus depopulatusque agrum
9 Carthaginiensem, cum Sardiniam inde peteret, quo
fama erat Hasdrubalem a Baliaribus nuper traiecisse,
classi Africam repetenti occurrit, levique certamine
in alto commisso septem inde naves cum sociis
navalibus cepit. Ceteras metus haud secus quam
tempestas passim disiecit.

Sardinians to rebel and had undoubtedly fomented that war. And the Sardinians' generals made the battle no less notable by their deaths. For Hostus, the son of Hampsicora, fell in battle, and also Hampsicora as he fled with a few horsemen, on hearing, not of the defeat only, but also of the death of his son, took his own life, doing this at night, that no one might come upon him and interfere with his attempt. For all the rest the same city of Cornus was a place of refuge, as before. Manlius with his victorious army attacked it and took it within a few days. Then other cities also which had revolted to Hampsicora and the Carthaginians gave hostages and surrendered. From these cities Manlius exacted tribute and grain in proportion to the resources of each or its guilt, and led his army back to Carales. There he launched his warships, took on board the soldiers he had brought with him, sailed for Rome, and reported to the senate the complete subjugation of Sardinia. He also turned over the tribute to the quaestors, the grain to the aediles, the captives to Quintus Fulvius, the praetor. B.C. 215

About the same time Titus Otacilius, the praetor,[1] sailed with his fleet from Lilybaeum across to Africa, and after laying waste the country about Carthage, was steering thence toward Sardinia, to which it was reported that Hasdrubal had recently crossed from the Balearic Islands, when he encountered the fleet returning to Africa; and in a slight engagement fought in open water he captured seven of their ships together with their crews. The rest were widely scattered by their fear quite as much as they had been by the storm.

[1] Here = *praefectus*, commander of the fleet.

A.U.C. 539
10 Per eosdem forte dies et Bomilcar cum militibus
ad supplementum Carthagine missis elephantisque
11 et commeatu Locros accessit. Quem ut incautum
opprimeret, Ap. Claudius per simulationem provinciae circumeundae Messanam raptim exercitu
12 ducto vento aestuque suo [1] Locros traiecit. Iam
inde Bomilcar ad Hannonem in Bruttios profectus
erat, et Locrenses portas Romanis clauserunt;
Appius magno conatu nulla re gesta Messanam
repetit.
13 Eadem aestate Marcellus ab Nola, quam praesidio
obtinebat, crebras excursiones in agrum Hirpinum
14 et Samnites Caudinos fecit adeoque omnia ferro
atque igni vastavit ut antiquarum cladium Samnio
memoriam renovaret. XLII. Itaque extemplo legati ad Hannibalem missi simul ex utraque gente ita
Poenum adlocuti sunt: "Hostes populi Romani,
2 Hannibal, fuimus primum per nos ipsi quoad nostra
arma, nostrae vires nos tutari poterant. Postquam
his parum fidebamus, Pyrrho regi nos adiunximus;
3 a quo relicti pacem necessariam accepimus, fuimusque
in ea per annos prope quinquaginta ad id tempus quo
4 tu in Italiam venisti. Tua nos non magis virtus
fortunaque quam unica comitas ac benignitas erga
cives nostros, quos captos nobis remisisti, ita con
ciliavit tibi ut te salvo atque incolumi amico non
modo populum Romanum sed ne deos quidem iratos,
5 si fas est dici, timeremus. At hercule non solum

[1] vento aestuque suo *Weissenborn*: aestuquaesuo *PR*: aestuque suo *R*[1]*?*(7).

---

[1] In the Samnite Wars, as narrated in books VII to X, especially their defeats at Suessula, 343 B.C., and at Sentinum, 295.

[2] The speech is, of course, that of their leader.

About the same time, moreover, as it happened, B.C. 215
Bomilcar arrived at Locri with the soldiers sent as reinforcements from Carthage and with elephants and supplies. In order to take him unawares Appius Claudius, with the pretence of making the round of his province, led his army in haste to Messana, and with wind and current in his favour crossed over to Locri. Already Bomilcar had left that place, to join Hanno among the Bruttii, and the Locrians closed their gates against the Romans. Appius, having accomplished nothing by his great effort, returned to Messana.

The same summer Marcellus from Nola, which he held with a garrison, made frequent raids into the country of the Hirpini and the Samnites about Caudium and laid waste the whole region with fire and sword so completely that he revived the Samnites' memory of their old disasters.[1] XLII. Accordingly ambassadors were sent at once to Hannibal from both tribes, and they addressed the Carthaginian thus:[2] "We were enemies of the Roman people, Hannibal, at first by ourselves, so long as our arms and our resources were able to defend us. When we had lost confidence in these, we attached ourselves to Pyrrhus, the king. Abandoned by him we accepted an inevitable peace, and have remained in that peace for about fifty years, down to the time when you came to Italy. It is not more your courage and success than your singular kindness and consideration toward our citizens, whom you captured and then sent back to us, that so won us over to you that, so long as you were a friend safe and sound, we not only did not fear the Roman people, but not even the anger of the gods, if it is right to say so. But in fact,

A.U.C. 539 incolumi et victore sed praesente te, cum ploratum prope coniugum ac liberorum nostrorum exaudire et flagrantia tecta posses conspicere, ita sumus aliquotiens hac aestate devastati ut M. Marcellus, non Hannibal, vicisse ad Cannas videatur, glorienturque Romani te, ad unum modo ictum vigentem, velut
6 aculeo emisso torpere. Per annos centum [1] cum populo Romano bellum gessimus, nullo externo adiuti nec duce nec exercitu, nisi quod per biennium Pyrrhus nostro magis milite suas auxit vires quam
7 suis viribus nos defendit. Non ego secundis rebus nostris gloriabor, duos consules ac duos consulares exercitus ab nobis sub iugum missos, et si qua alia
8 aut laeta aut gloriosa nobis evenerunt. Quae aspera adversaque tunc acciderunt minore indignatione re-
9 ferre possumus quam quae hodie eveniunt. Magni dictatores cum magistris equitum, bini consules cum binis consularibus exercitibus ingrediebantur finis nostros; ante explorato et subsidiis positis et sub
10 signis ad populandum ducebant; nunc propraetoris unius et parvi ad tuendam Nolam praesidii praeda sumus; iam ne manipulatim quidem sed latronum modo percursant totis finibus nostris neglegentius
11 quam si in Romano vagarentur agro. Causa autem haec est quod neque tu defendis et nostra iuventus, quae si domi esset tutaretur, omnis sub signis militat
12 tuis. Nec te nec exercitum tuum norim nisi, a quo

[1] centum *x*: prope centum A^2x: *om.* $P(1)$.

---

[1] *E.g.* Papirius Cursor, VIII. xxix ff.; again IX. xxxviii; five times consul.

[2] In disparagement of Marcellus, a proconsul; cf. xliii. 12.

while you are not merely safe and victorious, but also here present, although you could almost hear the wailing of our wives and children and could see the blazing houses, we have been so ravaged several times this summer that Marcus Marcellus, not Hannibal, appears to have been the victor at Cannae, and the Romans are boasting that you, having strength for but a single stroke, are inactive, as if you had spent your sting. For a hundred years we waged war with the Roman people, unaided either by commander or army from abroad, except that for two years Pyrrhus did not so much defend us with his resources as enlarge these by adding our soldiers. I shall not boast of our successes, that two consuls and two consular armies were sent under the yoke by us, nor of any other events which have brought us either joy or fame. But the hardships and defeats which then befel us we can relate with less indignation than the things that are happening today. Great dictators[1] and masters of the horse, two consuls and two consular armies, used each time to enter our territory. After first reconnoitring and posting reserves, and in regular array they would lead out for a raid. But now we are the prey of a single propraetor[2] and a small garrison assigned to the defence of Nola. Already they roam over our whole territory, not even in maniples, but after the manner of brigands, with less caution than if they were wandering in the country around Rome. The reason moreover is this: that you are not defending us, and at the same time our young men, who would be protecting us if they were at home, are all serving under your standards. I should be unacquainted both with you and your army if I were not to hold B.C. 215

A.U.C. 539 tot acies Romanas fusas stratasque esse sciam, ei facile esse ducam[1] opprimere populatores nostros vagos, sine signis palatos quo quemque trahit quamvis
13 vana praedae spes. Numidarum paucorum illi quidem praeda erunt praesidiumque miseris simul[2] nobis et Nolae ademeris, si modo, quos ut socios haberes dignos duxisti, haud[3] indignos iudicas quos in fidem receptos tuearis."

XLIII. Ad ea Hannibal respondit, omnia simul facere Hirpinos Samnitesque, et indicare clades suas et petere praesidium et queri indefensos se neglectos-
2 que. Indicandum autem primum fuisse, dein petendum praesidium, postremo ni inpetraretur, tum denique querendum frustra opem inploratam.
3 Exercitum sese non in agrum Hirpinum Samnitemve, ne et ipse oneri esset, sed in proxima loca sociorum populi Romani adducturum. Iis populandis et militem suum repleturum se et metu procul ab his[4]
4 summoturum hostis. Quod ad bellum Romanum attineret, si Trasumenni quam Trebiae, si Cannarum quam Trasumenni pugna nobilior esset, Cannarum quoque se[5] memoriam obscuram maiore et clariore victoria facturum.

5 Cum hoc responso muneribusque amplis legatos dimisit; ipse praesidio modico relicto in Tifatis pro-
6 fectus cetero exercitu ire Nolam pergit. Eodem Hanno ex Bruttiis cum supplemento Carthagine advecto atque elephantis venit. Castris haud procul

[1] ducam *z* : dicam *P*(1).

[2] miseris simul *Madvig* : misul *P* : misum P^3?*R* : missum R^1(7)*z* : simul erit *Gronovius*.

[3] haud A^v *Valla* : at it *PR* : ad id *C* : ad id R^2(14).

[4] his *P Walters, without comment* : iis *vulgate*.

[5] quoque se *Siesbye* : se quoque *P*(1).

it easy for one who, I know, has routed and laid low B.C. 215
so many Roman battle-lines to surprise our scattered plunderers, roaming without their standards wherever a man is drawn by even the vain hope of booty. To a few Numidians they will in any case fall a prey, and you will have sent us troops and at the same time will have rid Nola of its garrison, if only men whom you have considered worthy to be your allies are not judged by you unworthy to be taken under your protection and defended."

XLIII. To this Hannibal replied that the Hirpini and Samnites were doing everything at once, reporting their losses, and asking for troops, and complaining that they were undefended and neglected. But they ought first to have reported, then asked for protection, finally, if this was not obtained, they should then, and not sooner, have complained that help had been besought in vain. He would lead his army, not into the territory of the Hirpini or the Samnites, in order not to be another burden, but into the nearest lands of allies of the Roman people. By devastating these he would satisfy his own army and drive the frightened enemy to a distance from them. As for the Roman war, if the battle of Lake Trasumennus was more celebrated than that of the Trebia, if Cannae than Trasumennus, he would overshadow the memory even of Cannae by a greater and more famous victory.

With this answer and also with ample gifts he sent the ambassadors away. He himself set out, leaving a moderate force on Tifata, and proceeded with the rest of his army to Nola. Hanno also came thither from the land of the Bruttii with reinforcements brought from Carthage and with the elephants.

A.U.C. 539 positis longe alia omnia inquirenti conperta sunt
7 quam quae a legatis sociorum audierat. Nihil
enim Marcellus ita egerat ut aut fortunae aut temere
hosti commissum dici posset. Explorato cum firmis-
que praesidiis tuto receptu praedatum ierat, omniaque velut adversus praesentem Hannibalem cauta
8 provisaque fuerant. Tum, ubi sensit hostem adventare, copias intra moenia tenuit; per muros inambu-
lare senatores Nolanos iussit et omnia circa explorare
9 quae apud hostes fierent. Ex his Hanno, cum ad
murum successisset, Herennium Bassum et Herium
Pettium ad conloquium evocatos permissuque Mar-
10 celli egressos per interpretem adloquitur. Hannibalis virtutem fortunamque extollit: populi Romani
11 obterit senescentem cum viribus maiestatem. Quae
si paria essent, ut quondam fuissent, tamen expertis
quam grave Romanum imperium sociis, quanta
indulgentia Hannibalis etiam in captivos omnis
Italici nominis fuisset, Punicam Romanae societatem
12 atque amicitiam praeoptandam esse. Si ambo
consules cum suis exercitibus ad Nolam essent,
tamen non magis pares Hannibali futuros quam ad
Cannas fuissent, nedum praetor unus cum paucis et
13 novis militibus Nolam tutari possit. Ipsorum quam
Hannibalis magis[1] interesse capta an tradita Nola
poteretur; potiturum enim, ut Capua Nuceriaque

[1] magis *Harant* (*after* ipsorum *in* $A^{x}z$) : *om.* *P*(1).

Having pitched his camp not far away, Hannibal found on enquiry that everything was very different from what he had heard from the legates of his allies. For Marcellus had not done anything in such a way that it could be said to have been left to fortune or rashly left to the enemy. After reconnoitring, having strong forces and a safe refuge, he had gone out to forage, and every possible precaution had been taken, as though against Hannibal in person. Then on learning of the approach of the enemy, he kept his troops inside the walls. He ordered the senators of Nola to walk up and down on the walls, and to observe everything that went on among the enemy all around. Hanno, having come close to the wall, called out from their number Herennius Bassus and Herius Pettius to a conference, and when they came out with Marcellus' permission, he addressed them through an interpreter. He lauded Hannibal's courage and success. He belittled the majesty of the Roman people, as wasting away along with their resources. And if these qualities were evenly matched, he said, as once they had been, nevertheless those who had found out how burdensome was Roman rule to the allies, how great had been Hannibal's indulgence even to all captives who called themselves Italians, these were bound to prefer Carthaginian alliance and friendship to Roman. If both consuls were at Nola with their armies, still they would be no more a match for Hannibal than they had been at Cannae; much less could one praetor with a few raw soldiers defend Nola. It was their own concern more than Hannibal's whether he took Nola by capture or by surrender. For he would take it, as he had taken Capua and Nuceria. But what a difference B.C. 215

A.U.C. 539 potitus esset; sed quid inter Capuae ac Nuceriae fortunam interesset ipsos prope in medio sitos
14 Nolanos scire. Nolle ominari quae captae urbi casura[1] forent, et potius spondere, si Marcellum cum praesidio ac Nolam tradidissent, neminem alium quam ipsos legem qua in societatem amicitiamque Hannibalis venirent dicturum.

XLIV. Ad ea Herennius Bassus respondit multos annos iam inter Romanum Nolanumque populum amicitiam esse, cuius neutros ad eam diem paenitere, et sibi, si cum fortuna mutanda fides fuerit, sero
2 iam esse mutare. An dedituris se Hannibali fuisse accersendum Romanorum praesidium? Cum iis qui ad sese tuendos venissent omnia sibi et esse consociata et ad ultimum fore.

3 Hoc conloquium abstulit spem Hannibali per proditionem recipiendae Nolae. Itaque corona oppidum circumdedit, ut simul ab omni parte moenia adgrede-
4 retur. Quem ut successisse muris Marcellus vidit, instructa intra portam acie cum magno tumultu erupit. Aliquot primo impetu perculsi caesique sunt; dein concursu ad pugnantis facto aequatisque viribus atrox esse coepit pugna, memorabilisque inter paucas fuisset, ni ingentibus procellis effusus
5 imber diremisset pugnantis. Eo die commisso modico certamine atque inritatis animis in urbem Romani, Poeni in castra receperunt sese; nam[2]

[1] casura *Nipperdey*: cessura *P*(11)*A*[x].
[2] nam *Weissenborn*: tam *P*(1): tamen *M*[4].

there was between the lot of Capua and that of Nuceria the men of Nola themselves knew, being situated about half-way between them. He did not wish to forecast what would happen to the city if captured, but assured them instead that if they surrendered Marcellus and Nola with the garrison, no one but themselves should name the terms on which they might enter alliance and friendship with Hannibal. B.C. 215

XLIV. To this Herennius Bassus replied that for many years there had been friendship between the Roman people and that of Nola; that down to that time neither party regretted it, and for themselves, if with altered fortune they ought to have changed their loyalty, it was now too late to change. If they were going to surrender to Hannibal, had they needed to send for a Roman garrison? With the men who had come to defend them they had allied themselves in everything, and it would be so to the end.

This conference deprived Hannibal of the hope of getting Nola by treachery. And so he completely invested the town, in order to attack the walls from all sides at once. Marcellus, on seeing that Hannibal had approached the walls, drew up his line inside the gate and sallied out with a great uproar. Not a few were terrified by the first attack and slain. Then, when they had charged the attacking force and brought up equal numbers, the battle began to be a fierce one, and would have been among the most memorable, if a downpour of rain in heavy squalls had not separated the combatants. That day, after beginning an engagement of no importance and merely inflaming their passions, they withdrew, the Romans into the city, the Carthaginians to the camp. For of

A.U.C. 539 Poenorum prima eruptione perculsi ceciderunt haud
6 plus quam triginta,[1] Romani quinquaginta.[2] Imber[3]
continens per noctem totam usque ad horam tertiam diei insequentis tenuit. Itaque, quamquam utraque pars avidi certaminis erant, eo die tenuerunt sese tamen munimentis.

Tertio die Hannibal partem copiarum praedatum
7 in agrum Nolanum misit. Quod ubi animadvertit Marcellus, extemplo in aciem copias eduxit; neque Hannibal detractavit. Mille fere passuum inter urbem erant castraque; eo spatio—et sunt omnia
8 campi circa Nolam—concurrerunt. Clamor ex parte utraque sublatus proximos ex cohortibus iis quae in agros praedatum exierant ad proelium iam com-
9 missum revocavit. Et Nolani aciem Romanam auxerunt, quos conlaudatos Marcellus in subsidiis stare et saucios ex acie efferre iussit, pugna abstinere, ni ab se signum accepissent. XLV. Proelium erat anceps; summa vi et duces hortabantur et milites pugnabant. Marcellus victis ante diem tertium, fugatis ante paucos dies a Cumis, pulsis priore anno ab Nola ab eodem se duce, milite alio, instare iubet.
2 Non omnis esse in acie; praedantis vagari in agro; et[4] qui pugnent, marcere Campana luxuria, vino et scortis omnibusque lustris per totam hiemem con-
3 fectos. Abisse illam vim vigoremque, dilapsa[5] esse robora corporum animorumque quibus Pyrenaei Alpiumque superata sint iuga. Reliquias illorum

[1] triginta (XXX) PC^x (14) : XXXX R : trecenti *Gronovius*.
[2] quinquaginta *Gronovius* (*see next note*).
[3] imber R^2(7) : liber (*i.e.* L = 50 + iber) *P* : inber P^1?.
[4] agro; et *Alschefski* : agro sed *P*(1) : agris; et *Luchs*.
[5] dilapsa *z* : delapsa *P*(1).

[1] The small number is probably an error of the copyists.

the Carthaginians not more than thirty,[1] who were terrified by the first sally, fell, of the Romans fifty. The rain continued incessantly throughout the night to the third hour of the next day. And so, although both sides were eager for the fray, they nevertheless kept within their fortifications that day. B.C. 215

On the third day Hannibal sent a part of his forces into the country about Nola to plunder. On observing this Marcellus at once drew up his troops in line. And Hannibal did not refuse battle. There was about a mile between the city and the camp. In that space—and there is only a plain around Nola—they met each other. A shout raised on both sides recalled to a battle already begun the nearest men of the cohorts which had gone out to the farms for booty. And the men of Nola reinforced the Roman line. Marcellus praised them and ordered them to keep their place among the reserves and to carry off the wounded from the field; to refrain from fighting unless they should receive a signal from him. XLV. The battle was doubtful. The generals were doing their utmost in cheering on their men, the soldiers in fighting. Marcellus bids them attack men defeated two days before, driven from Cumae in flight a few days earlier, beaten back from Nola the previous year by himself, the same commander, and other soldiers. Not all of the enemy, he said, were in the line of battle; the booty-hunters were roaming about the country, and those who were fighting were weakened by Campanian luxury, exhausted by wine and harlots and every kind of dissipation the whole winter through. Gone was that force and energy, lost the strength of body and spirit with which they had crossed the ranges of the Pyrenees and the Alps.

A.U.C. 539

virorum vix arma membraque sustinentis pugnare.
4 Capuam Hannibali Cannas fuisse: ibi virtutem bellicam, ibi militarem disciplinam, ibi praeteriti temporis
5 famam, ibi spem futuri exstinctam. Cum haec exprobrando hosti Marcellus suorum militum animos erigeret, Hannibal multo gravioribus probris increpa-
6 bat: arma signaque eadem se noscere quae ad Trebiam Trasumennumque, postremo ad Cannas viderit habueritque; militem alium profecto se in hiberna Capuam duxisse, alium inde eduxisse.
7 "Legatumne Romanum et legionis unius atque alae magno certamine vix toleratis pugnam, quos binae
8 acies consulares numquam sustinuerunt? Marcellus tirone milite ac Nolanis subsidiis inultus nos iam iterum lacessit! Ubi ille miles meus est qui derepto ex equo C. Flaminio consuli caput abstulit? Ubi,
9 qui L. Paulum ad Cannas occidit? Ferrum nunc hebet? an dextrae torpent? an quid prodigii est aliud? Qui pauci plures vincere soliti estis, nunc paucis plures vix restatis? Romam vos expugna-
10 turos, si quis duceret, fortes lingua iactabatis: en,[1] in minore re[2] hic experiri vim virtutemque volo. Expugnate Nolam, campestrem urbem, non flumine, non mari saeptam. Hinc vos ex tam opulenta urbe

[1] en A^y *Valla, Madvig*: enim *P*(10).
[2] in minore re *Madvig*: minor res est *PM*²?A^y(13) *Valla*.

---

[1] Again disparagement of Marcellus, as in xlii. 10.
[2] A somewhat different account in XXII. vi. 4.
[3] Cf. XXII. xlix. 12.

Remnants only of those men were fighting, scarcely B.C. 215
able to hold up their weapons and their limbs. Capua had been Hannibal's Cannae. It was there that warlike courage had been extinguished, there the discipline of the soldier, there the past reputation, there the hope for the future. While by thus reviling the enemy Marcellus was raising the spirits of his soldiers, Hannibal was uttering much more serious reproaches; he recognized the same arms and standards which he had seen and had at the Trebia and Trasumennus, finally at Cannae; but as for the soldier, he had certainly led one man into winter quarters at Capua, and out of them a different man. "Are you," he said, "hardly able with great effort to hold out against a mere Roman lieutenant,[1] and an engagement with a single legion and its auxiliaries —you, whom two consular armies combined have never withstood? Marcellus with recruits and with reserves from Nola is now attacking us for the second time with impunity! Where is that soldier of mine who pulled Gaius Flaminius, the consul, down from his horse and carried away his head? [2] Where the man who slew Lucius Paulus at Cannae? [3] Is the sword now blunted? Or are your right hands benumbed? Or is it some other portent? You who, though few, were wont to defeat larger numbers, now in larger numbers with difficulty resist the few? You used to boast, brave men in speech, that if some one led you, you would take Rome by storm. Look you, in a less difficult situation, here and now I wish to test your might and courage. Take Nola by storm, a city of the plain, not fenced by a river nor by the sea. From this place, a city of such wealth, I will either lead you, laden with booty and

A.U.C. 539 praeda spoliisque onustos vel ducam quo voletis vel sequar."

XLVI. Nec bene nec male dicta profuerunt ad
2 confirmandos animos. Cum omni parte pellerentur, Romanisque crescerent animi, non duce solum adhortante sed Nolanis etiam per clamorem favoris indicem accendentibus ardorem pugnae, terga Poeni dederunt
3 atque in castra conpulsi sunt. Quae oppugnare cupientis milites Romanos Marcellus Nolam reduxit cum magno gaudio et gratulatione etiam plebis, quae
4 ante inclinatior ad Poenos fuerat. Hostium plus quinque milia [1] caesa eo die, vivi capti sescenti et signa militaria undeviginti et duo elephanti, quattuor in acie occisi; Romanorum minus mille interfecti.
5 Posterum diem indutiis tacitis sepeliendo utrimque caesos in acie consumpserunt. Spolia hostium
6 Marcellus Volcano votum cremavit. Tertio post die, ob iram, credo, aliquam aut spem liberalioris militiae, ducenti septuaginta duo equites, mixti Numidae et Hispani, ad Marcellum transfugerunt. Eorum forti fidelique opera in eo bello usi sunt saepe Romani.
7 Ager Hispanis in Hispania et Numidis in Africa post bellum virtutis causa datus est.

8 Hannibal, ab Nola remisso in Bruttios Hannone cum quibus venerat copiis, ipse Apuliae hiberna petit
9 circaque Arpos consedit. Q. Fabius ut profectum in

[1] quinque milia *Gronovius* : vel *P*(1); *cf.* xxxiv. 13.

spoils, or I will follow you whithersoever you shall desire." B.C. 215

XLVI. Neither encouragement nor reproaches had any effect in steadying their spirits. Since they were everywhere beaten back, while the Romans' courage rose, as not only the general exhorted them, but the men of Nola also kindled their ardour for battle by shouting as evidence of their support, the Carthaginians retreated and were forced back into the camp. The Roman soldiers were eager to assault the camp, but Marcellus led them back to Nola, in the midst of great rejoicing and congratulation on the part of the common people as well, who had previously been more inclined to the Carthaginians. Of the enemy more than five thousand were slain that day, six hundred captured alive, and nineteen military standards and two elephants were taken, four killed in battle. Of the Romans less than a thousand were slain. The next day they spent under a tacit armistice, burying those slain in the battle on both sides. Marcellus burned the spoils of the enemy, paying a vow to Vulcan. Two days later in anger on some account, I suppose, or in the hope of a more generous service, two hundred and seventy-two horsemen, partly Numidians, partly Spaniards, deserted to Marcellus. Their brave and loyal services were repeatedly employed by the Romans in that war. As a reward for their courage farm land was given after the war to the Spaniards in Spain, to the Numidians in Africa.

Hannibal, sending Hanno back from Nola into the country of the Bruttii with the forces with which he had come, himself sought winter quarters in Apulia and established himself near Arpi. Quintus Fabius,

A.U.C. 539 Apuliam Hannibalem audivit, frumento ab Nola Nea-
polique in ea castra convecto quae super Suessulam
erant, munimentisque firmatis et, praesidio quod per
hiberna ad obtinendum[1] locum satis esset relicto,
ipse Capuam propius movit castra agrumque Campa-
10 num ferro ignique est depopulatus, donec coacti
sunt Campani, nihil admodum viribus suis fidentes,
egredi portis et castra ante urbem in aperto com-
11 munire. Sex milia armatorum habebant, peditem
inbellem, equitatu plus poterant; itaque equestribus
proeliis lacessebant hostem.

12 Inter multos nobiles equites Campanos Cerrinus
Vibellius erat, cognomine Taurea. Civis indidem
erat, longe omnium Campanorum fortissimus eques,
adeo ut, cum apud Romanos militaret, unus eum
Romanus Claudius Asellus gloria equestri aequaret.
13 Tunc[2] Taurea, cum diu perlustrans oculis obequi-
tasset hostium turmis, tandem silentio facto, ubi
14 esset Claudius Asellus quaesivit et, quoniam verbis
secum de virtute ambigere solitus esset, cur non
ferro decerneret daretque opima spolia victus aut
victor caperet.

XLVII. Haec ubi Asello sunt nuntiata in castra, id modo moratus ut consulem percunctaretur liceretne extra ordinem in provocantem hostem pugnare,

[1] obtinendum *Madvig*: tenendum *x Gronovius*: petendum *P*(1).

[2] tunc *Walch*: hunc *P*(4): hic *DA*.

on hearing that Hannibal had gone into Apulia, brought in grain from Nola and Neapolis to the camp above Suessula, strengthened the fortifications, and left a garrison which was strong enough to hold the place through the winter season. He then moved his camp nearer to Capua and ravaged the Campanian territory with fire and sword, until the Campanians, who had no confidence at all in their own resources, were compelled to come out of the gates and fortify a camp in the open before the city. They had six thousand armed men, infantry unfit for war; but in cavalry they were more effective. Accordingly they kept harassing the enemy by cavalry battles. B.C. 215

Among the many distinguished Campanian horsemen was Cerrinus Vibellius, surnamed Taurea. A citizen of that state, he was far the bravest horseman of all the Campanians, so much so that while he served with the Romans only one Roman, Claudius Asellus, rivalled him in reputation as a cavalryman. At this time Taurea, looking all around again and again, rode up to the squadrons of the enemy's cavalry and, when silence was at last obtained, asked where Claudius Asellus was, and why, since he had been in the habit of disputing with him about their courage, did he not settle the matter with the sword and, if vanquished, give, or if victorious, take, the splendid spoils.[1]

XLVII. When this was reported to Asellus in the camp, he waited only to ask the consul whether he might fight out of the ranks against an enemy who

[1] Strictly speaking the *opima spolia* were those taken by a Roman general in command from the general of the enemy after a single combat; I. x. 4–7 (Romulus); IV. xx. 2 and 5–6 (Cossus); *Periocha* 20 (Marcellus).

A.U.C. 539 2 permissu eius arma extemplo cepit, provectusque ante stationes equo Tauream nomine compellavit
3 congredique ubi vellet iussit. Iam[1] Romani ad spectaculum pugnae eius frequentes exierant, et Campani non vallum modo castrorum sed moenia
4 etiam urbis prospectantes repleverant.[2] Cum iam ante ferocibus dictis rem nobilitassent, infestis hastis concitarunt equos; dein libero spatio inter se ludi-
5 ficantes sine vulnere pugnam extrahebant.[3] Tum Campanus Romano "Equorum" inquit "hoc non equitum erit certamen, nisi e campo in cavam hanc viam demittimus equos. Ibi nullo ad evagandum
6 spatio comminus conserentur manus." Dicto prope citius equum in viam Claudius deiecit.[4] Taurea verbis ferocior quam re "Minime sis" inquit "cantherium in fossam"; quae vox in rusticum inde proverbium
7 prodita est. Claudius, cum ea via[5] longe perequitasset,[6] nullo obvio hoste in campum rursus evectus, increpans ignaviam hostis, cum magno gaudio et
8 gratulatione victor in castra redit. Huic pugnae equestri rem—quam vera sit,[7] communis existimatio est—mirabilem certe adiciunt quidam annales: cum refugientem ad urbem Tauream Claudius sequeretur, patenti hostium porta[8] invectum per alteram, stupentibus miraculo hostibus, intactum evasisse.

[1] iam (13): hinc C^4M^1: in *PCMF*.

[2] repleverant $A^{v}z$ *Madvig*: -erunt *P*(1)*F*.

[3] extrahebant P^1?(1)*F*: extraherebant *P*: extrahere *Gronovius*.

[4] deiecit A^2 *Madvig*: delegit *PA*?(2)*F*: egit A^3x *Aldus*.

[5] ea via *Perizonius, Madvig*: exva *P*: ex via P^2?(1)*F*: cava *Madvig* (*later*).

[6] perequitasset, *P*(1)*F* *add* quia, P^1? via.

[7] quam vera sit *Gronovius*: quam vetatis *P*(4)*F*: quam etatis *DA*.

[8] porta *Ingerslev*: portae *P*(1)*F*.

challenged him. With the consul's permission he at B.C. 215 once took up his arms, and riding out in front of the guard-posts he addressed Taurea by name and bade him engage wherever he pleased. Already the Romans had gone out in crowds to that spectacle of a combat, and the Campanians who looked on had filled not only the earthwork of the camp but also the walls of the city. First calling attention to the affair by high-spirited words, they levelled spears and spurred their horses. Then, dodging each other in the open space, they prolonged the bloodless fray. Then the Campanian said to the Roman: "This will be a contest of horses, not of horsemen, unless we let our horses go down from the open field into this deep-cut road. There, with no room to avoid each other, we shall fight hand to hand." Almost sooner than said Claudius put his horse into the road. Taurea, more spirited in words than in action, said: "Never a nag, please, into a ditch!"[1]—words which have come down from that time as a farmer's parable. Claudius rode a long way on that road, and then riding back to the field without meeting any enemy, returned as victor to the camp, reviling the cowardice of his enemy in the midst of great rejoicing and congratulations. To this combat of horsemen some annals add what is certainly marvellous—how true, it is for everyone to judge—that, as Claudius was pursuing Taurea fleeing to the city, he rode in through the enemy's open gate and, while they were spellbound in amazement, escaped unharmed by the opposite gate.

[1] To be supplied is a verb, probably *demiseris*. Colloquial *sis* (= *si vis*, an insistent "please") merely strengthens the prohibition.

A.U.C. 539

XLVIII. Quieta inde stativa fuere, ac retro etiam
consul movit castra, ut sementem Campani facerent,
nec ante violavit agrum Campanum quam iam altae
2 in segetibus herbae pabulum praebere poterant. Id
convexit in Claudiana castra super Suessulam ibique
hiberna aedificavit. M. Claudio proconsuli imperavit
ut, retento Nolae necessario ad tuendam urbem
praesidio, ceteros milites dimitteret Romam, ne
3 oneri sociis et sumptui rei publicae essent. Et
Ti. Gracchus, a Cumis Luceriam in Apuliam legiones
cum duxisset, M. Valerium inde praetorem Brundisium cum eo quem Luceriae habuerat exercitum misit
tuerique oram agri Sallentini et providere quod ad
Philippum bellumque Macedonicum attineret iussit.
4 Exitu aestatis eius qua haec gesta perscripsimus litterae a P. et Cn. Scipionibus venerunt, quantas quamque prosperas in Hispania res gessissent; sed pecuniam in stipendium vestimentaque et frumentum
5 exercitui et sociis navalibus omnia deesse. Quod ad
stipendium attineat, si aerarium inops sit, se aliquam
rationem inituros quomodo ab Hispanis sumatur;[1]
cetera utique ab Roma mittenda esse, nec aliter aut
6 exercitum aut provinciam teneri posse. Litteris
recitatis nemo omnium erat quin et vera scribi et
postulari aequa fateretur; sed occurrebat animis
quantos exercitus terrestris navalisque tuerentur,
quantaque nova classis mox paranda esset, si bellum

[1] sumatur (sumat') *P*[1]*?* *Alschefski, Walters*: summat'q. *P*: sumant' *P*[2]*?R*[1]*?*(7)*F*.

---

[1] The time is early autumn.

[2] In the extreme south of Calabria; XXIV. xx. 16; XXV. i. 1.

[3] As told in XXII. xxii. and XXIII. xxvi ff.

[4] *I.e.* the senators present.

XLVIII. Thereafter the winter quarters were undisturbed, and the consul moved his camp back again, that the Campanians might do their sowing.[1] And he did not ravage the Campanian country until the growing grain in the fields was tall enough to furnish fodder. This he transported to the Claudian Camp above Suessula and there built winter barracks. He ordered Marcus Claudius, the proconsul, to keep at Nola only the garrison needed to defend the city, and to send away the rest of the soldiers to Rome, lest they be a burden to the allies and an expense to the state. And Tiberius Gracchus, after leading his legions from Cumae to Luceria in Apulia, sent thence Marcus Valerius, the praetor, to Brundisium with the army which he had had at Luceria, and ordered him to defend the coast of the Sallentine region[2] and to take measures concerning Philip and the Macedonian war. B.C. 215

At the end of the summer in which occurred the events I have described, there came a letter from Publius and Gnaeus Scipio, reporting how great and how successful had been their operations in Spain;[3] but that money for pay, also clothing and grain, were lacking for the army, and for the crews everything. So far as pay was concerned, if the treasury was empty, they would find some method of getting it from the Spaniards. Everything else, they said, must in any case be sent from Rome, and in no other way could either the army or the province be kept. After the reading of the letter, there was no one among them all[4] who did not admit that the statements were true and the demands fair. But they reflected what great forces on land and sea they were maintaining, and how large a new fleet must soon be made ready

A.U.C. 539 7 Macedonicum moveretur: Siciliam ac Sardiniam,
quae ante bellum vectigales fuissent, vix praesides
provinciarum exercitus alere; tributo sumptus
8 suppeditari; ipsum[1] tributum conferentium numerum tantis exercituum stragibus et ad Trasumennum
lacum et ad Cannas inminutum; qui superessent
pauci, si multiplici gravarentur stipendio, alia peri-
9 turos peste. Itaque nisi fide staretur,[2] rem publicam[3]
10 opibus non staturam. Prodeundum in contionem
Fulvio praetori esse, indicandas populo publicas
necessitates cohortandosque, qui redempturis auxis-
sent patrimonia, ut rei publicae, ex qua crevissent,
11 tempus commodarent conducerentque ea[4] lege praebenda quae ad exercitum Hispaniensem opus
essent, ut, cum pecunia in aerario esset, iis primis
12 solveretur. Haec praetor in contione; edixitque diem[5] quo vestimenta frumentum Hispaniensi
exercitui praebenda quaeque alia opus essent navalibus sociis esset locaturus. XLIX. Ubi ea dies
venit, ad conducendum tres societates aderant hominum undeviginti, quorum duo postulata fuere:
2 unum ut militia vacarent, dum[6] in eo publico essent,
alterum ut quae in naves inposuissent ab hostium
3 tempestatisque vi publico periculo essent. Utroque
impetrato conduxerunt, privataque pecunia res
publica administrata est. Ii mores eaque caritas
patriae per omnes ordines velut tenore uno pertine-

[1] ipsum, *P*(1)*F* *have* eum ipsum.
[2] staretur (staret') *P* *Walters*: staret (1)*F* *vulgate*.
[3] rem publicam *P*(2)*F*: res publica *Az*.
[4] ea *Sigonius*: ex *P*(1)*F*.
[5] -que diem *Riemann*: *om.* *P*(1).
[6] ut militia vacarent dum *Gronovius*: *hopeless confusion in* *P*(1)*F*.

[1] A direct tax paid by Roman citizens.

if a Macedonian war should begin; that Sicily and Sardinia, which before the war had paid taxes in kind, were hardly feeding the armies that garrisoned those provinces; that necessary expenses were met only by the property tax;[1] that the number of those who paid that particular tax had been diminished by such great losses of troops at Lake Trasumennus and also at Cannae; that if the few who survived should be burdened by a much greater levy, they would perish by another malady. And so they thought that, unless support should be found in credit, the state would not be sustained by its assets; that Fulvius, the praetor, must go before the assembly, inform the people of the public needs and exhort those who by contracts had increased their property to allow the state, the source of their wealth, time for payment, and to contract for furnishing what was needed for the army in Spain, on the condition that they should be the first to be paid, as soon as there was money in the treasury. To this effect the praetor addressed the people, and named a date on which he would let the contracts for furnishing clothing and grain to the army in Spain and whatever else was needed for the crews. XLIX. When that day came, three companies of nineteen members presented themselves to take the contracts. And their demands were two: one, that they should be exempt from military duty so long as they were in that public service, the other, that the cargoes which they shipped should be at the risk of the state, so far as concerned the violence of enemies and of storms. Both demands being obtained, they contracted, and the state was carried on by private funds. Such character and such love of country pervaded all the classes virtually without B.C. 215

A.U.C. 539 4 bat. Quemadmodum conducta omnia magno animo
sunt, sic summa fide praebita, nec quicquam parcius
militibus quam [1] si ex opulento aerario, ut quondam,
alerentur.

5 Cum hi commeatus venerunt, Iliturgi oppidum ab
Hasdrubale ac Magone et Hannibale Bomilcaris filio
6 ob defectionem ad Romanos oppugnabatur. Inter
haec trina castra hostium Scipiones cum in urbem
sociorum magno certamine ac strage obsistentium
pervenissent, frumentum, cuius inopia erat, advexe-
7 runt, cohortatique oppidanos ut eodem animo
moenia tutarentur quo pro se pugnantem Romanum
exercitum vidissent, ad castra maxima oppugnanda,
8 quibus Hasdrubal praeerat, ducunt. Eodem et duo
duces et duo exercitus Carthaginiensium, ibi rem
9 summam agi cernentes, convenerunt. Itaque
eruptione e castris pugnatum est. Sexaginta
hostium milia eo die in pugna fuerunt, sedecim circa
10 a Romanis. Tamen adeo haud dubia victoria fuit ut
plures numero quam ipsi erant Romani hostium
11 occiderint, ccperint amplius tria milia hominum,
paulo minus mille equorum, undesexaginta militaria
signa, septem elephantos, quinque in proelio occisis,
12 trinisque eo die castris potiti sint. Iliturgi obsidione
liberato ad Intibili oppugnandum Punici exercitus
traducti suppletis copiis ex provincia, ut quae maxime

[1] parcius militibus quam *Madvig* (*one line*), *but he added* datum (*before* quam) *with Weissenborn*: *om. P*(1)*F*.

---

[1] In southern Spain, on the upper course of the Baetis (Guadalquivir), destroyed by Scipio Africanus in 206 B.C.; XXVIII. xx.

exception. As all the supplies were magnanimously contracted for, so they were delivered with great fidelity, and nothing was furnished to the soldiers less generously than if they were being maintained, as formerly, out of an ample treasury. B.C. 215

When these supplies arrived, the town of Iliturgi,[1] because of its revolt to the Romans, was being besieged by Hasdrubal and Mago and Hannibal, the son of Bomilcar. Between these three camps of the enemy the Scipios made their way into a city of their allies with great effort and great loss to those that opposed them. And they brought grain, of which it had no supply, and encouraged the townspeople to defend their walls with the same spirit with which they had seen the Roman army fighting for them. Then they led their troops to an attack upon the largest camp, which Hasdrubal commanded. To it also came the other two generals and two armies of the Carthaginians, seeing that the whole issue was at stake there. Accordingly a sally from the camp opened the battle. Sixty thousand of the enemy were in the battle that day, about sixteen thousand on the Roman side. Yet so far was the victory from being uncertain that the Romans slew more than their own number, captured more than three thousand men, a little less than a thousand horses, fifty-nine military standards, seven elephants, five having been slain in battle. And they took the three camps that day. The siege of Iliturgi having been raised, the Carthaginian armies were led over to attack Intibili,[2] while their forces were recruited from a province which, more than any

[2] Apparently not far from Iliturgi; cf. Frontinus II. iii. 1. The only town of this name of which we hear elsewhere was on the east coast south of the Hiberus (Ebro).

A.U.C. 539 omnium belli avida, modo praeda aut merces esset,
13 et tum iuventute abundante. Iterum signis conlatis eadem fortuna utriusque partis pugnatum. Supra tredecim milia hostium caesa, supra duo capta cum signis duobus et quadraginta et novem elephantis.
14 Tum vero omnes prope Hispaniae populi ad Romanos defecerunt, multoque maiores ea aestate in Hispania quam in Italia res gestae.

other, was eager for war, if only there was booty or pay, and at that time was well supplied with young men. A second time there was a battle in regular line, with the same result for each side. Over thirteen thousand of the enemy were slain, over two thousand captured, with forty-two standards and nine elephants. Then indeed nearly all the peoples of Spain revolted to the Romans, and there were much greater achievements that summer in Spain than in Italy. B.C. 215

LIBRI XXIII PERIOCHA[1]

Campani ad Hannibalem defecerunt. Nuntius Cannensis victoriae Mago Carthaginem missus anulos aureos corporibus occisorum detractos in vestibulo curiae effudit, quos excessisse modii mensuram traditur. Post quem nuntium Hanno, vir ex Poenis nobilibus, suadebat senatui Carthaginiensium ut pacem a populo Romano peterent; nec tenuit obstrepente Barcina factione. Claudius Marcellus praetor ad Nolam eruptione adversus Hannibalem ex oppido facta prospere pugnavit. Casilinum a Poenis obsessum ita fame vexatum est ut lora et pelles scutis detractas et mures inclusi essent. Nucibus per Volturnum amnem a Romanis missis vixerunt. Senatus ex equestri ordine hominibus centum nonaginta septem suppletus est. L. Postumius praetor a Gallis cum exercitu caesus est. Cn. et P. Scipiones in Hispania Hasdrubalem vicerunt et Hispaniam suam fecerunt. Reliquiae Cannensis exercitus in Siciliam relegatae sunt, ne recederent inde nisi finito bello. Sempronius Gracchus consul Campanos cecidit. Claudius Marcellus praetor Hannibalis exercitum ad Nolam proelio fudit et vicit, primusque tot cladibus fessis Romanis meliorem spem belli dedit. Inter Philippum Macedoniae regem et Hannibalem societas iuncta est. Praeterea in Hispania feliciter a P. et Cn. Scipionibus, in Sardinia a[2] T. Manlio praetore adversus Poenos res gestas continet, a quibus Hasdrubal dux et Mago et Hanno capti. Exercitus Hannibalis per hiberna ita luxuriatus est ut corporis animique viribus enervaretur.

[1] For the *Periochae* cf. Vol. I, pp. xvii f.

[2] *The words* Cn. . . . a, *omitted in MSS., were added by O. Jahn.*

SUMMARY OF BOOK XXIII

The Campanians revolted to Hannibal. Mago, who was sent to Carthage to report the victory at Cannae, poured out before the entrance of the Senate House golden rings taken from bodies of the slain; and the tradition is that there were more than a peck of them. After that report Hanno, one of the Carthaginian nobles, tried to persuade the Carthaginian senate to sue for peace from the Roman people. And he did not carry it through, since the Barca faction protested loudly. Claudius Marcellus, a praetor, fought with success at Nola, making a sally from the city against Hannibal. Casilinum, beset by the Carthaginians, suffered so much from starvation that the besieged ate thongs, hides stripped off from shields, and rats. They lived on nuts sent down the river Volturnus by the Romans. The senate was recruited by one hundred and ninety-seven men from the equestrian order. Lucius Postumius, the praetor, was slain with his army by the Gauls. Gnaeus and Publius Scipio defeated Hasdrubal in Spain and made Spain their own. The remnant of the army of Cannae was relegated to Sicily, not to leave it except after the end of the war. Sempronius Gracchus, the consul, utterly defeated the Campanians. Claudius Marcellus, a praetor, routed and worsted Hannibal's army in battle at Nola, and was the first to give the Romans, exhausted by so many disasters, a better hope for the war. An alliance was formed between Philip, king of Macedonia, and Hannibal. The book also contains the successes gained over the Carthaginians by Publius and Gnaeus Scipio in Spain and by Titus Manlius, the praetor, in Sardinia. Hasdrubal, the general, and Mago and Hanno were captured by them. The army of Hannibal lived in such indulgence in winter quarters as to be weakened in body and spirit.

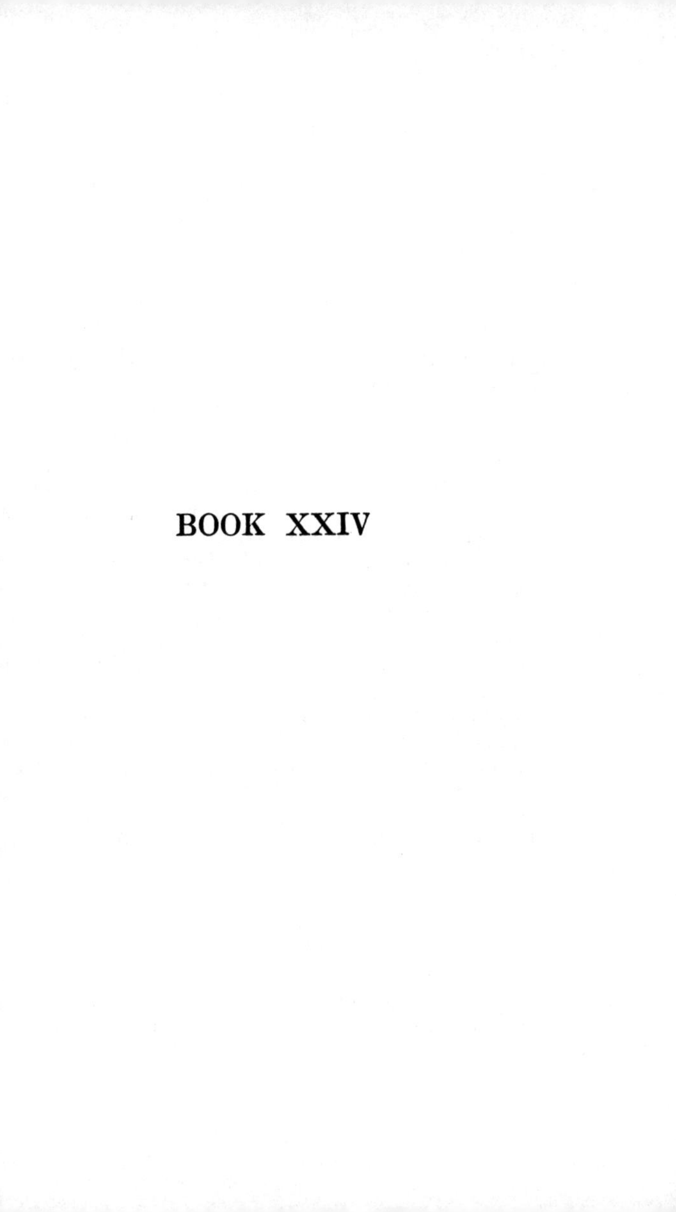

BOOK XXIV

LIBER XXIV

A.U.C. 539 I. Ut ex Campania in Bruttios reditum est, Hanno adiutoribus et ducibus Bruttiis Graecas urbes temptavit, eo facilius in societate manentes Romana quod Bruttios, quos et oderant et metuebant, Car-
2 thaginiensium partis factos cernebant. Regium primum temptatum est diesque aliquot ibi nequiquam absumpti. Interim Locrenses frumentum lignaque et cetera necessaria usibus ex agris in urbem rapere, etiam ne quid relictum praedae hostibus esset, et in dies maior omnibus portis multitudo
3 effundi; postremo sescenti[1] modo relicti in urbe erant, qui reficere muros ac[2] portas, telaque in pro-
4 pugnacula congerere cogebantur. In permixtam omnium aetatium ordinumque multitudinem et vagantem in agris magna ex parte inermem Hamilcar Poenus[3] equites emisit, qui violare quemquam vetiti, tantum ut ab urbe excluderent fuga dissi-
5 patos, turmas obiecere. Dux ipse loco superiore capto, unde agros urbemque posset conspicere, Bruttiorum cohortem adire muros atque evocare

[1] sescenti (DC) *W. Heraeus*: ob *P*: oc *P*[1]*?*: hoc (1): hi *x*: ii *z*.
[2] ac *x*: *om. P*(1).
[3] Poenus *P*(1): Poenos *A*[2].

---

[1] He had been with Hannibal around Nola, and was sent back to the country of the Bruttii; XXIII. xlvi. 8.

BOOK XXIV

I. Having returned from Campania to the land of the Bruttii, Hanno,[1] with the Bruttii as supporters and guides, attacked the Greek cities,[2] which were all the more ready to remain in alliance with Rome because they saw that the Bruttii, whom they both hated and feared, had gone over to the side of the Carthaginians. Regium was the first city to be attacked, and some days were spent there to no purpose. Meantime the Locrians hastily brought grain and wood and the other things needed to supply their wants from the farms into the city, also that no booty might be left for the enemy. And every day a larger crowd poured out of all the gates. Finally there were left in the city only six hundred men, who were made to repair walls and gates and to carry arms to the battlements. Against the multitude made up of all ages and classes, wandering about the country, many of the unarmed, Hamilcar the Carthaginian sent out his cavalry. Forbidden to injure anyone, they interposed their squadrons merely to shut off from the city those who had scattered in flight. The commander himself, after capturing higher ground from which he could see the country and the city, ordered a cohort of Bruttii B.C. 215

[2] Operations against Regium, Locri and Croton, barely mentioned in XXIII. xxx. 6 ff., are given here in greater detail. It is late autumn, 215 B.C.

A.U.C. 539

principes Locrensium ad conloquium iussit et polli-
centes amicitiam Hannibalis adhortari ad urbem tra-
6 dendam. Bruttiis in conloquio nullius rei primo fides
est; deinde, ut Poenus apparuit in collibus et refugientes pauci aliam omnem multitudinem in potestate
hostium esse adferebant, tum metu victi consulturos
7 se populum responderunt. Advocataque extemplo
contione, cum et levissimus quisque novas res
novamque societatem mallent et, quorum propinqui
extra urbem interclusi ab hostibus erant, velut
8 obsidibus datis pigneratos haberent animos, pauci
magis taciti probarent constantem fidem quam
prolatam[1] tueri auderent, haud dubio in speciem
9 consensu fit ad Poenos deditio. L. Atilio praefecto
praesidii quique cum eo milites Romani erant clam
in portum deductis atque impositis in navis, ut
Regium deveherentur, Hamilcarem Poenosque ea
condicione ut foedus extemplo aequis legibus fieret in
10 urbem acceperunt. Cuius rei prope non servata
fides deditis est, cum Poenus dolo dimissum Romanum incusaret, Locrenses profugisse ipsum cau-
11 sarentur. Insecuti etiam equites sunt, si quo casu
in freto aestus morari aut deferre naves in terram
posset. Et eos quidem quos sequebantur non sunt
adepti: alias a Messana traicientis freto Regium
12 naves conspexerunt. Milites erant Romani a

[1] prolatam *P*(4) *Conway*: probatam *DA*: propalam *Walch.*

---

[1] Not directly opposite Messana, but about seven miles to the southeast.

to go up to the walls and call out the chief men of B.C. 215 the Locrians to a conference, and with a promise of Hannibal's friendship to encourage them to surrender the city. In the conference the Bruttians at first were not believed at all. Then, when the Carthaginians were seen on the hills, and a few returning fugitives repeatedly asserted that all the rest of the multitude were in the power of the enemy, overcome by fear, they answered that they would consult the people. An assembly being at once called, all the fickle preferred political change and a new alliance; also those whose relations had been shut off outside the city by the enemy had mortgaged their affections, having virtually given hostages. And the few silently approved of steadfast loyalty, rather than dared to declare and defend it. Hence surrender to the Carthaginians was voted with apparently unquestioned unanimity. After Lucius Atilius, commander of the garrison, and the Roman soldiers who were with him had been secretly led down to the harbour and put on ships to be carried to Regium, they admitted Hamilcar and the Carthaginians into the city on condition that a treaty be made at once on fair terms. The promise of such a treaty was almost broken after they surrendered, when the Carthaginian charged that the Roman had been allowed by trickery to go away, while the Locrians pleaded that he had escaped unaided. Also the cavalry pursued him in the hope that possibly the current in the strait might delay the ships or bring them to shore. They did not indeed overtake the men they were pursuing, but they sighted other ships crossing the strait from Messana to Regium.[1] It was the Roman soldiers sent by Claudius, the

A.U.C. 539

Claudio praetore missi ad obtinendam urbem prae-
13 sidio. Itaque Regio extemplo abscessum est. Locrensibus iussu Hannibalis data pax ut liberi suis legibus viverent, urbs pateret Poenis, portus in potestate Locrensium esset, societas eo iure staret ut Poenus Locrensem Locrensisque Poenum pace ac bello iuvaret.

II. Sic a freto Poeni reducti frementibus Bruttiis quod Regium ac Locros, quas urbes direpturos se de-
2 stinaverant, intactas reliquissent. Itaque per se ipsi conscriptis armatisque iuventutis suae quindecim milibus ad Crotonem oppugnandum pergunt
3 ire, Graecam et ipsam urbem et maritimam, plurimum accessurum opibus, si in ora maris urbem ac portum[1] moenibus validam tenuissent, credentes.
4 Ea cura angebat quod neque non accersere ad auxilium Poenos satis audebant, ne quid non pro sociis egisse viderentur et, si Poenus rursus magis arbiter pacis quam adiutor belli fuisset, ne in libertatem Crotonis, sicut ante Locrorum, frustra pugnaretur.
5 Itaque optimum visum est ad Hannibalem mitti legatos caverique ab eo ut receptus Croto Brut-
6 tiorum esset. Hannibal cum praesentium eam consultationem esse respondisset et ad Hannonem eos reiecisset, ab Hannone nihil certi ablatum.
7 Nec[2] diripi volebat nobilem atque opulentam urbem et sperabat, cum Bruttius oppugnaret, Poenos nec

[1] ac portum *P*(1) : portu ac *x*.
[2] nec *Riemann* : nec eo *P*(1) : nec enim *A*³.

praetor, to garrison and hold the city. And so the siege of Regium was at once raised. Peace was granted the Locrians by Hannibal's order: they were, namely, to live in freedom under their own laws, the city to be open to the Carthaginians, the harbour in the power of the Locrians, the alliance to rest upon this basis: that the Carthaginian should help the Locrian, the Locrian the Carthaginian, in peace and in war. B.C. 215

II. Thus the Carthaginians were withdrawn from the strait, though the Bruttians were indignant because they had left Regium and Locri untouched, the cities which they had counted upon plundering. And so without aid they enlisted and armed 15,000 of their young men and set out to besiege Croton, another Greek city and on the sea, believing that it would be a great addition to their resources if they should hold a fortified city and harbour on the sea-coast. It troubled them that they did not quite dare not to call the Carthaginians to their aid, for fear they might seem to have failed to act as became allies. At the same time they feared that, if the Carthaginian should again be rather an arbiter of peace than a helper in war, fighting to secure freedom for Croton might be profitless, as previously for Locri. And thus it seemed best to send legates to Hannibal and gain assurance from him that Croton when captured should belong to the Bruttians. Hannibal having replied that decision in the matter lay with those on the ground, thus referring them to Hanno, they obtained no definite answer from Hanno. He did not wish a city well-known and rich to be plundered, and he was hoping that, while the Bruttian was besieging them and the Carthaginians

A.U.C. 539 probare nec iuvare eam oppugnationem appareret,
8 eo maturius ad se defecturos. Crotone nec consilium unum inter populares nec voluntas erat. Unus velut morbus invaserat omnes Italiae civitates ut plebes ab optimatibus dissentirent, senatus Romanis
9 faveret, plebs ad Poenos rem traheret. Eam dissensionem in urbe perfuga nuntiat Bruttiis: Aristomachum esse principem plebis tradendaeque auctorem urbis, et in vasta urbe lateque moenibus disiectis[1] raras stationes custodiasque senatorum esse; quacumque custodiant plebis homines, ea patere aditum.
10 Auctore ac duce perfuga Bruttii corona cinxerunt urbem acceptique ab plebe primo impetu omnem
11 praeter arcem cepere. Arcem optimates tenebant praeparato iam ante ad talem casum perfugio. Eodem Aristomachus perfugit, tamquam Poenis, non Bruttiis auctor urbis tradendae fuisset.

III. Urbs Croto murum in circuitu patentem duodecim milia passuum habuit ante Pyrrhi in Italiam
2 adventum. Post vastitatem eo bello factam vix pars dimidia habitabatur; flumen, quod medio oppido fluxerat, extra frequentia tectis loca praeterfluebat,
3 et arx procul eis erat[2] quae habitabantur. Sex milia aberat ab[3] urbe nobili[4] templum ipsa urbe

[1] moenibus disiectis *Jacobs*: omnibus disiectis moenibus *P*(1).

[2] erat *H. J. Müller* (*after* arx *Weissenborn*; *before* et *Walters*): *om. P*(1).

[3] ab *z*: in *P*(1): inde *Gronovius*.

[4] nobili *PM*^{3}*A*^{2}: nobile *P*^{2}(1).

obviously neither approving nor helping the siege, B.C. 215
they would all the more promptly come over to his side. At Croton there was among the citizens no one policy or common preference. One malady, so to speak, had attacked all the city-states of Italy, that the common people were at odds with the upper class, the senate inclining to the Romans, the common people drawing the state to the side of the Carthaginians. This disagreement in the city was reported to the Bruttians by a deserter: that Aristomachus was the leader of the plebeians and advised surrender of the city; also that in the sparsely inhabited city, with its walls at a great distance, there were only scattered posts and guards of the senators; that wherever plebeians were on guard there was free access to the city. With the deserter as adviser and leader the Bruttians completely encircled the city, and being admitted by the plebeians, they took the whole city by assault, with the exception of the citadel. The optimates held the citadel, having previously prepared a place of refuge for such an emergency. To it Aristomachus also fled, as though he had advised surrendering the city to the Carthaginians, not to the Bruttians.

III. The city of Croton had a wall with a circuit of twelve miles before the coming of Pyrrhus to Italy. Since the desolation caused by that war scarcely half of the city was inhabited.[1] The river which had flowed through the middle of the city now flowed past, outside the quarters which had numerous houses, and the citadel was far from the inhabited portions. Six miles from the famous city was a temple more

[1] According to XXIII. xxx. 6 the city now had less than 2000 inhabitants.

A.U.C. 539
nobilius[1] Laciniae Iunonis, sanctum omnibus circa
4 populis. Lucus ibi frequenti silva et proceris abietis
arboribus saeptus laeta in medio pascua habuit, ubi
omnis generis sacrum deae pecus pascebatur sine
5 ullo pastore, separatimque greges sui cuiusque
generis nocte remeabant ad stabula, numquam
6 insidiis ferarum, non fraude violati hominum. Magni
igitur fructus ex eo pecore capti, columnaque inde
aurea solida facta et sacrata est; inclitumque
templum divitiis etiam, non tantum sanctitate fuit.
7 Ac miracula aliqua adfingunt, ut plerumque tam
insignibus locis: fama est aram esse in vestibulo
templi, cuius cinerem nullo[2] umquam moveri[3]
8 vento. Sed[4] arx Crotonis una parte imminens mari,
altera vergente in agrum, situ tantum naturali
quondam munita, postea et muro cincta est qua per
aversas rupes ab Dionysio Siciliae tyranno per dolum
9 fuerat capta. Ea tum arce satis, ut videbatur, tuta
Crotoniatum optimates tenebant se, circumsedente
10 cum Bruttiis eos etiam plebe sua. Postremo Bruttii,
cum suis viribus inexpugnabilem viderent arcem,
11 coacti necessitate Hannonis auxilium inplorant. Is
condicionibus ad deditionem compellere Crotoniates

[1] nobilius, *before this* $P(1)$ *have* erat.
[2] nullo *P Gronovius*: nullus $P^3(1)$.
[3] moveri *Gronovius*: move *P*: movet $P^3(1)$: moveat *z*.
[4] vento. Sed *Gronovius*: ventos et *PCR*: vento et P^x: ventus et $C^x M?DA$.

---

[1] Cp. XXIII. xxxiii. 4. At that temple, the most celebrated shrine in Magna Graecia, Polybius found and used Hannibal's own inscription in Punic and Greek, recording his successes (Polyb. III. xxxiii. 18; lvi. 4), a document which Livy barely mentions (XXVIII. xlvi. 16). A single column of the temple still stands on the promontory. Livy is correct in regard to the distance from the city of Croton (*ca.* 9 km.).

famous than the city itself, that of Lacinian Juno,[1] B.C. 215
revered by all the surrounding peoples. There a sacred grove, which was enclosed by dense woods and tall fir-trees, had in its centre luxuriant pastures, where cattle of all kinds, being sacred to the goddess, used to pasture without any shepherd. And at night the flocks of each kind would return separately to their stalls, being never harmed by wild beasts lying in wait, nor by the dishonesty of men. Therefore great profits were made from the cattle, and out of the profits a massive golden column[2] was wrought and consecrated. And the temple was famous for its wealth also, not merely for its sanctity. They give it some pretended marvels also, as generally in places so noted. It is reported that in the space in front of the temple there is an altar whose ashes are never stirred by any wind. But the citadel of Croton, on one side overhanging the sea, while the other slopes down toward the country, was once protected merely by its natural situation, but later encircled with a wall also, where, along the cliffs on the farther side, it had been taken by ruse of Dionysius,[3] tyrant of Sicily. In that citadel, sufficiently safe, as it seemed, the optimates of Croton were at the time maintaining themselves, besieged even by their own plebs as well as by the Bruttians. Finally the Bruttians, seeing that the citadel was for their resources impregnable, were of necessity constrained to beg aid of Hanno. He attempted to compel the Crotonians to surrender on condition that they

[2] Coelius the historian said that Hannibal, finding it was not merely plated, decided to carry it away, but was deterred by a dream; Cicero *de Div.* I. 48.

[3] Who captured Croton about 389 B.C. and is said to have held it twelve years.

A.U.C. 539 conatus ut coloniam Bruttiorum eo deduci anti-
quamque frequentiam recipere vastam ac desertam
bellis urbem paterentur, omnium neminem praeter
12 Aristomachum movit. Morituros se adfirmabant
citius quam inmixti Bruttiis in alienos ritus mores
13 legesque ac mox linguam etiam verterentur. Aristomachus unus, quando nec suadendo ad deditionem
satis valebat nec, sicut urbem prodiderat, locum prodendae arcis inveniebat, transfugit ad Hannonem.
14 Locrenses brevi post legati, cum permissu Hannonis
arcem intrassent, persuadent ut traduci se in Locros
15 paterentur nec ultima experiri vellent. Iam hoc ut sibi
liceret impetraverant et ab Hannibale missis ad id
ipsum legatis. Ita Crotone excessum est deductique
Crotoniatae ad mare naves conscendunt. Locros
omnis multitudo abeunt.

16 In Apulia ne hiems quidem quieta inter Romanos
atque Hannibalem erat. Luceriae Sempronius con-
17 sul, Hannibal haud procul Arpis hibernabat. Inter
eos levia proelia ex occasione aut opportunitate
huius aut illius partis oriebantur, meliorque eis Romanus et in dies cautior tutiorque ab insidiis fiebat.

IV. In Sicilia Romanis omnia mutaverat mors
Hieronis regnumque ad Hieronymum nepotem eius
translatum, puerum vixdum libertatem, nedum domi-
2 nationem modice laturum. Eam aetatem, id inge-

[1] The entire population, while "Crotonians" refers primarily to the optimates.

[2] For Hiero's family see the table on p. 338.

permit a colony of Bruttians to be established there, B.C. 215
and allow the city, desolate and depopulated by wars, to recover its old-time numbers. But among them all he prevailed upon no one except Aristomachus. They claimed that they would sooner die than mingle with the Bruttians and change to the rites, customs and laws, and presently even the language, of another people. Aristomachus, since he was unable by persuasion to bring them to surrender and could find no opportunity to betray the citadel, as he had betrayed the city, alone went over to Hanno. Soon after that the Locrian legates entered the citadel with Hanno's consent and persuaded them to allow themselves to be transferred to Locri, and not to risk desperate measures. Permission to that effect they had already obtained from Hannibal, having sent legates for that very purpose. So Croton was evacuated, and the Crotonians were led down to the sea and went on shipboard. They went, the whole number of them,[1] to Locri.

In Apulia even the winter was not without conflict between the Romans and Hannibal. Sempronius, the consul, was wintering at Luceria, Hannibal not far from Arpi. Skirmishes between them kept occurring as opportunity offered, or the favourable moment for one side or the other. And in consequence the Romans were better soldiers, daily more cautious and safer from surprise attacks.

IV. In Sicily everything had been changed for the Romans by the death of Hiero [2] and the transfer of the kingdom to his grandson Hieronymus, a boy hardly able to keep his independence under control, much less absolute power. Such was the age, such

A.U.C. 539 nium tutores atque amici ad praecipitandum in omnia vitia acceperunt. Quae ita futura cernens Hiero ultima senecta voluisse dicitur liberas Syracusas relinquere, ne sub dominatu puerili per ludibrium bonis artibus partum firmatumque interiret regnum.
3 Huic consilio eius summa ope obstitere filiae, nomen regium penes puerum futurum ratae, regimen rerum omnium penes se virosque suos Adranodorum et
4 Zoippum, qui tutorum[1] primi relinquebantur. Non facile erat nonagensimum iam agenti annum, circumsesso dies noctesque muliebribus blanditiis, liberare animum et convertere ad publicam a privata curam.
5 Itaque tutores modo quindecim puero relinquit, quos precatus est moriens ut fidem erga populum Romanum quinquaginta annos ab se cultam inviolatam servarent iuvenemque suis potissimum vestigiis insistere vellent et disciplinae in qua eductus esset.
6 Haec mandata. Cum expirasset, tutores testamento prolato pueroque in contionem producto—
7 erat autem quindecim tum ferme annorum—paucis, qui per contionem ad excitandos clamores dispositi erant, adprobantibus testamentum, ceteris velut patre amisso in orba civitate omnia timentibus . . .[2]
8 Funus fit regium, magis amore civium et caritate
9 quam cura suorum celebre. Brevi deinde ceteros

[1] *The loss of a line in P(1) reduced five words apparently to* andranorum; *restored by Gronovius from Polybius.*

[2] *The lost words may have covered the transfer of power to Hieronymus (Madvig). Or, more briefly, it may have been merely the assumption of control by the guardians, e.g.* munus suscipiunt (*i.e.* tutores, § 6); *then perhaps followed* Tum funus, *etc.* (*Weissenborn*).

the disposition which guardians and friends took in hand, to throw him into all the vices. Hiero, seeing that this would happen, is said in his extreme old age to have wished to leave Syracuse free, that kingly power gained and confirmed by good qualities might not come to an end in disgrace under the tyranny of a boy. This his plan was opposed might and main by his daughters, who thought the boy would have the kingly title, but that complete control would be in their hands and those of their husbands, Adranodorus and Zoippus, who were being left as the principal guardians. It was not easy for a man now in his ninetieth year,[1] surrounded day and night by the blandishments of women, to be independent and turn his attention from the personal to the public interest. Accordingly he merely left fifteen guardians for the boy, and dying entreated them to keep inviolate that loyalty to the Roman people which he had maintained for fifty years[2] and to choose above all to have the young man tread in his footsteps and continue the training in which he had been brought up. Such were his instructions. After he had breathed his last the guardians produced the will and brought the boy, at that time about fifteen years old, before an assembly of the people. While a few men, who had been posted in all parts of the assembly to start applause, showed approval of the will, while the rest, as if deprived of a father and in an orphaned city, had only fears, the guardians ⟨took charge⟩. Then came the king's funeral, honoured rather by the love and regard of the citizens than by the grief of his B.C. 215

[1] He lived more than ninety years according to Polybius VII. viii. 7.

[2] In fact 48 years (263-215 B.C.).

A.U.C. 539 tutores summovet Adranodorus, iuvenem iam esse
dictitans Hieronymum ac regni potentem; de-
ponendoque tutelam ipse, quae cum pluribus communis erat, in se unum omnium vires convertit.

V. Vix quidem ulli vel[1] bono moderatoque regi
facilis erat favor apud Syracusanos, succedenti
2 tantae caritati Hieronis; verum enimvero Hieronymus, velut suis vitiis desiderabilem efficere vellet
avum, primo statim conspectu omnia quam disparia
3 essent ostendit. Nam qui per tot annos Hieronem
filiumque eius Gelonem nec vestis habitu nec alio
ullo insigni differentes a ceteris civibus vidissent, ei
conspexere purpuram ac diadema ac satellites arma-
4 tos, quadrigisque etiam alborum equorum interdum
5 ex regia procedentem more Dionysi tyranni. Hunc
tam superbum apparatum habitumque convenientes
sequebantur contemptus omnium hominum, superbae
aures, contumeliosa dicta, rari aditus non alienis
modo sed tutoribus etiam, libidines novae, inhumana
6 crudelitas. Itaque tantus omnis terror invaserat ut
quidam ex tutoribus aut morte voluntaria aut fuga
7 praeverterent metum suppliciorum. Tres ex iis,
quibus solis aditus in domum familiarior erat, Adranodorus et Zoippus, generi Hieronis, et Thraso quidam,
de aliis quidem rebus haud magnopere audiebantur;
8 tendendo autem duo ad Carthaginienses, Thraso ad
societatem Romanam, certamine ac studiis interdum
9 in se convertebant animum adulescentis, cum coniu-

[1] ulli vel *Conway*: ulli PC^3(11): vel *Madvig*.

---

[1] See note on XXIII. xxx. 11.

[2] In xxv. 1–2 the blame for his conduct is laid upon the guardians. The youth reigned only thirteen months; Polybius VII. vii. 3.

family. Soon afterwards Adranodorus removed the rest of the guardians, saying that Hieronymus was now a young man and capable of ruling. And laying down his own guardianship, which was shared with a number of others, he took to himself alone the powers of them all. B.C. 215

V. It would have been difficult for any king, even a good one and self-controlled, to find favour with the Syracusans as successor to Hiero, so beloved. But certainly Hieronymus at his very first appearance showed how different everything was, just as if he wished by his vices to make them regret his grandfather. For, though through so many years they had seen Hiero and his son Gelo [1] not differing from the rest of the citizens in garb or in any other distinction, they beheld purple and a diadem and armed attendants and a man who came forth from the palace sometimes even in a chariot with four white horses after the manner of Dionysius the tyrant. This haughty state and costume were suitably attended by contempt shown towards everyone, by haughty ears, insulting words, infrequent access, not only for outsiders but even for his guardians, by unheard-of lusts, by inhuman cruelty.[2] Consequently such alarm had laid hold of all that some of the guardians anticipated the dreaded punishments either by suicide or by flight. Three of them, who alone had more intimate access to the palace, Adranodorus and Zoippus, the sons-in-law of Hiero, and a certain Thraso, were not indeed much listened to on other matters; but as two of them were inclining to the Carthaginians, Thraso to alliance with Rome, by their partisan rivalry they were occasionally attracting the young man's attention, when a conspiracy

A.U.C. 539 ratio in tyranni caput facta indicatur per Callonem
quendam, aequalem Hieronymi et iam inde a puero
10 in omnia familiaria iura adsuetum. Index unum ex
coniuratis Theodotum, a quo ipse appellatus erat,
nominare potuit. Qui conprensus extemplo tradi-
tusque Adranodoro torquendus, de se ipse haud
11 cunctanter fassus conscios celabat. Postremo, cum
omnibus intolerandis patientiae humanae cruciati-
bus laceraretur, victum malis se simulans avertit
12 ab consciis in insontes indicium, Thrasonem esse
auctorem consilii mentitus, nec nisi tam potenti duce
13 confisos rem tantam ausuros fuisse; addit socios[1] ab
latere tyranni quorum capita vilissima fingenti inter
dolores gemitusque occurrere. Maxime animo
tyranni credibile indicium Thraso nominatus fecit;
itaque extemplo traditur ad supplicium, adiectique
14 poenae ceteri iuxta insontes. Consciorum nemo,
cum diu socius consilii torqueretur, aut latuit aut
fugit; tantum illis in virtute ac fide Theodoti fiduciae
fuit tantumque ipsi Theodoto virium ad arcana
occultanda.

VI. Ita, quod unum vinculum cum Romanis societatis erat, Thrasone sublato e medio extemplo haud
2 dubie ad defectionem res spectabat; legatique ad
Hannibalem missi ac remissi ab eo cum Hannibale,
nobili adulescente, Hippocrates et Epicydes, nati

[1] fuisse; addit socios *Madvig* (*a line*): *om. P*(1).

---

[1] Zoippus had been sent about this time to Egypt; xxvi. 1.

[2] Livy mentions only Hannibal's envoys. Polybius gives the names of two sent from Hieronymus' court, viz. Polyclitus and Philodemus (VII. ii. 2).

[3] This Hannibal was only a trierarch; *ibid.* § 3.

formed against the life of the tyrant was revealed by one Callo, of the same age as Hieronymus and from boyhood accustomed to all the rights of intimacy. The informer was able to name but one of the conspirators, Theodotus, by whom he had himself been approached. And Theodotus, at once seized and handed over for torture to Adranodorus,[1] confessed without hesitation in regard to himself, but did not reveal his accomplices. Finally, racked by all the tortures which pass human endurance, pretending to be mastered by his sufferings, he turned informer against the innocent instead of against his accomplices, and falsely stated that Thraso was responsible for the plan: that they would not have ventured upon such an undertaking if they had not relied upon so powerful a leader. He also named attendants of the tyrant as associates, men whose lives, it occurred to him, as he was fabricating between pains and groans, were of the least account. His mentioning Thraso made the information particularly credible to the mind of the tyrant. Accordingly Thraso was forthwith handed over for execution, and the rest, equally innocent, shared his punishment. Not one of the accomplices either hid himself or fled, though their partner in the plot was long under torture. Such confidence was theirs in the courage and loyalty of Theodotus, and such will-power to keep secrets did Theodotus himself possess. B.C. 215

VI. Thus as soon as Thraso, who was the sole link to an alliance with the Romans, had been removed from their midst, matters at once tended unquestionably toward defection. And ambassadors [2] were sent to Hannibal, and he sent back with a young noble named Hannibal [3] also Hippocrates and Epicydes,

A.U.C. 539

Carthagine sed oriundi ab Syracusis exule avo, Poeni
3 ipsi materno genere. Per hos iuncta societas
Hannibali ac Syracusano tyranno, nec invito Hanni-
4 bale apud tyrannum manserunt. Appius Claudius
praetor, cuius Sicilia provincia erat, ubi ea accepit
extemplo legatos ad Hieronymum misit. Qui cum
sese ad renovandam societatem quae cum avo fuisset
venisse dicerent, per ludibrium auditi dimissique
sunt ab quaerente per iocum Hieronymo quae
5 fortuna eis pugnae ad Cannas fuisset; vix credibilia
enim legatos Hannibalis narrare; velle quid veri sit
scire, ut ex eo utram spem sequatur consilium capiat.
6 Romani, cum serio legationes audire coepisset redituros se ad eum dicentes esse, monito magis eo
quam rogato ne fidem temere mutaret proficiscuntur.
7 Hieronymus legatos Carthaginem misit ad foedus ex
societate cum Hannibale pacta faciendum. Convenit
ut, cum Romanos Sicilia expulissent—id autem brevi
fore, si naves atque exercitum misissent—, Himera
amnis, qui ferme mediam [1] dividit, finis regni Syracu-
8 sani ac Punici imperii esset. Aliam deinde, inflatus
adsentationibus eorum qui eum non Hieronis tantum
sed Pyrrhi etiam regis, materni avi, iubebant meminisse, legationem misit, qua aecum censebat Sicilia
sibi omni cedi, Italiae imperium proprium quaeri
9 Carthaginiensi populo. Hanc levitatem ac iacta-

[1] mediam *Riemann*: *om.* *P*(1): insulam (*after* dividit) *z* *Weissenborn*.

---

[1] Pyrrhus seems to have been his mother's grandfather; see table on p. 338.

who were born at Carthage but Syracusans by origin B.C. 215 (their grandfather being an exile), Carthaginians themselves on the mother's side. Through these men an alliance was made between Hannibal and the tyrant of Syracuse, and with Hannibal's consent they remained with the tyrant. Appius Claudius, the praetor, whose province was Sicily, on learning of this, forthwith sent legates to Hieronymus. While they were saying that they had come to renew the alliance which they had had with his grandfather, they were heard with derision and dismissed by Hieronymus, who in jest asked what success they had had in the battle at Cannae; for Hannibal's envoys reported what was scarcely to be believed. He wished to know, he said, what the truth was, that he might accordingly determine from which side he had the more to hope. The Romans departed, saying that they would return to him when he began to give a sober hearing to embassies, and warning rather than asking him not to be rash in changing his loyalty. Hieronymus sent ambassadors to Carthage to make a treaty in accordance with the alliance arranged with Hannibal. The agreement was that, after they had driven the Romans out of Sicily (and this would be shortly done if *they* would send ships and an army), the river Himera, which nearly divides the island in halves, should be the boundary of the kingdom of Syracuse and the Carthaginian empire. Thereupon, puffed up by the flatteries of those who bade him remember not Hiero only but also King Pyrrhus, his maternal grandfather,[1] Hieronymus sent another embassy, through which he declared it was fair for them to yield all Sicily to him, and for the Carthaginian people to seek their own dominion over Italy.

A.U.C. 539 tionem animi neque mirabantur in iuvene furioso
neque arguebant, dummodo averterent eum ab
Romanis.

VII. Sed omnia in eo praecipitia ad exitium
fuerunt. Nam cum praemissis Hippocrate atque
Epicyde cum binis milibus armatorum ad temptandas
2 urbes quae praesidiis tenebantur Romanis, et ipse in
Leontinos cum cetero omni exercitu—erant autem
ad quindecim milia peditum equitumque—profectus
3 erat,[1] liberas aedis coniurati—et omnes forte militabant—imminentes viae angustae, qua descendere
4 ad forum rex solebat, sumpserunt. Ibi cum instructi
armatique ceteri transitum expectantes starent, uni
ex eis—Dinomeni fuit nomen—, quia custos corporis
erat partes datae sunt ut, cum adpropinquaret ianuae
rex, per causam aliquam in angustiis sustineret ab
5 tergo agmen. Ita ut convenerat factum est. Tamquam laxaret elatum pedem ab stricto nodo, moratus
turbam Dinomenes tantum intervalli fecit ut, cum in
praetereuntem sine armatis regem impetus fieret,
confoderetur aliquot prius vulneribus quam succurri
6 posset. Clamore et tumultu audito in Dinomenem
iam haud dubie obstantem tela coniciuntur, inter
quae tamen duobus acceptis vulneribus evasit.
7 Fuga satellitum, ut iacentem videre regem, facta est.
Interfectores pars in forum ad multitudinem laetam
libertate, pars Syracusas pergunt ad praeoccupanda
8 Adranodori regiorumque aliorum consilia. Incerto

[1] erat *P*(1) *Conway* : esset *A*[2] *Walters*.

---

[1] Northwest of Syracuse and looking down on a lake and the plain of Catana; captured by Marcellus, xxx. 1.

At this trifling and boastful spirit in a madcap youth they did not wonder, nor find fault either, provided they made him break with the Romans. B.C. 215

VII. But in everything he was on the verge of ruin. For after sending Hippocrates and Epicydes in advance, each with two thousand armed men, to attack the cities which were held by Roman garrisons, he too setting out with all the rest of the army—and they were about fifteen thousand infantry and cavalry—had gone to Leontini.[1] The conspirators, all of whom, as it happened, were in the army, took possession of an empty house looking down upon the narrow street by which the king used to go down to the market-place. There, while the rest, drawn up under arms, were to stand waiting for him to pass, one of them—his name was Dinomenes—, as being a body-guard, was assigned the rôle of halting, on some pretext, the column following the king in the narrow street, when he approached the door of the house. This was carried out as had been arranged. Dinomenes, raising one foot and pretending to loosen a knot drawn too tight, delayed the crowd and caused such a gap that, when the attack on the king was made as he passed without guards, he was stabbed with several thrusts before help could reach him. On hearing the shouting and uproar they hurled their weapons at Dinomenes, who was now obviously blocking the way. In the midst of these, however, he escaped with only two wounds. The guards fled as soon as they saw the king lying there. Of the assassins some proceeded to the market-place and into a crowd which rejoiced in its freedom, some to Syracuse to forestall the designs of Adranodorus and the other supporters of the king. In the unsettled

A.U.C. 539 rerum statu Ap. Claudius bellum oriens ex propinquo
cum cerneret, senatum litteris certiorem fecit Siciliam Carthaginiensi populo et Hannibali conciliari;
9 ipse adversus Syracusana consilia ad provinciae
regnique fines omnia convertit praesidia.

10 Exitu anni eius Q. Fabius ex auctoritate senatus
Puteolos, per bellum coeptum frequentari emporium,
11 communiit praesidiumque inposuit. Inde Romam
comitiorum causa veniens in eum quem primum diem
comitialem habuit comitia edixit atque ex itinere
12 praeter urbem in campum descendit. Eo die cum
sors praerogativae Aniensi iuniorum exisset eaque
T. Otacilium M. Aemilium Regillum consules diceret,
tum Q. Fabius silentio facto tali oratione est
usus:

VIII. " Si aut pacem in Italia aut id bellum eumque hostem haberemus in quo neglegentiae laxior
locus esset, qui vestris studiis, quae in campum ad
mandandos quibus velitis honores adfertis, moram
ullam offerret, is mihi parum meminisse videretur
2 vestrae libertatis; sed cum in hoc bello, in hoc hoste
numquam ab ullo duce sine ingenti nostra clade
erratum sit, eadem vos cura qua in aciem armati
descenditis inire suffragium ad creandos consules
decet et sibi sic quemque dicere: 'Hannibali
3 imperatori parem consulem nomino.' Hoc anno

---

[1] In 241 B.C. Hiero as a faithful ally for 22 years was allowed to keep the eastern end of the island (about one-fourth, and not including Messana).

[2] The Delayer, consul this year and the next (five times in all), dictator in 217 B.C.

[3] Thus he retains full military authority, which would not be the case if he had entered the city; cp. ix. 2.

state of affairs Appius Claudius, seeing a war beginning near at hand, informed the senate by letter that Sicily was being won over to the Carthaginian people and Hannibal. For his own part, to meet the schemes of the Syracusans, he concentrated all his garrisons on the frontier between the province and the kingdom.[1] B.C. 215

At the end of that year Quintus Fabius [2] by the authority of the senate fortified and garrisoned Puteoli, which as a commercial centre had grown in population during the war. Then, while on his way to Rome to hold the elections, he proclaimed them for the first date available for an election, and without stopping passed the city and came down to the Campus.[3] On the day set the right to vote first fell to the century of the younger men of the Aniensis tribe, and it named Titus Otacilius and Marcus Aemilius Regillus as consuls. Thereupon Quintus Fabius, after silence had been made, spoke somewhat as follows:

VIII. "If we had either peace in Italy or such a war and such an enemy that there was ample room for carelessness, should someone interpose any delay to the enthusiasm which you bring to the Campus in order to entrust magistracies to the men of your choice, such a man would seem to me forgetful of your freedom. But since in this war, in dealing with this enemy, never has a mistake been made by any commander without huge losses to us, you ought in electing consuls to enter the polls with the same seriousness with which you go into battle-line under arms, and each man should say to himself: 'I name as consul a man who is a match for Hannibal the general.' This year at Capua, when Vibellius

A.U.C. 539 ad Capuam Vibellio Taureae, Campano summo equiti, provocanti summus Romanus eques Asellus
4 Claudius est oppositus. Adversus Gallum quondam provocantem in ponte Anienis T. Manlium fidentem
5 et animo et viribus misere maiores nostri. Eandem causam haud multis annis post fuisse non negaverim cur M. Valerio non diffideretur adversus similiter provocantem arma capienti Gallum ad certamen.
6 Quem ad modum pedites equitesque optamus ut validiores, si minus, ut pares hosti habeamus, ita duci
7 hostium parem imperatorem quaeramus. Cum qui est summus in civitate dux eum legerimus, tamen repente lectus, in annum creatus adversus veterem ac perpetuum imperatorem comparabitur, nullis neque temporis nec iuris inclusum angustiis quo minus ita omnia gerat administretque ut tempora postulabunt
8 belli; nobis autem in apparatu ipso ac tantum inco-
9 hantibus res annus circumagitur. Quoniam quales viros creare vos consules deceat satis est dictum, restat ut pauca de eis in quos praerogativae favor
10 inclinavit dicam. M. Aemilius Regillus flamen est Quirinalis, quem neque mittere a sacris neque retinere possumus ut non deum aut belli deseramus
11 curam. T. Otacilius sororis meae filiam uxorem atque ex ea liberos habet; ceterum non ea vestra in me maioresque meos merita sunt ut non potiorem privatis necessitudinibus rem publicam habeam.

---

[1] Cf. XXIII. xlvii.
[2] Cf. VII. x. 2 ff.
[3] Also in Book VII (xxvi. 2 ff.).

Taurea, a distinguished Campanian knight, challenged, Asellus Claudius, a distinguished Roman knight, was matched against him.[1] Against the Gaul who once challenged at the bridge over the Anio our ancestors sent Titus Manlius,[2] who relied upon his courage and his strength. There was the same reason, I am inclined to admit, why not many years later Marcus Valerius[3] found no lack of confidence in him when he took up arms for the fray against a Gaul who made a like challenge. Just as we desire to have foot and horse stronger than those of the enemy, if not, then a match for him, so let us seek a general who is a match for the commander of the enemy. When we shall have chosen the man who is the greatest commander in the state, nevertheless, although suddenly chosen, elected for a single year, he will be pitted against an experienced permanent general, hampered by no restrictions of time or authority to prevent him from doing and directing everything as the phases of the war shall require. But with us the year rolls round in mere preparation and while we are just beginning. Having sufficiently stated what kind of men you ought to elect as consuls, it remains for me to say a few words in regard to those to whom the favour of the first century to vote has inclined. Marcus Aemilius Regillus is the flamen of Quirinus, and we can neither send him away from the sacred rites nor keep him at home without abandoning our responsibility for the gods or else for the war. Titus Otacilius has my sister's daughter as his wife and children by her. But not so slight are your favours to my ancestors and myself that I can fail to hold the state of more account than personal ties. Any one of the B.C. 215

A.U.C. 539

12 Quilibet nautarum vectorumque tranquillo mari gubernare potest; ubi saeva orta tempestas est ac turbato mari rapitur vento navis, tum viro et guberna-
13 tore opus est. Non tranquillo navigamus, sed iam aliquot procellis submersi paene sumus; itaque quis ad gubernacula sedeat summa cura providendum ac praecavendum vobis est. In minore te experti, T. Otacili, re sumus; haud sane cur ad maiora tibi
14 fidamus documenti quicquam dedisti. Classem hoc anno, cui tu praefuisti, trium rerum causa paravimus, ut Africae oram popularetur, ut tuta nobis Italiae litora essent, ante omnia ne supplementum cum stipendio commeatuque ab Carthagine Hannibali
15 transportaretur. Create consulem T. Otacilium, non dico si omnia haec, sed si aliquid eorum rei publicae praestitit. Sin autem te classem obtinente,[1] ea [2] etiam velut pacato mari quibus non erat opus [3] Hannibali tuta atque integra ab domo vene-
16 runt, si ora Italiae infestior hoc anno quam Africae fuit, quid dicere potes cur te potissimum ducem
17 Hannibali hosti opponamus? [4] Si consul esses, dictatorem dicendum exemplo maiorum nostrum censeremus, nec tu id indignari posses, aliquem in civitate Romana meliorem bello haberi quam te. Magis nullius interest quam tua, T. Otacili, non
18 imponi cervicibus tuis onus sub quo concidas. Ego magnopere oro [5] suadeoque,[6] eodem animo quo si

[1] obtinente *C^2M^3BDA* : obtinentes *P*(4)*A^x*.

[2] ea *H. J. Müller* : *om. P*(1).

[3] non erat opus *Riemann* (*after H. J. M.*): *om.* P(1): *various emendations.*

[4] opponamus *Salmasius* : -pugnabant *FC?RM* : -ponant *DAz Walters* (*inserting* hi).

[5] oro *Hertz* : moneo *Alschefski* : *om. P*(1).

sailors and passengers can steer when the sea is calm. When a savage storm comes and the ship is swept over a rough sea by the wind, then there is need of a man and a pilot. We are not sailing a calm sea, but have been almost sunk already by a number of squalls. And so who is to sit at the helm is for you to decide with the greatest seriousness and foresight. In a lesser affair we have tested you, Titus Otacilius. Certainly you have not shown any reason why we should trust you for greater things. This year we equipped the fleet which you commanded for three purposes: to ravage the coast of Africa, to make our Italian shores safe, but above all to prevent reinforcements with pay and supplies from being brought over from Carthage for Hannibal. Citizens, elect Titus Otacilius consul, if he has performed, I do not say all of these things, but some part of them, for the state. But if, while you, Titus Otacilius, commanded the fleet, even the things he did not need came to Hannibal from home safe and intact, as though he had conquered the sea, if the coast of Italy has been more unsafe this year than that of Africa, what reason can you give why we are to match you by preference as commander against such an enemy as Hannibal? If you were consul we should propose the appointment of a dictator, following the precedent of our ancestors, and you could not be incensed that some one in the Roman state was considered a better man in war than you. It is to no one's interest more than yours, Titus Otacilius, that no such burden be placed on your shoulders that you may fall beneath it. I earnestly entreat and urge you, citizens, that the same spirit which you B.C. 215

[6] suadeoque *P*(4): suadeo *BDA*.

A.U.C. 539 stantibus vobis in acie armatis repente deligendi duo imperatores essent quorum ductu atque auspicio
19 dimicaretis, hodie quoque consules creetis quibus sacramento liberi vestri dicant, ad quorum edictum conveniant, sub quorum tutela atque cura militent.
20 Lacus Trasumennus et Cannae tristia ad recordationem exempla, sed ad praecavendas[1] similes[2] clades[3] documento sunt. Praeco, Aniensem iuniorum in suffragium revoca."

IX. Cum T. Otacilius halociter eum continuare consulatum velle vociferaretur atque obstreperet,
2 lictores ad eum accedere consul iussit et, quia in urbem non inierat protinus in campum ex itinere profectus, admonuit cum securibus sibi fasces prae-
3 ferri.[1] Interim praerogativa suffragium init creatique in ea consules Q. Fabius Maximus quartum M. Marcellus tertium. Eosdem consules ceterae
4 centuriae sine variatione ulla dixerunt. Et praetor unus refectus Q. Fulvius Flaccus, novi alii creati, T. Otacilius Crassus iterum,[2] Q. Fabius consulis filius, qui tum aedilis curulis erat, P. Cornelius Lentulus.
5 Comitiis praetorum perfectis senatus consultum factum, ut Q. Fulvio extra ordinem urbana provincia esset isque potissimum consulibus ad bellum profectis
6 urbi praeesset. Aquae magnae bis eo anno fuerunt

[1] praecavendas *Stroth*: -enda *P*(2) *Conway*: -endum *Axz*.
[2] similes *PC?RM*: simile *BDAxz*: similia C^4 *Conway*.
[3] clades *Stroth*: utiles *P*(10): utile *C*: utili M^5: utilia *z*.

---

[1] Removed when a magistrate entered the city, as an indication that there his sentence was subject to appeal.
[2] His first praetorship was in 217 B.C.; XXII. x. 10.

would show if, while standing armed in battle-line, B.C. 215
you had suddenly to choose two generals under whose command and auspices you should fight, be yours today also in electing consuls to whom your sons shall repeat the oath, in response to whose edict they shall assemble, under whose guardian care they shall serve. The Lake of Trasumennus and Cannae are sad examples to recall, but to guard against like disasters they are a warning. Herald, summon the Aniensis century of the younger men to vote again!"

IX. While Titus Otacilius was fiercely and noisily shouting that Fabius wanted to have his consulship prolonged, the consul ordered the lictors to go up to him, and, as he had not entered the city, having gone without a halt directly to the Campus, he warned Otacilius that the fasces carried before the consul had their axes.[1] Meanwhile the leading century proceeded to vote, and in it were elected consuls Quintus Fabius Maximus for the fourth time and Marcus Marcellus for the third time. The rest of the centuries without exception named the same men as consuls. And of the praetors one, Quintus Fulvius Flaccus, was reëlected, the others newly created, Titus Otacilius Crassus for the second time,[2] Quintus Fabius, son of the consul and at the time curule aedile, and Publius Cornelius Lentulus. The election of praetors being now completed, the senate decreed[3] that Quintus Fulvius by special designation should have the duties of city praetor, and that he, and no one else, should be in charge of the city when the consuls took the field. There were great floods twice

[3] Ordinarily praetors received their particular assignment of duty by casting lots or by agreement.

A.U.C. 539 Tiberisque agros inundavit cum magna strage
tectorum pecorumque et hominum pernicie.
A.U.C. 540 7 Quinto anno secundi Punici belli Q. Fabius Maximus quartum M. Claudius Marcellus tertium consulatum ineuntes plus solito converterant in se civitatis
animos; multis enim annis tale consulum par non
8 fuerat. Referebant senes sic Maximum Rullum
cum P. Decio ad bellum Gallicum, sic postea Papirium
Carviliumque adversus Samnites Bruttiosque et
Lucanum cum Tarentino populum consules de-
9 claratos. Absens Marcellus consul creatus, cum ad
exercitum esset; praesenti Fabio atque ipso comitia
10 habente consulatus continuatus. Tempus ac necessitas belli ac discrimen summae rerum faciebant ne
quis aut in eam rem[1] exemplum exquireret aut
suspectum cupiditatis imperii consulem haberet;
11 quin laudabant potius magnitudinem animi quod,
cum summo imperatore esse opus rei publicae sciret
seque eum haud dubie esse, minoris invidiam suam,
si qua ex ea re oreretur, quam utilitatem rei publicae
fecisset.

X. Quo die magistratum inierunt consules, senatus
2 in Capitolio est habitus decretumque omnium primum ut consules sortirentur conpararentve[2] inter
se uter censoribus creandis comitia haberet, prius-
3 quam ad exercitum proficisceretur. Prorogatum

[1] eam rem *M. Müller*: *om.* *P*(1).
[2] -ve *z*: -quae *or* -que *P*(1).

---

[1] For 295 B.C.; X. xxiv. 1.
[2] For 272 B.C.

that year and the Tiber overflowed the farms with great destruction of buildings and cattle and much loss of life. B.C. 215

In the fifth year of the Second Punic War, Quintus Fabius Maximus entering his fourth consulship and Marcus Claudius Marcellus his third attracted the attention of the citizens more than was usual. For many years there had been no such pair of consuls. Old men recalled that thus Maximus Rullus had been declared consul [1] with Publius Decius for the Gallic war, thus, later on,[2] Papirius and Carvilius against the Samnites and Bruttians and the people of Lucania and of Tarentum. Marcellus was made consul in his absence, being with the army; for Fabius, who was present and himself conducted the election, his consulship was continued. The times and the straits of war and danger to the existence of the state deterred any one from searching for a precedent for that,[3] and from suspecting the consul of greed for power. On the contrary they praised his high-mindedness, in that, knowing the state had need of a great commander, and that he was himself undoubtedly that man, he counted his own unpopularity, should any be the consequence, as of less moment than the advantage of the state. B.C. 214

X. On the day on which the consuls entered upon office the senate met on the Capitol, and it was decreed first of all that the consuls should decide by lot or by mutual arrangement which of them should hold the election for naming the censors before leaving for the army. Then for all who were with

[3] *I.e.*, immediate reëlection, which a plebiscite of 217 B.C. had made legal for the duration of the war in Italy; cf. XXVII. vi. 7 f.

A.U.C. 540 deinde imperium omnibus qui ad exercitus erant iussique in provinciis manere, Ti. Gracchus Luceriae, ubi cum volonum exercitu erat, C. Terentius Varro
4 in agro Piceno, M. Pomponius in Gallico; et praetores[1] prioris anni pro praetoribus, Q. Mucius obtineret Sardiniam, M. Valerius ad Brundisium orae maritimae, intentus adversus omnes motus
5 Philippi Macedonum regis, praeesset. P. Cornelio Lentulo praetori Sicilia decreta provincia, T. Otacilio classis eadem quam adversus Carthaginienses priore anno habuisset.

6 Prodigia eo anno multa nuntiata sunt, quae quo magis credebant simplices ac religiosi homines, eo plura nuntiabantur: Lanuvi in aede intus Sospitae
7 Iunonis corvos nidum fecisse; in Apulia palmam viridem arsisse; Mantuae stagnum effusum Mincio amni cruentum visum; et Calibus creta et Romae in
8 foro bovario sanguine pluvisse; et in vico Insteio fontem sub terra tanta vi aquarum fluxisse ut serias doliaque quae in eo loco erant provoluta velut
9 impetus[2] torrentis tulerit; tacta de caelo atrium publicum in Capitolio, aedem in campo Volcani, Vacunae[3] in Sabinis publicamque viam, murum ac
10 portam Gabiis. Iam alia vulgata miracula erant:

[1] praetores *Gronovius*: praetorum *Drakenborch*: pr̄ *P*(2).
[2] impetus *P*(1): impetu *x Gronovius*.
[3] Vacunae *Hertz*: vocem *P*(1): arcem *z*.

---

[1] Cf. XXIII. xxxii. 1.
[2] Cf. XXIII. xxxi. 15; XXIV. xliv. 8.
[3] A street leading up to the Collis Latiaris (part of the Quirinal), not far from the Curia.

the army their commands were continued, and they were ordered to remain in their assignments, Tiberius Gracchus at Luceria, where he was with the army of slave-volunteers,[1] Gaius Terentius Varro in the Picene district, Marcus Pomponius in the Gallic; and that of the praetors of the previous year, now as propraetors, Quintus Mucius should govern Sardinia and Marcus Valerius should be in command of the sea-coast at Brundisium, watchful against all movements of Philip, King of the Macedonians. Sicily was assigned as his province to Publius Cornelius Lentulus, the praetor, and to Titus Otacilius the same fleet which he had had against the Carthaginians the previous year. B.C. 214

Prodigies [2] in large numbers—and the more they were believed by men simple and devout, the more of them used to be reported—were reported that year: that at Lanuvium ravens had made a nest inside the temple of Juno Sospita; that in Apulia a green palm took fire; that at Mantua a lake, the overflow of the river Mincius, appeared bloody; and at Cales it rained chalk, and at Rome in the Cattle Market blood; and that on the Vicus Insteius [3] an underground spring flowed with such a volume of water that the force of a torrent, as it were, overturned the jars, great and small, that were there and carried them along; that the Atrium Publicum on the Capitol, the temple of Vulcan in the Campus, that of Vacuna [4] and a public street in the Sabine country, the wall and a gate at Gabii were struck by lightning. Moreover other marvels were widely

[4] Honoured especially by the Sabines, and known to modern readers chiefly in Horace's *post fanum putre Vacunae*; *Epist.* I. x. 49.

A.U.C. 540 hastam Martis Praeneste sua sponte promotam; bovem in Sicilia locutum; infantem in utero matris in Marrucinis "Io triumphe" clamasse; ex muliere Spoleti virum factum; Hadriae aram in caelo speciesque hominum circum eam cum candida veste visas
11 esse. Quin Romae quoque in ipsa urbe, secundum apum examen in foro visum—quod mirabile est, quia rarum—adfirmantes quidam legiones se armatas in Ianiculo videre concitaverunt civitatem ad arma,
12 cum qui in Ianiculo essent negarent quemquam ibi praeter adsuetos collis eius cultores adparuisse.
13 Haec prodigia hostiis maioribus procurata sunt ex haruspicum responso, et supplicatio omnibus deis quorum pulvinaria Romae essent indicta est.

XI. Perpetratis quae ad pacem deum pertinebant, de re publica belloque gerendo et quantum copiarum et ubi quaeque essent consules ad senatum rettule-
2 runt. Duodeviginti legionibus bellum geri placuit: binas consules sibi sumere, binis Galliam Siciliamque
3 ac Sardiniam obtineri; duabus Q. Fabium praetorem Apuliae, duabus volonum Ti. Gracchum circa Luceriam praeesse; singulas C. Terentio proconsuli ad Picenum et M. Valerio ad classem circa Brundi-
4 sium relinqui; duas urbi praesidio esse. Hic ut numerus legionum expleretur, sex novae legiones

---

[1] *I.e.*, draped *lecti* with their cushions, kept in the temples of such gods as received the special honour of a *lectisternium*, a feast at which images of gods reclined in pairs; XXII. x. 9.

[2] Not including those in Spain. Similarly in § 5 no mention is made of a fleet for Spain.

circulated: that the spear of Mars at Praeneste moved B.C. 214
of itself; that an ox in Sicily spoke; that among the Marrucini an infant in its mother's womb shouted "Hail, triumph!"; that at Spoletium a woman was changed into a man; that at Hadria an altar was seen in the sky, and about it the forms of men in white garments. In fact at Rome also, actually in the city, directly after the appearance of a swarm of bees in the Forum—a wonder because it is rare—certain men, asserting that they saw armed legions on the Janiculum, aroused the city to arms, whereas those who were on the Janiculum denied that anyone had been seen there except the usual dwellers on that hill. Atonement was made for these prodigies with full-grown victims on the advice of the soothsayers, and a season of prayer to all the gods who had festal couches [1] at Rome was proclaimed.

XI. The rites which concerned peace with the gods being now completed, the consuls laid before the senate the condition of the state and the conduct of the war, and what forces there were and where severally stationed. It was voted to carry on the war with eighteen legions; [2] that each consul should take two; that with two legions in each case Gaul and Sicily and Sardinia should be held; that with two legions Quintus Fabius, a praetor, should be in charge of Apulia, and that with two legions of slave-volunteers Tiberius Gracchus should be in command in the region of Luceria; that one legion each should be left for Gaius Terentius, the proconsul, in the Picene district and for Marcus Valerius for service with the fleet near Brundisium; that two should form the garrison of the city. To make up this number of legions six new legions had to be enrolled.

A.U.C. 540

5 erant scribendae. Eas primo quoque tempore consules scribere iussi et classem parare, ut cum eis navibus quae pro Calabriae litoribus in statione essent, centum quinquaginta longarum classis navium eo
6 anno expleretur. Dilectu habito et centum navibus novis deductis Q. Fabius comitia censoribus creandis habuit; creati M. Atilius Regulus et P. Furius Philus.

Cum increbresceret rumor bellum in Sicilia esse,
7 T. Otacilius eo cum classe proficisci iussus est. Cum deessent nautae, consules ex senatus consulto edixerunt ut, qui L. Aemilio C. Flaminio censoribus milibus aeris quinquaginta ipse aut pater eius census fuisset usque ad centum milia, aut cui postea tanta res [1] esset facta, nautam unum cum sex mensum stipendio daret; qui supra centum milia usque ad trecenta
8 milia, tris nautas cum stipendio annuo; qui supra trecenta milia usque ad deciens aeris, quinque nautas; qui supra deciens, septem; senatores octo
9 nautas cum annuo stipendio darent. Ex hoc edicto dati nautae, armati instructique ab dominis, cum triginta dierum coctis cibariis naves conscenderunt. Tum primum est factum ut classis Romana sociis navalibus privata inpensa paratis conpleretur.

XII. Hic maior solito adparatus praecipue conterruit Campanos, ne ab obsidione Capuae bellum eius
2 anni Romani inciperent. Itaque legatos ad Hannibalem oratum miserunt ut Capuam exercitum admoveret: ad eam oppugnandam novos exercitus

[1] tanta res *Weissenborn* : res tanta *z* : tanta *P*(1).

---

[1] Meaning chiefly *remiges*, who pulled the long oars and were in general slaves; cf. XXVI. xxxv.

The consuls were ordered to enroll them as soon as possible, and to furnish a fleet, so that, including the ships at anchor defending the coast of Calabria, the fleet should amount that year to a hundred and fifty warships. After conducting the levy and launching a hundred new ships, Quintus Fabius held an election for the choosing of censors. Marcus Atilius Regulus and Publius Furius Philus were elected. B.C. 214

As the rumour that there was a war in Sicily spread more widely, Titus Otacilius was ordered to set sail thither with his fleet. Owing to the lack of sailors [1] the consuls in accordance with a decree of the senate issued an edict that a man who in the censorship of Lucius Aemilius and Gaius Flaminius [2] had been rated—either he or his father—at from 50,000 to 100,000 asses, or if his property had since increased to that amount, should furnish one sailor provided with six months' pay; that one who had more than 100,000 and up to 300,000 should furnish three sailors and a year's pay; he who had over 300,000 and up to a million asses, five sailors; he who had over a million, seven; that senators should furnish eight sailors and a year's pay. The sailors furnished in accordance with this edict went on board armed and equipped by their masters, and with cooked rations for thirty days. It was the first time that a Roman fleet was manned with crews secured at private expense.

XII. This extraordinary preparation particularly alarmed the Campanians, for fear the Romans might begin that year's war with a siege of Capua. Accordingly they sent legates to Hannibal to beg him to bring his army to Capua. New armies, they said,

[2] *I.e.* 220 B.C.; XXIII. xxiii. 5.

A.U.C. 540 scribi Romae, nec ullius urbis defectioni magis infensos
3 eorum animos esse. Id quia tam trepide nuntiabant,
maturandum Hannibal ratus, ne praevenirent Romani, profectus Arpis ad Tifata in veteribus castris
4 super Capuam consedit. Inde Numidis Hispanisque
ad praesidium simul castrorum simul Capuae relictis
cum cetero exercitu ad lacum Averni per speciem
sacrificandi, re ipsa ut temptaret Puteolos quodque
5 ibi praesidium erat, descendit. Maximus, postquam
Hannibalem Arpis profectum et regredi in Campaniam adlatum est, nec die nec nocte intermisso
6 itinere ad exercitum redit, et Ti. Gracchum ab
Luceria Beneventum copias admovere, Q. Fabium
praetorem—is filius consulis erat—ad Luceriam
Graccho succedere iubet.

7 In Siciliam eodem tempore duo praetores profecti,
P. Cornelius ad exercitum, T. Otacilius qui mari-
8 timae orae reique navali praeesset. Et ceteri in
suas quisque provincias profecti, et quibus prorogatum imperium erat easdem quas priori anno
regiones obtinuerunt.

XIII. Ad Hannibalem, cum ad lacum Averni esset,
quinque nobiles iuvenes ab Tarento venerunt, partim
ad Trasumennum lacum, partim ad Cannas capti dimissique domos cum eadem comitate qua usus ad-
2 versus omnes Romanorum socios Poenus fuerat. Ei
memores beneficiorum eius perpulisse magnam partem se iuventutis Tarentinae referunt ut Hannibalis

[1] Probably in connection with the necromancy practised at Avernus.

were being enrolled at Rome for besieging it, and the defection of no city had more embittered the Romans. Since they reported this with such excitement, Hannibal, thinking he must make haste, lest he be anticipated by the Romans, set out from Arpi and established himself by Tifata in his old camp above Capua. Then leaving Numidians and Spaniards to defend the camp and Capua at the same time, he came down with the rest of his army to the Lake of Avernus, with the pretext of sacrificing,[1] in reality to attack Puteoli and the garrison which was there. Maximus, on being informed that Hannibal had left Arpi and was returning to Campania, without interrupting his journey by day or night returned to the army. And he ordered Tiberius Gracchus to bring his troops from Luceria to Beneventum, and Quintus Fabius, the praetor—he was the consul's son—, to relieve Gracchus at Luceria. B.C. 214

Two praetors set out at the same time for Sicily, Publius Cornelius to the army, and Titus Otacilius to take command of the sea-coast and of naval operations. And the others set out for their several assignments, and those whose commands had been prolonged held the same regions as in the previous year.

XIII. While Hannibal was at the Lake of Avernus five noble young men came to him from Tarentum, some of whom had been captured at the Lake of Trasumennus, others at Cannae, and sent to their homes with that same courtesy which the Carthaginian had shown toward all allies of the Romans. Mindful of his favours, they reported that they had induced a large part of the young men of Tarentum to prefer the friendship and alliance of Hannibal to

A.U.C. 540

amicitiam ac societatem quam populi Romani mallent, legatosque ab suis missos rogare Hanni-
3 balem ut exercitum propius Tarentum admoveat: si signa eius, si castra conspecta a Tarento sint, haud ullam intercessuram moram quin in deditionem veniat[1] urbs; in potestate iuniorum plebem, in manu
4 plebis rem Tarentinam esse. Hannibal conlaudatos eos oneratosque ingentibus promissis domum ad coepta maturanda redire iubet: se in tempore adfuturum esse. Hac cum spe dimissi Tarentini.
5 Ipsum ingens cupido incesserat Tarenti potiundi. Urbem esse videbat cum opulentam nobilemque, tum maritimam et in Macedoniam opportune versam, regemque Philippum hunc portum, si transiret in Italiam, quoniam[2] Brundisium Romani haberent,
6 petiturum. Sacro inde perpetrato ad quod venerat et, dum ibi moratur, pervastato agro Cumano usque ad Miseni promunturium Puteolos repente agmen convertit ad opprimendum praesidium Romanum.
7 Sex milia hominum erant et locus munimento quoque, non natura modo tutus. Triduum ibi moratus Poenus ab omni parte temptato praesidio, deinde, ut nihil procedebat, ad populandum agrum Neapolitanum magis ira quam potiundae urbis spe processit.

8 Adventu eius in propincum agrum mota Nolana est plebs, iam diu aversa ab Romanis et infesta senatui suo. Itaque legati ad arcessendum Hannibalem cum haud dubio promisso tradendae urbis

[1] in deditionem veniat (*a line*) *Conway*: *om.* *P*(1): (*after* urbs) dedatur A^2: ei tradatur *Madvig*: in potestatem eius tradatur *Weissenborn*.

[2] quoniam *Madvig, Conway*: *om.* *P*(1).

those of the Roman people; and that, as legates B.C. 214
sent by their people, they asked Hannibal to bring his army nearer to Tarentum. If his standards, if his camp should be seen from Tarentum there would be no delay in the surrender of the city; that the common people were in the power of the younger men, the Tarentine state in the hands of the common people. Hannibal praised them and overwhelmed them with great promises, and bade them return home to carry out their undertaking promptly; that he would be there at the right moment. With this hope the Tarentines were sent away. He himself had conceived a great desire to gain possession of Tarentum. He saw that the city was not only rich and famous but also a seaport, and favourably placed in the direction of Macedonia, and that accordingly King Philip, if he should cross into Italy, would make for this port, since the Romans held Brundisium. Then, after accomplishing the rite for which he had come, and devastating the territory of Cumae as far as the promontory of Misenum, while he lingered there, he suddenly headed his column toward Puteoli, to surprise the Roman garrison. There were six thousand men and the place was defended by a wall also, not merely by nature. There the Carthaginian tarried three days, attacking the garrison from every side; and then, when he met with no success, he set out to ravage the territory of Neapolis, rather in anger than with the hope of taking the city.

His coming into a neighbouring region aroused the common people of Nola, who had long been estranged from the Romans and hostile to their own senate. Consequently legates came to invite Hannibal, bringing a definitive promise to surrender the city.

A.U.C. 540

9 venerunt. Praevenit inceptum eorum Marcellus
consul a primoribus accitus. Die uno Suessulam a
Calibus, cum Volturnus amnis traicientem moratus
10 esset, contenderat; inde proxima nocte sex milia
peditum, equites trecentos, qui[1] praesidio senatui
11 essent, Nolam intromisit. Et uti a consule omnia
inpigre facta sunt ad praeoccupandam Nolam, ita
Hannibal tempus terebat, bis iam ante nequiquam
temptata re segnior ad credendum Nolanis factus.

XIV. Isdem diebus et Q. Fabius consul ad Casilinum temptandum, quod praesidio Punico tenebatur, venit et ad Beneventum velut ex composito parte altera Hanno ex Bruttiis cum magna peditum equitumque manu, altera Ti. Gracchus ab Luceria accessit.
2 Qui primo oppidum intravit, deinde, ut Hannonem.
tria milia ferme ab urbe ad Calorem fluvium castra
posuisse et inde agrum populari audivit, et ipse
egressus moenibus mille ferme passus ab hoste
3 castra locat. Ibi contionem militum habuit.
Legiones magna ex parte volonum habebat, qui iam
alterum annum libertatem tacite mereri quam
postulare palam maluerant. Senserat tamen hibernis egrediens murmur in agmine esse quaerentium,
4 en umquam liberi militaturi essent, scripseratque
senatui non tam quid desiderarent quam quid meruissent: bona fortique opera eorum se ad eam diem

[1] trecentos, qui A^2x : quingentos, qui *Weissenborn* : *om.* *P*(1).

---

[1] Since Hannibal had captured the city; XXIII. xix. 15 f.; xx. 1.

Marcellus, the consul, was called in by the leading men and forestalled their undertaking. From Cales he had hastened in one day to Suessula, though the river Volturnus had delayed his crossing. Thence he sent six thousand infantry and three hundred horsemen that night into Nola, to defend the senate. And whereas the consul did everything with energy, in order to anticipate him in occupying Nola, Hannibal was wasting time, having twice already made the vain attempt, and being now less inclined to believe the men of Nola. B.C. 214

XIV. At the same time not only did Quintus Fabius, the consul, come to Casilinum, to attack the city, held by a Carthaginian garrison,[1] but also, as if by prearrangement, Hanno, with a large force of infantry and cavalry, from the land of the Bruttii, came to Beneventum from one side, while on the other side Tiberius Gracchus came to it from Luceria. The latter at first entered the town, and then, on hearing that Hanno had pitched his camp about three miles from the city by the river Calor, and from that point was ravaging the country, he likewise left the city and pitched camp about a mile from the enemy. There he held an assembly of the soldiers. The legions he had were largely made up of slave-volunteers, who now for two years had preferred silently to earn their freedom rather than openly to demand it. Yet as he came out of winter quarters he had been aware that there was murmuring in the column, as they asked whether they were ever at all to serve as free men. And he had written to the senate, not so much what they wanted as what they had deserved; that he had had good and brave service from them up to that time, and that they lacked

A.U.C. 540

usum, neque ad exemplum iusti militis quicquam eis
5 praeter libertatem deesse. De eo permissum ipsi erat faceret quod e re publica duceret esse. Itaque priusquam cum hoste manum consereret, pronuntiat tempus venisse eis libertatis quam diu sperassent
6 potiundae; postero die signis conlatis dimicaturum puro ac patenti campo, ubi sine ullo insidiarum metu
7 vera virtute geri res posset. Qui caput hostis rettulisset, eum se extemplo liberum iussurum esse; qui loco cessisset, in eum servili supplicio animadversu-
8 rum; suam cuique fortunam in manu esse. Libertatis auctorem eis non se fore solum, sed consulem M. Marcellum, sed universos patres, quos consultos ab
9 se de libertate eorum sibi permisisse. Litteras inde consulis ac senatus consultum recitavit; ad quae clamor cum ingenti adsensu est sublatus. Pugnam poscebant signumque ut daret extemplo ferociter
10 instabant. Gracchus proelio in posterum diem pronuntiato contionem dimisit. Milites laeti, praecipue quibus merces navatae in unum diem operae libertas futura erat, armis expediendis diei [1] relicum consumunt.

XV. Postero die ubi signa coeperunt canere, primi omnium parati instructique ad praetorium conveniunt. Sole orto Gracchus in aciem copias educit; nec hostes moram dimicandi fecerunt.
2 Decem [2] septem milia peditum erant, maxima ex parte Bruttii ac Lucani, equites mille ducenti, inter quos pauci admodum Italici, ceteri Numidae fere

[1] diei *x Gronovius*: que *P*: quod P^2(1): A^2 *adds* diei fuit.
[2] decem *P*(2): C^2A *add* et.

nothing toward the standard of the real soldier except their freedom. In this matter he had been given permission to do whatever he thought to be for the good of the state. And so, before engaging the enemy, he announced that the time had come for them to gain the freedom for which they so long had hoped; that the next day he would fight, standards against standards, in a clear and open field, where without any fear of ambush the battle could be fought with pure courage. Whoever should bring back the head of an enemy would by his order be a free man at once. Whoever retreated from his post would meet the punishment of a slave. Each man's fortune was in his own hand. The giver of their freedom would be not merely himself, but the consul Marcus Marcellus, but the whole senate, for they had been consulted by him and had given him permission in the matter of their freedom. He then read the letter of the consul and the decree of the senate. Upon that a shout was raised with great applause. They clamoured for battle and with high spirit insisted that he give the signal at once. Gracchus announced a battle for the morrow and dismissed the assembly. The soldiers were happy, especially those for whom freedom was to be the reward of a single day's service, and spent the rest of the day in putting their arms in order. B.C. 214

XV. On the next day, when the signals began to sound, these soldiers were the first of all to assemble at headquarters, ready and in formation. After sunrise Gracchus led his troops out into line, and the enemy did not delay the battle. They had seventeen thousand infantry, mostly Bruttians and Lucanians, twelve hundred cavalry, among them very few

A.U.C. 540 3 omnes Maurique. Pugnatum est et acriter et diu;
quattuor horis neutro inclinata est pugna. Nec alia
magis Romanum impediebat res quam capita hostium
4 pretia libertatis facta; nam ut quisque hostem
inpigre occiderat, primum capite aegre inter turbam
tumultumque abscidendo terebat tempus; deinde
occupata dextra tenendo caput fortissimus quisque
pugnator esse desierat, segnibus ac timidis tradita
5 pugna erat. Quod ubi tribuni militum Graccho nuntiaverunt, neminem stantem iam vulnerari hostem,
carnificari iacentes, et in dextris militum pro gladiis
humana capita esse, signum dari propere iussit, pro-
6 icerent capita invaderentque hostem: claram satis et
insignem virtutem esse nec dubiam libertatem futuram strenuis viris. Tum redintegrata pugna est,
7 et eques etiam in hostes emissus. Quibus cum
inpigre Numidae occurrissent,[1] nec segnior equitum
quam peditum pugna esset, iterum in dubium
adducta res. Cum utrimque duces, Romanus Brut-
tium Lucanumque totiens a maioribus suis victos
subactosque, Poenus mancipia Romana et ex ergas-
8 tulo militem verbis obtereret, postremo pronuntiat
Gracchus esse nihil quod de libertate sperarent, nisi
eo die fusi fugatique hostes essent. XVI. Ea
demum vox ita animos accendit ut renovato clamore,
velut alii repente facti, tanta vi se in hostem intule-

[1] occurrissent *xz*: concurrissent *P*(1).

Italians, nearly all the rest Numidians and Mauri. B.C. 214 The battle was fierce and long; for four hours it did not incline either way. And nothing hampered the Romans more than that enemies' heads were made the price of freedom. For when a man had boldly slain an enemy, in the first place he was wasting time in cutting off the head with difficulty in the confusion and turmoil; and then, as his right hand was occupied in holding the head, the bravest had ceased to be fighters, while the battle was turned over to the spiritless and the fearful. When the tribunes of the soldiers reported this to Gracchus: that they were not wounding a single enemy standing, but butchering the fallen; and that in the soldier's right hands there were human heads instead of swords, he ordered the command at once given that they should throw away the heads and attack the enemy. Their courage, he said, was sufficiently clear and conspicuous, and for active men freedom would be beyond a doubt. Thereupon the battle was renewed, and the cavalry also charged the enemy. Since the Numidians met this charge gallantly and the cavalry battle was no less spirited than that of the infantry, the issue was for the second time made doubtful. While the commanders on both sides heaped abuse, the Roman on the Bruttians and Lucanians, so many times defeated and subdued by their ancestors, the Carthaginian on the Roman slaves and prison-house soldiers, Gracchus finally declared that they had no reason to hope for freedom, unless on that day the enemy should be routed and put to flight. XVI. Those words at last so fired their courage that, as though they were suddenly different men, they raised a shout again and charged the enemy

A.U.C. 540

2 rint ut sustineri ultra non possent. Primo antesignani Poenorum, dein signa perturbata, postremo
tota inpulsa acies; inde haud dubie terga data,
ruuntque fugientes in castra adeo pavidi trepidique
ut ne in portis quidem aut vallo quisquam restiterit,
ac prope continenti agmine Romani insecuti novum
de integro proelium inclusi hostium vallo ediderint.
3 Ibi sicut pugna inpeditior in angustiis, ita caedes
atrocior fuit. Et adiuvere captivi, qui rapto inter
tumultum ferro conglobati et ab tergo ceciderunt
4 Poenos et fugam impedierunt. Itaque minus duo
milia hominum ex tanto exercitu, et ea maior pars
equitum, cum ipso duce effugerunt; alii omnes
caesi aut capti; capta et signa duodequadraginta.
5 Ex victoribus duo milia ferme cecidere. Praeda
omnis praeterquam hominum captorum militi concessa est; et pecus exceptum est quod intra dies
triginta domini cognovissent.

6 Cum praeda onusti in castra redissent, quattuor
milia ferme volonum militum, quae pugnaverant
segnius nec in castra inruperant simul, metu poenae
7 collem haud procul castris ceperunt. Postero die
per tribunos militum inde deducti contione militum
8 advocata a Graccho superveniunt. Ubi cum proconsul veteres milites primum, prout cuiusque virtus
atque opera in ea pugna fuerat, militaribus donis
9 donasset, tunc quod ad volones attineret, omnes ait

[1] Livy often applies Roman military terms to the enemy's army. Here *signa* suggests a second line somewhat like the Roman *principes*. Cf. XXII. v. 7 for *antesignani*.

with such force that they could no longer be withstood. At first the front line [1] of the Carthaginians, then the second was in confusion; finally the whole line was forced back. Then it was unmistakeable flight, and fleeing they dashed into their camp in such fright and excitement that no one halted even at the gates or on the wall. And the Romans, pursuing in almost unbroken column, fought an entirely new battle while hemmed in by the enemies' wall. There the battle was indeed more hampered in a confined space, but the slaughter was more savage. And they were aided by the captives, who, seizing weapons during the confusion and advancing in a mass, slashed the Carthaginians from the rear and also hindered their flight. And so out of that great army less than two thousand men, mainly cavalry at that, escaped along with the general himself. All the rest were slain or captured. Captured were also thirty-eight standards. Of the victors about two thousand fell. All the booty except the captives was given to the soldiers. Cattle also were excepted, if the owners should identify them within thirty days. B.C. 214

When they had returned to camp laden with booty, about four thousand of the slave-volunteeers, who had fought with less spirit and had not dashed into the camp with the others, for fear of punishment occupied a hill not far from the camp. The next day they were brought down by military tribunes and arrived after an assembly of the soldiers had been called by Gracchus. There the proconsul first presented military decorations to the old soldiers, to each according to his valour and his part in that battle; and then he said that, so far as the slave-volunteers

A.U.C. 540 malle laudatos a se, dignos indignosque, quam quemquam eo die castigatum esse. Quod bonum faustum
felixque rei publicae ipsisque esset, omnes eos
10 liberos esse iubere. Ad quam vocem cum clamor
ingenti alacritate sublatus esset, ac nunc conplexi
inter se gratulantesque, nunc manus ad caelum
tollentes bona omnia populo Romano Gracchoque
11 ipsi precarentur, tum Gracchus "Priusquam omnes
iure libertatis aequassem" inquit, "neminem nota
12 strenui aut ignavi militis notasse volui; nunc exsoluta
iam fide publica, ne discrimen omne virtutis ignaviaeque pereat, nomina eorum qui detractatae pugnae
memores secessionem paulo ante fecerunt referri ad
me iubebo, citatosque singulos iure iurando adigam,
13 nisi quibus[1] morbus causa erit, non aliter quam
stantes cibum potionemque, quoad stipendia facient,
capturos esse. Hanc multam ita aequo animo
feretis, si reputabitis nulla ignaviae nota leviore vos
14 designari potuisse." Signum deinde colligendi vasa
dedit; militesque praedam portantes agentesque
per lasciviam ac iocum ita ludibundi Beneventum
15 rediere ut ab epulis per celebrem festumque diem
16 actis, non ex acie reverti viderentur. Beneventani
omnes turba effusa cum obviam ad portas exissent,
complecti milites, gratulari, vocare in hospitium.
17 Adparata convivia omnibus in propatulo aedium

[1] quibus C^2M^2 : quis *A* : que *P*(2) : cui *Weissenborn* : queis *Gronovius*.

---

[1] Thus the good things could be seen through the open door, as in XXV. xii. 15: *apertis ianuis in propatulo epulati sunt*.

were concerned, he preferred to have all of them, the worthy and the unworthy, praised by himself, rather than to have any one of them punished that day; that, with the prayer that it might be good and happy and fortunate for the state and for the men themselves, he ordered them all to be free. At these words they raised a shout with great enthusiasm, and now embracing and congratulating each other, now raising their hands to heaven, they prayed for every blessing for the Roman people and for Gracchus himself. Thereupon Gracchus said: "Before making you all equals by the right of freedom, I wished to stamp not one man of you with the mark of a brave or of a cowardly soldier. But now, the promise made in the name of the state being already fulfilled, to prevent the loss of every distinction between valour and cowardice, I shall order the names of those who, remembering their refusal to fight, left us a while ago to be reported to me; and summoning them one by one I shall make them swear that, excepting men who shall have illness as an excuse, they will take food and drink standing only, so long as they shall be in the service. This penalty you will bear with patience, if you will reflect that you could not have been marked with any slighter sign of cowardice." He then gave the signal to pack baggage, and the soldiers carrying and driving their booty returned with sport and mirth so gaily to Beneventum that they seemed to be returning from a feast on a day of general festivity, not from a battle. All the people of Beneventum, having come out *en masse* to the gates to meet them, embraced the soldiers, congratulated them, invited them into their houses. Feasts had been made ready by all in the atria[1] of B.C. 214.

A.U.C. 540 fuerant; ad ea invitabant Gracchumque orabant ut epulari permitteret militibus; et Gracchus ita permisit, si[1] in publico epularentur omnes ante suas
18 quisque fores. Prolata omnia. Pilleati aut lana alba velatis capitibus volones epulati sunt, alii accubantes, alii stantes, qui simul ministrabant vesce-
19 banturque. Digna res visa ut simulacrum celebrati eius diei Gracchus, postquam Romam rediit, pingi iuberet in aede Libertatis quam pater eius in Aventino ex multaticia pecunia faciendam curavit dedicavitque.

XVII. Dum haec ad Beneventum geruntur, Hannibal depopulatus agrum Neapolitanum ad Nolam
2 castra movet. Quem ubi adventare consul sensit, Pomponio propraetore cum eo exercitu qui super Suessulam in castris erat accito ire obviam hosti parat
3 nec moram dimicandi facere. C. Claudium Neronem cum robore equitum silentio noctis per aversam maxime ab hoste portam emittit circumvectumque occulte subsequi sensim agmen hostium iubet et, cum coortum proelium videret, ab tergo se obicere.
4 Id errore viarum an exiguitate temporis Nero exsequi
5 non potuerit incertum est. Absente eo cum proelium commissum esset, superior quidem haud dubie Romanus erat; sed quia equites non adfuere in

[1] si *Sigonius*: ut *x*: *om.* *P*(1).

---

[1] The *pilleus* was evidence of freedom, as was the *lana alba*.

[2] The closing words are possibly copied from an inscription on the temple. The father was consul in 238 B.C.

their houses. To these they invited the soldiers and implored Gracchus to allow the soldiers to feast. And Gracchus did permit them, provided they all feasted in the open, each before the door of his house. Everything was brought out. Wearing caps[1] or white woollen headbands the volunteers feasted, some reclining, and some standing served and ate at the same time. This seemed to deserve the order Gracchus gave on his return to Rome for a representation of that day of festivity to be painted in the Temple of Liberty which his father, with money yielded by fines, caused to be built on the Aventine and dedicated.[2] B.C. 214

XVII. While these things were going on about Beneventum, Hannibal, after ravaging the territory of Neapolis, removed his camp to Nola. When the consul learned of his approach, summoning Pomponius, the propraetor, with the army which was in camp[3] above Suessula, he prepared to advance to meet the enemy and to engage without delay. He sent Gaius Claudius Nero with the best of the cavalry out by the gate farthest from the enemy in the silence of the night, and commanded him to ride around unseen and follow the enemy's column slowly, and when he saw that the battle had begun, to throw himself upon their rear. Whether it was by losing the way that Nero was unable to carry this out, or from the shortness of the time, is uncertain. After the battle had begun in his absence, the Roman indeed unquestionably had the upper hand; but since the cavalry were not there at the right moment, the

[3] *Castra Claudiana*; XXIII. xxxi. 3 and elsewhere. Pomponius must have been relieved of his duties in the North (x. 3).

A.U.C. 540 tempore, ratio compositae rei turbata est. Non ausus insequi cedentes Marcellus vincentibus suis
6 signum receptui dedit. Plus tamen duo milia hostium eo die caesa traduntur, Romani minus
7 quadringenti. Solis fere occasu Nero diem noctemque nequiquam fatigatis equis hominibusque, ne viso quidem hoste rediens, adeo graviter est ab consule increpitus ut per eum stetisse diceret [1] quo minus accepta ad Cannas redderetur hosti clades.
8 Postero die Romanus in aciem descendit, Poenus, tacita etiam confessione victus castris se tenuit. Tertio die silentio noctis omissa spe Nolae potiundae, rei numquam prospere temptatae, Tarentum ad certiorem spem proditionis proficiscitur.

XVIII. Nec minore animo res Romana domi quam
2 militiae gerebatur. Censores, vacui ab operum locandorum cura propter inopiam aerarii, ad mores hominum regendos animum adverterunt castigandaque vitia quae, velut diutinis morbis aegra corpora
3 ex sese gignunt, eo [2] nata bello erant. Primum eos citaverunt qui post Cannensem pugnam rem publicam deseruisse [3] dicebantur. Princeps eorum M.
4 Caecilius Metellus quaestor tum forte erat. Iusso deinde eo ceterisque eiusdem noxae reis causam

[1] diceret *z* : diceretur *P*(1).
[2] eo C^2 : aea *P* : ea *C* : *om.* P^2?(10).
[3] pugnam rem publicam deseruisse A^2x : *om.* *P*(1) : *the gap indicated in PA, probably a single line, is variously supplied, e.g.* cladem a re publica defecisse *Walters.*

---

[1] Cannae was avenged by this Nero and his colleague Livius at the Metaurus, 207 B.C.; XXVII. xlviii f.; xlix. 5.

prearranged plan for the battle was ruined. Marcellus, B.C. 214 not venturing to pursue the retreating, gave his men, victorious though they were, the signal to retire. More than two thousand of the enemy, however, are said to have been slain that day, of the Romans less than four hundred. About sunset Nero, returning with his horses and men exhausted to no purpose by their efforts for a day and a night, without even seeing the enemy, was sternly rebuked by the consul, who went so far as to say that it was his fault that the disaster suffered at Cannae was not paid back to the enemy.[1] On the next day the Roman went into line of battle, while the Carthaginian, beaten, as he tacitly admitted also, remained in camp. The third day, giving up hope of capturing Nola, an undertaking which had never prospered, he set out in the dead of night for Tarentum, led by a surer hope of its betrayal.

XVIII. And it was with no less spirit that the Roman state was administered at home than in the field. The censors, freed from the charge of contracting for public works on account of the emptiness of the treasury, turned their attention to the control of morals and the punishment of vices which had sprung from that war, just as bodies suffering from long illnesses of themselves produce defects. First they summoned those who after the battle of Cannae were said to have abandoned the state. The foremost among them, Marcus Caecilius Metellus,[2] happened at this time to be quaestor. Inasmuch as he and the rest of those guilty of the same offence, on being ordered to plead their cases, proved unable

[2] For his plan to leave Italy cf. XXII. liii. 5, where his praenomen is Lucius.

A.U.C. 540 dicere, cum purgari nequissent, pronuntiarunt verba
orationemque eos adversus rem publicam habuisse,
quo coniuratio deserendae Italiae causa fieret.
5 Secundum eos citati nimis callidi exsolvendi iuris
iurandi interpretes, qui captivorum ex itinere re-
gressi clam in castra Hannibalis solutum quod iura-
6 verunt redituros rebantur. His superioribusque illis
equi adempti qui publicum equom habebant, tribuque
7 moti aerarii omnes facti. Neque senatu modo aut
equestri ordine regendo cura se censorum tenuit; nomina omnium ex iuniorum tabulis excerpserunt qui
quadriennio non militassent, quibus neque vacatio
8 iusta militiae neque morbus causa fuisset. Et ea
supra duo milia nominum [1] in aerarios relata tribuque
9 omnes moti; additumque tam truci censoriae notae
triste senatus consultum, ut ei omnes quos censores
notassent pedibus mererent mitterenturque in
Siciliam ad Cannensis exercitus reliquias, cui militum
generi non prius quam pulsus Italia hostis esset
finitum stipendiorum tempus erat.

10 Cum censores ob inopiam aerarii se iam locationi-
bus abstinerent aedium sacrarum tuendarum curu-
liumque equorum praebendorum ac similium his

[1] nominum *P*(1) *Aldus* : hominum *xz Madvig.*

---

[1] So ten of them pretended to think, XXII. lxi. 8. Another version (*ib.* 4 and lviii. 8) had only a single perjurer.

[2] Transfer to one of the four city tribes was a degradation, but, since the reform of 312 B.C., *aerarii* ("taxpayers only") were allowed to vote and serve in the army.

to clear themselves, the censors gave their verdict B.C. 214
that in conversation and formal speeches they had attacked the state, in order to form a conspiracy to desert Italy. Next after them were summoned those who had been too crafty in interpreting the discharge of an oath,—those of the captives who, after setting out and then returning secretly to Hannibal's camp, thought the oath they had sworn, that they would return, had been discharged.[1] From these men and those mentioned above their horses, if they had such from the state, were taken away, and all were ejected from their tribes and made *aerarii*.[2] And the diligence of the censors did not confine itself to regulating the senate and the order of the knights. From the lists of the younger men they culled the names of all who during four years had not served, without having had a legitimate exemption from the service or ill health as an excuse. And of these above two thousand names were placed on the list of the *aerarii*, and they all were ejected from their tribes. And to this relentless stigma of the censors was added a severe decree of the senate that all of those whom the censors had stigmatised should serve on foot and be sent to Sicily, to the remnant of the army of Cannae. For this class of soldiers the term of service was not at an end until the enemy should be driven out of Italy.

Since the censors on account of the emptiness of the treasury now refrained from letting contracts for the maintenance of temples and the furnishing of horses[3] used in religious processions and for similar

[3] The two-wheeled vehicles (*tensae*) which carried attributes of the Capitoline deities in procession to the Circus were usually drawn by four horses.

A.U.C. 540

11 rerum, convenire[1] ad eos frequentes qui hastae huius generis adsueverant, hortarique[2] censores ut omnia perinde agerent locarent ac si pecunia in aerario esset: neminem nisi bello confecto pecuniam
12 ab aerario petiturum esse. Convenere deinde domini eorum quos Ti. Sempronius ad Beneventum manu emiserat arcessitosque se ab triumviris mensariis esse dixerunt ut pretia servorum acciperent; ceterum non ante quam bello confecto accepturos esse.
13 Cum haec inclinatio animorum plebis ad sustinendam inopiam aerarii fieret, pecuniae quoque pupillares
14 primo, deinde viduarum coeptae conferri, nusquam eas tutius sanctiusque deponere credentibus qui deferebant quam in publica fide; inde si quid emptum paratumque pupillis ac viduis foret, a quaestore
15 perscribebatur. Manavit ea privatorum benignitas ex urbe etiam in castra, ut non eques, non centurio stipendium acciperet, mercennariumque increpantes vocarent qui accepisset.

XIX. Q. Fabius consul ad Casilinum castra habebat, quod duum milium Campanorum et septingentorum militum Hannibalis tenebatur praesidio.
2 Praeerat Statius Metius, missus ab Cn. Magio Atellano, qui eo anno medix tuticus erat, servitiaque

[1] convenire *H. J. Müller*: convenere *P*(1).
[2] hortarique *P*(1): hortatique *z Madvig, adding* sunt *after* censores.

[1] At sales and the letting of contracts a spear (*hasta*) symbolised the authority of the state, and gave its name to the proceedings.

matters, those who had been in the habit of such bidding [1] came in large numbers to the censors, and urged them to take action and let contracts at once for everything, just as if there were money in the treasury; that no one would claim his money from the treasury until the war was over. Then came the owners of the slaves Tiberius Sempronius had manumitted at Beneventum, and said they had been summoned by the bank commissioners [2] to receive the price of their slaves; but that they would not receive it until the war was over. Such being now the tendency of the people to relieve the poverty of the treasury, funds, first of wards, and then of widows and single women, began also to be turned in; for those who brought in the sums believed that nowhere could they deposit them with a sense of greater safety and honesty than under the guarantee of the state. Thereafter when anything was purchased or provided for wards and widows and single women, it was paid for by an order of a quaestor. This generosity of private citizens spread from the city also even to the camps, so that no knight, no centurion accepted pay, and the man who did accept was reproachfully called a hireling. B.C. 214

XIX. Quintus Fabius, the consul, had his camp near Casilinum, which was held by a garrison of two thousand Campanians and seven hundred of Hannibal's soldiers. In command was Statius Metius, who had been sent by Gnaeus Magius, of Atella (who was the *medix tuticus* [3] that year), and Metius had armed slaves and plebeians without distinction, in order to

[2] Cf. XXIII. xxi. 6. These emergency officials (*triumviri mensarii*) evidently served for some years; cf. XXVI. xxxvi. 8.

[3] Cf. XXIII. xxxv. 13; XXVI. vi. 13.

A.U.C. 540 et plebem promiscue armarat, ut castra Romana invaderet intento consule ad Casilinum oppugnan-
3 dum. Nihil eorum Fabium fefellit. Itaque Nolam ad collegam mittit: altero exercitu, dum Casilinum oppugnatur, opus esse qui Campanis opponatur;
4 vel ipse relicto Nolae praesidio modico veniret, vel, si eum Nola teneret necdum securae res ab Hannibale essent, se Ti. Gracchum proconsulem a Bene-
5 vento acciturum. Hoc nuntio Marcellus duobus militum milibus Nolae in praesidio relictis cum cetero exercitu Casilinum venit, adventuque eius Campani
6 iam moventes sese quieverunt. Ita ab duobus consulibus Casilinum oppugnari coepit. Ubi cum multa succedentes temere moenibus Romani milites acciperent vulnera neque satis inceptu[1] succederet, Fabius omittendam rem parvam ac iuxta magnis difficilem abscedendumque inde censebat, cum res
7 maiores instarent; Marcellus multa magnis ducibus sicut non adgredienda, ita semel adgressis non dimittenda esse dicendo, quia magna famae momenta in utramque partem fierent, tenuit ne inrito incepto
8 abiretur. Vineae inde omniaque alia operum machinationumque genera cum admoverentur, Campanique Fabium orarent ut abire Capuam tuto liceret,
9 paucis egressis Marcellus portam qua egrediebantur occupavit, caedesque promiscue omnium circa portam primo, deinde inruptione facta etiam in urbe

[1] inceptu (*dative*) *P*(6): -tus *M*: -tis *A*: -tum *x Gronovius*: -to *Luchs*.

---

[1] Catapults, towers, rams, etc. Movable sheds protected the besiegers.

[2] Livy touches lightly upon Marcellus' apparent ruthlessness; cf. xxxix. 7.

make an attack upon the Roman camp while the consul was occupied with the siege of Casilinum. Of all this nothing escaped Fabius. So he sends word to his colleague at Nola that he needs the other army, to face the Campanians while Casilinum was being besieged: either Marcellus should leave a suitable garrison at Nola and come in person, or if Nola held him back and there was still danger from Hannibal, he would himself summon Tiberius Gracchus, the proconsul, from Beneventum. On receiving this message Marcellus left two thousand soldiers as a garrison at Nola, and with the rest of his army came to Casilinum; and upon his arrival the Campanians, who were already bestirring themselves, became inactive. So began the siege of Casilinum by the two consuls. Since in this operation the Roman soldiers rashly approaching the walls were receiving many wounds and the undertaking was not successful, Fabius thought that they should give up a small affair which was as difficult as great ventures, and that they must leave the place, since greater matters were impending. Marcellus, saying that, while there were many places which great generals ought not to attack, yet, once the attack has begun, they should not give them up, since reputation has great influence in both directions, carried his point, not to depart while their attempt was unsuccessful. Then while sheds and all other kinds of siege-works and apparatus[1] were being brought up, and the Campanians were begging Fabius for permission to go to Capua in safety, after a few had left the city, Marcellus occupied the gate by which they were leaving. And a general slaughter began,[2] first around the gate, and then, as the troops burst in, B.C. 214

A.U.C. 540 10 fieri coepta est. Quinquaginta fere primo egressi
Campanorum, cum ad Fabium confugissent, prae-
sidio eius Capuam pervenerunt. Casilinum inter
conloquia cunctationemque petentium fidem per
11 occasionem captum est, captivique Campanorum
quive[1] Hannibalis militum erant Romam missi
atque ibi in carcere inclusi sunt; oppidanorum
turba per finitimos populos in custodiam divisa.

XX. Quibus diebus a Casilino re bene gesta recessum est, eis Gracchus in Lucanis aliquot cohortes
in ea regione conscriptas cum praefecto socium in
2 agros hostium praedatum misit. Eos effuse palatos
Hanno adortus haud multo minorem quam ad Beneventum acceperat reddidit hosti cladem atque in
Bruttios raptim, ne Gracchus adsequeretur, concessit.
3 Consules Marcellus retro unde venerat Nolam rediit,
Fabius in Samnites ad populandos agros recipiendas-
4 que armis quae defecerant urbes processit. Caudi-
nus Samnis gravius devastatus: perusti late agri,
5 praedae pecudum hominumque actae; oppida vi
capta Conpulteria, Telesia, Compsa inde, Fugifulae
et Orbitanium ex Lucanis, Blanda et Apulorum
6 Aecae oppugnatae. Milia hostium in his urbibus
viginti quinque capta aut occisa, et recepti perfugae
trecenti septuaginta; quos cum Romam misisset
consul, virgis in comitio caesi omnes ac de saxo

[1] quive *P*(1) *Conway*: quique *z*.

even inside the city. About fifty Campanians who had left the city first sought refuge with Fabius and, escorted by his men, reached Capua. Casilinum was captured, as opportunity offered during the conversations and the delay due to those who begged a promise of protection. And the captives, whether Campanians or of Hannibal's soldiers, were sent to Rome and there imprisoned. The mass of the townspeople were distributed among the neighbouring communities to be guarded. B.C. 214

XX. At the same time that they left Casilinum after their success, Gracchus in Lucania sent a number of cohorts which had been enlisted in that region, under the command of a prefect of the allies, into the enemy's farm lands to plunder. Hanno attacked as they were widely scattered, inflicting upon the enemy in return a defeat not much less serious than that which he had received near Beneventum, and withdrew hastily into the land of the Bruttians, that Gracchus might not overtake him. Of the consuls, Marcellus returned to Nola, whence he had come, Fabius advanced into Samnium, to lay waste their farms and to recover by force the cities which had revolted. Samnium around the Caudine Pass was more thoroughly laid waste. Farms were burned over far and wide, cattle and men carried off as booty. Conpulteria, Telesia and Compsa, towns of that region, were taken by storm, also Fugifulae and Orbitanium in Lucania. Blanda and, in Apulia, Aecae were taken after a siege. In these cities twenty-five thousand of the enemy were captured or slain, and three hundred and seventy deserters recovered. These were all sent to Rome by the consul, scourged in the Comitium and hurled from

A.U.C. 540 7 deiecti. Haec a Q. Fabio intra paucos dies gesta.
Marcellum ab gerundis rebus valetudo adversa Nolae
8 tenuit. Et a praetore Q. Fabio, cui circa Luceriam
provincia erat, Acuca oppidum per eos dies vi captum
stativaque ad Ardaneas communita.
9 Dum haec in aliis [1] locis ab Romanis geruntur, iam
Tarentum pervenerat Hannibal cum maxima omni-
10 um quacumque ierat clade; in Tarentino demum
agro pacatum incedere agmen coepit. Nihil ibi
violatum neque usquam via excessum est; apparebatque non id modestia militum sed ducis iussu [2] ad
11 conciliandos animos Tarentinorum fieri. Ceterum
cum prope moenibus successisset,[3] nullo ad conspectum primum agminis, ut rebatur, motu facto
12 castra ab urbe ferme passus mille locat. Tarenti
triduo ante quam Hannibal ad moenia accederet a
M. Valerio propraetore, qui classi ad Brundisium
13 praeerat, missus M. Livius impigre [4] conscripta
iuventute dispositisque ad omnes portas circaque
muros qua res postulabat stationibus die ac nocte
iuxta intentus neque hostibus neque dubiis sociis loci
14 quicquam praebuit ad temptandum.[5] Diebus aliquot frustra ibi absumptis Hannibal, cum eorum
nemo qui ad lacum Averni se [6] adissent aut ipsi
venirent aut nuntium litterasve mitterent, vana
promissa se temere secutum cernens castra inde

[1] in aliis *Madvig, Emend.*: maliis *P* : aliis P^2(1) *Madvig*^{4}.

[2] sed ducis iussu *Wölfflin* : aut ducis usi *P*(2) : aut ducis sed *x Sigonius, Madvig* : aut ducis nisi *Ax Walters* : aut ducis iussu sed M^3?.

[3] successisset *Gronovius* : accessisset *P*(1).

[4] impigre *Weissenborn* : inpriore *P*(1).

[5] temptandum, *PM add* q. (-que *CRBA*): quare M^2? *Gronovius*.

[6] se *Madvig* : *om. P*(1).

the Rock.[1] Such were the acts of Fabius within a few days, while Marcellus was kept out of employment by illness at Nola. And the praetor Quintus Fabius, whose field of duty was around Luceria, stormed the town of Acuca about that time and fortified a permanent camp at Ardaneae.[2] B.C. 214

While the Romans were thus employed elsewhere, Hannibal had now reached Tarentum, leaving the most complete devastation wherever he had passed. Not until it had entered the territory of Tarentum did his column begin to advance peaceably. There they did no damage, and nowhere did they leave the road. And it was plain that this was not due to the self-restraint of the soldiers, but to the commander's orders, for the purpose of winning over the Tarentines. But when he had come quite close to the walls, and there was no movement at the first sight of his column, as he supposed there would be, he pitched camp about a mile from the city. In Tarentum three days before Hannibal approached the walls, Marcus Livius, who had been sent by Marcus Valerius, the propraetor in command of the fleet at Brundisium, actively enlisted young men, posted guards at all the gates and along the walls, wherever required, and alert by night as well as by day, he left neither the enemy nor wavering allies any opening for an attack. After spending some days there to no purpose, Hannibal, since none of the men who had come before him at the Lake of Avernus either came in person or sent a messenger or letter, saw that he had rashly followed empty promises and moved his camp away. Even then he left the

[1] The Tarpeian Rock of the Capitol (site still disputed).
[2] The same as Herdonea, XXV. xxi. 1; XXVII. i. 3.

A.U.C. 540 15 movit, tum quoque intacto agro Tarentino, quamquam simulata lenitas nihildum profuerat, tamen spe labefactandae fidei haud absistens. Salapiam ut venit, frumentum ex agris Metapontino atque Heracleensi—iam enim aestas exacta erat et hibernis
16 placebat locus—conportat. Praedatum inde Numidae Maurique per Sallentinum agrum proximosque Apuliae saltus dimissi; unde ceterae praedae haud multum, equorum greges maxime abacti, e quibus ad quattuor milia domanda equitibus divisa.

XXI. Romani, cum bellum nequaquam contemnendum in Sicilia oreretur morsque tyranni duces magis inpigros dedisset Syracusanis quam causam aut animos mutasset, M. Marcello alteri consulum
2 eam provinciam decernunt. Secundum Hieronymi caedem primo tumultuatum in Leontinis apud milites fuerat vociferatumque ferociter parentandum
3 regi sanguine coniuratorum esse. Deinde libertatis restitutae dulce auditu nomen crebro usurpatum et spes [1] facta ex pecunia regia largitionis militiaeque fungendae potioribus ducibus et relata tyranni foeda scelera foedioresque libidines adeo mutavere animos ut insepultum iacere corpus paulo ante
4 desiderati regis paterentur. Cum ceteri ex coniuratis ad exercitum obtinendum remansissent, Theodotus et Sosis regiis equis quanto maximo

[1] et spes (*or* spesque) *Madvig* : spes *P*(1) : spe *Conway.*

---

[1] Cf. XXIII. xlviii. 3.

territory of Tarentum unharmed, as he did not give B.C. 214
up his hope of weakening their loyalty, although his pretended clemency had had no effect as yet. Arrived at Salapia, he brought in grain from the districts of Metapontum and Heraclea; for the summer was now over, and he thought well of the place for winter quarters. From it Numidians and Mauri were sent out to plunder in the Sallentine territory[1] and the nearest forests of Apulia. From these places not many other cattle were driven off as booty, but chiefly herds of horses, about four thousand of which were distributed among the cavalry to be broken.

XXI. The Romans, inasmuch as a war that was by no means to be despised was breaking out in Sicily, and the death of the tyrant had given energetic commanders to the Syracusans, and had not changed the situation or their feelings, assigned that country to Marcus Marcellus, one of the consuls, as his province. Directly after the assassination of Hieronymus there was at first an uproar among the soldiers at Leontini, and a fierce outcry that they must offer sacrificial vengeance to the dead king in the blood of the conspirators. Later the frequent mention of restored freedom—a word sweet to the ears—and the hope of a largess out of the king's money, and of serving under better generals, also the enumeration of the shameful crimes and still more shameful lusts of the tyrant, so changed their feelings that they allowed the body of the king, whose loss they had just been regretting, to lie unburied. Although the rest of the conspirators had remained, in order to keep their hold on the army, Theodotus[2] and Sosis hastened to

[2] Cf. v. 10 ff.

A.U.C. 540 cursu poterant, ut ignaros omnium regios opprime-
5 rent, Syracusas contendunt. Ceterum praevenerat
non fama solum, qua nihil in talibus rebus est celerius,
6 sed nuntius etiam ex regiis servis. Itaque Adranodorus et Insulam et arcem et alia quae poterat
7 quaeque opportuna erant praesidiis firmarat. Hexapylo Theodotus ac Sosis post solis occasum iam
obscura luce invecti, cum cruentam regiam vestem
atque insigne capitis ostentarent, travecti per
Tycham simul ad libertatem simul ad arma vocantes,
8 in Achradinam convenire iubent. Multitudo pars
procurrit in vias, pars in vestibulis stat, pars ex
tectis fenestrisque prospectant et quid rei sit rogi-
9 tant. Omnia luminibus conlucent strepituque vario
conplentur. Armati locis patentibus congregantur;
inermes ex Olympii Iovis templo spolia Gallorum
Illyriorumque, dono data Hieroni a populo Romano
10 fixaque ab eo, detrahunt, precantes Iovem ut volens
propitius praebeat sacra arma pro patria, pro deum
11 delubris, pro libertate sese armantibus. Haec quoque multitudo stationibus per principes regionum
urbis dispositis adiungitur. In Insula inter cetera
Adranodorus praesidiis firmarat horrea publica.
12 Locus saxo quadrato saeptus atque arcis in modum
emunitus capitur ab iuventute quae praesidio eius

---

[1] The oldest quarter of Syracuse, Ortygia. Cf. Cicero's description of the city, *Verr.* IV. 117 ff.

[2] The great northern gate of the Wall of Dionysius; xxxii. 4 ff.; XXV. xxiv. 2f., etc.; v. Appendix.

[3] A quarter that included a level tract, in which lay the market-place (xxii. 12), but not the rocky heights to the northward facing the sea; frequently mentioned below; v. Appendix.

Syracuse on the king's horses at the greatest possible speed, to surprise his supporters while they were in complete ignorance. However, not only rumour, than which nothing is swifter in such cases, but also a messenger, one of the royal slaves, had anticipated them. And so Adranodorus had garrisoned the Island [1] and the citadel and such other places as were possible and of advantage. By the Hexapylon [2] after sunset Theodotus and Sosis rode into the city in the twilight, showing the bloody garment of the king and his diadem. Then riding across the quarter of Tycha, and calling people to freedom and at the same time to arms, they bid them assemble in Achradina.[3] Of the populace some dash into the streets, some stand before the entrance to their houses, some look out from roofs and windows and keep asking what it means. Everywhere there are bright lights, every place filled with mingled noises. The armed gather in open spaces; those without arms take down from the Temple of Olympian Jupiter [4] the spoils of Gauls and Illyrians, presented by the Roman people to Hiero and hung up there by him. And this they did with a prayer to Jupiter that he graciously consent to furnish consecrated arms to men arming themselves for their native city, for the temples of the gods, for liberty. This crowd also was added to the guard stationed by the leading citizens of the quarters. On the Island Adranodorus had garrisoned, among other positions, the public granaries. This place, which was walled about with squared stone and made strong like a citadel, was captured by the young B.C. 214

[4] On the market-place; built by Hiero; not to be confused with the much older and larger temple west of the Great Harbour; xxxiii. 3; cf. Cicero *op. cit.* 119.

A.U.C. 540 loci adtributa erat, mittuntque nuntios in Achradinam horrea frumentumque in senatus potestate esse.

XXII. Luce prima populus omnis, armatus inermisque, in Achradinam ad curiam convenit. Ibi pro Concordiae ara, quae in eo sita loco erat, ex principibus unus nomine Polyaenus contionem et liberam et
2 moderatam habuit. Servitutis formidines [1] indignitatesque homines expertos adversus notum malum inritatos esse: discordia civilis quas inportet clades, audisse magis a patribus Syracusanos quam ipsos
3 vidisse. Arma quod inpigre ceperint, laudare; magis laudaturum, si non utantur nisi ultima necessitate
4 coacti. In praesentia legatos ad Adranodorum mitti placere qui denuntient ut in potestate senatus ac populi sit, portas Insulae aperiat, reddat praesi-
5 dium. Si tutelam alieni regni suum regnum velit facere, eundem se censere multo acrius ab Adrano-
6 doro quam ab Hieronymo repeti libertatem. Ab hac contione legati missi sunt. Senatus inde haberi coeptus est, quod sicut regnante Hierone manserat publicum consilium, ita post mortem eius ante eam diem nulla de re neque convocati neque consulti
7 fuerant. Ut ventum ad Adranodorum est, ipsum

[1] servitutis formidines *Weissenborn*: servitudinis *P*(4): servitutis *M*[3]*DA*[2]: servitu onus *A*: servitii onus *Walters.*

---

[1] A council, rather than a senate in the Roman sense.

men who had been assigned to its defence; and they B.C. 214
sent messengers into Achradina to say that the granaries and the grain were under the authority of the senate.[1]

XXII. At daybreak all the people, armed and unarmed, gathered at the Senate House in Achradina. There, standing on the altar of Concord,[2] which had been erected on that spot, one of the leading men, Polyaenus by name, delivered a speech at once outspoken and restrained. He said that men who had experienced the terrors of slavery and its humiliations had been inflamed against an evil which they knew. As for civil strife, the Syracusans had heard from their fathers, rather than seen for themselves, what disasters it brings. He praised them for having taken up arms readily, and would praise them the more willingly if they did not use them except when compelled by absolute necessity. For the present he approved of sending representatives to Adranodorus, to instruct him to put himself under the authority of the senate and people, open the gates of the Island and surrender the citadel. At the same time, if Adranodorus should try to turn a regency into a kingship of his own, he favoured reclaiming their freedom from Adranodorus much more fiercely than from Hieronymus. After this speech representatives were sent directly. Then began a session of the senate, which in the reign of Hiero had indeed continued to be the council of state, yet since his death had not been called together nor consulted about anything until that day. When the legates reached Adranodorus, he for his part was

[2] This altar and the Senate House were in the market-place; 12 f.

A.U.C. 540 quidem movebat et civium consensus et cum aliae
occupatae urbis partes, tum pars Insulae vel muni-
8 tissima prodita atque alienata. Sed evocatum eum
ab legatis Damarata uxor, filia Hieronis, inflata
adhuc regiis animis ac muliebri spiritu, admonet
9 saepe usurpatae Dionysi tyranni vocis, qua pedibus
tractum, non insidentem equo relinquere tyrannidem
dixerit debere. Facile esse momento quo quis
velit cedere possessione magnae fortunae; facere
10 et parare eam difficile atque arduum esse. Spatium
sumeret ad consultandum ab legatis; eo uteretur ad
arcessendos ex Leontinis milites, quibus si pecuniam
regiam pollicitus esset, omnia in potestate eius
11 futura. Haec muliebria consilia Adranodorus neque
tota aspernatus est neque extemplo accepit, tuti-
orem ad opes adfectandas ratus esse viam, si in
12 praesentia tempori cessisset. Itaque legatos renuntiare iussit futurum se in senatus ac populi
potestate.

Postero die luce prima patefactis Insulae portis in
13 forum Achradinae venit. Ibi in aram Concordiae,
ex qua pridie Polyaenus contionatus erat, escendit
orationemque eam orsus est qua primum cuncta-
14 tionis suae veniam petivit: se enim clausas habuisse
portas, non separantem suas res a publicis, sed
strictis semel gladiis timentem qui finis caedibus
esset futurus, utrum, quod satis libertati foret,
contenti nece tyranni essent, an quicumque aut

moved by the agreement of the citizens, also by the occupation of other quarters of the city, and especially by the betrayal and loss of the most strongly fortified part of the Island. But his wife Damarata, daughter of Hiero and still puffed up with princely pride and a woman's boldness, called him aside from the legates and reminded him of the oft-repeated utterance of Dionysius the tyrant, that one should leave a tyranny, not on horseback, but dragged by the feet. It was easy, she said, to give up the possession of an exalted station at any moment one wished; to create and achieve it was difficult and all but impossible. He should gain time for deliberation from the legates. He should use it to summon the soldiers from Leontini, and if he should promise them money from the royal treasury everything would be in his power. These feminine counsels Adranodorus neither wholly rejected nor at once adopted, thinking it a safer way to gain power if for the moment he should yield to the crisis. And so he bade the legates report that he would be under the authority of the senate and people. B.C. 214

On the following day at dawn he opened the gates of the Island and came to the market-place of Achradina. There he mounted the altar of Concord, from which Polyaenus had addressed the people the day before, and began a speech in which he first begged pardon for his hesitation. For he had kept the gates closed, he said, not that he wished to separate his cause from that of the people, but because he feared what limit there would be to slaughter, when swords should once be drawn; whether they would be content with the death of the tyrant, which would be sufficient to secure freedom,

A.U.C. 540 propinquitate aut adfinitate aut aliquis ministeriis
regiam contigissent alienae culpae rei trucidarentur.
15 Postquam animadverterit eos qui liberassent patriam
servare etiam liberatam velle atque undique consuli
in medium, non dubitasse quin et corpus suum et
cetera omnia quae suae fidei tutelaeque essent,
quoniam eum qui mandasset suus furor absumpsisset,
16 patriae restitueret. Conversus deinde ad interfectores tyranni ac nomine appellans Theodotum ac
17 Sosin, " Facinus " inquit " memorabile fecistis; sed
mihi credite, incohata vestra gloria, nondum perfecta
est periculumque ingens manet, nisi paci et concordiae consulitis, ne libera efferatur res publica."

XXIII. Post hanc orationem claves portarum pecu-
niaeque regiae ante pedes eorum posuit. Atque illo
quidem die dimissi ex contione laeti circa fana omnia
deum supplicaverunt cum coniugibus ac liberis;
postero die comitia praetoribus creandis habita.
2 Creatus in primis Adranodorus, ceteri magna ex
parte interfectores tyranni; duos etiam absentes,
3 Sopatrum ac Dinomenen, fecerunt. Qui auditis[1]
quae Syracusis acta erant pecuniam regiam quae in
Leontinis erat Syracusas devectam quaestoribus ad
4 id ipsum creatis tradiderunt. Et ea quae in Insula
erat Achradinam tralata est; murique ea pars quae
ab cetera urbe nimis firmo munimento intersaepiebat
Insulam consensu omnium deiecta est. Secutae

[1] auditis *Gronovius* : -tiis *P* : -tis iis P^{1}?(3) *Madvig* : -tis his *D*.

or on the other hand every one who either by blood B.C. 214 or marriage or certain duties was connected with the palace would be slain, as being chargeable with another's guilt. After he observed that those who had freed their native city wished also to keep her free, and that the common good was the aim of all, he had not hesitated to surrender to the city his own person and in addition all that had been confided to his honour and protection, since the man who had given that charge had been destroyed by his own madness. Turning then to the assassins of the tyrant and addressing Theodotus and Sosis by name, he said: "It is a memorable deed that you have done. But believe me, your glory is but begun, not yet finished, and unless you provide for peace and harmony there remains a very great danger that this may be the funeral of the liberated state."

XXIII. After this speech he laid the keys of the gates and those of the royal treasure at their feet. And they, dismissed from the assembly and happy that day at least, with their wives and children gave thanks at all the temples of the gods. On the next day elections for the naming of magistrates were held. Among the first so named was Adranodorus, the rest largely assassins of the tyrant. Two who were not even present, Sopater and Dinomenes, were elected. These, hearing what had been done at Syracuse, brought the royal treasure that was at Leontini to Syracuse and turned it over to treasurers elected for that very purpose. The money that was on the Island was also transferred to Achradina. And that part of the wall which shut off the Island from the rest of the city by a needlessly strong fortification was thrown down by common consent. The other

A.U.C. 540 et ceterae res hanc inclinationem animorum ad
libertatem.[1]

5 Hippocrates atque Epicydes audita morte tyranni,
quam Hippocrates etiam nuntio interfecto celare voluerat, deserti a militibus, quia id tutissimum ex
6 praesentibus videbatur, Syracusas rediere. Ubi ne
suspecti obversarentur tamquam novandi res aliquam occasionem quaerentes, praetores primum,
7 dein per eos senatum adeunt. Ab Hannibale se
missos praedicant ad Hieronymum tamquam amicum ac socium paruisse imperio eius cuius imperator
8 suus voluerit. Velle ad Hannibalem redire; ceterum,
cum iter tutum non sit vagantibus passim per totam
Siciliam Romanis, petere ut praesidii dent aliquid
quo Locros in Italiam perducantur; gratiam magnam
9 eos parva opera apud Hannibalem inituros. Facile
res impetrata; abire enim duces regios cum peritos
militiae, tum egentes eosdem atque audaces cupiebant; sed quod volebant non quam maturato opus
10 erat naviter expediebant. Interim iuvenes militares
et adsueti militibus, nunc apud eos ipsos, nunc apud
transfugas, quorum maxima pars ex navalibus
sociis Romanorum erat, nunc etiam apud infimae
plebis homines crimina serebant in senatum opti-
11 matesque: illud[2] moliri clam eos atque struere ut
Syracusae per speciem reconciliatae societatis in

[1] libertatem, *PCRM add* -que.
[2] illud *Luchs*: ut *P*(1): et *x*: id *Gronovius*.

---

[1] For their service under Hieronymus, cf. vii. 1.

measures also were in keeping with this trend toward freedom. B.C. 214

Hippocrates and Epicydes, on hearing of the tyrant's death, which Hippocrates had wished to keep secret even by slaying the messenger, were deserted by the soldiers and returned to Syracuse,[1] since that course seemed safest in the circumstances. There, to avoid going about under suspicion as seeking some opportunity for a revolution, they first came before the magistrates, and then through them before the senate. They stated that, having been sent by Hannibal to Hieronymus as his friend and ally, they had obeyed the orders of the man to whom their own commander wished them to be obedient. They wished to return to Hannibal; but since the way was unsafe while the Romans were at large everywhere in Sicily, they asked the senators to give them some escort to conduct them to Locri [2] in Italy. The senate, they said, would gain great favour with Hannibal by a small service. This request was readily granted; for the senate greatly desired the departure of the king's generals, as men skilled in military art, and, what was more, needy also and daring. But they took no active steps to carry out their wish with the required promptness. Meanwhile the generals, as young men of military training and familiar with soldiers, at one time in the presence of these, at another among the deserters, the majority of whom were from the crews of the Romans, at another even among the lowest of the people, made charges against the senate and the aristocrats: that they were secretly working and contriving that Syracuse under the guise of a reëstablished alliance should be subject to the

[2] Cf. i. 2 ff.

A.U.C. 540 dicione Romanorum sint, dein factio ac pauci auctores foederis renovati dominentur.

XXIV. His audiendis credendisque opportuna multitudo maior in dies Syracusas confluebat, nec Epicydi solum spem novandarum rerum, sed Adrano-
2 doro etiam praebebat. Qui fessus tandem uxoris vocibus monentis nunc illud esse tempus occupandi res, dum turbata omnia nova atque incondita libertate essent, dum regiis stipendiis pastus obversaretur miles, dum ab Hannibale missi duces adsueti militibus iuvare possent incepta, cum Themisto, cui Gelonis filia nupta erat, rem consociatam paucos post dies Aristoni cuidam tragico actori, cui et alia arcana com-
3 mittere adsuerat, incaute aperit. Huic et genus et fortuna honesta erant, nec ars, quia nihil tale apud Graecos pudori est, ea deformabat. Itaque fidem potiorem [1] ratus quam patriae debebat, indicium ad
4 praetores defert. Qui ubi rem haud vanam esse certis indiciis conpererunt, consultis senioribus et [2] auctoritate eorum praesidio ad fores posito ingressos curiam Themistum atque Adranodorum interfece-
5 runt. Et cum tumultus ab re in speciem atrociore causam aliis ignorantibus ortus esset, silentio tandem
6 facto indicem in curiam introduxerunt. Qui cum ordine omnia edocuisset: principium coniurationis factum ab Harmoniae Gelonis filiae nuptiis, quibus
7 Themisto iuncta esset; Afrorum Hispanorumque auxiliares instructos ad caedem praetorum princi-

[1] potiorem, *PCRM add* -que: priorem potioremque *Alschefski*.

[2] et *F*(1): ex *Luchs*: et ex *Walters*.

Romans, and that then a faction, that is, a few who B.C. 214
supported the renewal of the treaty, should rule.

XXIV. Ready to hear and believe these charges, a daily larger multitude was flocking to Syracuse and giving not Epicydes only, but also Adranodorus, the hope of a revolution. The latter was at length wearied by admonitions of his wife: that it was now the time to seize the power, while everything was confused by the new freedom not yet organized; while the soldiers one met were fattened on the king's pay; while generals sent by Hannibal and familiar with the soldiers could aid the undertaking. Accordingly he formed a plot with Themistus, whose wife was Gelo's daughter, and after a few days rashly revealed it to one Aristo, a tragic actor, to whom he had been in the habit of confiding other secrets. This man's family and station were respectable and not tarnished by his artistic profession, since among the Greeks nothing of the sort brings discredit. And so thinking that the loyalty he owed to his native city took precedence, he reports the matter to the magistrates. They, finding from trustworthy information that this was not unfounded, conferred with the older men, placed a guard at the doors on their advice, and when Themistus and Adranodorus had entered the senate, slew them. And after the confusion resulting from an act even more terrible in appearance than in reality, since others were unaware of the reason, they at length secured silence and brought the informer into the Senate House. He first told everything in order: that the conspiracy had taken its start from the marriage of Gelo's daughter Harmonia, uniting her with Themistus; that African and Spanish auxiliaries had been made ready for the

A.U.C. 540 pumque aliorum, bonaque eorum praedae futura
8 interfectoribus pronuntiatum; iam mercennariorum manum, adsuetam imperiis Adranodori, paratam fuisse ad Insulam rursus occupandam; singula deinde quae per quosque agerentur, totamque viris armisque instructam coniurationem ante oculos posuit. Et senatui quidem tam iure caesi quam
9 Hieronymus videbantur: ante curiam variae atque incertae rerum multitudinis clamor erat. Quam ferociter minitantem in vestibulo curiae corpora coniuratorum eo metu compresserunt ut silentes inte-
10 gram plebem in contionem sequerentur. Sopatro mandatum ab senatu et a collegis ut verba faceret.

XXV. Is, tamquam reos ageret, ab [1] ante acta vita orsus, quaecumque post Hieronis mortem sceleste atque impie facta essent, Adranodorum ac Themi-
2 stum arguit fecisse: quid enim sua sponte [2] Hieronymum, puerum ac vixdum pubescentem facere potuisse? Tutores ac magistros eius sub aliena invidia regnasse; itaque aut ante Hieronymum aut
3 certe cum Hieronymo perire eos debuisse. At illos debitos iam morti destinatosque, alia nova scelera post mortem tyranni molitos, palam primo, cum clausis Adranodorus Insulae portis hereditatem regni creverit et quae procurator tenuerat pro domino
4 possederit; proditus deinde ab eis qui in Insula

[1] ab *xz*: *om.* *P*(1).
[2] sponte, *P*(1) *add* fecisse.

slaughter of the magistrates and other leading B.C. 214 citizens, and the announcement made that their property would be spoil for the assassins; moreover that a force of mercenaries accustomed to the orders of Adranodorus had been provided, to occupy the Island again. He then set forth in detail what was to be done, and by whom, and pictured the whole conspiracy manned and armed. And to the senators indeed they appeared to have been slain with as much justice as Hieronymus. But in front of the Senate House there was shouting by the mixed crowd unacquainted with the situation. Uttering wild threats, they were checked by the corpses of the conspirators before the entrance to the Senate House, in such fear that they silently followed the orderly populace to the assembly. Sopater was instructed by the senate and his colleagues to speak.

XXV. Beginning with their previous life, just as if he were prosecuting them, he charged that every act of violence or impiety committed since the death of Hiero had been done by Adranodorus and Themistus. For what could Hieronymus, a boy who had hardly reached puberty, have done of his own motion? His guardians and teachers, shielded by the embitterment directed against another, had been the real kings. Accordingly they ought to have perished either before Hieronymus or at least with Hieronymus. But though doomed already and marked for death, they had contrived fresh crimes since the death of the tyrant, at first openly, when Adranodorus, closing the gates of the Island, took over the kingdom as his own inheritance and as owner entered into possession of what he had held as agent: again when, betrayed by those who were on the Island, beset by the whole

A.U.C. 540 erant, circumsessus ab universa civitate quae Achradinam tenuerit, nequiquam palam atque aperte
petitum regnum clam et dolo adfectare conatus sit,
5 et ne beneficio quidem atque honore potuerit vinci,
cum inter liberatores patriae insidiator ipse libertatis
6 creatus esset praetor. Sed animos eis regios regias
coniuges fecisse, alteri Hieronis, alteri Gelonis filias
7 nuptas. Sub hanc vocem ex omnibus partibus
contionis clamor oritur nullam earum vivere debere
8 nec quemquam superesse tyrannorum stirpis. Ea
natura multitudinis est: aut servit humiliter aut
superbe dominatur; libertatem, quae media est, nec
9 suscipere [1] modice nec habere sciunt; et non ferme
desunt irarum indulgentes ministri, qui avidos atque
intemperantes suppliciorum animos ad sanguinem
10 et caedes inritent; sicut tum extemplo praetores
rogationem promulgarunt, acceptaque paene prius
quam promulgata est, ut omnes regiae stirpis interficerentur; missique a praetoribus Damaratam
Hieronis et Harmoniam Gelonis filiam, coniuges
Adranodori et Themisti, interfecerunt.

XXVI. Heraclia erat filia Hieronis, uxor Zoippi,
qui legatus ab Hieronymo ad regem Ptolomaeum
2 missus voluntarium consciverat exilium. Ea cum
ad se quoque veniri [2] praescisset, in sacrarium ad
penates confugit cum duabus filiis [3] virginibus,
3 resolutis crinibus miserabilique alio habitu, et ad ea

[1] suscipere *x*: cupere *x*: stupere *P*(2): struere *Conway*: sibi parare *M. Müller*.

[2] veniri *x Gronovius*: venire *P*(1).

[3] filiis *Weissenborn conj.* (*cf.* XXXVIII. lvii. 2): filiabus *P*(1).

---

[1] Cf. v. 7.

[2] Ptolemy IV Philopator, XXIII. x. 11.

body of citizens holding Achradina, he attempted B.C. 214
secretly and craftily to win the kingdom which he had sought in vain openly and above board, and could not be won over even by the bestowal of public office. For among those who gained liberty for the state, he, a plotter against liberty himself, had been elected a magistrate. But their autocratic temper was due to their royal consorts, Hiero's daughter married to the one, Gelo's daughter to the other. Following this statement there arose in all parts of the assembly a shout that none of those women ought to live, nor any one of the family of the tyrants to survive. This is the nature of the mass: either it is a humble slave or a haughty master. As for freedom, which is the mean, they know no moderation either in assuming or in keeping it. And angry passions usually do not lack complaisant helpers, to provoke to bloodshed those who are immoderately eager for punishment; as in this case the magistrates forthwith proposed a bill—and it was adopted almost before it was proposed—that all members of the royal family should be put to death. And by order of the magistrates men were sent who put to death Damarata the daughter of Hiero and Harmonia the daughter of Gelo, being the wives of Adranodorus and Themistus.

XXVI. Heraclia was the daughter of Hiero and wife of Zoippus,[1] who was sent as ambassador to King Ptolemy [2] by Hieronymus and had accepted voluntary exile. She, having learned in advance that they were coming to her house also, fled into the chapel of the household gods with her two maiden daughters, her hair dishevelled and her general appearance moving to pity. And in addition were

A.U.C. 540 addidit preces, nunc per deos, nunc[1] per memoriam
Hieronis patris Gelonisque fratris, ne se innoxiam
4 invidia Hieronymi conflagrare sinerent: nihil se ex
regno illius praeter exilium viri habere; neque
fortunam suam eandem vivo Hieronymo fuisse quam
sororis, neque interfecto eo causam eandem esse.
5 Quid quod si Adranodoro consilia processissent, illa
cum viro fuerit regnatura, sibi cum ceteris servien-
6 dum? Si quis Zoippo nuntiet interfectum Hieronymum ac liberatas Syracusas, cui dubium esse quin
extemplo conscensurus sit navem atque in patriam
7 rediturus? Quantum spes hominum falli! in liberata
patria coniugem eius ac liberos de vita dimicare,
8 quid obstantes libertati aut legibus? Quod ab se cuiquam periculum, a sola ac prope vidua et puellis in
orbitate degentibus esse? At enim periculi quidem
nihil ab se timeri, invisam tamen stirpem regiam esse.
9 Ablegarent ergo procul ab Syracusis Siciliaque et
asportari Alexandriam iuberent, ad virum uxorem, ad
10 patrem filias. Aversis auribus animisque cum conclamassent[2] ne tempus tereretur[3] ferrum quosdam
11 expedientes cernebat; tum omissis pro se precibus,
puellis ut saltem parcerent orare institit, a qua aetate
etiam hostes iratos abstinere; ne tyrannos ulciscendo
12 quae odissent scelera ipsi imitarentur. Inter haec
abstractam a penetralibus iugulant; in virgines

[1] per deos, nunc *Ruperti*: *om.* *P*(1).

[2] cum conclamassent *Novák*: cassae *P*: cassae *or* casse (1): *variously emended*: adstare *Madvig*: questa est *Koch*.

[3] tereretur A^2: terrerentur *P*(4): tererentur *A*: tererent *Madvig*.

her prayers, now by the gods, now by the memory of B.C. 214
her father Hiero and her brother Gelo, that they should not allow her innocent self to perish by the fire of resentment against Hieronymus. Nothing had she gained by his reign except the exile of her husband; and while Hieronymus lived, her station had not been so high as her sister's, nor was their situation the same after his death. What of it that, if Adranodorus' plans had succeeded, the sister would have reigned with her husband, while she herself and all the rest must be slaves? If someone should inform Zoippus that Hieronymus had been slain and Syracuse set free, who would have any doubt that he would forthwith board ship and return to his native city? How the hopes of men were disappointed! In his native city, now set free, his wife and children were fighting for their lives, offering what obstacle to freedom and laws? What danger to anyone was there from herself, a lone woman, virtually a widow, and from maidens living as orphans? But they might say that no danger was indeed feared from her, that nevertheless the royal family was hated. Therefore they should send them far from Syracuse and Sicily and bid them to be carried away to Alexandria, the wife to her husband, the daughters to their father. When they paid no attention whatever and shouted not to waste time, she could see some men drawing swords. Then ceasing entreaties for herself, she urgently begged them at least to spare the girls—an age on which even enraged enemies do not lay hands; that in taking vengeance on the tyrants they should not themselves imitate the crimes which they hated. While still speaking, they dragged her away from the altar and cut her throat,

A.U.C. 540 deinde respersas matris cruore impetum faciunt. Quae alienata mente simul luctu metuque velut captae furore eo cursu se ex sacrario proripuerunt ut, si effugium patuisset in publicum, impleturae urbem
13 tumultu fuerint. Tum quoque haud magno aedium spatio inter medios tot armatos aliquotiens integro corpore evaserunt tenentibusque, cum tot ac tam validae eluctandae manus essent, sese eripuerunt.
14 Tandem vulneribus confectae, cum omnia replessent sanguine, exanimes corruerunt. Caedemque per se miserabilem miserabiliorem casus fecit, quod paulo post nuntius venit, mutatis repente ad misericordiam
15 animis, ne interficerentur. Ira deinde ex misericordia orta, quod adeo festinatum ad [1] supplicium neque locus paenitendi aut regressus ab ira relictus
16 esset. Itaque fremere multitudo et in locum Adranodori ac Themisti—nam ambo praetores fuerant—comitia poscere, quae nequaquam ex sententia praetorum futura essent.

XXVII. Statutus est comitiis dies; quo necopinantibus omnibus unus ex ultima turba Epicyden nominavit, tum inde alius Hippocratem; crebriores deinde hae voces et cum haud dubio adsensu multi-
2 tudinis esse. Et erat confusa contio non populari modo sed militari quoque turba, magna ex parte etiam perfugis, qui omnia novare cupiebant, per-
3 mixtis. Praetores dissimulare primo et trahenda re morae [2] esse [3]; postremo, victi consensu et sedi-

[1] ad *P*(1): id *Madvig, Emend.*

[2] morae *M. Müller*: *om. P*(1).

[3] esse, *for* et trahenda re esse (*PRD*: et -dam rem esse *C*²*MBA*) *Madvig and Walters read* extrahenda re; sed.

then turned their attack upon the girls spattered with their mother's blood. Beside themselves for grief and fear, as though insane, they dashed out of the chapel with such speed that, if there had been any escape to the street, they would have caused a riot throughout the city. Even as it was, in the limited space of the house, amidst so many armed men, they several times escaped unharmed and tore themselves away from those who tried to hold them, although they had to fight off hands so many and so strong. At last exhausted by wounds, after staining everything with their blood, they fell lifeless. The slaughter, in itself pitiful, was made still more pitiful by the coincidence that shortly after came the word that they were not to be put to death, for animosity had suddenly changed to pity. From pity then came anger, that such haste to punish had been made, and no chance left for a change of mind or a cooling of anger. And so the multitude complained, and to replace Adranodorus and Themistus—for both had been magistrates—they clamoured for an election, which would not prove at all to the liking of the magistrates. B.C. 214

XXVII. A day was set for the election, and on that day, to the surprise of everybody, one man on the outskirts of the crowd nominated Epicydes, then after him another named Hippocrates, whereupon these shouts were repeated and with evident approval of the multitude. And the assembly was disturbed by the crowd not only of citizens but also of soldiers, even deserters in large part mingling with them and eager for any change. The magistrates at first ignored them and by postponing delayed matters. Finally, compelled by the general

A.U.C. 540

4 tionem metuentes, pronuntiant eos praetores. Nec illi primo statim creati nudare quid vellent, quamquam aegre ferebant et de indutiis dierum decem legatos isse ad Appium Claudium et inpetratis eis alios qui de foedere antiquo renovando agerent
5 missos. Ad Murgantiam tum classem navium centum Romanus habebat, quonam evaderent motus ex caedibus tyrannorum orti Syracusis quove eos ageret nova atque insolita libertas opperiens.
6 Per eosdem dies cum ad Marcellum venientem in Siciliam legati Syracusani missi ab Appio essent, auditis condicionibus pacis Marcellus, posse rem convenire ratus, et ipse legatos Syracusas qui coram cum praetoribus de renovando foedere agerent misit.
7 Et iam ibi nequaquam eadem quies ac tranquillitas erat. Postquam Punicam classem accessisse Pachynum adlatum est, dempto timore Hippocrates et Epicydes nunc apud mercennarios milites, nunc apud transfugas prodi Romano Syracusas criminabantur.
8 Ut vero Appius naves ad ostium portus, quo [1] aliae [2] partis hominibus animus accederet, in statione habere coepit, ingens in speciem criminibus vanis
9 accesserat fides; ac primo etiam tumultuose decurrerat multitudo ad prohibendos, si in terram egrederentur.

[1] quo *x Gronovius*: quid *P*(1).

[2] aliae *P*(1)*x Hertz*: alius *A*²: amicae *Madvig*: suae *Bauer*. *For the old form* aliae *cf. Cicero de Divinatione* II. 30 (*twice*).

---

[1] Now a legatus of Marcellus; praetor in Sicily the previous year; vi. 4; vii. 8.

agreement and fearing an uprising, they declared B.C. 214
Epicydes and Hippocrates magistrates. And at first the newly elected did not reveal their intentions, although they were indignant that legates had gone to Appius Claudius [1] to sue for a ten days' truce, and that, this being secured, others had been sent to negotiate the renewal of the old treaty. At that time the Roman commander had a fleet of a hundred ships off Murgantia,[2] waiting to see what would be the outcome of the disturbances at Syracuse due to the massacre of the tyrant's family, and to what the new and unwonted freedom would prompt them.

About the same time Marcellus was just arriving in Sicily, and the Syracusan ambassadors were sent to him by Appius. After hearing the peace terms, Marcellus thought agreement could be reached, and himself sent ambassadors to Syracuse to treat in person with the magistrates for a renewal of the treaty. And by this time the situation there was by no means so orderly and peaceful. When word was received that a Carthaginian fleet had reached the promontory of Pachynum,[3] Hippocrates and Epicydes, relieved of their fear, kept making the charge, now before the mercenaries, now among the deserters, that Syracuse was being betrayed to the Roman. But from the time Appius began to keep ships at anchor at the harbour mouth in order to encourage the men of the other party, the false charges apparently had received strong confirmation. And at first the crowd had even rushed down in disorder to keep them off in case they should be landing.

[2] A seaport of unknown situation. Another town of the same name was in the interior, to the east of Henna.

[3] Little more than thirty miles south of Syracuse.

A.U.C. 540

XXVIII. In hac turbatione rerum in contionem vocari placuit. Ubi cum alii alio tenderent nec procul seditione res esset, Apollonides, principum unus, orationem salutarem ut in tali tempore habuit:
2 nec spem salutis nec perniciem propiorem umquam
3 civitati ulli fuisse. Si enim uno animo omnes vel ad Romanos vel ad Carthaginienses inclinent, nullius
4 civitatis statum fortunatiorem ac beatiorem fore; si alii alio trahant res, non inter Poenos Romanosque bellum atrocius fore quam inter ipsos Syracusanos, cum intra eosdem muros pars utraque suos exercitus,
5 sua arma, suos habitura sit duces. Itaque ut idem omnes sentiant summa vi agendum esse. Utra societas sit utilior, eam longe minorem ac levioris
6 momenti consultationem esse; sed tamen Hieronis potius quam Hieronymi auctoritatem sequendam in sociis legendis, vel quinquaginta annis feliciter expertam amicitiam nunc incognitae, quondam
7 infideli praeferendam. Esse etiam momenti aliquid ad consilium quod Carthaginiensibus ita pax negari possit, ut non utique in praesentia bellum cum eis geratur: cum Romanis extemplo aut pacem aut
8 bellum habendum. Quo minus cupiditatis ac studii visa est oratio habere, eo plus auctoritatis habuit. Adiectum est praetoribus ac delectis senatorum militare etiam consilium; iussi et duces ordinum
9 praefectique auxiliorum simul consulere. Cum saepe acta res esset magnis certaminibus, postremo, quia

XXVIII. In this confused state of affairs it was decided to summon the people to an assembly. There while some inclined in one direction, some in another, and an uprising was not far away, Apollonides, one of the leading citizens, made a speech which was well-advised, considering the crisis. He said that neither the prospect of safety nor that of destruction had ever been nearer to any state. For if with one mind they should all incline, whether to the Romans or to the Carthaginians, no state would be in a more highly favoured and happier condition. If they pulled in different directions, war between Carthaginians and Romans would not be more cruel than that among the Syracusans themselves, since within the same walls each side would have its own armies, its own weapons, its own generals. Accordingly they must make the greatest effort to reach agreement. Which alliance was the more advantageous was a question decidedly subordinate and of far less weight. Yet Hiero's authority ought to be followed in choosing allies rather than that of Hieronymus; in other words, a friendship which had proved happy for fifty years should be preferred to one unknown at present and formerly faithless. For their decision it was also of considerable importance that they could decline the Carthaginians' offer of peace without necessarily waging war with them at once. With the Romans they must straightway have either peace or war. The less of party passion the speech seemed to have, the greater was its influence. To the magistrates and picked senators they added a military council also. Commanders of units and prefects of auxiliaries as well were ordered to take part in the deliberations. After the question had been repeatedly debated with B.C. 214

A.U.C. 540 belli cum Romanis gerendi ratio nulla apparebat, pacem fieri placuit mittique legatos ad rem cum eis[1] confirmandam.

XXIX. Dies haud ita multi intercesserunt, cum ex Leontinis legati praesidium finibus suis orantes venerunt; quae legatio peropportuna visa ad multitudinem inconditam ac tumultuosam exonerandam
2 ducesque eius ablegandos. Hippocrates praetor ducere eo transfugas iussus; secuti multi ex mercennariis auxiliis quattuor milia armatorum effecerunt.
3 Et mittentibus et missis ea laeta expeditio fuit; nam et illis, quod iam diu cupiebant, novandi res occasio data est, et hi sentinam quandam urbis rati exhaustam laetabantur. Ceterum levaverunt modo in praesentia velut corpus aegrum, quo mox in
4 graviorem morbum recideret. Hippocrates enim finitima provinciae Romanae primo furtivis excursionibus vastare coepit; deinde, cum ad tuendos sociorum agros missum ab Appio praesidium esset, omnibus copiis impetum in oppositam stationem cum
5 caede multorum fecit. Quae cum essent nuntiata Marcello, legatos extemplo Syracusas misit qui pacis fidem ruptam esse dicerent nec belli defuturam umquam causam, nisi Hippocrates atque Epicydes non ab Syracusis modo, sed tota procul Sicilia ablegaren-
6 tur. Epicydes, ne aut reus criminis absentis fratris praesens esset, aut deesset pro parte sua concitando bello, profectus et ipse in Leontinos, quia satis eos

[1] cum eis *P*(1), *but after* mittique: *after* rem *Gronovius*.

great contention, finally, as they evidently had no means of carrying on a war with the Romans, it was decided to make an alliance with them, and to send ambassadors for the ratification. B.C. 214

XXIX. Not many days had elapsed, when ambassadors from Leontini arrived, pleading for a force to defend their territory. The request of this embassy seemed very timely for the purpose of relieving the city of a disorderly and turbulent multitude and of sending away its leaders. Hippocrates as magistrate was ordered to lead the deserters thither. Many of the mercenary auxiliaries followed, making four thousand armed men. That enterprise gave joy both to the senders and the sent; for the one party were given a long-desired opportunity for revolution, and the other rejoiced also to think that the dregs of the city had been drained off. But they relieved the diseased body, so to speak, merely for the moment, only to have it relapse presently into a more serious ailment. For Hippocrates began, at first with stealthy raids, to ravage lands on the border of the Roman province. Later, when Appius had sent troops to protect the farms of the allies, he made an attack with all his forces upon the unit on guard-duty facing him, and many were slain. Marcellus, being informed of this, at once sent legates to Syracuse, to say that the promised peace had been broken, and that a reason for war would never be wanting unless Hippocrates and Epicydes should be sent far away, not merely from Syracuse, but from all Sicily. Epicydes, to avoid being present under an accusation brought against his absent brother, or else failing to do his part in provoking war, went likewise to Leontini; and seeing that its citizens were sufficiently

A.U.C. 540 adversus populum Romanum concitatos cernebat,
7 avertere etiam ab Syracusanis coepit: nam ita eos pacem pepigisse cum Romanis ut quicumque populi sub regibus fuissent [1] suae dicionis essent, nec iam libertate contentos esse nisi etiam regnent ac domi-
8 nentur. Renuntiandum igitur eis esse Leontinos quoque aequom censere liberos [2] esse, vel quod in solo urbis suae tyrannus ceciderit, vel quod ibi primum conclamatum ad libertatem relictisque
9 regiis ducibus Syracusas concursum sit.[3] Itaque aut eximendum id de foedere esse, aut legem eam
10 foederis non accipiendam. Facile multitudini persuasum; legatisque Syracusanorum et de caede stationis Romanae querentibus et Hippocratem atque Epicydem abire seu Locros seu quo alio mallent, dummodo Sicilia cederent, iubentibus ferociter responsum est neque mandasse sese Syracu-
11 sanis ut pacem pro se cum Romanis facerent, neque
12 teneri alienis foederibus. Haec ad Romanos Syracusani detulerunt, abnuentes Leontinos in sua potestate esse: itaque integro secum foedere bellum Romanos cum iis gesturos, neque sese defuturos ei bello, ita ut in potestatem redacti suae rursus dicionis essent, sicut pax convenisset.

XXX. Marcellus cum omni exercitu profectus in

[1] fuissent *Madvig*[4]: fuissent et *P*(1) *Conway*: fuissent ei *Riemann*.
[2] liberos *P*(1) *Conway*: liberos se *Madvig*.
[3] sit *Weissenborn* (*before* concursum *z*): *om.* *P*(1).

aroused against the Roman people, began also to estrange them from the Syracusans. For, he explained, the Syracusans had made an alliance with the Romans with the provision that all the states which had been subject to the kings should be under their rule; that now they were not satisfied with freedom, without also being lords and masters. They must therefore report to them that the Leontinians likewise thought it right that they should be free, either because it was on the soil of their city that the tyrant fell, or because there for the first time men shouted the summons to liberty, and deserting the king's generals flocked to Syracuse. Accordingly either that clause, he said, must be removed from the treaty, or else an alliance on such terms was not to be accepted. The multitude was easily persuaded, and when the legates of the Syracusans complained of the slaughter of the Roman guard-post and also bade Hippocrates and Epicydes go away to Locri or wherever they preferred, provided they withdrew from Sicily, the people replied with spirit that they had not instructed the Syracusans to make a treaty for them with the Romans, and that they were not bound by treaties not of their own making. This was reported to the Romans by the Syracusans, who stated that the men of Leontini were not subject to their authority; and that consequently the Romans would make war upon them without violating the treaty made with Syracuse; also that they would themselves not refuse to give help in the war, on condition that, when reduced to subjection, the Leontini should again be under their authority, as had been settled in the treaty. B.C. 214

XXX. Marcellus, proceeding with his whole army

A.U.C. 540

Leontinos, Appio quoque accito ut altera parte adgrederetur, tanto ardore militum est usus ab ira inter condiciones pacis interfectae stationis ut primo impe-
2 tu urbem expugnarent. Hippocrates atque Epicydes, postquam capi muros refringique portas videre, in arcem sese cum paucis recepere; inde clam nocte
3 Herbesum perfugiunt. Syracusanis octo milium armatorum agmine profectis domo ad Mylan flumen nuntius occurrit captam urbem esse, cetera falsa
4 mixta veris ferens: caedem promiscuam militum atque oppidanorum factam, nec quicquam puberum arbitrari superesse; direptam urbem, bona locuple-
5 tium donata. Ad nuntium tam atrocem constitit agmen, concitatisque omnibus duces—erant autem Sosis ac Dinomenes—quid agerent consultabant.
6 Terroris speciem haud vanam mendacio praebuerant verberati ac securi percussi transfugae ad duo milia
7 hominum; ceterum Leontinorum militumque aliorum nemo post captam urbem violatus fuerat, suaque omnia eis, nisi quae primus tumultus captae urbis
8 absumpserat, restituebantur. Nec ut Leontinos irent, proditos ad caedem commilitones querentes, perpelli potuere, nec ut eodem loco certiorem nun-
9 tium expectarent. Cum ad defectionem inclinatos animos cernerent praetores, sed eum motum haud diuturnum fore, si duces amentiae sublati essent,
10 exercitum ducunt Megara, ipsi cum paucis equitibus

---

[1] Probably between Syracuse and Leontini, perhaps on the Mylas.

[2] Leontini.

[3] The *praetores*, having taken the field, are now generals, as repeatedly below.

[4] On the coast north of Syracuse; destroyed by Marcellus, xxv. 2.

to Leontini and summoning Appius also to make an attack from the other side, found such enthusiasm in his soldiers, due to anger aroused by the slaughter of men of the guard while negotiations were pending, that they took the city at the first assault. Hippocrates and Epicydes, on seeing that the walls were being taken and gates forced, sought refuge with a few men in the citadel. Thence they fled secretly by night to Herbesus.[1] The Syracusans, who had set out from home in a column of eight thousand men, were met at the river Mylas by a messenger, reporting that the city [2] had been captured, but for the rest mingling the false with the true: that a general massacre of soldiers and townspeople had occurred, and no adults, he thought, had survived; that the city had been plundered, the property of the wealthy given away. On hearing news so terrible the column halted, and in the general excitement the commanders—and they were Sosis and Dinomenes—considered what they should do. The appearance of well-founded alarm had been lent to the falsehood by the scourging and beheading of deserters, about two thousand men. But not one of the Leontinians or of the other soldiers had been injured after the capture of the city; and, except what had been lost in the first confusion of the capture of the city, all their property was being restored to them. And the soldiers, complaining that their comrades had been betrayed to their death, could neither be induced to go to Leontini nor to wait at the same spot for more trustworthy news. The generals,[3] seeing them inclined to mutiny, but that the outbreak would not last long if the leaders in folly should be removed, led the army to Megara:[4] and then with a few B.C. 214

A.U.C. 540
Herbesum proficiscuntur spe territis omnibus per
11 proditionem urbis potiundae. Quod ubi frustra eis
fuit inceptum, vi agendum rati postero die Megaris
castra movent, ut Herbesum omnibus copiis oppug-
12 narent. Hippocrates et Epicydes non tam tutum
prima specie quam unum spe undique abscisa consilium esse rati, ut se militibus permitterent et
adsuetis magna ex parte sibi et tum fama caedis
commilitonum accensis, obviam agmini procedunt.
13 Prima forte signa sescentorum Cretensium erant,
qui apud Hieronymum meruerant sub eis et Hannibalis beneficium habebant, capti ad Trasumennum
14 inter Romanorum auxilia dimissique. Quos ubi ex
signis armorumque habitu cognovere, Hippocrates
atque Epicydes ramos oleae ac velamenta alia
supplicum porrigentes orare ut reciperent sese,
receptos tutarentur, neu proderent Syracusanis, a
quibus ipsi mox trucidandi populo Romano dede-
rentur. XXXI. Enimvero conclamant bonum ut
animum haberent; omnem se cum illis fortunam
2 subituros. Inter hoc conloquium signa constiterant
tenebaturque agmen, necdum quae morae causa
foret pervenerat ad duces. Postquam Hippocraten
atque Epicyden adesse [1] pervasit rumor, fremitusque
toto agmine erat haud dubie adprobantium adventum

[1] adesse *z Madvig*: esse $A^x x$: *om.* *P*(1): adesse ordines *Weissenborn*.

[1] They were archers.

horsemen they went themselves to Herbesus, in the B.C. 214 hope of getting possession of the city by treachery, owing to the general alarm. When this undertaking disappointed them, they thought they must use force, and moved their camp from Megara the next day, to attack Herbesus with all their troops. Hippocrates and Epicydes, thinking that their plan to put themselves at the mercy of the soldiers, who were in large part used to them and also at that time inflamed by the report of the slaughter of their comrades, was not so much one which at first sight promised safety, as it was the only possible plan in a desperate situation, went out to meet the column. The first unit happened to be that of six hundred Cretans, who had served under them in the army of Hieronymus and were under obligations to Hannibal, as they had been captured among the Roman auxiliaries at Lake Trasumennus and allowed to go free. Recognizing them from their standards and the character of their weapons,[1] Hippocrates and Epicydes, holding out olive branches and in addition the woollen bands of suppliants, implored them to admit them and, having done so, to protect and not betray them to the Syracusans, to be themselves presently surrendered by the same to the Roman people for brutal execution.

XXXI. And in fact the Cretans shouted to them to take courage, saying they would share every lot with them. During this conversation the standards had halted and the column was being held up. And word had not yet reached the generals as to what was the cause of the delay. When the report that Hippocrates and Epicydes were there did reach them, and down the whole length of the column there was a shout of evident joy over their coming, at once the

A.U.C. 540 eorum, extemplo praetores citatis equis ad prima
3 signa perrexerunt. Qui mos ille, quae licentia
Cretensium esset rogitantes, conloquia serendi cum
hoste iniussuque praetorum miscendi eos agmini
suo, conprehendi inicique catenas iusserunt Hippo-
4 crati. Ad quam vocem tantus extemplo primum a
Cretensibus clamor est ortus, deinde exceptus ab
aliis, ut facile, si ultra tenderent, appareret eis ti-
5 mendum esse. Solliciti incertique rerum suarum
Megara, unde profecti erant, referri signa iubent
nuntiosque de statu praesenti Syracusas mittunt.

6 Fraudem quoque Hippocrates addit inclinatis ad
omnem suspicionem animis et Cretensium quibusdam
ad itinera insidenda missis velut interceptas litteras
7 quas ipse composuerat, recitat: "Praetores Syracusani consuli Marcello." Secundum salutem, ut
adsolet, scriptum erat recte eum atque ordine fecisse,
8 quod in Leontinis nulli pepercisset. Sed omnium
mercennariorum militum eandem esse causam, nec
umquam Syracusas quieturas donec quicquam ex-
ternorum auxiliorum aut in urbe aut in exercitu suo
9 esset. Itaque daret operam ut eos qui cum suis
praetoribus castra ad Megara haberent in suam
potestatem redigeret ac supplicio eorum liberaret
10 tandem Syracusas. Haec cum recitata essent, cum
tanto clamore ad arma discursum est ut praetores
11 inter tumultum pavidi abequitaverint Syracusas. Et
ne fuga quidem eorum seditio conpressa est, impetus-
que in Syracusanos milites fiebant; nec ab ullo

---

[1] Mention of one brother is meant to include the other, Epicydes; xxiv. 1; xxxv. 4.

[2] Only the heading is quoted verbatim, with suppression of the conventional greeting.

generals made their way at a gallop to the head B.C. 214
of the column. Asking what a practice, what a breach of discipline, it was on the part of the Cretans to join in conversation with an enemy and to admit the men to their own column without orders from the generals, they ordered them to be arrested and Hippocrates[1] to be put in chains. Upon that command such an outcry was first raised by the Cretans, and then caught up by others, that it was easy to see that if they took any further steps they would have to fear for themselves. Troubled and uncertain as to their own situation, they ordered a retreat to Megara, from which they had set out, and sent messengers to Syracuse to report how matters stood.

While men were inclined to suspect everything, Hippocrates also resorted to a ruse. After sending some of the Cretans to lie in wait by the roads, with the pretence that it had been intercepted, he publicly read a letter written by himself: "The magistrates of Syracuse to the Consul Marcellus."[2] Following the customary greeting it was stated that he had been entirely right in sparing no one at Leontini; but that the situation of all the mercenary soldiers was the same, and Syracuse would never have peace so long as there were any foreign auxiliaries in either the city or its army. Therefore he should take measures to reduce to submission the men who were encamped at Megara under the command of their own generals, and by their punishment to set Syracuse free at last. After this had been read, they rushed to arms with such shouting that during the confusion the generals rode away in alarm to Syracuse. And the mutiny was not quelled even by their flight; but attacks were repeatedly made on the Syracusan soldiers.

A.U.C. 540 temperatum foret, ni Epicydes atque Hippocrates
12 irae multitudinis obviam issent, non a misericordia
aut humano consilio, sed ne spem reditus praeci-
derent sibi et, cum ipsos simul milites fidos haberent
13 simul obsides, tum cognatos quoque eorum atque
amicos tanto merito primum, dein pignore sibi
14 conciliarent. Expertique quam vana aut levi aura
mobile volgus esset, militem nancti ex eo numero qui
in Leontinis circumsessi erant, subornant, ut Syracusas perferret nuntium convenientem eis quae ad
15 Mylan falso nuntiata erant, auctoremque se exhi-
bendo ac velut visa quae dubia erant narrando
concitaret iras hominum.

XXXII. Huic non apud volgum modo fides fuit,
sed senatum quoque in curiam introductus movit.
Haud vani quidam homines palam ferre perbene
detectam in Leontinis esse avaritiam et crudelitatem
Romanorum. Eadem, si intrassent Syracusas, aut
foediora etiam, quo maius ibi avaritiae praemium
2 esset, facturos fuisse. Itaque claudendas cuncti
portas et custodiendam urbem censere. Sed non
ab iisdem omnes timere nec eosdem odisse: ad
militare genus omne partemque magnam plebis
3 invisum esse nomen Romanum; praetores optima-
tiumque pauci, quamquam inflati vano nuntio erant,
tamen ad propius praesentiusque malum cautiores
4 esse. Et iam ad Hexapylum erant Hippocrates

[1] Since the soldiers would virtually be hostages, to ensure the support of many friends and relatives in the city.

Nor would they have spared any of them, had not B.C. 214
Epicydes and Hippocrates opposed the enraged multitude, not out of pity and a humane intent, but in order not to cut off the hope of their own return, and that they might not only keep the men themselves as loyal soldiers and at the same time hostages, but also win over their relatives and friends, first by so great a service, and then by the personal security.[1] And having learned how empty or faint a breath moves the crowd, they took a soldier from among those who had been besieged at Leontini and bribed him to carry to Syracuse a message in agreement with what had been falsely reported at the Mylas, and by showing himself to vouch for it and by relating the doubtful as things that he had seen, to inflame men's anger.

XXXII. This man was not only believed by the common people, but on being admitted to the Senate House, he stirred the senate as well. Some men of consequence openly declared it was very well that the avarice and cruelty of the Romans had been revealed at Leontini; that if they had entered Syracuse they would have done the same things or even more terrible, in proportion to the greater prize for avarice there. Accordingly, they all voted that the gates should be closed and the city guarded. But not all were afraid of the same persons or hated the same men. Among the whole military class and a large part of the common people the Roman name was hated. As for the generals and a few of the best citizens, although they had been misled by the false news, they were nevertheless more circumspect in the face of a danger more immediately impending. And already Hippocrates

A.U.C. 540 atque Epicydes, serebanturque conloquia per propinquos popularium qui in exercitu erant, ut portas aperirent sinerentque communem patriam defendi ab
5 impetu Romanorum. Iam unis foribus Hexapyli apertis coepti erant recipi, cum praetores intervenerunt. Et primo imperio minisque, deinde auctoritate deterrendo, postremo, ut omnia vana erant, obliti maiestatis precibus agebant ne proderent patriam tyranni ante satellitibus et tum corruptoribus
6 exercitus. Sed surdae ad ea omnia [1] aures concitatae multitudinis erant, nec minore intus vi quam foris portae effringebantur, effractisque omnibus toto
7 Hexapylo agmen receptum est. Praetores in Achradinam cum iuventute popularium confugiunt. Mercennarii milites perfugaeque et quidquid regiorum militum Syracusis erat agmen hostium augent.
8 Ita Achradina quoque primo impetu capitur, praetorumque nisi qui inter tumultum effugerunt omnes
9 interficiuntur. Nox caedibus finem fecit. Postero die servi ad pilleum vocati et carcere vincti emissi; confusaque haec omnis multitudo Hippocraten atque Epicyden creant praetores; Syracusaeque, cum breve tempus libertas adfulsisset, in antiquam servitutem reciderant.

XXXIII. Haec nuntiata cum essent Romanis, ex Leontinis mota sunt extemplo castra ad Syracusas.

[1] ad ea omnia *Böttcher*: ad omnia *Madvig*: aditomnium *P*: adeo omnium $P^{2?}$(1).

---

[1] Cf. xvi. 18.

and Epicydes were at the Hexapylon, and there were communications through intermediaries who were relatives of citizens in the army: that they should open the gates and allow the defence of the city, their common home, against attack by the Romans. By this time one of the gates of the Hexapylon had been opened, and by it they had begun to be admitted, when the generals intervened. And at first by their military authority and by threats, then by using their personal influence to restrain them, finally, when all was without affect, disregarding dignity they prayed them not to betray their native city to former minions of the tyrant and present seducers of the army. But the ears of the excited crowd were deaf to all that; and the gates were being forced with no less violence from within than from without, and when all had been forced, the column was admitted through the whole breadth of the Hexapylon. The generals with the younger citizens flee for refuge to Achradina. The mercenary soldiers and deserters and such royal troops as were at Syracuse swell the column of the enemy. Thus Achradina also is taken by assault, and all the magistrates, except those who escaped in the midst of the uproar, are slain. Night put an end to the slaughter. On the next day slaves were called to wear the cap of freedom [1] and criminals in chains released from prison; and all this assorted multitude elected Hippocrates and Epicydes generals. And Syracuse, after the light of liberty had shone upon it for a short time, had fallen back into its old-time servitude. B.C. 214

XXXIII. When these facts were reported to the Romans, the camp was at once removed from Leontini

A.U.C. 540

2 Et ab Appio legati per portum missi forte in quinqueremi erant. Praemissa quadriremis cum intrasset
3 fauces portus, capitur; legati aegre effugerunt. Et iam non modo pacis sed ne belli quidem iura relicta erant, cum Romanus exercitus ad Olympium—Iovis id templum est—mille et quingentos passus ab urbe
4 castra posuit. Inde quoque legatos praemitti placuit; quibus, ne intrarent urbem, extra portam Hippocrates atque Epicydes obviam cum suis pro-
5 cesserunt. Romanus orator non bellum se Syracusanis sed opem auxiliumque adferre ait, et eis qui ex media caede elapsi perfugerint ad se, et eis qui metu oppressi foediorem non exilio solum sed etiam
6 morte servitutem patiantur; nec caedem nefandam sociorum inultam Romanos passuros. Itaque, si eis qui ad se perfugerint tutus in patriam reditus pateat,[1] caedis auctores dedantur, et libertas legesque Syracusanis restituantur, nihil armis opus esse; si ea non fiant, quicumque in mora sit bello perse-
7 cuturos. Ad ea Epicydes, si qua ad se mandata haberent, responsum eis ait se daturos fuisse; cum in eorum ad quos venerint manu res Syracusana esset,
8 tum reverterentur. Si bello lacesserent, ipsa re intellecturos nequaquam idem esse Syracusas ac

[1] pateat *Crévier*: pateat et *Walters*: pateret *P*(1).

---

[1] Westward of the Great Harbour, plainly visible from the Island and from part of Achradina. Near this great temple the Athenians had encamped, as also the Carthaginians, in other sieges. Two columns still stand.

to Syracuse. And, as it happened, legates had been sent by Appius by way of the harbour on a five-banker. The four-banker sent in advance was captured on entering the narrows. The legates barely escaped. And now there remained no longer any rights even of war, not to say of peace, when the Roman army pitched camp at the Olympium, that is, the Temple of Jupiter,[1] a mile and a half from the city. From this place also it was decided to send legates in advance. To prevent their entering the city, Hippocrates and Epicydes and their retinue advanced beyond the gate to meet them. The speaker for the Romans said he was not bringing war, but aid and comfort to the Syracusans, both to those who, escaping from the midst of the slaughter, had sought refuge with the Romans, and to those who, subdued by their fear, were enduring a slavery more shameful, not only than exile, but even than death; and that the Romans would not leave the atrocious slaughter of their allies unavenged. Accordingly, if a safe return to their native city should be open to those who had sought refuge with the Romans, if those responsible for the slaughter should be surrendered and their freedom and laws restored to the Syracusans, there was no need of arms. If those conditions should not be met, the Romans would wage war against every man who caused delay. In reply Epicydes said that, if their message had been addressed to his colleague and himself, they would have given them an answer. When the Syracusan state should be under the control of the men to whom they came, then let them return. Should they make war, they would find from actual experience that to attack Syracuse was by no means the same as B.C. 214

A.U.C. 540 Leontinos oppugnare. Ita legatis relictis portas clausit.

9 Inde terra marique simul coeptae oppugnari Syracusae, terra ab Hexapylo, mari ab Achradina, cuius murus fluctu adluitur. Et quia, sicut Leontinos terrore ac primo impetu ceperant, non diffidebant vastam disiectamque spatio urbem parte aliqua se invasuros, omnem apparatum oppugnandarum urbium muris admoverunt. XXXIV. Et habuisset tanto impetu coepta res fortunam, nisi unus homo Syra-
2 cusis ea tempestate fuisset. Archimedes is erat, unicus spectator caeli siderumque, mirabilior tamen inventor ac machinator bellicorum tormentorum operumque quibus quicquid[1] hostes ingenti mole
3 agerent ipse perlevi momento ludificaretur. Muros per inaequalis ductos[2] colles, pleraque alta et difficilia aditu, submissa quaedam et quae planis vallibus adiri possent, ut cuique aptum visum est loco, ita
4 genere omni tormentorum instruxit. Achradinae murum, qui, ut ante dictum est, mari adluitur, segaginta[3] quinqueremibus Marcellus oppugnabat.
5 Ex ceteris navibus sagittarii funditoresque et velites etiam, quorum telum ad remittendum inhabile imperitis est, vix quemquam sine vulnere consistere
6 in muro patiebantur; hi, quia spatio missilibus opus est, procul muro tenebant naves: iunctae aliae binae

[1] quicquid *Madvig*: *om.* *P*(1): si quid *Weissenborn.*
[2] muros . . . ductos *Weissenborn*: murus . . . ductus *P*(1): murum . . . ductum *z* *Madvig.*
[3] sexaginta *Böttcher*: ex (*for* LX *or* ex LX) *P*(1).

---

[1] Livy does not mention Archimedes' celebrity as a mathematician.
[2] The number sixty agrees with Polybius VIII. 4(6). 1.

to attack Leontini. So he left the ambassadors and closed the gates. B.C. 214

Thereupon began the siege of Syracuse at the same time by land and by sea, by land from the side of the Hexapylon, by sea from that of Achradina, the wall of which is washed by the waves. And because, having taken Leontini by a panic and the first assault, the Romans did not doubt that at some point they would make their way into a city immense and widely scattered, they brought all their equipment for besieging cities up to the walls. XXXIV. And an undertaking begun with so vigorous an assault would have met with success if one man had not been at Syracuse at that time. It was Archimedes, an unrivalled observer of the heavens and the stars, more remarkable, however, as inventor and contriver of artillery and engines of war, by which with the least pains he frustrated whatever the enemy undertook with vast efforts.[1] The walls, carried along uneven hills, mainly high positions and difficult to approach, but some of them low and accessible from level ground, were equipped by him with every kind of artillery, as seemed suited to each place. The wall of Achradina, which, as has been said already, is washed by the sea, was attacked by Marcellus with sixty five-bankers.[2] From most[3] of the ships archers and slingers, also light-armed troops, whose weapon is difficult for the inexpert to return,[4] allowed hardly anyone to stand on the wall without being wounded; and these men kept their ships at a distance from the wall, since range is needed for missile weapons.

[3] "Most," since *ceterae* is contrasted with *aliae* in § 6 (eight in Polybius).

[4] Owing to the skill required in using the thong (*amentum*).

A.U.C. 540 quinqueremes demptis interioribus remis, ut latus
7 lateri adplicaretur, cum exteriore ordine remorum
velut una navis agerentur, turres contabulatas
machinamentaque alia quatiendis muris portabant.
8 Adversus hunc navalem apparatum Archimedes
variae magnitudinis tormenta in muris disposuit.
In eas quae procul erant navis saxa ingenti pondere
emittebat, propiores levioribus eoque magis crebris
9 petebat telis; postremo, ut sui volnere intacti tela
in hostem ingererent, murum ab imo ad summum
crebris cubitalibus fere cavis aperuit, per quae cava
pars sagittis, pars scorpionibus modicis ex occulto
10 petebant hostem. Quae [1] propius [2] subibant naves,
quo interiores ictibus tormentorum essent, in eas
tollenone super murum eminente ferrea manus,
firmae catenae inligata, cum iniecta prorae esset
gravique libramento plumbi [3] recelleret ad solum,
11 suspensa prora navem in puppim statuebat; dein remissa subito velut ex muro cadentem navem cum ingenti trepidatione nautarum ita undae adfligebat [4]
ut, etiamsi recta reciderat,[5] aliquantum aquae acci-
12 peret. Ita maritima oppugnatio est elusa omnisque
spes eo [6] versa ut totis viribus terra adgrederentur.

[1] quae *P*(1) : quia *Madvig* : *om. Walters.*

[2] propius *P*(1), *adding* quaedam (*retained by Madvig, Walters* : *om. x Crévier*).

[3] plumbi *P*(10) : blumbi *C* : plumbum *Heller, Conway.*

[4] adfligebat *Sigonius* : -bant *P*(1) *Walters.*

[5] reciderat *Gronovius* : recciderant *PCR* : reciderant *M*: -eret *BA*²*?Madvig* : -erent *DA*.

[6] eo *Böttcher* : ea *P*² : est *C* : ad(versa) *P*(10).

---

[1] Livy seems to mean the width on the inside, while Polybius gives a palm (three inches) as the width of a loophole on the outside (VIII. 7. 6).

Other five-bankers, paired together, with the inner oars removed, so that side was brought close to side, were propelled by the outer banks of oars like a single ship, and carried towers of several stories and in addition engines for battering walls. To meet this naval equipment Archimedes disposed artillery of different sizes on the walls. Against ships at a distance he kept discharging stones of great weight; nearer vessels he would attack with lighter and all the more numerous missile weapons. Finally, that his own men might discharge their bolts at the enemy without exposure to wounds, he opened the wall from bottom to top with numerous loopholes about a cubit wide,[1] and through these some, without being seen, shot at the enemy with arrows, others from small scorpions. As for the ships which came closer, in order to be inside the range of his artillery, against these an iron grapnel, fastened to a stout chain, would be thrown on to the bow by means of a swing-beam projecting over the wall. When this[2] sprung backward to the ground owing to the shifting of a heavy leaden weight, it would set the ship on its stern, bow in air. Then, suddenly released, it would dash the ship, falling, as it were, from the wall, into the sea, to the great alarm of the sailors, and with the result that, even if she fell upright, she would take considerable water. Thus the assault from the sea was baffled, and all hope shifted to a plan to attack from the land with all their forces. But that

B.C. 214

[2] Literally the grappling hook; but here, as if the *ferrea manus* might serve as a name for the entire crane, the reference is in fact to another part, viz. the beam, the after end of which sank to the ground inside the wall when the leaden weight was shifted. Polybius, VIII. 6(8). 1–4, gives a more detailed account.

A.U.C. 540
13 Sed ea quoque pars eodem omni apparatu tormentorum instructa erat Hieronis inpensis curaque per
14 multos annos, Archimedis unica arte. Natura etiam
adiuvabat loci, quod saxum, cui inposita muri funda-
menta sunt, magna parte ita proclive est ut non
solum missa tormento, sed etiam quae pondere suo
provoluta essent, graviter in hostem inciderent.
15 Eadem causa ad subeundum arduum aditum insta-
16 bilemque ingressum praebebat. Ita consilio habito,
quoniam[1] omnis conatus ludibrio esset, absistere
oppugnatione atque obsidendo tantum arcere terra
marique commeatibus hostem placuit.

XXXV. Interim Marcellus cum tertia fere parte
exercitus ad recipiendas urbes profectus quae in motu
rerum ad Carthaginienses defecerant, Helorum atque
2 Herbesum dedentibus ipsis recipit, Megara vi capta
diruit ac diripuit ad reliquorum ac maxime Syracusa-
3 norum terrorem. Per idem fere tempus et Himilco,
qui ad Pachyni promunturium classem diu tenuerat,
ad Heracleam, quam vocant Minoam, quinque et viginti milia peditum, tria equitum, duodecim elephantos
exposuit, nequaquam cum quantis copiis ante tenue-
4 rat ad Pachynum classem; sed, postquam ab Hippocrate occupatae Syracusae erant, profectus Carthaginem adiutusque ibi et ab legatis Hippocratis et litteris Hannibalis, qui venisse tempus aiebat Siciliae
5 per summum decus repetendae, et ipse haud vanus

[1] quoniam *Alschefski*: quo (*for* quom?) *P*(1): quod $\dot{A}^2x$: quando *Luchs*.

side also had been provided with the same complete equipment of artillery, at the expense and the pains of Hiero during many years, by the unrivalled art of Archimedes. The nature of the place [1] also helped, in that the rock on which the foundations of the wall were laid is generally so steep that not only missiles from a machine, but also whatever rolled down of its own weight fell heavily upon the enemy. The same circumstance made approach to the wall difficult and footing unsteady. So, after a war council, since every attempt was being balked, it was decided to give up the assault and merely by a blockade to cut off the enemy by land and sea from their supplies. B.C. 214

XXXV. Meanwhile Marcellus set out with about a third of his army to recover the cities which in the unsettled state of affairs had gone over to the Carthaginians. Helorus and Herbesus he did recover by their own surrender; Megara he took by assault, destroyed and plundered, to terrify the others and especially the Syracusans. About the same time also Himilco, who had long kept his fleet off the promontory of Pachynum, landed at Heraclea,[2] called Minoa, 25,000 infantry, 3,000 cavalry and twelve elephants, a very much larger force than that with which he had previously kept his fleet off Pachynum. But after Syracuse had been seized by Hippocrates, Himilco went to Carthage and was aided there both by the legates of Hippocrates and by a letter from Hannibal, who said the time had come to recover Sicily in the most honourable manner. Himilco

[1] Evidently meaning the northern face of Epipolae, the great triangle at whose western apex stood the fortress of Euryalus; cf. XXV. xxiv. 4; xxv. 2; v. Appendix.

[2] West of Agrigentum, on the south coast.

A.U.C. 540

praesens monitor facile perpulerat ut quantae maxime[1]
possent peditum equitumque copiae in Siciliam
6 traicerentur. Adveniens Heracleam, intra paucos
inde dies Agrigentum recepit; aliarumque civitatium,
quae partis Carthaginiensium erant, adeo accensae
sunt spes ad pellendos Sicilia Romanos ut postremo
etiam qui obsidebantur Syracusis animos sustulerint.
7 Et parte copiarum satis defendi urbem posse rati, ita
inter se munera belli partiti sunt ut Epicydes praeesset custodiae urbis, Hippocrates Himilconi coniunctus bellum adversus consulem Romanum gereret.
8 Cum decem milibus peditum, quingentis equitibus
nocte per intermissa custodiis loca profectus castra
9 circa Acrillas urbem ponebat. Munientibus super-
venit Marcellus ab Agrigento iam occupato, cum
frustra eo praevenire hostem festinans tetendisset,
rediens, nihil minus ratus quam illo tempore ac loco
10 Syracusanum sibi exercitum obvium fore; sed tamen
metu Himilconis Poenorumque, ut quibus nequaquam
eis copiis quas habebat par esset, quam poterat
maxime intentus atque agmine ad omnes casus composito ibat. XXXVI. Forte ea cura quae adversus Poenos praeparata erat[2] adversus Siculos usui fuit. Castris ponendis incompositos ac dispersos nanctus eos et
plerosque inermes quod peditum fuit circumvenit;
eques levi certamine inito cum Hippocrate Acras
perfugit.

[1] maxime *PBDA* : maximae *CRM Madvig.*
[2] erat *x* : *om. P*(1) *Walters, who rejects* quae (*or* q. *P*(7)).

---

[1] To the west of Syracuse, as was Acrae, xxxvi. 1.

himself, being an influential adviser, present in B.C. 214 person, had easily prevailed upon them to send across to Sicily the largest possible forces of infantry and cavalry. Arrived at Heraclea, he recovered Agrigentum within a few days. And the hopes of the other city-states which were on the side of the Carthaginians were so fired to drive the Romans out of Sicily that finally even those who were besieged at Syracuse took courage. And thinking the city could be sufficiently defended by a part of the forces, they so divided the military duties that Epicydes should be in charge of the defence of the city, and Hippocrates, together with Himilco, should carry on the war against the Roman consul. With 10,000 infantry and five hundred horse he set out by night through places unguarded and pitched camp near the city of Acrillae.[1] As they were fortifying, Marcellus arrived, returning from Agrigentum, which was already occupied, since it was in vain that he had endeavoured to anticipate the enemy by hastening thither. Nothing was farther from his thoughts than that a Syracusan army should meet him there at that time. Nevertheless, from fear of Himilco and the Carthaginians, being no match for them with the forces he had, he was advancing with all possible alertness and with a column so formed as to meet any emergency. XXXVI. The precaution which had been taken against Carthaginians served him, as it happened, against Sicilians. Coming upon them after they had broken ranks and were scattered in the act of pitching camp and mostly unarmed, he overwhelmed all the infantry. The cavalry, after a slight engagement, fled with Hippocrates to Acrae.

A.U.C. 540

2 Ea pugna deficientes ab Romanis cum cohibuisset
Siculos, Marcellus Syracusas redit; et post paucos dies
Himilco adiuncto Hippocrate ad flumen Anapum, octo
3 ferme inde milia, castra posuit. Sub idem forte [1]
tempus et naves longae quinque et quinquaginta
Carthaginiensium cum Bomilcare [2] in magnum por-
4 tum Syracusas ex alto decurrere, et Romana item classis, triginta quinqueremes, legionem primam Panor-
mi exposuere; versumque ab Italia bellum—adeo
uterque populus in Siciliam intentus fuit [3]—videri
5 poterat. Legionem Romanam quae exposita Panor-
mi erat venientem Syracusas praedae haud dubie sibi
6 futuram Himilco ratus via decipitur. Mediterraneo
namque Poenus itinere duxit; legio maritimis locis
classe prosequente ad Appium Claudium Pachynum
cum parte copiarum obviam progressum pervenit.
7 Nec diutius Poeni ad Syracusas morati sunt: et
Bomilcar simul parum fidens navibus suis duplici facile
numero classem habentibus Romanis, simul inutili
mora cernens nihil aliud ab suis quam inopiam
adgravari sociorum, velis in altum datis in Africam
8 transmisit, et Himilco, secutus nequiquam Marcellum
Syracusas, si qua priusquam maioribus copiis iun-
geretur occasio pugnandi esset, postquam ea nulla

[1] idem forte P^2(4) *Madvig*: itemfor *P*: idem fere *A Walters*.

[2] Bomilcare *P*(1), *adding* classis (*to which* $A^x x$ *add* praefecto), *rejected by Kästner*.

[3] fuit *Bekker, Madvig*: fuisse *P*(1), *joined with* videri.

---

[1] The small river of Syracuse, emptying into the Great Harbour. Near its mouth was a Roman camp; xxxiii. 3.

[2] Now Palermo; the chief city of Carthaginian Sicily, until taken by the Romans in 254 B.C.; Polybius I. xxxviii. fin.

Marcellus, by that battle having restrained the Sicilians inclined to revolt from the Romans, returned to Syracuse. And a few days later Himilco was joined by Hippocrates and pitched camp by the river Anapus,[1] about eight miles away. About the same time it so happened that fifty-five warships of the Carthaginians under Bomilcar sailed from the open sea into the Great Harbour of Syracuse, and also a Roman fleet of thirty quinqueremes debarked the first legion at Panormus.[2] And the war could be considered as now diverted from Italy, so intent were both nations upon Sicily. Himilco, thinking that the legion which had been landed at Panormus would certainly fall a prey to him on its way to Syracuse, was baffled by its route. For the Carthaginian led his troops along an inland road, while the legion, escorted by the fleet, made its way along the coast to Appius Claudius, who with a part of his forces had advanced as far as Pachynum [3] to meet it. And so the Carthaginians did not tarry longer near Syracuse. On the one hand Bomilcar, lacking confidence in his own ships, since the Romans had a fleet of fully double the number, and at the same time seeing that by useless delay the lack of supplies for the allies was only intensified by his forces, put out to sea and crossed over to Africa. On the other hand Himilco first followed Marcellus to Syracuse to no purpose, in the hope that there might be some opportunity for an engagement before he should unite with larger forces. Then, when no such opportunity fell to him, and he B.C. 214

[3] Probably an error for Pelorum, the north-eastern promontory of Sicily, since, with Agrigentum in the hands of the Carthaginians, the route via the western and southern coasts (much longer in any case) would have been impracticable.

A.U.C. 540 contigerat tutumque ad Syracusas et munimento
9 et viribus hostem cernebat, ne frustra adsidendo spec-
tandoque obsidionem sociorum tempus tereret, castra
inde movit, ut quocumque vocasset defectionis ab
Romano spes admoveret exercitum ac praesens suas
10 res foventibus adderet animos. Murgantiam primum
prodito ab ipsis praesidio Romano recipit, ubi frumenti
magna vis commeatusque omnis generis convecti erant
Romanis.

XXXVII. Ad hanc defectionem erecti sunt et aliarum civitatium animi, praesidiaque Romana aut pelle-
bantur arcibus aut prodita per fraudem opprimeban-
2 tur. Henna, excelso loco ac praerupto undique sita,
cum loco inexpugnabilis erat, tum praesidium in arce
validum praefectumque praesidii haud sane oppor-
3 tunum insidiantibus habebat. L. Pinarius erat, vir
acer et qui plus in eo ne posset decipi quam in fide
Siculorum reponeret. Et tum intenderant eum ad
cavendi omnia curam tot auditae proditiones defec-
4 tionesque urbium et clades praesidiorum. Itaque
nocte dieque iuxta parata instructaque omnia custodiis ac vigiliis erant, nec ab armis aut loco suo miles
5 abscedebat. Quod ubi Hennensium principes, iam
pacti cum Himilcone de proditione praesidii, animad-
verterunt, nulli occasioni fraudis Romanum patere,
6 palam erat [1] agendum. Urbem arcemque suae
potestatis aiunt debere esse, si liberi in societatem,

[1] palam erat *Lipsius*: patuerat *P*: placuerat *P*[2](1): per vim erat *Salmasius*.

---

[1] Cf. xxvii. 5.

[2] The most commanding city-site in Sicily, with its citadel 3200 ft. above the sea. Described by Cicero *in Verr.* IV. 107. Henna was the centre of the worship of Demeter and Persephone; cf. xxxix. 8.

saw the enemy safe near Syracuse thanks to his fortifications and military strength, fearing to waste time in besieging him in vain and watching the blockade of the allies, he moved his camp away. His purpose was to bring up his army to any point to which the hope of revolting from the Romans might call him, and by his presence to give encouragement to those who inclined to support his cause. Murgantia [1] was first recovered, after the inhabitants had betrayed the Roman garrison. There a great quantity of grain and supplies of every kind had been accumulated for the Romans. B.C. 214

XXXVII. Upon this revolt, feeling was aroused in other city-states, and Roman garrisons were being either driven out of citadels or betrayed by treachery and slain. Henna,[2] perched on a lofty site with cliffs on every side, was not only impregnable from its position, but also had a strong garrison in its citadel and a garrison commander who was certainly no easy prey to plotters. This was Lucius Pinarius, a man of high spirit and one who gave more weight to precautions against possible deception than to the honour of Sicilians. And at this time the news of so many cities betrayed and in revolt and of so many garrisons destroyed had made him more intent upon guarding against every danger. Accordingly every position had been prepared and provided with guards and sentinels night and day; and the soldier did not leave his arms and his post. When this was noticed by the leading men of Henna, who had already made an agreement with Himilco to betray the garrison, namely, that the Roman left no opportunity for treachery, they were forced to act openly. They said that city and citadel ought to be under their own control, if as free men

A.U.C. 540 non servi in custodiam traditi essent Romanis.
7 Itaque claves portarum reddi sibi aequom censent: bonis sociis fidem suam maximum vinculum esse, et ita sibi populum Romanum senatumque gratias habiturum, si volentes ac non coacti mansissent in
8 amicitia. Ad ea Romanus se in praesidio impositum esse dicere ab imperatore suo clavesque portarum et custodiam arcis ab eo accepisse, quae nec suo nec Hennensium arbitrio haberet, sed eius qui commisis-
9 set. Praesidio decedere apud Romanos capital esse, et nece liberorum etiam suorum eam noxiam[1] parentes sanxisse. Consulem Marcellum haud procul esse: ad eum mitterent legatos cuius iuris atque
10 arbitrii res[2] esset. Se vero negare illi missuros testarique, si verbis nihil agerent, vindictam aliquam
11 libertatis suae quaesituros. Tum Pinarius: at illi, si ad consulem gravarentur mittere, sibi saltem darent populi concilium, ut sciretur, utrum paucorum ea denuntiatio an universae civitatis esset. Consensa in posterum diem contio.

XXXVIII. Postquam ab eo conloquio in arcem sese recepit, convocatis militibus[3] "Credo ego vos audisse, milites" inquit, "quem ad modum praesidia Romana ab Siculis circumventa et oppressa sint per hos dies.
2 Eam vos fraudem deum primo benignitate, dein vestra ipsi virtute dies noctesque perstando ac pervigilando

[1] noxiam *Weissenborn*: *om.* *P*(1).
[2] res *Crévier, Fabri*: *om.* *P*(1) *Walters.*
[3] militibus A^2x: quibus *P*(2)*A?*: aliquibus C^4: sociis *x*: suis *Gronovius.*

they had entered into alliance with the Romans, B.C. 214 and had not been consigned to custody as slaves. Consequently they said they thought it right that the keys of the gates should be restored to them. For good allies their loyalty was the strongest bond, and the Roman people and senate would be grateful to them only in case they remained in their friendship willingly and not under compulsion. In reply to this the Roman commandant said that he had been placed at his post by his general and had received from him both the keys to the gates and the guarding of the citadel, to keep them, not at his own discretion nor that of the people of Henna, but of the man who had confided them to him. To leave one's post was among the Romans a capital offence, and fathers had punished that crime with the death even of their own sons. The consul Marcellus was not far away; they should send legates to him who had the right to decide the matter. But they said that they would not send them, and asserted that if they accomplished nothing by words, they would seek some means of recovering their freedom. Upon that Pinarius said that, if they objected to sending to the consul, very well, let them at least give him an assembly of the people, that it might be known whether their demand was that of a few men or of the whole city. They agreed to an assembly on the next day.

XXXVIII. Returning from that conference to the citadel, he called his men together and said: "I believe you have heard, soldiers, how in these days Roman garrisons have been beset and overwhelmed by Sicilians. Such treachery you have escaped, thanks first to the favour of the gods, and then to your own courage, by standing guard day and night

A.U.C. 540 in armis vitastis. Utinam relicum tempus nec patien-
3 do infanda nec faciendo traduci posset![1] Haec occulta in fraude cautio est qua usi adhuc sumus; cui quoniam parum succedit, aperte ac propalam claves portarum reposcunt; quas simul tradiderimus, Carthaginiensium extemplo Henna erit, foediusque hic trucidabimur quam Murgantiae praesidium inter-
4 fectum est. Noctem unam aegre ad consultandum sumpsi, qua vos certiores periculi instantis facerem. Orta luce contionem habituri sunt ad criminandum
5 me concitandumque in vos populum. Itaque crastino die aut vestro aut Hennensium sanguine Henna inundabitur. Nec praeoccupati spem ullam nec occupantes periculi quicquam habebitis; qui prior
6 strinxerit ferrum, eius victoria erit. Intenti ergo omnes armatique signum expectabitis. Ego in contione ero et tempus, quoad omnia instructa sint,
7 loquendo altercandoque traham. Cum toga signum dedero, tum mihi undique clamore sublato turbam invadite ac sternite omnia ferro; et cavete quicquam[2]
8 supersit cuius[3] aut vis aut fraus timeri possit. Vos, Ceres mater ac Proserpina, precor, ceteri superi infernique di, qui hanc urbem, hos sacratos lacus lucosque colitis, ut ita nobis volentes propitii adsitis, si vitandae, non inferendae fraudis causa hoc consilii
9 capimus. Pluribus vos, milites, hortarer, si cum armatis dimicatio futura esset; inermes, incautos ad

[1] posset $A^x z$: possit *Valla*: potest *P*(1).
[2] quicquam *P*(1) *Conway*: quisquam $C^2 x$ *Madvig*.
[3] cuius *Alschefski*: quiusa *P*: a quibus P^2(1).

under arms. Would that the remaining time B.C. 214
could be passed without either suffering or committing atrocities! In covert trickery the method of defence is that which we have so far employed. Since the trick does not succeed, they demand back the keys of the gates openly and above board. And the moment we surrender them, Henna will be in the hands of the Carthaginians, and we shall be more cruelly slaughtered here than was the garrison slain at Murgantia. With difficulty I have gained for deliberation one night in which to inform you of the impending danger. At daybreak they are to hold an assembly for the purpose of accusing me and arousing the people against you. And so tomorrow Henna will be deluged either with your blood or with that of the Hennensians. If forestalled, you will have no hope, nor any danger if you forestall them. Who first draws the sword will have the victory. Therefore, alert and armed, you will all await the signal. I shall be in the assembly, and I will kill time in speaking and disputing, until everything is ready. When I give the signal with my toga, then do you from all sides raise a shout, attack the crowd, and strike down everyone with the sword; and see to it that no one survives whose violence or treachery can be feared. Mother Ceres and Proserpina, and all the other gods, above and below, who inhabit this city, these hallowed lakes and groves, I pray that ye attend us with your favour and support, if so be that we are taking this step for the purpose of guarding against treachery, not of practising it. I should exhort you, soldiers, at greater length if your battle were to be with armed men. Unarmed and off their guard, you will massacre them to your hearts' content.

A.U.C. 540 satietatem trucidabitis; et consulis castra in propinquo sunt, ne quid ab Himilcone et Carthaginiensibus timeri possit."

XXXIX. Ab hac adhortatione dimissi corpora curant. Postero die alii aliis locis ad obsidenda itinera claudendosque oppositi[1] exitus; pars maxima super theatrum circaque, adsueti et ante
2 spectaculo contionum, consistunt. Productus ad populum a magistratibus praefectus Romanus cum consulis de ea re ius ac potestatem esse, non suam,
3 et pleraque eadem quae pridie dixisset, et primo sensim ac pauci, mox plures[2] reddere claves, dein iam una voce id omnes iuberent cunctantique et differenti ferociter minitarentur nec viderentur ultra vim ultimam dilaturi, tum praefectus toga signum, ut
4 convenerat, dedit, milites que intenti dudum ac parati alii superne in aversam contionem clamore sublato decurrunt, alii ad exitus theatri conferti
5 obsistunt. Caeduntur Hennenses cavea inclusi coacervanturque non caede solum sed etiam fuga, cum super aliorum alii capita ruerent, et[3] integri[4]
6 sauciis,[5] vivi mortuis incidentes cumularentur. Inde passim discurritur et urbis captae modo fugaque et caedes omnia tenet nihilo remissiore militum ira quod

[1] oppositi A^x *Valla*: opsiti *A*: -positis M^2: -ponitis *P*(2).

[2] pauci, mox plures *Riemann*: plus *P*(1): plures A^xz *Madvig*: pauci *Weissenborn*.

[3] et *Madvig*: *om.* *P*(1).

[4] integri *P*(1): -gris M^9 *Conway*.

[5] sauciis *BDA*: -ci *P*: -ii P^2(4)M^9 *Conway*.

And the consul's camp is near; I tell you this that B.C. 214
you may have no possible fear from Himilco and the Carthaginians."

XXXIX. Dismissed immediately after this exhortation, they took food and rest. On the following day they were posted in different places, to occupy the roads and close the ways of escape. The majority took their positions above and around the theatre, being already familiar with the sight of an assembly. The Roman commandant, being brought before the people by the magistrates, said that right and authority in the matter belonged to the consul, not to himself, and in general the same things he had said the day before. And at first insensibly and only a few, presently a larger number, then all, now with one voice kept bidding him to deliver the keys; and when he delayed and postponed, they repeated savage threats and apparently would not further postpone violence, their last resort. Thereupon the prefect gave the signal with his toga, as had been agreed, and the soldiers, alert and ready long before, dashed down, some of them from above, upon the rear of the assembly with a shout, while others, massed at the exits of the theatre, blocked the way. The men of Henna, shut up in the cavea, were slain and piled together not only owing to the slaughter, but also by the panic, since they rushed down over each others' heads, and as the unharmed fell upon the wounded, the living upon the dead, they were lying in heaps. Thence the soldiers scattered in every direction, and, just as in a captured city, flight and slaughter were in complete possession, while the wrath of the soldiers was not a whit less intense because they were slaying an unarmed

A.U.C. 540

turbam inermem caedebant quam si periculum par et
7 ardor certaminis eos inritaret. Ita Henna aut malo
aut necessario facinore retenta.

Marcellus nec factum inprobavit et praedam Hennensium militibus concessit, ratus timore deterritos
8 proditionibus praesidiorum Siculos. Atque ea clades,
ut urbis in media Sicilia sitae claraeque vel ob insignem munimento naturali locum vel ob sacrata omnia vestigiis raptae quondam Proserpinae, prope uno
9 die omnem Siciliam pervasit; et quia caede infanda
rebantur non hominum tantum sed etiam deorum
sedem violatam esse, tum vero etiam qui[1] ante dubii
10 fuerant defecere ad Poenos. Hippocrates inde
Murgantiam, Himilco Agrigentum sese recepit, cum
acciti a proditoribus nequiquam ad Hennam exercitum
11 admovissent. Marcellus retro in Leontinos redit
frumentoque et commeatibus aliis in castra convectis,
praesidio modico ibi relicto ad Syracusas obsidendas
12 venit. Inde Appio Claudio Romam ad consulatum
petendum misso T. Quinctium Crispinum in eius
13 locum classi castrisque praeficit veteribus; ipse
hibernacula quinque milia passuum ab Hexapylo—
Leonta vocant locum—communiit aedificavitque.
Haec in Sicilia usque ad principium hiemis gesta.

XL. Eadem aestate et cum Philippo rege quod
2 iam ante suspectum fuerat motum bellum est. Legati

[1] etiam qui *Madvig* : qui etiam *P*(1).

[1] As in Cicero *in Verr.* IV. 107 the very place reminds one how Pluto carried off Proserpina from the meadows below Henna.

crowd, than if equal danger and ardour for the fray were spurring them on. So by an act, it may have been criminal, it may have been unavoidable, Henna was held. B.C. 214

Marcellus, without reproving the act, allowed the soldiers to plunder the Hennensians, thinking the frightened Sicilians had been deterred from betraying their garrisons. And as was natural in the case of a city in the heart of Sicily and famous, whether for the remarkable natural defences of its site, or as hallowed everywhere by the footprints of Proserpina, long ago carried away,[1] news of the massacre made its way over the whole of Sicily almost in a single day. And then in truth, since they thought that the abode, not of men only but also of gods, had been desecrated by an atrocious massacre, even those who till then had wavered went over to the Carthaginians. Hippocrates thereupon went back to Murgantia, Himilco to Agrigentum, after bringing up their army to Henna to no purpose at the summons of the traitors. Marcellus returned to Leontini, had grain and other supplies brought into the camp, left a suitable garrison there and came to Syracuse to carry on the siege. He then relieved Appius Claudius, to sue for the consulship at Rome, and in his place put Titus Quinctius Crispinus in command of the fleet and the old camp.[2] As for himself, he fortified and built winter quarters five miles from the Hexapylon—Leon they call the place. Such were the events in Sicily up to the beginning of the winter.

XL. The same summer the war with King Philip also that for some time had been foreshadowed broke

[2] Cf. xxxiii. 3; XXV. xxvi. 4. The new winter camp was northwest of Syracuse.

A.U.C. 540 ab Orico ad M. Valerium praetorem venerunt, praesidentem classi Brundisio Calabriaeque circa litoribus, nuntiantes Philippum primum Apolloniam temptasse lembis biremibus centum viginti flumine adverso sub-
3 vectum; deinde, ut ea res tardior spe fuerit, ad Oricum clam nocte exercitum admovisse; eamque urbem, sitam in plano neque moenibus neque viris atque armis validam, primo impetu oppressam esse.
4 Haec nuntiantes orabant ut opem ferret hostemque haud dubium Romanis mari ac terra a maritimis urbibus arceret, quae ob nullam aliam causam nisi
5 quod imminerent Italiae, peterentur. M. Valerius duorum milium praesidio relicto praepositoque[1] eis P. Valerio legato cum classe instructa parataque et, quod longae naves militum capere non poterant in
6 onerarias inpositis altero die Oricum pervenit; urbemque eam levi tenente praesidio quod rex[2] recedens inde reliquerat haud magno certamine
7 recepit. Legati eo ab Apollonia venerunt, nuntiantes in obsidione sese, quod deficere ab Romanis nollent, esse neque sustinere ultra vim Macedonum
8 posse, ni[3] praesidium mittatur Romanum. Facturum se quae vellent pollicitus, duo milia delectorum mili-

[1] praepositoque *Crévier*: q. *or* que *only* *P*(1).
[2] rex *Fabri* (*before* reliquerat *Gronovius*): *om.* *P*(1).
[3] ni *Riemann*: nil *P*: nisi $P^{2?}$(1).

[1] In southern Illyria (Albania), at the south end of the bay behind the Acroceraunian Mountains, almost directly opposite Brundisium.

out. Legates came from Oricum[1] to Marcus Valerius, the praetor,[2] who with his fleet was guarding Brundisium and the neighbouring coast of Calabria. They reported that Philip had first sailed up the river with a hundred and twenty small vessels having two banks of oars and attacked Apollonia;[3] and that then, when the undertaking proved slower than he anticipated, had secretly moved his army to Oricum by night; also that that city, situated in a plain and not strong either in walls or armed men, had been taken by assault. Making this report, they begged him to lend aid and by land and sea to keep an undoubted enemy of the Romans away from the coast cities, which were being attacked for no other reason than that they faced Italy. Marcus Valerius, after leaving a garrison of two thousand soldiers and placing Publius Valerius, his lieutenant, in command of them, with his fleet drawn up and in readiness, while such soldiers as the warships could not accommodate had been placed on transports, came on the second day to Oricum; and as only a small garrison which the king had left when he withdrew held the city, he recaptured it after slight resistance. To it came legates from Apollonia, reporting that they were being besieged because they refused to revolt from the Romans and could no longer withstand the attack of the Macedonians, unless a Roman force should be sent. Valerius promised to do as they desired, and sent two thousand picked soldiers in B.C. 214

[2] Strictly propraetor; x. 4; xx. 12.

[3] The city, in southern Illyria, and allied with Rome since 229 B.C., lay near the river Aoüs and about seven miles inland, about thirty miles north of Oricum. Later it attracted young Romans pursuing their studies, *e.g.* Octavian.

A.U.C. 540 tum navibus longis mittit ad ostium fluminis cum
praefecto socium Q. Naevio Crista, viro inpigro et
9 perito militiae. Is expositis in terram militibus navi-
busque Oricum retro, unde venerat, ad ceteram classem remissis, milites procul a flumine per viam minime
ab regiis obsessam duxit et nocte, ita ut nemo hostium
10 sentiret, urbem est ingressus. Diem insequentem
quievere, dum praefectus iuventutem Apolloniatium
armaque et urbis vires inspiceret. Ubi ea visa
inspectaque satis animorum fecere, simulque ab
exploratoribus conperit quanta socordia ac negle-
11 gentia apud hostes esset, silentio noctis ab urbe sine
ullo tumultu egressus castra hostium adeo neglecta
atque aperta intravit ut satis constaret prius mille
hominum vallum intrasse quam quisquam sentiret,
ac, si caede abstinuissent, pervenire ad tabernaculum
12 regium potuisse. Caedes proximorum portae excitavit hostes. Inde tantus terror pavorque omnis
occupavit ut non modo alius quisquam arma caperet
13 aut castris pellere hostem conaretur, sed etiam ipse
rex, sicut somno excitus erat, prope seminudus
fugiens militi quoque, nedum regi, vix decoro habitu,
ad flumen navisque perfugerit. Eodem et alia turba
14 effusa est. Paulo minus tria milia militum in castris
aut capta aut occisa; plus tamen hominum aliquanto
15 captum quam caesum est. Castris direptis Apol-
loniatae catapultas, ballistas tormentaque alia quae

[1] *I.e.* the Aoüs.

warships to the mouth of the river[1] under the command of a prefect of the allies, Quintus Naevius Crista, a man of action and an experienced soldier. He landed his men, sent the ships back to the rest of the fleet at Oricum, his starting-point, led his soldiers at a distance from the river along the road least beset by the king's troops and entered the city by night, so that no one of the enemy was aware of it. The following day they rested, that the prefect might inspect the young men of Apollonia and the arms and resources of the city. The result of that inspection gave him sufficient encouragement, and he learned also from scouts what carelessness and indifference there was among the enemy. Thereupon in the silence of the night and without making any noise he went out of the city and entered the enemy's camp, so neglected and open that a thousand men had entered the wall before anyone was aware of it, so it was generally asserted; also, that if they had refrained from slaughter, they could have reached the king's tent. The slaughter of the men nearest to the gate aroused the enemy. Then such alarm and panic took possession of them all that not only did no one else seize his arms and attempt to drive the enemy out of the camp, but even the king himself, fleeing almost half-naked, just as he was when awakened, fled to the river and his ships in a garb scarcely seemly even for a common soldier, much less a king. Thither the rest of the disorderly crowd also poured out. Little fewer than three thousand soldiers were either captured or slain in the camp; a considerably larger number of men were captured than slain. After plundering the camp the Apollonians carried away the catapults, ballistae and other

A.U.C. 540 oppugnandae urbi conparata erant ad tuenda moenia, si quando similis fortuna venisset, Apolloniam devexere; cetera omnis praeda castrorum Romanis
16 concessa est. Haec cum Oricum essent nuntiata, M. Valerius classem extemplo ad ostium fluminis duxit,
17 ne navibus capessere fugam rex posset. Itaque Philippus, neque terrestri neque navali certamini satis fore parem se fidens, subductis navibus atque incensis terra Macedoniam petiit magna ex parte inermi exercitu spoliatoque. Romana classis cum M. Valerio Orici hibernavit.

XLI. Eodem anno in Hispania varie res gestae. Nam priusquam Romani amnem Hiberum transirent, ingentes copias Hispanorum Mago et Hasdrubal fude-
2 runt; defecissetque ab Romanis ulterior Hispania, ni P. Cornelius raptim traducto exercitu Hiberum dubiis
3 sociorum animis in tempore advenisset. Primo ad Castrum Album—locus est insignis caede magni
4 Hamilcaris—castra Romani habuere. Arx erat munita et convexerant ante frumentum; tamen, quia omnia circa hostium plena erant, agmenque Romanum inpune incursatum ab equitibus hostium fuerat et ad duo milia aut moratorum aut palantium per agros interfecta, cessere inde Romani propius pacata loca et
5 ad montem Victoriae castra communivere. Eo Cn. Scipio cum omnibus copiis et Hasdrubal Gisgonis filius, tertius Carthaginiensium dux, cum exercitu iusto

[1] Probably modern Alicante, on the coast and northeast of Carthago Nova; built by Hamilcar Barca, who fell in battle there 229–8 B.C.

[2] Situation unknown.

engines which had been provided for a siege of the city to Apollonia, in order to defend their walls, if ever a similar situation should arise. All the remaining booty of the camp was left to the Romans. When this news reached Oricum, Marcus Valerius at once led his fleet to the mouth of the river, to prevent the king from escaping by ship. And so Philip, believing he would not be quite equal to a battle either on land or sea, stranded his ships, set fire to them, and started for Macedonia with an army in large part disarmed and despoiled. The Roman fleet wintered at Oricum under the command of Marcus Valerius. B.C. 214

XLI. In the same year operations in Spain were chequered. For Mago and Hasdrubal, before the Romans should cross the Ebro, routed immense forces of Spaniards. And Farther Spain would have revolted from the Romans if Publius Cornelius had not hastily led his army across the Hiberus and arrived in the nick of time, while the allies were still wavering. At first the Romans had their camp at Castrum Album,[1] noted as the place where the great Hamilcar fell. The citadel had been fortified and they had previously brought in grain. Yet the country all around was filled with the enemy, and the Roman column had been attacked with impunity by the enemy's cavalry and about two thousand men, either straggling or scattered over the farms, had been slain. The Romans therefore retired from the place to a position nearer peaceful regions and fortified a camp at Victory Mountain.[2] Thither came Gnaeus Scipio with all his troops, and Hasdrubal the son of Gisgo, making three Carthaginian generals and a complete army; and all three established themselves across

A.U.C. 540 advenit, contraque castra Romana trans fluvium
6 omnes consedere. P. Scipio cum expeditis clam
profectus ad loca circa visenda haud fefellit hostes,
oppressissentque eum in patentibus campis, ni
tumulum in propinquo cepisset. Ibi quoque cir-
7 cumsessus adventu fratris obsidione eximitur. Castulo, urbs Hispaniae valida ac nobilis et adeo con-
iuncta societate Poenis ut uxor inde Hannibali esset,
8 ad Romanos defecit. Carthaginienses Iliturgim
oppugnare adorti, quia praesidium ibi Romanum
erat, videbanturque inopia maxime eum locum
9 expugnaturi. Cn. Scipio, ut sociis praesidioque ferret
opem, cum legione expedita profectus inter bina castra cum magna caede hostium urbem est ingressus et
10 postero die eruptione aeque felici pugnavit. Supra
duodecim milia hominum caesa duobus proeliis, plus
mille hominum captum cum sex et triginta militari-
11 bus signis. Ita ab Iliturgi recessum est. Bigerra inde
urbs—socii [1] et hi [2] Romanorum erant [3]—a Carthaginiensibus oppugnari coepta est. Eam obsidionem
sine certamine adveniens Cn. Scipio solvit.

XLII. Ad Mundam exinde castra Punica mota et
2 Romani eo confestim secuti sunt. Ibi signis conlatis
pugnatum per quattuor ferme horas; egregieque
vincentibus Romanis signum receptui est datum,
quod Cn. Scipionis femur tragula confixum erat

[1] socii *Hertz*: socie *P*: socia P^1(1) *Walters*.
[2] hi *P Hertz*: hec *or* haec P^1(1) *Walters*.
[3] erant *PCR*^{1}*M*: erat C^2(13).

---

[1] In the upper valley of the Baetis (Guadalquivir), on the main road from the Pyrenees to Gades.

[2] Imilce, if Silius Italicus (III. 97 and 106) is correct.

[3] On the left bank of the Baetis, southwest of Castulo; cf. XXIII. xlix. 5, where the form was Iliturgi.

the river, opposite the Roman camp. Publius Scipio, who set out secretly to reconnoitre with unencumbered troops, did not escape the notice of the enemy, and they would have overwhelmed him in the open meadows if he had not captured a hill near by. Even there he was beset, but by the arrival of his brother he escaped a siege. Castulo[1] revolted to the Romans, a strong and famous city of Spain, so closely joined to the Carthaginians by alliance that Hannibal's wife[2] was from that place. The Carthaginians attempted to capture Iliturgis,[3] because there was a Roman garrison there, and it seemed that they would take the town mainly by starvation. Gnaeus Scipio, to lend aid to the allies and the garrison, set out with an unencumbered legion, passing between their two camps, and after slaying many of the enemy entered the city, and on the following day engaged them in an equally successful sally. Over twelve thousand men were slain in the two battles, more than a thousand men captured, with thirty-six military standards. So they withdrew from Iliturgis. Then began the siege of Bigerra[4]—these also were allies of the Romans—by the Carthaginians. Gnaeus Scipio on his arrival raised the siege without an engagement. B.C. 214

XLII. Thereupon the Carthaginian camp was removed to Munda,[5] and the Romans promptly followed them thither. There they fought in pitched battle for about four hours, and though the Romans were winning a brilliant victory, the signal for recall was given, because Gnaeus Scipio's thigh had been

[4] Site unknown.

[5] Near Corduba. This is the first mention of Caesar's Munda; probably Montilla.

A.U.C. 540 pavorque circa eum ceperat milites, ne mortiferum
3 esset vulnus. Ceterum haud dubium fuit quin,
nisi ea mora intervenisset, castra eo die Punica capi
potuerint. Iam[1] non milites solum sed elephanti
etiam usque ad vallum acti erant, superque ipsas
fossas[2] novem et triginta elephanti pilis confixi.
4 Hoc quoque proelio ad duodecim milia hominum
dicuntur caesa, prope tria capta cum signis militari-
5 bus septem et quinquaginta. Ad Auringem inde
urbem Poeni recessere et, ut territis instaret, secutus
Romanus. Ibi iterum Scipio lecticula in aciem in-
latus conflixit, nec dubia victoria fuit; minus tamen
dimidio hostium quam antea, quia pauciores super-
6 fuerant qui pugnarent, occisum. Sed gens nata
instaurandis reparandisque bellis, Magone ad conquisitionem militum a fratre misso, brevi replevit
exercitum animosque ad temptandum de integro
7 certamen fecit; Galli[3] plerique milites, iique[4]
pro parte totiens intra paucos dies victa, iisdem
animis quibus priores[5] eodemque eventu pugnavere.
8 Plus octo milia hominum caesa, et haud[6] multo minus
quam mille captum et signa militaria quinquaginta
octo. Et spolia plurima Gallica fuere, aurei torques
armillaeque, magnus numerus. Duo etiam insignes
reguli Gallorum—Moeniacoepto et Vismaro nomina

[1] iam $P(1)$: nam *Madvig.*

[2] ipsas fossas *Riemann*: ipsas $P(2)$: ipsos *Ax*: ipsum *x*: fossas *Madvig.*

[3] Galli A^y *Valla*: alii $P(1)$ *Madvig.*

[4] iique A^y *Valla*: sique $P(1)$: quippe *Madvig.*

[5] priores *Valla*: pr. orta $P(11)A?$: prius *x.*

[6] et haud $P(2)$ *Conway*: et non *A*: haud *z Madvig.*

pierced by a light javelin, and fear that the wound B.C. 214 might prove fatal had seized the soldiers around him. But there was no doubt that, if this delay had not occurred, the Carthaginian camp could have been captured that day. Already not only soldiers but the elephants also had been driven even up to the wall, and just as they crossed the trenches thirty-nine elephants were struck down by heavy javelins. In this battle also about twelve thousand men are said to have been slain, about three thousand captured, with fifty-seven military standards. The Carthaginians then retired to the city of Aurinx,[1] and the Roman followed, to threaten men already terrified. There Scipio again engaged, being carried into battle-line in a litter, and the victory was not to be questioned. Less than half as many of the enemy as before, however, were slain, because fewer men had survived to fight. But, as Mago was sent by his brother to recruit soldiers, a race adapted by nature to renew wars and to make fresh preparations for them soon refilled the army and gave them the spirit to essay another conflict. The soldiers were mostly Gauls,[2] and they fought with the same spirit as their predecessors for the side which had been beaten so many times within a few days, and with the same result. More than eight thousand men were slain, and not much less than a thousand captured, also fifty-eight military standards. And the spoils were largely Gallic, golden collars and armbands—a great number of them. Also two conspicuous princes of the Gauls —Moeniacoeptus and Vismarus were their names

[1] Perhaps the same as Orongis, XXVIII. iii. 2.

[2] From Celtic tribes already established in Spain, even in the southwest.

A.U.C. 540 erant—eo proelio ceciderunt. Octo elephanti capti,
tres occisi.
9 Cum tam prosperae res in Hispania essent, verecundia Romanos tandem cepit, Saguntum oppidum, quae causa belli esset, octavum iam annum sub
10 hostium potestate esse. Itaque id oppidum vi pulso
praesidio Punico receperunt cultoribusque antiquis,
11 quos ex iis vis reliquerat belli, restituerunt; et Tur-
detanos, qui contraxerant eis cum Carthaginiensibus
bellum, in potestatem redactos sub corona vendiderunt
urbemque eorum delerunt.

XLIII. Haec in Hispania Q. Fabio M. Claudio
2 consulibus gesta. Romae cum tribuni plebis novi magistratum inissent, extemplo censoribus P. Furio et M.
Atilio a M. Metello tribuno plebis dies dicta ad popu-
3 lum est—quaestorem eum proximo anno adempto
equo tribu moverant atque aerarium fecerant propter
coniurationem deserendae Italiae ad Cannas factam
—sed novem tribunorum auxilio vetiti causam in
4 magistratu dicere dimissique fuerunt.[1] Ne lustrum
perficerent, mors prohibuit P. Furi; M. Atilius
magistratu se abdicavit.
5 Comitia consularia habita ab Q. Fabio Maximo
consule. Creati consules ambo absentes Q. Fabius
Maximus, consulis filius, et Ti. Sempronius Gracchus

[1] fuerunt *Crévier*: fuerant *P*(1): *om. Ussing, Walters.*

---

[1] Livy's own chronology would make it four complete years; XXI. vii. ff.; xv. 5; XXIV. ix. 7.

[2] Cf. XXI. vi. 1. Better known is the tribe of the same name in southern Baetica.

[3] Cf. xviii. 3 and 6; XXVII. xi. 12. The scene was Canusium, after Cannae.

—fell in that battle. Eight elephants were captured, three slain. B.C. 214

The situation in Spain being so favourable, the Romans came at last to be ashamed that the town of Saguntum, which was the cause of the war, had been by that time seven years [1] in the power of the enemy. Accordingly the Carthaginian garrison was driven out by force, and recovering the town the Romans restored it to its former inhabitants—such of them as the violence of war had spared. And as for the Turdetani,[2] who had brought on the war between Saguntum and the Carthaginians, they reduced them to subjection, sold them under the garland and destroyed their city.

XLIII. Such were the events in Spain in the consulship of Quintus Fabius and Marcus Claudius. At Rome, immediately after the newly elected tribunes of the plebs had entered upon office, a day was set by Marcus Metellus, a tribune of the plebs, for the censors Publius Furius and Marcus Atilius to appear at the bar of the people. In his quaestorship the year before they had taken away his horse, removed him from his tribe and made him an aerarian on account of the conspiracy formed at Cannae to desert Italy.[3] But by the aid of nine tribunes they were forbidden to plead their cause while in office and were released. From completing the ceremony of purification they were prevented by the death of Publius Furius. Marcus Atilius abdicated his office.

For the consulship the election was conducted by Quintus Fabius Maximus, the consul. Elected consuls, both in absence, were Quintus Fabius Maximus, the consul's son, and Tiberius Sempronius Gracchus, the latter for the second time. Two men

A.U.C. 540

6 iterum. Praetores fiunt duo qui tum aediles curules erant, P. Sempronius Tuditanus et Cn. Fulvius Centumalus, et cum illis[1] M. Atilius et[2] M. Aemilius
7 Lepidus. Ludos scenicos per quadriduum eo anno primum factos ab curulibus aedilibus memoriae
8 proditur. Aedilis Tuditanus hic erat[3] qui ad Cannas pavore aliis in tanta clade torpentibus per medios hostes duxit.

A.U.C. 541

9 His[4] comitiis perfectis auctore Q. Fabio consule designati consules Romam accersiti magistratum inierunt, senatumque de bello ac provinciis suis praetorumque et de exercitibus quibus quique praeessent consuluerunt; (XLIV) itaque provinciae atque exercitus divisi: bellum cum Hannibale consulibus mandatum et exercituum unus quem ipse Sempronius habuerat, alter quem Fabius consul;
2 eae binae erant legiones. M. Aemilius praetor, cuius peregrina sors erat, iuris dictione M. Atilio collegae, praetori urbano, mandata, Luceriam provinciam haberet legionesque duas quibus Q. Fabius,
3 qui tum consul erat, praetor praefuerat. P. Sempronio provincia Ariminum, Cn. Fulvio Suessula cum binis item legionibus evenerunt, ut Fulvius urbanas legiones duceret, Tuditanus a M. Pomponio acciperet.
4 Prorogata imperia provinciaeque, M. Claudio Sicilia

[1] cum illis *Walters* : cum iis *M. Müller* : *om.* *P*(1).
[2] M. Atilius et *Madvig* : *om.* *P*(1).
[3] erat $C^2M^xA^2$: erit *P*(1) *Walters*.
[4] duxit. His *Madvig*[4] (Iis *Weissenborn*) : auxiliis *P*(1).

---

[1] Cf. XXII. l. 6 ff.
[2] Gallia was the more recent name of this "province," *ager Gallicus* in x. 3.
[3] With the important Roman camp near it, the *castra Claudiana*; xvii. 2; xlvii. 12; XXIII. xxxi. 3.

who were at the time curule aediles, Publius Sempronius Tuditanus and Gnaeus Fulvius Centumalus, were made praetors, and with them Marcus Atilius and Marcus Aemilius Lepidus. Tradition has it that at the festival given that year by the curule aediles four days had dramatic performances for the first time. The aedile Tuditanus was the man who at Cannae, when others were paralyzed by fear in such a disaster, led his men through the midst of the enemy.[1] B.C. 214

These elections being completed, the consuls designate were summoned to Rome, as proposed by Quintus Fabius, the consul, entered upon office and consulted the senate in regard to the war and the provinces, their own and those of the praetors, and as to the armies which they should respectively command; (XLIV) and the provinces and armies were divided as follows: the war with Hannibal was assigned to the consuls, and two armies, one which Sempronius himself, and the other which Fabius had commanded as consul. These were of two legions each. Marcus Aemilius, the praetor to whom fell jurisdiction in cases involving foreigners, was to assign his judicial function to his colleague Marcus Atilius, the city praetor, and have Luceria as his province, and two legions which Quintus Fabius, who was now consul, had commanded as praetor. To Publius Sempronius Ariminum fell as his assignment,[2] to Gnaeus Fulvius, Suessula,[3] likewise with two legions in each case, so assigned that Fulvius should take with him the legions at the city, and Tuditanus take over from Marcus Pomponius his legions. Commands and assignments were continued as follows: for Marcus Claudius Sicily, with the B.C. 213

A.U.C. 541 finibus eis quibus regnum Hieronis fuisset, P. Lentulo
propraetori provincia vetus, T. Otacilio classis—
5 exercitus nulli additi novi—, M. Valerio Graecia
Macedoniaque cum legione et classe quam haberet,
Q. Mucio cum vetere exercitu—duae autem legiones
erant—Sardinia, C. Terentio legio una [1] cui iam
6 praeerat ac [2] Picenum. Scribi praeterea duae
urbanae legiones iussae et viginti milia sociorum.
His ducibus, his copiis adversus multa simul aut mota
aut suspecta bella muniverunt Romanum imperium.
7 Consules duabus urbanis legionibus scriptis supple-
mentoque in alias lecto, priusquam ab urbe moverent,
8 prodigia procurarunt quae nuntiata erant. Murus ac
portae . . .,[3] et Ariciae etiam Iovis aedes de caelo
tacta fuerat. Et alia ludibria oculorum auriumque
credita pro veris: navium longarum species in flumine
Tarracinae quae nullae erant visas, et in Iovis Vici-
lini templo, quod in Compsano agro est, arma con-
crepuisse, et flumen Amiterni cruentum fluxisse.
9 His procuratis ex decreto pontificum profecti consules,
Sempronius in Lucanos, in Apuliam Fabius. Pater
10 filio legatus ad Suessulam in castra venit. Cum
obviam filius progrederetur lictoresque verecundia
maiestatis eius taciti anteirent, praeter undecim fasces
equo praevectus senex, ut consul animadvertere
proximum lictorem iussit et is ut descenderet ex

[1] legio una *P*(1): cum legione una *Aldus*.
[2] ac *Weissenborn*: et *x Gronovius*: *om. P*(1).
[3] portae (*or* -te) *P*(1), *followed by* tactae (*or* -te), *into which a town name has been corrupted*: porta Caietae *Luterbacher, Walters*.

---

[1] Cf. XXIII. i. 1. In that southern part of Samnium Jupiter had the rare epithet Vicilinus.

boundaries which Hiero's kingdom had had; for B.C. 213
Publius Lentulus, as propraetor, the old province; for Titus Otacilius the fleet; and for them new armies were not added. So also for Marcus Valerius Greece and Macedonia, with the legion and the fleet which he had; for Quintus Mucius Sardinia, with its old army—there were two legions; for Gaius Terentius one legion which he already commanded, and Picenum. It was further ordered that two city legions should be enrolled, also twenty thousand allies. With these generals, these forces, they defended the Roman empire at the same time against many wars, either already begun or foreshadowed.

The consuls, after enrolling two legions for the city and enlisting recruits to reinforce the others, before setting out from the city made expiation for the prodigies which had been reported. The wall and gates at . . . and at Aricia even the temple of Jupiter had been struck by lightning. And for eyes and ears there were other illusions, accepted as real: that in the river at Tarracina forms of warships which had no existence had been seen; and that in the temple of Jupiter Vicilinus, in the territory of Compsa,[1] there was a sound of clashing arms; and that the river at Amiternum ran with blood. These portents being expiated according to a decree of the pontiffs, the consuls set out, Sempronius for Lucania, Fabius for Apulia. The father came as his son's lieutenant to the camp at Suessula. While the son was advancing to meet him and the lictors out of respect for the father's dignity were silent as they preceded the consul, the old man rode past eleven fasces. And not until the consul had ordered the last lictor to take notice and the latter had called

A.U.C. 541 equo inclamavit, tum demum desiliens "Experiri" inquit "volui, fili, satin' scires consulem te esse."

XLV. In ea castra Dasius Altinius Arpinus clam nocte cum tribus servis venit promittens, si sibi prae-
2 mio foret, se Arpos proditurum esse. Eam rem ad consilium cum rettulisset Fabius, aliis pro transfuga verberandus necandusque videri ancipitis animi communis hostis, qui post Cannensem cladem, tamquam cum fortuna fidem stare oporteret, ad Hannibalem de-
3 scisset traxissetque ad defectionem Arpos; tum, quoniam [1] res Romana contra spem votaque eius velut resurgere ab stirpibus videatur, novam referre proditionem proditis polliceatur, aliunde stet [2] semper, aliunde sentiat, infidus socius, vanus hostis; id [3] ad Faleriorum Pyrrhique proditorem tertium transfugis
4 documentum esset. Contra ea consulis pater Fabius temporum oblitos homines in medio ardore belli, tamquam in pace, libera de quoque arbitria agere
5 aiebat, ut,[4] cum illud potius agendum atque cogitandum sit, si quo modo fieri possit, ne qui socii a populo Romano desciscant, id non cogitent,[5] documentum autem dicant [6] statui oportere, si quis resipiscat et

[1] quoniam C^4x: quia M^2A^2: quam *P*(11).
[2] aliunde stet *Gronovius*: aliunde ipse stet *Conway*: aliiudicioestet *P*(10)*C?*.
[3] id *Madvig*: om. *P*(1).
[4] ut *Weissenborn*: et *P*(1): qui *Gronovius*.
[5] id non cogitent *Gronovius*: et non vocitent *P*(1): et ut novos concilient *Madvig*.
[6] dicant *Valla*: dicatur *P*(1).

---

[1] A famous story. Gellius (II. ii. 13) gives the brief version of Claudius Quadrigarius.

out the order to dismount, did the father leap to the ground and say: "I wished to find out, son, whether you were quite aware that you are consul."[1] B.C. 213

XLV. To that camp came Dasius Altinius of Arpi secretly by night with three slaves, promising that if rewarded he would betray Arpi.[2] When Fabius brought the matter before the council, the others thought that as a deserter he should be scourged and put to death, a waverer and an enemy to both sides, who after the disaster at Cannae, as if loyalty should side with success, had gone over to Hannibal and dragged Arpi into revolt. But now, because, contrary to his expectation and his wishes, the Roman state seemed to be springing up again, as it were from the roots, he was promising to present the betrayed with a new betrayal, and always taking part with one side, but with the other in heart, faithless as an ally, inconstant as an enemy. To the betrayers of Falerii[3] and of Pyrrhus[4] he should be added as a third example to deserters. On the contrary the consul's father Fabius said that men were forgetting the situation, when they exercised free judgment in each individual case in the midst of the heat of war, as though in peace, the result was that, although the thing to be done and to be borne in mind was rather to prevent any allies—if this was somehow possible—from abandoning the Roman people, they were not bearing that in mind. On the contrary, they were saying that, if a man came to his senses and turned his eyes to the previous alliance, he ought to be made a

[2] In northern Apulia, east of Luceria and not far from the Adriatic; cf. iii. 16; xii. 3, 5; XXIII. xlvi. 8.

[3] Cf. V. xxvii. 2 ff.

[4] This story was told in the lost XIIIth book (cf. *Epit.*).

A.U.C. 541

6 antiquam societatem respiciat. Quod si abire ab
Romanis liceat, redire ad eos non liceat, cui dubium
esse quin brevi desperata[1] ab sociis Romana res
foederibus Punicis omnia in Italia iuncta visura
7 sit?[2] Se tamen non eum esse qui Altinio fidei quicquam censeat habendum, sed mediam secuturum
8 consilii viam. Neque enim[3] pro hoste neque pro
socio in praesentia habitum libera custodia haud
procul a castris placere in aliqua fida civitate
eum[4] servari per belli tempus; perpetrato bello
tum consultandum utrum prior defectio plus merita
9 sit poenae, an hic reditus veniae. Fabio adsensum
est, Calenisque legatis traditus et ipse et comites;
et auri satis magnum pondus, quod secum tum
10 attulerat, ei servari iussum. Calibus eum interdiu
solutum custodes sequebantur, nocte clausum ad-
11 servabant. Arpis domi primum desiderari quae-
rique est coeptus; dein fama per totam urbem volgata
tumultum, ut principe amisso, fecit, metuque rerum
12 novarum extemplo nuntii missi. Quibus nequaquam
offensus Poenus, quia et ipsum ut ambiguae fidei
virum suspectum iam pridem habebat et causam
nactus erat tam ditis hominis bona possidendi
13 vendendique; ceterum, ut irae magis quam
avaritiae datum crederent homines, crudelitatem
14 quoque aviditati[5] addidit, coniugemque eius ac
liberos in castra accitos, quaestione prius habita

[1] desperata *Madvig*: desiderata *P*(1): deserta *z*.
[2] res . . . visura sit *P*(1): re . . . visuri sint *Madvig*.
[3] enim *Weissenborn*: eum *P*(1) *Madvig*.
[4] eum *P*(1): om. *Aldus, Madvig*.
[5] aviditati *Stroth*: gravitatem *P*(1).

---

[1] *I.e.* to Hannibal.

warning example. If then it was permissible to leave B.C. 213 the Romans, but not to return to them, who could doubt that soon the Roman state, despaired of by the allies, would see the whole of Italy joined together by Carthaginian treaties? For himself, however, he was not the man to think that any trust should be placed in Altinius, but would follow a middle course. He thought it best, namely, that Altinius should not be treated as either enemy or ally for the present, that under qualified arrest he should be guarded for the duration of the war in some loyal city-state not far from the camp. When the war was over they should then deliberate whether his previous defection deserved punishment more than his present return merited pardon. They agreed with Fabius, and the man was turned over to representatives of Cales, himself and his companions. And it was ordered that the gold—and the weight of it was considerable—which he had then brought with him should be kept for him. At Cales he was free to go about by day followed by guards, at night confined and watched by them. At Arpi it was in his house that he was first missed and search for him began. Then the report spreading through the city caused the usual commotion when a leading man is missing, and for fear of a rebellion they at once sent messengers.[1] The Carthaginian was by no means displeased at this news, since he had long regarded the man himself with suspicion, as unsettled in his loyalty, and also he now had an excuse for taking possession of the property of a man of such wealth and selling it. But that men might believe he was yielding to anger rather than greed, he added cruelty also to avarice, that is, he summoned the wife and children to the camp, and,

A.U.C. 541 primum de fuga Altini, dein quantum auri argentique domi relictum esset, satis cognitis omnibus vivos combussit.

XLVI. Fabius ab Suessula profectus Arpos primum institit oppugnare. Ubi cum a quingentis[1] fere passibus castra posuisset, contemplatus ex propinquo situm urbis moeniaque, quae pars tutissima moenibus erat, quia maxime neglectam custodia vidit, ea potissimum
2 adgredi statuit. Comparatis omnibus quae ad urbes oppugnandas usui sunt centurionum robora ex toto exercitu delegit tribunosque viros fortes eis praefecit, et milites sescentos, quantum satis visum est, attribuit eosque, ubi quartae vigiliae signum cecinisset, ad eum
3 locum scalas iussit ferre. Porta ibi humilis et angusta erat infrequenti via per desertam partem urbis. Eam portam scalis prius transgressos murum aperire[2] ex interiore parte aut claustra refringere iubet et tenentes partem urbis cornu signum dare ut ceterae copiae admoverentur: parata omnia atque instructa
4 sese[3] habiturum. Ea inpigre facta, et quod impedimentum agentibus fore videbatur, id maxime ad fallendum adiuvit. Imber ab nocte media coortus custodes vigilesque dilapsos e stationibus subfugere
5 in tecta coegit, sonitusque[4] primo largioris procellae strepitum molientium portam exaudiri prohibuit, lentior deinde aequaliorque accidens auribus magnam

[1] a quingentis *Gronovius* : ad (= a D) *P*(4).
[2] murum aperire *Crévier* : aperire *Madvig* : amurumperire *P* (-pergere P^2(4)) : ad murum pergere C^2BDA.
[3] sese A^2 *Aldus* : esse *P*(1) : *om. Conway.*
[4] sonitusque A^2?*x Madvig*: sonituque *P*(2)*A*? *Walters.*

after investigating first the flight of Altinius, then B.C. 213
how much gold and silver had been left in his house, now fully informed, he burned them alive.

XLVI. Fabius setting out from Suessula first pressed the siege of Arpi. There he pitched his camp at a distance of about five hundred paces, and after observing the situation of the city and the walls at close range, he decided to attack just at that part of the city which was best defended by walls, because he saw that that was the most carelessly guarded. He assembled everything useful for siege operations, selected from the entire army the pick of the centurions, and placed tribunes who were brave men in command of them. And he assigned them six hundred soldiers—all that seemed necessary—and ordered them to carry ladders to that place, when the trumpet should sound for the fourth watch. There was a low, narrow gate there, as the street, leading through a deserted part of the city, was not much frequented. He ordered them first to climb over the wall by means of their ladders, and then to open that gate from the inside, or else break down the bars, and then, holding a part of the city, to give the signal on a trumpet for the rest of the troops to move up. He would have everything ready and in order. These commands were carried out with spirit, and a circumstance which seemed likely to hamper action proved of the greatest help to secrecy. Heavy rain beginning at midnight forced the guards and sentries to slip away from their posts and run to cover. And the sound, at first of a heavier shower, prevented the noise they made in forcing the gate from being heard clearly, and then, gentler and more monotonous as they listened, it lulled a great many

A.U.C. 541 6 partem hominum sopivit. Postquam portam tenebant, cornicines, in via paribus intervallis dispositos,
7 canere iubent, ut consulem excirent. Id ubi factum
ex composito est, signa efferri consul iubet ac paulo
ante lucem per effractam portam urbem ingreditur.

XLVII. Tum demum hostes excitati sunt iam et
2 imbre conquiescente et propinqua luce. Praesidium
in urbe erat Hannibalis, quinque milia ferme armatorum, et ipsi Arpini tria milia hominum armarant.
Eos primos Poeni, ne quid ab tergo fraudis esset,
3 hosti opposuerunt. Pugnatum primo in tenebris
angustisque viis est. Cum Romani non vias tantum
sed tecta etiam proxima portam[1] occupassent, ne peti
4 superne ac volnerari possent, cogniti inter se quidam
Arpinique et Romani atque inde conloquia coepta
fieri, percunctantibus Romanis quid sibi vellent
5 Arpini, quam ob noxam Romanorum aut quod meri-
tum Poenorum pro alienigenis ac barbaris Italici
adversus veteres socios Romanos bellum gererent et
vectigalem ac stipendiariam Italiam Africae facerent,
6 Arpinis purgantibus ignaros omnium se venum a
principibus datos Poeno, captos oppressosque a
7 paucis esse. Initio orto plures cum pluribus conloqui;
postremo praetor Arpinus ab suis ad consulem deductus, fideque data inter signa aciesque Arpini repente

[1] portam *Drakenborch*: portae $C^2M^3?A^2$: porta $P(2)A?$.

of the men to sleep. Once in possession of the gate, they ordered the trumpeters, posted at equal intervals along the road, to sound, in order to summon the consul. This done according to agreement, the consul orders the standards to be carried out of the camp, and a little before daylight enters the city through the gate they had forced. B.C. 213

XLVII. Not until then were the enemy aroused, as the noise of the rain was now lessening and daylight approaching. In the city there was a garrison of Hannibal's, about five thousand armed men, and the citizens of Arpi also had armed three thousand men. These were the first troops with which the Carthaginians, to prevent any treachery in the rear, confronted the enemy. They fought at first in darkness and in narrow streets. The Romans gained possession not only of the streets but also of the houses nearest to the gate, that they might not be attacked and wounded from above. Thereupon some Arpini and Romans recognized each other and then began conversations. The Romans asked what the Arpini meant, for what offence on the part of the Romans, or for what service on the part of the Carthaginians they, although Italians, were waging war for foreigners and barbarians against their old allies the Romans, and making Italy a tributary and a taxpayer to Africa. The Arpini pleaded as excuse that in complete ignorance they had been sold by their leading citizens to the Carthaginian and captured and overpowered by a few men. With that beginning larger groups conversed with larger. Finally the magistrate of Arpi was escorted by fellow-citizens to the consul, and after promises had been given in the midst of standards and battle-lines, the

A.U.C. 541 pro Romanis adversus Carthaginiensem arma verte-
8 runt. Hispani quoque, paulo minus mille homines, nihil praeterea cum consule pacti quam ut sine fraude Punicum emitteretur praesidium, ad consulem
9 transtulerunt signa. Carthaginiensibus portae patefactae emissique cum fide incolumes ad Hannibalem
10 Salapiam venerunt. Arpi sine clade ullius praeterquam unius veteris proditoris, novi perfugae, resti-
11 tuti ad Romanos. Hispanis duplicia cibaria dari iussa; operaque eorum forti ac fideli persaepe res publica usa est.

12 Cum consul alter in Apulia, alter in Lucanis esset, equites centum duodecim nobiles Campani per speciem praedandi ex hostium agro permissu magistratuum ab Capua profecti ad castra Romana, quae super Suessulam erant, venerunt; stationi militum qui essent dixerunt: conloqui sese cum praetore velle.
13 Cn. Fulvius castris praeerat; cui ubi nuntiatum est, decem ex eo numero iussis inermibus deduci ad se, ubi quae postularent audivit—nihil autem aliud petebant quam ut Capua recepta bona sibi restitue-
14 rentur—, in fidem omnes accepti. Et ab altero praetore Sempronio Tuditano oppidum Atrinum expugnatum. Amplius septem milia[1] hominum capta et
15 aeris argentique signati aliquantum. Romae foedum incendium per duas noctes ac diem unum tenuit. Solo aequata omnia inter Salinas ac portam Carmen-

[1] septem milia *P*(4) *in numerals* (Iↄↄ ∞ ∞) : LXX *A*.

---

[1] *I.e.* Gracchus; xliv. 9.
[2] Situation unknown.

Arpini suddenly fought for the Romans, turning their B.C. 213 weapons against the Carthaginians. The Spanish troops also, hardly fewer than a thousand men, after making no other terms with the consul than that the Punic garrison be allowed to go without injury, brought their standards over to the consul. The gates were opened for the Carthaginians, they were allowed to leave, as promised, and came unharmed to Hannibal at Salapia. Arpi, with the loss of no man but a single veteran traitor and recent deserter, was restored to the Romans. To the Spaniards double rations were ordered to be issued, and the state repeatedly availed itself of their brave and faithful service.

While one consul was in Apulia, the other[1] in Lucania, a hundred and twelve noble Campanian horsemen, setting out from Capua, with permission of the magistrates, under pretext of plundering the enemy's country, came to the Roman camp above Suessula. They told the guards outside who they were; that they wished to speak with the praetor. Gnaeus Fulvius was in command of the camp, and on being informed, he ordered that ten of their number be disarmed and brought to him. After he had heard their demands—and they made no other request than that upon the recovery of Capua their property should be restored to them, they were all taken under his protection. And the other praetor, Sempronius Tuditanus, took the town of Atrinum[2] by storm. More than seven thousand men were captured and a considerable amount of coined copper and silver. At Rome a terrible fire lasted two nights and a day. Everything between the Salinae and Porta Carmentalis was levelled to the ground,

A.U.C. 541 talem cum Aequimaelio Iugarioque vico et[1] templis
16 Fortunae ac matris Matutae. Et extra portam late
vagatus ignis sacra profanaque multa absumpsit.

XLVIII. Eodem anno P. et Cn. Cornelii, cum in
Hispania res prosperae essent multosque et veteres
reciperent socios et novos adicerent, in Africam quo-
2 que spem extenderunt. Syphax erat rex Numidarum
3 subito Carthaginiensibus hostis factus; ad eum centuriones tres legatos miserunt qui cum eo amicitiam
societatemque facerent et pollicerentur, si perse-
veraret urguere bello Carthaginienses, gratam eam
rem fore senatui populoque Romano et adnisuros ut in
tempore et bene cumulatam gratiam referant.
4 Grata ea legatio barbaro fuit; conlocutusque cum
legatis de ratione belli gerundi, ut veterum militum
verba audivit, quam multarum rerum ipse ignarus
esset, ex conparatione tam ordinatae disciplinae
5 animum advertit. Tum id[2] primum ut pro bonis
ac fidelibus sociis facerent oravit, ut duo legationem
referrent ad imperatores suos, unus apud sese magister
rei militaris remaneret[3]: rudem ad pedestria bella
Numidarum gentem esse, equis tantum habilem;
6 ita iam inde a principiis gentis maiores suos bella

[1] et *Madvig*: in *P*(1).
[2] tum id *Crévier*: id tum *Riemann*: tum *P*(1).
[3] remaneret *A*[2] *Riemann*: retieret *P*: rediret *C*[4](10): restaret *Walters*.

---

[1] The devastated area was that along the river from the Aventine to the Capitoline, including part of the southeast slope (Aequimaelium) of the latter, and the street (Vicus Iugarius) leading to the Forum. The temples mentioned were near the Tiber and close together; cf. XXXIII. xxvii. 4.

including the Aequimaelium and Vicus Iugarius,[1] B.C. 213
also the Temples of Fortune and Mater Matuta. Outside the gate also the fire spread to a distance and destroyed many buildings sacred [2] and profane.

XLVIII. The same year Publius and Gnaeus Cornelius, in consequence of their success in Spain and their recovery of many old allies and the addition of new allies, enlarged their hopes in the direction of Africa as well. There was Syphax, king of the Numidians,[3] who had suddenly become an enemy of the Carthaginians. To him they sent three centurions as legates, to establish friendship and alliance with him, and to promise that if he should continue to embarrass the Carthaginians by war, it would be acceptable to the senate and the Roman people, and they would endeavour to return the favour at the right moment and with generous interest. This embassy pleased the barbarian, and he conferred with the ambassadors on the conduct of the war; and hearing what was said by experienced soldiers, he noted, from comparison with so well-ordered a system, how many things he did not know himself. Then, as the first act befitting good and faithful allies, be begged that two of the legates might report to their generals, and one remain with him as instructor in tactics. He said the Numidian nation was inexpert in infantry warfare, of service only as horsemen. This was the way their ancestors from their earliest history had waged war, thus they had

[2] Among these was the Temple of Spes, one of three in the Forum Holitorium, outside the wall; XXI. lxii. 4; XXV. vii. 6.

[3] *I.e.* of the western Numidians, the Masaesulians, in Algeria and Oran; XXVIII. xvii. 5.

A.U.C. 541 gessisse, ita se a pueris insuetos. Sed habere
hostem pedestri fidentem Marte, cui si aequari robore
7 virium velit, et sibi pedites comparandos esse. Et ad
id multitudine hominum regnum abundare, sed ar-
mandi ornandique et instruendi eos artem ignorare.
Omnia, velut forte congregata turba, vasta [1] ac
8 temeraria esse. Facturos se in praesentia quod vellet
legati respondent, fide accepta ut remitteret extemplo eum, si imperatores sui non comprobassent
9 factum. Q. Statorio nomen fuit, qui ad regem
remansit. Cum duobus Romanis rex tres a [2] Numidis [3]
legatos in Hispaniam misit ad accipiendam fidem ab
10 imperatoribus Romanis. Isdem mandavit ut protinus
Numidas qui intra praesidia Carthaginiensium auxili-
11 ares essent [4] ad transitionem perlicerent. Et Statorius ex multa iuventute regi pedites conscripsit
ordinatosque proxime morem Romanum instruendo
et decurrendo signa sequi et servare ordines docuit,
12 et operi aliisque iustis militaribus ita adsuefecit
ut brevi rex non equiti magis fideret quam pediti con-
latisque aequo campo signis iusto proelio Carthagi-
13 niensem hostem superaret. Romanis quoque in
Hispania legatorum regis adventus magno emolumento fuit; namque ad famam eorum transitiones
crebrae ab Numidis coeptae fieri.

Ita cum Syphace Romanis coepta amicitia est. Quod ubi Carthaginienses acceperunt, extemplo

[1] vasta *Rubens* : suasca PR^1 : suaisca P^2?(12).

[2] rex tres a *Conway* : relata *P*(1) : rex tres *Alschefski* : rex *Weissenborn*.

[3] Numidis *P*(4) : -das BA^2.

[4] essent *z* : erant A^2x : *om.* *P*(1).

themselves been trained from boyhood. But he B.C. 213
had an enemy who relied upon infantry battles, and if he wished to be a match for him in military strength he too must acquire infantry. And for that purpose his kingdom was supplied with men in great numbers, but they did not understand the art of arming and equipping them and placing them in battle-line. Everything was formless and unmethodical, as if a mob had been gathered by chance. The legates replied that for the present they would do as he desired, after receiving his pledge to send back the man at once, if their generals should not approve of their action. Quintus Statorius was the name of the one who remained with the king. With the two Romans the king sent three legates from the Numidians to Spain, to receive confirmation from the Roman generals. He further instructed them at once to persuade Numidians who were auxiliaries in the forces of the Carthaginians to desert them. And Statorius out of the mass of young men enrolled infantry for the king, organized them almost in the Roman manner, taught them in formation and evolution to follow standards and keep their ranks, and to such an extent accustomed them to fortifying and other regular duties of the soldier that in a short time the king had as much confidence in his infantry as in his cavalry, and in a regular engagement in formal array on level ground he defeated the Carthaginian enemy. The Romans also in Spain profited greatly by the coming of the king's representatives. For upon the news of their arrival desertions by the Numidians began to be frequent.

Thus began the friendship of the Romans with Syphax. When the Carthaginians learned of the

A.U.C. 541 ad Galam in parte altera Numidiae—Maesuli ea gens vocatur—regnantem legatos mittunt. XLIX. Filium Gala Masinissam habebat septem decem annos natum, ceterum iuvenem ea indole ut iam tum appareret maius regnum opulentiusque quam quod accepisset
2 facturum. Legati, quoniam Syphax se Romanis iunxisset, ut potentior societate eorum adversus
3 reges populosque Africae esset, docent melius fore Galae quoque Carthaginiensibus iungi quam primum, antequam Syphax in Hispaniam aut Romani in Africam transeant; opprimi Syphacem nihildum praeter nomen ex foedere Romano habentem posse.
4 Facile persuasum Galae, filio deposcente id bellum, ut mitteret exercitum; qui Carthaginiensibus legionibus coniunctus[1] magno proelio Syphacem devicit. Triginta milia eo proelio hominum caesa dicuntur.
5 Syphax cum paucis equitibus in Maurusios ex acie Numidas—extremi prope Oceanum adversus Gadis colunt—refugit, adfluentibusque ad famam eius undi-
6 que barbaris ingentis brevi copias armavit cum quibus in Hispaniam angusto diremptam freto traiceret. Sed[2] Masinissa cum victore exercitu advenit; isque ibi cum Syphace ingenti gloria per se sine ullis Carthaginiensium opibus gessit bellum.

[1] coniunctus *Madvig*: -iis *P*: -i *P*²*?*: -is (1).
[2] Sed *H. J. Müller*: *om.* *P*(1): eo *or* et *Madvig*: ceterum *Luchs*: interim *Weissenborn*.

---

[1] The eastern part, adjoining Carthaginian territory. Cirta (Constantine) was Syphax's capital, until it fell to Masinissa in 203 B.C.; XXX. xii.

matter they at once sent legates to Gala, who reigned in the other part of Numidia,[1] his people being called the Maesulians. XLIX. Gala had a son Masinissa,[2] seventeen years old, but a young man of such promise that even then it was evident that he would make the kingdom larger and richer than what he had received. The legates stated that, inasmuch as Syphax had attached himself to the Romans, in order, through alliance with them, to be more powerful against the kings and peoples of Africa, it would be well for Gala too to attach himself as soon as possible to the Carthaginians, before Syphax should cross into Spain or the Romans into Africa. Syphax could be surprised, they said, while he had as yet no advantage from his treaty with the Romans except the name. They easily persuaded Gala to send an army, as his son was begging for the command; and reinforced by the Carthaginian legions, Masinissa defeated Syphax in a great battle. Thirty thousand men are said to have been slain in that battle. Syphax with a few horsemen fled from the field to the Maurusian Numidians, who live far away, near the Ocean opposite Gades. And as the barbarians on hearing of him flocked together from all sides, he soon armed immense forces with which to cross into Spain, separated only by a narrow strait. But Masinissa came with his victorious army, and there by himself, without any help from the Carthaginians, he carried on war against Syphax with great distinction. B.C. 213

[2] Who fought against the Romans in Spain down to the time of Gala's death in 206 B.C., and then became an ally of Rome, and a friend of Scipio. At present he must have been nearer twenty-seven, since he died in 149 B.C. at 92 (*Epit.* 48 fin.; cf. 50).

A.U.C. 541 7 In Hispania nihil memorabile gestum praeterquam quod Celtiberum iuventutem eadem mercede qua pacta cum Carthaginiensibus erat imperatores
8 Romani ad se perduxerunt, et nobilissimos Hispanos supra trecentos in Italiam ad sollicitandos populares qui inter auxilia Hannibalis erant miserunt. Id [1] modo eius anni in Hispania [2] ad memoriam insigne est, quod mercennarium militem in castris neminem ante quam tum Celtiberos Romani habuerunt.

[1] Id modo . . . habuerunt *P*(1) : *spurious Geyer.*
[2] eius (*or* eris) anni in Hispania *P*(1) : *spurious Conway.*

In Spain nothing notable occurred except that the B.C. 213
Roman commanders attracted to their side the young men of the Celtiberians at the same pay at which these had made an agreement with the Carthaginians, and more than three hundred Spaniards of the highest rank were sent to Italy to win over their fellow-countrymen who were among Hannibal's auxiliaries. This is the only occurrence of that year in Spain that is worthy of record, since the Romans had no mercenary soldiers in their camps previous to the Celtiberians whom they had at that time.

LIBRI XXIV PERIOCHA

HIERONYMUS Syracusanorum rex, cuius pater Hiero amicus populi Romani fuerat, ad Carthaginienses defecit et propter crudelitatem superbiamque a suis interfectus est. Tib. Sempronius Gracchus proconsul prospere adversus Poenos et Hannonem ducem ad Beneventum pugnavit servorum maxime opera, quos liberos esse iussit. Claudius Marcellus consul in Sicilia, quae prope tota ad Poenos defecerat, Syracusas obsedit. Philippo Macedonum regi bellum indictum est, qui ad Apolloniam nocturno proelio oppressus fugatusque in Macedoniam cum prope inermi exercitu profugit. Ad id bellum gerendum M. Valerius praetor missus. Res praeterea in Hispania a P. et Cn. Scipionibus adversus Carthaginienses gestas continet;[1] a quibus Syphax rex Numidiae in amicitiam adscitus, qui a Masinissa Massyliorum rege pro Carthaginiensibus pugnante victus in Hispaniam ad Scipionem cum magna manu transiit contra Gades, ubi angusto freto Africa et Hispania dirimuntur. Celtiberi quoque in amicitiam recepti sunt, quorum auxiliis adscitis tunc primum mercennarium militem Romana castra habuerunt.

[1] *The following lines (to the end) appear to be a later addition, Zangemeister, Wölfflin.*

SUMMARY OF BOOK XXIV

Hieronymus, king of the Syracusans, whose father[1] Hiero had been a friend of the Roman people, revolted to the Carthaginians and on account of his cruelty and haughtiness was slain by his own men. Tiberius Sempronius Gracchus as proconsul fought with success against the Carthaginians and Hanno their general near Beneventum, chiefly by the help of the slaves, whom he ordered to be free men. Claudius Marcellus, the consul, in Sicily, which had almost entirely revolted to the Carthaginians, besieged Syracuse. War was declared against Philip, king of the Macedonians, and he, surprised at Apollonia in a battle at night and put to flight, fled with an army almost disarmed into Macedonia. Marcus Valerius, a praetor, was sent to conduct that war. Furthermore the book contains what was accomplished against the Carthaginians in Spain by Publius and Gnaeus Scipio, by whom Syphax, king of Numidia, was won over to friendship. Syphax, defeated by Masinissa, king of the Massylians,[2] who was fighting for the Carthaginians, crossed over with a large force to Scipio in Spain, from a point opposite Gades, where Africa and Spain are parted by a narrow strait.[3] The Celtiberians also were admitted to friendship, and by their enrollment as auxiliaries Roman camps then for the first time had mercenary soldiers.

[1] An error for grandfather.

[2] *I.e.* the Maesulians.

[3] The statement that Syphax actually crossed over to Spain conflicts with the text (xlix. 6).

THE FAMILY OF HIERO

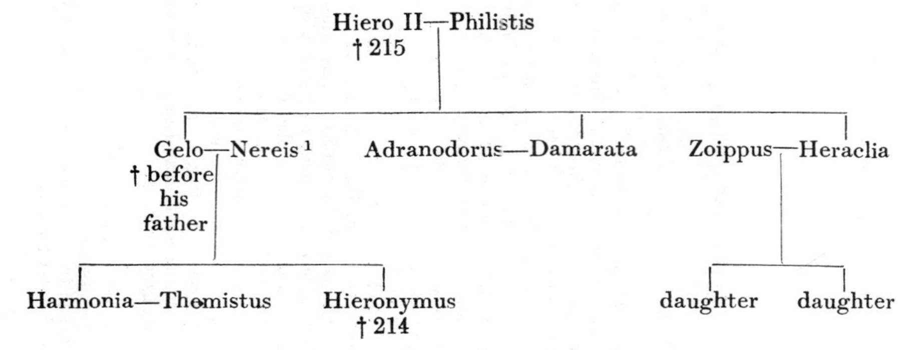

[1] A grand-daughter, rather than daughter, of Pyrrhus.

BOOK XXV

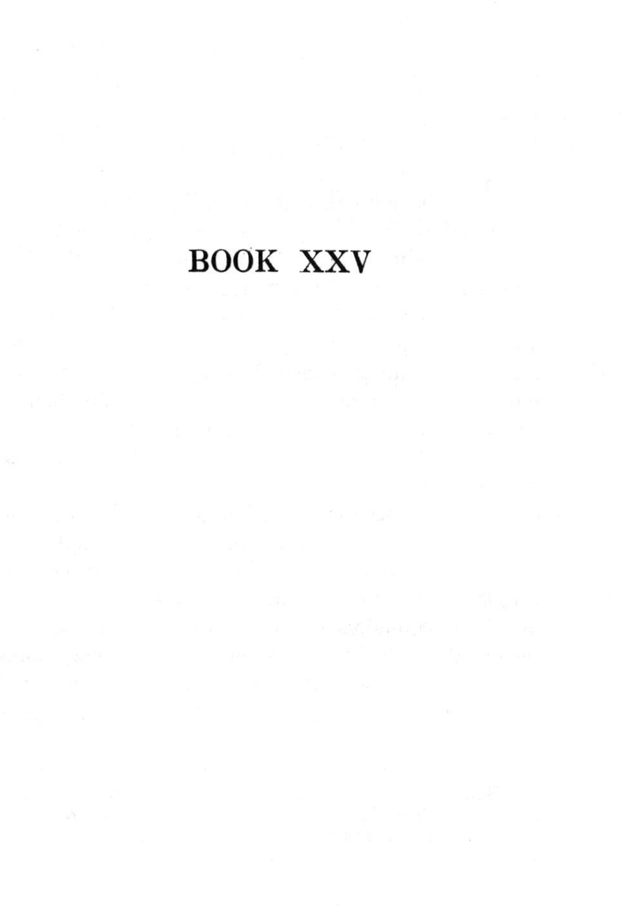

LIBER XXV

A.U.C. 541 I. Dum haec in Africa atque in Hispania geruntur,
Hannibal in agro Sallentino aestatem consumpsit
spe per proditionem urbis Tarentinorum potiundae.
Ipsorum interim Sallentinorum ignobiles urbes ad
2 eum defecerunt. Eodem tempore in Bruttiis ex
duodecim populis qui anno priore ad Poenos desciverant Consentini et Tauriani in fidem populi Romani
3 redierunt; et plures redissent, ni T. Pomponius
Veientanus, praefectus socium, prosperis aliquot
populationibus in agro Bruttio iusti ducis speciem
nactus tumultuario exercitu coacto cum Hannone
4 conflixisset. Magna ibi vis hominum, sed inconditae
turbae agrestium servorumque, caesa aut capta est.
Minimum iacturae fuit quod praefectus inter ceteros
est captus, et tum temerariae pugnae auctor et ante
publicanus omnibus malis artibus et rei publicae et
5 societatibus infidus damnosusque. Sempronius
consul in Lucanis multa proelia parva, haud ullum
dignum memoratu fecit et ignobilia oppida Lucanorum aliquot expugnavit.

---

[1] Hannibal is now in the southern part of Calabria, three days' march from Tarentum; cf. viii. 12. He had previously been near Arpi, in Apulia; XXIV. xlv. 11 ff.

BOOK XXV

I. WHILE these things were being done in Africa and Spain, Hannibal spent the summer in the Sallentine region,[1] in the hope of getting possession of the city of Tarentum through treachery. Meantime, however, Sallentine cities of no importance went over to his side. At the same time among the Bruttians, out of twelve states which in the previous year had revolted to the Carthaginians, Consentia and Taurianum returned to their allegiance to the Roman people; and more would have returned if a prefect of the allies, Titus Pomponius Veientanus, who by successfully ravaging Bruttian territory a number of times gained the appearance of a regularly appointed general, had not gathered a hastily mustered army and engaged Hanno. A great many men were slain or captured there, an ill-organized mass, however, of rustics and slaves. It was the smallest part of the loss that, along with the rest, the prefect was captured, who was responsible at that time for a reckless battle, and had previously been a tax-farmer possessed of all the dishonest devices, faithless and ruinous both to the state and to the companies. Sempronius, the consul, fought many small engagements in Lucania, not one worthy of record, and took by storm a number of unimportant Lucanian towns. B.C. 213

A.U.C. 541

6 Quo diutius trahebatur bellum et variabant secundae adversaeque res non fortunam magis quam
animos hominum, tanta religio, et ea magna ex parte
externa, civitatem incessit ut aut homines aut dei
7 repente alii viderentur facti. Nec iam in secreto
modo atque intra parietes abolebantur Romani ritus,
sed in publico etiam ac foro Capitolioque mulierum
turba erat nec sacrificantium nec precantium deos
8 patrio more. Sacrificuli ac vates ceperant hominum
mentes, quorum numerum auxit rustica plebs, ex
incultis diutino bello infestisque agris egestate et
metu in urbem conpulsa, et quaestus ex alieno errore
facilis, quem velut concessae artis usu exercebant.
9 Primo secretae bonorum indignationes exaudiebantur; deinde ad patres et iam ad[1] publicam
10 querimoniam excessit res. Incusati graviter ab
senatu aediles triumvirique capitales quod non prohiberent, cum emovere eam multitudinem e foro ac
disicere adparatus sacrorum conati essent, haud
11 procul afuit quin violarentur. Ubi potentius iam
esse id malum apparuit quam ut minores per magistratus sedaretur, M. Aemilio praetori urbano[2]
negotium ab senatu datum est ut eis religionibus
12 populum liberaret. Is et in contione senatus consultum recitavit et edixit ut quicumque libros vaticinos precationesve aut artem sacrificandi con-

[1] et iam ad *Alschefski* : etiamad *P*(1) : etiam ac *Weissenborn.*

[2] urbano (*i.e.* urb.) *P*(1) : *om. as gloss Walters.*

---

[1] Forsaken, as they felt, by their own gods, the populace were turning to foreign divinities and strange cults.

[2] An error of Livy for Marcus Atilius; XXIV. xliv. 2, where Aemilius, *praetor peregrinus,* assigns his duties to Atilius,

The longer the war dragged on and success and failure altered the situation, and quite as much so the attitude of men, superstitious fears, in large part foreign at that, invaded the state to such a degree that either men or else gods suddenly seemed changed. And now not only in secret and within the walls of houses were Roman rites abandoned, but in public places also and in the Forum and on the Capitol there was a crowd of women who were following the custom of the fathers neither in their sacrifices nor in prayers to the gods.[1] Petty priests and also prophets had taken hold on men's minds. And the number of these was increased by the mass of rustics forced by want and fear into the city from their farms neglected and endangered because of the long war, and by easy profit from the delusion of others—a trade which they plied as though it were sanctioned. At first good men's indignation was voiced in private; then the matter reached the senate and now even official complaints. The aediles and the three police magistrates were roundly censured by the senate because they did not stop it; and after they had attempted to drive that crowd out of the Forum and to scatter the properties required for the rites, they narrowly escaped violence. Now that the disorder appeared to be too strong to be quelled by the lower magistrates, the senate assigned to Marcus Aemilius,[2] the city praetor, the task of freeing the people from such superstitions. He read the decree of the senate in an assembly, and also issued an edict that whoever had books of prophecies or prayers or a ritual of sacrifice set down in writing should bring all such B.C. 213

praetor urbanus, and takes a command in Apulia. The error is repeated in iii. 12 and xii. 3.

A.U.C. 541 scriptam haberet, eos libros omnis litterasque ad se
ante kal. Apriles deferret, neu quis in publico
sacrove loco novo aut externo ritu sacrificaret.

II. Aliquot publici sacerdotes mortui eo anno sunt,
L. Cornelius Lentulus pontifex maximus et C.
Papirius C. f. Masso pontifex et P. Furius Philus
augur et C. Papirius L. f. Masso decemvir sacrorum.
2 In Lentuli locum M. Cornelius Cethegus, in Papiri
Cn. Servilius Caepio pontifices suffecti sunt, augur
creatus L. Quinctius Flamininus, decemvir sacrorum
L. Cornelius Lentulus.

3 Comitiorum consularium iam adpetebat tempus;
sed quia consules bello [1] intentos avocare non placebat, Ti. Sempronius consul comitiorum causa dictatorem dixit C. Claudium Centonem. Ab eo magister
4 equitum est dictus Q. Fulvius Flaccus. Dictator
primo comitiali die creavit consules Q. Fulvium Flac-
cum magistrum equitum et Ap. Claudium Pulchrum,
5 cui Sicilia provincia in praetura fuerat. Tum praetores creati Cn. Fulvius Flaccus, C. Claudius Nero,
M. Iunius Silanus, P. Cornelius Sulla. Comitiis
6 perfectis dictator magistratu abiit. Aedilis curulis
fuit eo anno cum M. Cornelio Cethego P. Cornelius
Scipio, cui post Africano fuit cognomen. Huic
petenti aedilitatem cum obsisterent tribuni plebis,
negantes rationem eius habendam esse, quod

[1] bello $P^{1}?x$: a bello $P(10)$.

---

[1] Exact compliance with written directions being essential, as in the Roman religion, to seize the texts was in effect to suppress the cults.

[2] Cf. xii. 10 f.

[3] Scipio was probably only 22, but the famous law fixing statutory ages for the different offices (Lex Villia annalis) was not passed until 180 B.C.; XL. xliv. 1.

books and writings [1] to him before the first of April, B.C. 213 and that no one should sacrifice in a public or consecrated place according to a strange or foreign rite.

II. A number of priests of the state died that year: Lucius Cornelius Lentulus, pontifex maximus, and Gaius Papirius Masso, son of Gaius, a pontifex, and Publius Furius Philus, an augur, and Gaius Papirius Masso, son of Lucius, a decemvir in charge of rites.[2] In place of Lentulus they made Marcus Cornelius Cethegus a pontiff and Gnaeus Servilius Caepio in that of Papirius; Lucius Quinctius Flamininus was named augur, Lucius Cornelius Lentulus, decemvir in charge of rites.

For the consular elections the time was now approaching, but because the consuls were occupied with the war and it was not thought advisable to call them away, Tiberius Sempronius, the consul, named Gaius Claudius Cento dictator to hold the elections. He in turn named Quintus Fulvius Flaccus master of the horse. On the first day available for elections the dictator announced the choice as consuls of Quintus Fulvius Flaccus, master of the horse, and Appius Claudius Pulcher, who as praetor had had Sicily as his province. Then the following were elected praetors: Gnaeus Fulvius Flaccus, Gaius Claudius Nero, Marcus Junius Silanus, Publius Cornelius Sulla. Having finished the elections, the dictator laid down his office. Curule aedile that year, together with Marcus Cornelius Cethegus, was Publius Cornelius Scipio,[3] who was later called Africanus. When he was a candidate for the aedileship, and the tribunes of the plebs tried to oppose him, saying that he ought not to be considered because he did

A.U.C. 541

7 nondum ad petendum legitima aetas esset, "Si me" inquit "omnes Quirites aedilem facere volunt, satis annorum habeo." Tanto inde favore ad suffragium ferendum in tribus discursum est ut tribuni
8 repente incepto destiterint. Aedilicia largitio haec fuit: ludi Romani pro temporis illius copiis magnifice facti et diem unum instaurati, et congii olei in vicos
9 singulos dati . . . .[1] L. Villius Tappulus et M. Fundanius Fundulus aediles plebei aliquot matronas apud populum probri accusarunt; quasdam ex eis
10 damnatas in exilium egerunt. Ludi plebei per biduum instaurati et Iovis epulum fuit ludorum causa.

A.U.C. 542

III. Q. Fulvius Flaccus tertium Appius Claudius
2 consulatum ineunt. Et praetores provincias sortiti sunt, P. Cornelius Sulla urbanam et peregrinam, quae duorum ante sors fuerat, Cn. Fulvius Flaccus Apuliam, C. Claudius Nero Suessulam, M. Iunius
3 Silanus Tuscos. Consulibus bellum cum Hannibale et binae legiones decretae; alter a Q. Fabio superioris anni consule, alter a Fulvio Centumalo acciperet;
4 praetorum Fulvi Flacci quae Luceriae sub Aemilio praetore, Neronis Claudi quae in Piceno sub C. Terentio fuissent legiones essent; supplementum in eas ipsi scriberent sibi. M. Iunio in Tuscos

[1] *Numeral missing, perhaps* L *preceding* L. (*Engelmann*) *at end of line in P.*

---

[1] The *ludi Romani* or *maximi* occurred in mid-September and lasted four days. For repetition cf. XXIII. xxx. 16.

[2] A *congius* held about three quarts.

[3] As in wartime cases to be heard by the *praetor peregrinus* would be much reduced in number, he could be spared for service at the front; XXIV. xliv. 2.

[4] A military base in Campania, southeast of Capua, half-way to Nola. Its Castra Claudiana lay near the entrance to the Caudine Pass. Cf. XXIII. xxxi. 3; XXIV. xvii. 2; xliv. 3.

not have the legal age for candidacy, he said, "If all the citizens want to make me aedile I have years enough." Thereupon with such enthusiasm they separated to form by tribes in order to cast their votes, that the tribunes suddenly gave up their attempt. The generosity of the aediles consisted in celebrating the Roman Games [1] splendidly, for the resources of that time, and in repeating them for one day; also in giving . . . measures [2] of oil for each precinct. Lucius Villius Tappulus and Marcus Fundanius Fundulus as plebeian aediles brought before the people charges of immorality against a number of matrons. Some of these being convicted, they drove them into exile. The Plebeian Games were repeated for two days, and on account of the festival a banquet for Jupiter was held. B.C. 213

III. Quintus Fulvius Flaccus and Appius Claudius entered upon their consulship, the former for the third time. And the praetors received by lot the following assignments: Publius Cornelius Sulla, the duties of praetor urbanus and praetor peregrinus,[3] previously two separate offices; Gnaeus Fulvius Flaccus, Apulia, Gaius Claudius Nero, Suessula,[4] Marcus Junius Silanus, Etruria. To the consuls were assigned by decree the war with Hannibal and two legions each. The one was to take over his troops from Quintus Fabius, consul in the previous year, the other from Fulvius Centumalus. Of the praetors, Fulvius Flaccus was to have the legions which had been at Luceria under the praetor Aemilius, Nero Claudius the one [5] which had been in the Picene district under Gaius Terentius. They were themselves to enlist more recruits for the same. To Marcus Junius the B.C. 212

[5] Terentius Varro had had only one legion; XXIV. xliv. 5.

A.U.C. 542
5 legiones urbanae prioris anni datae. Ti. Sempronio
Gracco et P. Sempronio Tuditano imperium provinciaeque Lucani et Gallia cum suis exercitibus
6 prorogatae; item P. Lentulo qua vetus provincia in
Sicilia esset, M. Marcello Syracusae et qua Hieronis
regnum fuisset; T. Otacilio classis, Graecia M.
Valerio, Sardinia Q. Mucio Scaevolae, Hispaniae P.
7 et Cn. Corneliis. Ad veteres exercitus duae urbanae
legiones a consulibus scriptae, summaque trium et
viginti legionum eo anno effecta est.

8 Dilectum consulum M. Postumii Pyrgensis cum
9 magno prope motu rerum factum impediit. Publicanus erat Postumius, qui multis annis parem fraude
avaritiaque neminem in civitate habuerat praeter
T. Pomponium Veientanum, quem populantem
temere agros in Lucanis ductu Hannonis priore anno
10 ceperant Carthaginienses. Hi, quia publicum periculum erat a vi tempestatis in iis quae portarentur
ad exercitus et ementiti erant falsa naufragia et ea
ipsa quae vera renuntiaverant fraude ipsorum facta
11 erant, non casu. In veteres quassasque naves
paucis et parvi pretii rebus impositis, cum mersissent
eas in alto exceptis in praeparatas scaphas nautis,
12 multiplices fuisse merces ementiebantur. Ea fraus
indicata M. Aemilio praetori priore anno fuerat ac
per eum ad senatum delata nec tamen ullo senatus

[1] Cf. XXIV. xliv. 4; vii. 9.
[2] Cf. i. 3 f.

city legions of the previous year were given for Etruria. For Tiberius Sempronius Gracchus and Publius Sempronius Tuditanus their commands and provinces, Lucania and Gaul, with their armies, were continued. And the same was done for Publius Lentulus, within the limits of the old province in Sicily, and for Marcellus, whose province was Syracuse and up to the former boundaries of Hiero's kingdom.[1] The fleet was assigned to Titus Otacilius, Greece to Marcus Valerius, Sardinia to Quintus Mucius Scaevola, the Spanish provinces to Publius and Gnaeus Cornelius. In addition to the old armies two city legions were enrolled by the consuls, and the total that year amounted to twenty-three legions. B.C. 212

The consular levy was hampered by the conduct of Marcus Postumius of Pyrgi, which almost occasioned a serious insurrection. Postumius was a tax-farmer, who in many years had had no equal in dishonesty and avarice in the state, except Titus Pomponius Veientanus, whom the Carthaginians under Hanno's command had captured in the preceding year, while he was rashly ravaging the country in Lucania.[2] These men, since the state assumed the risk from violent storms in the case of shipments to the armies, had falsely reported imaginary shipwrecks, and even those which they had correctly reported had been brought about by their own trickery, not by accident. They would put small cargoes of little value on old, battered vessels, sink them at sea, after taking off the crews in small boats that were in readiness, and then falsely declare that the shipments were far more valuable. This dishonesty had been reported in the previous year to Marcus Aemilius, the praetor, and by him brought before the senate, but it was not branded by

A.U.C. 542 consulto notata, quia patres ordinem publicanorum
13 in tali tempore offensum nolebant. Populus severior
vindex fraudis erat, excitatique tandem duo tribuni
plebis, Spurius et L. Carvilii, cum rem invisam
infamemque cernerent, ducentum milium aeris
14 multam M. Postumio dixerunt. Cui certandae cum
dies advenisset, conciliumque tam frequens plebis
adesset ut multitudinem area Capitolii vix caperet,
15 perorata causa una spes videbatur esse si C. Servilius
Casca tribunus plebis, qui propinquus cognatusque
Postumio erat, priusquam ad suffragium tribus
16 vocarentur, intercessisset. Testibus datis tribuni
populum summoverunt, sitellaque lata est, ut sorti-
17 rentur ubi Latini suffragium ferrent. Interim
publicani Cascae instare ut concilio diem eximeret;
populus reclamare; et forte in cornu primus sedebat
Casca, cui simul metus pudorque animum versabat.
18 Cum in eo parum praesidii esset, turbandae rei causa
publicani per vacuum summoto locum cuneo inrupe-
19 runt iurgantes simul cum populo tribunisque. Nec
procul dimicatione res erat cum Fulvius consul
tribunis "Nonne videtis" inquit "vos in ordinem
coactos esse et rem ad seditionem spectare, ni
propere dimittitis plebis concilium?"

IV. Plebe dimissa senatus vocatur et consules

[1] It was left for the people to confirm or remit such a fine; cf. XXXVII. li. 4 f.; lviii. 1; Cicero, *Phil.* XI. 18; *de Leg.* III. 6.

[2] The witnesses were to watch the balloting.

[3] *I.e.* such Latins as were present at Rome. In which of the tribes they should vote was determined by the tribunes, who cast lots.

[4] Any action interfering with a tribune's duties or privileges was held equivalent to degrading him from office; cf. XLIII. 16. 9 f.

any decree of the senate, because the senators were unwilling to offend the tax-farmers as a class at such a crisis. The people proved a more unsparing avenger of dishonesty; namely, two tribunes of the plebs, Spurius and Lucius Carvilius, were at length aroused, and seeing that the affair was unpopular and notorious, imposed a fine of two hundred thousand asses upon Marcus Postumius. When the day for his protest against this fine arrived, the assembly of the commons [1] was so large that the open space on the Capitol could scarcely contain the crowd. After the arguments were concluded, there seemed to be but one hope, namely, if Gaius Servilius Casca, a tribune of the plebs who was a blood-relative of Postumius, should interpose his veto before the tribes should be called to vote. The tribunes provided witnesses,[2] cleared the people away, and the urn was brought, that they might determine by lot in which tribe the Latins [3] should vote. Meantime the tax-farmers pressed Casca to adjourn that day's hearing before the assembly. The people protested; and it so happened that the first seat at the end of the platform was occupied by Casca, whose mind was swayed at once by fear and shame. Finding in him no sufficient protection, the publicans, in order to prevent action, rushed in a wedge through the space cleared by removal of the crowd, while at the same time they reviled the people and the tribunes. And it had almost come to a battle when Fulvius, the consul, said to the tribunes, "Do you not see that you are reduced to the ranks,[4] and that this means an insurrection if you do not promptly dismiss the popular assembly?" B.C. 212

IV. The assembly being dismissed, the senate was summoned and the consuls brought up the matter

A.U.C. 542 referunt de concilio plebis turbato vi atque audacia
2 publicanorum: M. Furium Camillum, cuius exilium ruina urbis secutura[1] fuerit, damnari se ab iratis
3 civibus passum esse; decemviros ante eum, quorum legibus ad eam diem viverent, multos postea principes
4 civitatis iudicium de se populi passos: Postumium Pyrgensem suffragium populo Romano extorsisse, concilium plebis sustulisse, tribunos in ordinem coegisse, contra populum Romanum aciem instruxisse, locum occupasse, ut tribunos a plebe intercluderet,
5 tribus in suffragium vocari prohiberet. Nihil aliud a caede ac dimicatione continuisse homines nisi patientiam magistratuum, quod cesserint in praesentia furori atque audaciae paucorum vincique se ac populum
6 Romanum passi sint et comitia, quae reus vi atque armis prohibiturus erat, ne causa quaerentibus dimicationem daretur, voluntate ipsi sua sustulerint.
7 Haec cum ab optimo quoque pro atrocitate rei accepta[2] essent, vimque eam contra rem publicam et pernicioso exemplo factam senatus decresset,
8 confestim Carvilii tribuni plebis omissa multae certatione rei capitalis diem Postumio dixerunt ac, ni vades daret, prendi a viatore atque in carcerem
9 duci iusserunt. Postumius vadibus datis non adfuit.

[1] secutura *Alschefski*: secura *P*(1).
[2] accepta *Madvig*: acta *P*(1).

---

[1] Cf. V. xxxii. 9; xxxiii. 1.

of the disturbance in the popular assembly owing to the violence and audacity of the publicans. Marcus Furius Camillus,[1] it was said, a man whose exile would have been followed by the ruin of the city, had allowed himself to be condemned by the angry citizens; that before his time the decemvirs, under whose laws they were then still living, and later many leading men in the state, had submitted to the judgment of the people in their cases; that Postumius of Pyrgi had wrested the vote from the Roman people, had brought to naught an assembly of the plebs, reduced the tribunes to the ranks, drawn up a battle-line against the Roman people, had taken his position, to separate the tribunes from the people and to prevent the tribes from being summoned to vote. Nothing had restrained men from slaughter and battle but the forbearance of the magistrates in yielding for the moment to the mad audacity of a few men, and in allowing themselves and the Roman people to be worsted, also in that, as regards the voting, which the defendant would have prevented by force of arms, they had of their own accord suspended it, to avoid giving excuse to those eager for the fray. These words were interpreted by all the best citizens as deserved by an outrageous occurrence, and the senate declared that this violence had been employed against the state, setting a dangerous precedent. Thereupon the Carvilii, tribunes of the people, in place of the procedure to fix the amount of the fine, at once named a day for Postumius' appearance on a capital charge, and ordered that if he did not furnish sureties he should be seized by an attendant and taken to prison. Postumius furnished sureties, but did not appear. B.C. 212

A.U.C. 542 Tribuni plebem rogaverunt plebesque ita scivit, si M. Postumius ante kal. Maias non prodisset citatusque eo die non respondisset neque excusatus esset, videri eum in exilio esse bonaque eius venire,
10 ipsi aqua et igni placere interdici. Singulis deinde eorum qui turbae ac tumultus concitatores fuerant, rei capitalis diem dicere ac vades poscere coeperunt.
11 Primo non dantis, deinde etiam eos qui dare possent in carcerem coiciebant; cuius rei periculum vitantes plerique in exilium abierunt.

V. Hunc fraus publicanorum, deinde fraudem
2 audacia protegens exitum habuit. Comitia inde pontifici maximo creando sunt habita; ea comitia
3 novus pontifex M. Cornelius Cethegus habuit. Tres ingenti certamine petierunt, Q. Fulvius Flaccus consul, qui et ante bis consul et censor fuerat, et T. Manlius Torquatus, et ipse duobus consulatibus et censura insignis, et P. Licinius Crassus, qui aedili-
4 tatem curulem petiturus erat. Hic senes honoratosque iuvenis in eo certamine vicit. Ante hunc intra centum annos et viginti nemo praeter P. Cornelium Calussam pontifex maximus creatus fuerat qui sella curuli non sedisset.

5 Consules dilectum cum aegre conficerent, quod inopia iuniorum non facile in utrumque, ut et novae urbanae legiones et supplementum veteribus scri-
6 beretur, sufficiebat, senatus absistere eos incepto

The tribunes put the question to the plebs and the plebs ordained that, if Marcus Postumius should not appear before the first of May, and on being summoned on that day should not reply nor be excused, it should be understood that he was in exile, and be decided that his property should be sold and himself refused water and fire. The tribunes then began to name a day for the appearance on a capital charge of each of those who had been instigators of riot and sedition, and to demand sureties from them. At first they threw into prison those who did not give security, and then even those who were able to do so. Avoiding this danger many went into exile. B.C. 212

V. Such was the outcome of dishonesty on the part of the publicans and of audacity seeking to cover dishonesty. Next was held an election for the choice of a pontifex maximus. This election was conducted by a new pontiff, Marcus Cornelius Cethegus. Three men canvassed with great rivalry: Quintus Fulvius Flaccus, the consul, who had been consul twice before and also censor, and Titus Manlius Torquatus, likewise distinguished by two consulships and a censorship, and Publius Licinius Crassus, who was only about to be a candidate for a curule aedileship. This young man defeated in that contest old men who had held high offices. Before him for a hundred and twenty years no one who had not occupied a curule chair had been elected pontifex maximus, except Publius Cornelius Calussa.

The consuls were finding it difficult to complete the levy, since the scant supply of young men was hardly sufficient for the two purposes, enrollment of new legions for the city and replacements for the old ones. The senate accordingly forbade them to give

A.U.C. 542 vetuit et triumviros binos creari iussit, alteros qui citra, alteros qui ultra quinquagensimum lapidem in pagis forisque et conciliabulis omnem copiam inge-
7 nuorum inspicerent et, si qui roboris satis ad ferenda arma habere viderentur, etiamsi nondum militari
8 aetate essent, milites facerent; tribuni plebis, si iis videretur, ad populum ferrent ut, qui minores septem decem annis sacramento dixissent, iis perinde stipendia procederent ac si septem decem annorum
9 aut maiores milites facti essent. Ex hoc senatus consulto creati triumviri bini conquisitionem ingenuorum per agros habuerunt.

10 Eodem tempore ex Sicilia litterae Marci Marcelli de postulatis militum qui cum P. Lentulo militabant in senatu recitatae sunt. Cannensis reliquiae cladis hic exercitus erat, relegatus in Siciliam, sicut ante dictum est, ne ante Punici belli finem in Italiam reportarentur. VI. Hi permissu Lentuli primores equitum centurionumque et robora ex legionibus peditum legatos in hiberna ad M. Marcellum mise-
2 runt, e quibus unus potestate dicendi facta: "Consulem te, M. Marcelle, in Italia[1] adissemus, cum primum de nobis, etsi non iniquum, certe triste senatus consultum factum est, nisi hoc sperassemus,

[1] Italia *x*: italiam *P*(1).

---

[1] For *fora* and *conciliabula*, cf. xxii. 4; XXXIX. xiv. 7; xviii. 2; XL. xxxvii. 3 f.; XLIII. xiv. 10. *A forum* was a Roman settlement, usually on an important road (*e.g.* Forum Appii), but lacking the status of a *colonia*. A *conciliabulum* was a petty administrative centre for rural districts (*pagi*).

[2] Cf. XXIII. xxv. 7; XXIV. xviii. 9.

up the attempt and ordered the appointment of two commissions of three officials each, to inspect in rural districts, market-towns and local centres [1] all possible freeborn men within fifty miles, the other beyond that distance, and any that seemed to them strong enough to bear arms, even if not yet of military age, they were to recruit. The tribunes of the plebs, if they should see fit, were to bring before the people a bill that, in the case of those who had taken the military oath at less than seventeen years, their campaigns should run just as if they had been recruited at seventeen years or older. In accordance with this decree of the senate two commissions of three members each were appointed and they conducted the search for freeborn men in the country. B.C. 212

At the same time a letter from Marcus Marcellus in Sicily was read in the senate concerning demands of the soldiers serving under Publius Lentulus. This army was the remnant of the disaster at Cannae, and, as has been said above, was relegated to Sicily, not to be brought back to Italy before the end of the Punic War.[2] VI. These men with Lentulus' permission sent their leading knights and centurions and picked men from the infantry of the legions to Marcus Marcellus at his winter quarters as their representatives, and one of them, receiving permission to speak, said: "In your consulship,[3] Marcus Marcellus, and in Italy we should have come to you already, directly after the senate made in our case a decree that, if not unjust, was surely severe, had it not been our hope that we were being sent into a province thrown

[3] But at the time of the *senatus consultum* Marcellus was not consul, but praetor, and the men in question were in his own army; cf. XXIII. xxiv. 1; xxv. 7.

A.U.C. 542 in provinciam nos morte regum turbatam ad grave
3 bellum adversus Siculos simul Poenosque mitti, et
sanguine nostro vulneribusque nos senatui[1] satis-
facturos esse, sicut patrum memoria qui capti a
Pyrrho ad Heracleam erant adversus Pyrrhum ipsum
4 pugnantes satisfecerunt. Quamquam quod ob meri-
tum nostrum suscensuistis, patres conscripti, nobis
5 aut suscensetis? Ambo mihi consules et universum
senatum intueri videor, cum te, M. Marcelle, intueor,
quem si ad Cannas consulem habuissemus, melior et
6 rei publicae et nostra fortuna esset. Sine, quaeso,
priusquam de condicione nostra queror, noxam
cuius arguimur nos purgare. Si non deum ira nec
fato, cuius lege immobilis rerum humanarum ordo
seritur, sed culpa periimus ad Cannas, cuius tandem
7 ea culpa fuit? Militum an imperatorum? Equidem
miles nihil umquam dicam de imperatore meo, cui
praesertim gratias sciam ab senatu actas quod non
desperaverit de re publica, cui post fugam ab Cannis[2]
8 per omnes annos prorogatum imperium. Ceteros
item ex reliquiis cladis eius, quos tribunos militum
habuimus, honores petere et gerere et provincias
9 obtinere audivimus. An vobis vestrisque liberis
ignoscitis facile, patres conscripti, in haec vilia capita
saevitis?[3] Et consuli primoribusque aliis civitatis
fugere, cum spes alia nulla esset, turpe non fuit,
10 milites utique morituros in aciem misistis? Ad

[1] nos senatui *Bentley*: nostris senatui *Crévier*: nostratui *PA?*(2).

[2] ab Cannis *Gronovius*: actamnis *P*: actamnisi P^2*?*(1): Cannensem A^y.

[3] saevitis A^2: saeviret *PA?*(11): saevire P^xCM^1: saevire libet *Hertz.*

---

[1] Cf. V. xxxviii.

into confusion by the death of its kings, to carry on a serious war against Sicilians and Carthaginians combined, and that by our blood and wounds we were to give satisfaction to the senate, just as in the time of our fathers the men who had been captured by Pyrrhus at Heraclea had done by fighting against Pyrrhus himself. And yet for what desert of ours have you been angry at us, conscript fathers, or are now angry? It seems that I am looking at both consuls and the entire senate when I look at you, Marcus Marcellus. If we had had you as consul at Cannae the lot of the state, and of ourselves as well, would be a better one. Before I complain of our plight, permit us, I pray, to clear ourselves of the offence of which we are charged. If it was not by anger of the gods nor by Fate, according to whose law the chain of human events is unalterably linked, but by a fault that we were undone at Cannae, whose fault, pray, was it? Of the soldiers or of the generals? For my part I, a soldier, will never say anything about my general, especially since I know that he was thanked by the senate because he did not lose hope for the state, and that after the flight from Cannae his command was continued year after year. The others too who survived that disaster, the men whom we had as our tribunes of the soldiers, canvass for offices, we have heard, and hold them, and govern provinces. Can it be, conscript fathers, that you readily pardon yourselves and your sons, but are cruel to these creatures of no account? And while it was no disgrace to the consul and other leading men in the state to flee, since there was no other hope, did you send your common soldiers into battle to die inevitably? At the Allia [1] almost the entire B.C. 212

A.U.C. 542 Alliam prope omnis exercitus fugit; ad Furculas
Caudinas ne expertus quidem certamen arma
tradidit hosti, ut alias pudendas clades exercituum
11 taceam; tamen tantum afuit ab eo ut ulla ignominia
iis exercitibus quaereretur ut et urbs Roma per eum
exercitum qui ab Allia Veios transfugerat recipera-
12 retur, et Caudinae legiones, quae sine armis redierant
Romam, armatae remissae in Samnium eundem
illum hostem sub iugum miserint qui hac sua igno-
13 minia laetatus fuerat. Cannensem vero quisquam
exercitum fugae aut pavoris insimulare potest, ubi
plus quinquaginta milia hominum ceciderunt, unde
consul cum equitibus septuaginta fugit, unde nemo
superest nisi quem hostis caedendo fessus reliquit?
14 Cum captivis redemptio negabatur, nos vulgo
homines laudabant quod rei publicae nos reservasse-
mus, quod ad consulem Venusiam redissemus et
15 speciem iusti exercitus fecissemus; nunc deteriore
condicione sumus quam apud patres nostros fuerunt [1]
captivi. Quippe illis arma tantum atque ordo mili-
tandi locusque in quo tenderent in castris est mutatus,
quae tamen semel navata rei publicae opera et uno
16 felici proelio recuperarunt; nemo eorum relegatus
in exilium est, nemini spes emerendi stipendia
adempta, hostis denique est datus, cum quo dimi-
cantes aut vitam semel aut ignominiam finirent;
17 nos, quibus, nisi quod commisimus ut quisquam ex
Cannensi acie miles Romanus superesset, nihil obici
potest, non solum a patria procul Italiaque sed ab

[1] fuerunt *J. H. Voss*: fuerant *P*(1).

---

[1] Cf. IX. iv. The following phrase is exaggerated.

army fled; at the Caudine Forks,[1] without even attempting a battle, the army surrendered its weapons to the enemy, not to mention other shameful defeats of armies. But so far were men from devising any disgrace for those armies that the city of Rome was recovered by the army which had fled from the Allia over to Veii, and the Caudine legions, which had returned to Rome without their arms, were sent back armed into Samnium and sent under the yoke that same enemy who had exulted in a disgrace now their own. But at Cannae can any one accuse the army of panic and fright, where more than fifty thousand men fell, whence the consul fled with seventy horsemen, and of which no one survives except the man whom the enemy, tired of slaying, spared? At the time when ransom was refused to captives, men were everywhere praising us because we had saved ourselves for the state, had returned to the consul at Venusia and had formed the semblance of a regular army. But now we are in a worse situation than in our fathers' time were captives. For in their case only their arms and their rank and the position of their tents when in camp were changed. These, however, they recovered by a single service rendered to the state and one victory. Not one of them was sent into exile, not one of them was deprived of the hope of serving out his term; in fine they were given an enemy, so that in battle with him they might once for all end either life or disgrace. But we, against whom no charge can be brought except that we are to blame for the survival of any Roman soldier from the battle-line at Cannae, have been sent far away, not only from our native city and Italy, but also from the enemy, that there B.C. 212

A.U.C. 542 18 hoste etiam relegati sumus, ubi senescamus in exilio,
ne qua spes, ne qua occasio abolendae ignominiae,
ne qua placandae civium irae, ne qua denique bene
19 moriendi sit. Neque ignominiae finem nec virtutis
praemium petimus; modo experiri animum et virtutem exercere liceat. Laborem et periculum petimus,
20 ut virorum, ut militum officio fungamur. Bellum in
Sicilia iam alterum annum ingenti dimicatione geritur; urbes alias Poenus, alias Romanus expugnat;
peditum, equitum acies concurrunt; ad Syracusas
21 terra marique geritur res; clamorem pugnantium
crepitumque armorum exaudimus resides ipsi ac
segnes, tamquam nec manus nec arma habeamus.
Servorum legionibus Ti. Sempronius consul totiens
iam cum hoste signis conlatis pugnavit; operae
22 pretium habent libertatem civitatemque. Pro servis
saltem ad hoc bellum emptis vobis simus; congredi
cum hoste liceat et pugnando quaerere libertatem.
Vis tu mari, vis terra, vis acie, vis urbibus oppugnandis
23 experiri virtutem? Asperrima quaeque ad laborem
periculumque deposcimus, ut quod ad Cannas faci-
undum fuit quam primum fiat, quoniam, quidquid
postea viximus,[1] id omne destinatum ignominiae est."

VII. Sub haec dicta ad genua Marcelli procu-
buerunt. Marcellus id nec iuris nec potestatis suae
esse dixit; senatui scripturum se omniaque de
2 sententia patrum facturum esse. Eae litterae ad
novos consules allatae ac per eos in senatu recitatae
sunt, consultusque de iis litteris ita decrevit senatus:

[1] viximus *P*(1): vivimus *Luchs*: vixerimus *Harant*.

---

[1] XXIV. xvi. 9.

we may grow old in exile, that we may have no hope, B.C. 212
no opportunity of wiping out disgrace, none of appeasing the anger of our citizens, none even of dying bravely. It is neither an end of our disgrace nor a reward for our courage that we ask. Only let us prove our spirit and put our courage into practice. It is for hardship and danger we are asking, that we may do the duty of men and soldiers. The war in Sicily has now been carried on with intensity for two years. Some cities are being stormed by the Carthaginian, some by the Roman. Infantry and cavalry clash in battle-line. At Syracuse the war goes on by land and by sea. The cries of men in battle and the din of arms can be heard by us, who are ourselves unemployed and listless, as if we had neither hands nor weapons. With legions of slaves Tiberius Sempronius, the consul, has engaged the enemy again and again in battle formation. As a reward for their service they have freedom [1] and citizenship. Reckon us at least slaves purchased for this war; let us engage the enemy and by fighting earn freedom. Do you wish, sir, to test our courage on sea, on land, in battle-line, in besieging cities? We demand all the worst in hardship and danger, in order that what should have been done at Cannae be done as soon as possible, since every day that we have since lived has been marked for disgrace."

VII. At the close of this speech they fell at Marcellus' knees. Marcellus said the matter was neither within his competence nor his authority; he would write to the senate and do everything according to the opinion of the fathers. The letter was delivered to the new consuls and by them read in the senate. And after discussion of the letter the senate decreed

A.U.C. 542

3 militibus, qui ad Cannas commilitones suos pugnantis deseruissent, senatum nihil videre cur res publica
4 committenda esset. Si M. Claudio proconsuli aliter videretur, faceret quod e re publica fideque sua duceret, dum ne quis eorum munere vacaret neu dono militari virtutis ergo donaretur neu in Italiam reportaretur donec hostis in terra Italia esset.

5 Comitia deinde a praetore urbano de senatus sententia plebique scitu sunt habita, quibus creati sunt quinqueviri muris turribus [1] reficiendis, et triumviri bini, uni sacris conquirendis donisque persignandis,
6 alteri reficiendis aedibus Fortunae et matris Matutae [2] intra portam Carmentalem et Spei extra portam, quae priore anno incendio consumptae fuerant.

7 Tempestates foedae fuere; in Albano monte biduum continenter lapidibus pluvit. Tacta de caelo multa, duae in Capitolio aedes, vallum in castris multis locis
8 supra Suessulam, et duo vigiles exanimati; murus turresque quaedam Cumis non ictae modo fulminibus sed etiam decussae. Reate saxum ingens visum volitare, sol rubere solito magis sanguineoque similis.
9 Horum prodigiorum causa diem unum supplicatio fuit, et per aliquot dies consules rebus divinis operam dederunt, et per eosdem dies sacrum novemdiale fuit.

10 Cum Tarentinorum defectio iam diu et in spe

[1] turribus *P*(1): et turribus *Weissenborn*: turribusque *A*[y].
[2] Matutae *z*: *om.* *P*(1).

---

[1] Cf. XXIV. xlvii. 15 f.

as follows: that to soldiers who had deserted their comrades in battle at Cannae the senate saw no reason why the welfare of the state should be entrusted. If Marcus Claudius, the proconsul, should take a different view, he should do what he thought to accord with the interest of the state and his own conscience, provided that no one of them should be exempt from duties, or be decorated for valour, or be brought back to Italy, so long as the enemy should be in the land of Italy. B.C. 212

Elections were then held by the praetor urbanus in accordance with a decision of the senate and a plebiscite, and at these there were elected five commissioners for the restoration of the walls and towers, and two boards of three, one to recover sacred vessels and register temple gifts, the other to rebuild the Temple of Fortune and that of Mater Matuta inside Porta Carmentalis, and that of Hope outside the gate—temples that had been destroyed by fire the preceding year.[1]

There were terrible storms; on the Alban Mount it rained stones steadily for two days. Many things were struck by lightning: two temples on the Capitol, the embankment of the camp above Suessula in many places, and two sentries were killed. At Cumae the wall and certain towers were not merely struck by the bolts but even thrown down. At Reate a huge stone seemed to fly, the sun to be redder than usual and of a bloody colour. On account of these prodigies there was a single day of prayer, and for several days the consuls devoted themselves to religious rites; and about the same time there was a nine days' observance.

While a revolt of the Tarentines had long been

A.U.C. 542 Hannibali et in suspicione Romanis esset, causa forte
11 extrinsecus maturandae eius intervenit. Phileas
Tarentinus diu iam per speciem legationis Romae
cum esset, vir inquieti animi et minime otium, quo
tum diutino senescere videbatur, patientis, aditum
sibi ad obsides Tarentinos et Thurinos [1] invenit.
12 Custodiebantur in atrio Libertatis minore cura, quia
nec ipsis nec civitatibus eorum fallere Romanos
13 expediebat. Hos crebris conloquiis sollicitatos corruptis aedituis duobus cum primis tenebris custodia
eduxisset, ipse comes occulti itineris factus profugit.
Luce prima volgata per urbem fuga est, missique
qui sequerentur ab Tarracina comprensos omnis
retraxerunt. Deducti in comitium virgisque adprobante populo caesi de saxo deiciuntur.

VIII. Huius atrocitas poenae duarum nobilissimarum in Italia Graecarum civitatium animos
2 inritavit cum publice, tum etiam singulos privatim,
ut quisque tam foede interemptos aut propinquitate
3 aut amicitia contingebat. Ex iis tredecim fere
nobiles iuvenes Tarentini coniuraverunt, quorum
4 principes Nico et Philemenus erant. Hi priusquam
aliquid moverent, conloquendum cum Hannibale
rati, nocte per speciem venandi urbe egressi ad eum
5 proficiscuntur. Et cum haud procul castris abessent,
ceteri silva prope viam sese occuluerunt, Nico et

[1] Tarentinos et Thurinos *Heusinger*: Thurinos *P* (*cf.* viii. 1): Tarentinos $P^{1?}$(1).

---

[1] As in XXIV. xx. 6.

hoped for by Hannibal and suspected by the Romans, a reason for expediting the same happened to come from without. Phileas of Tarentum, a man of restless spirit and quite unable to endure the long inactivity in which he seemed to be losing his powers, had been at Rome for a long time, nominally as an ambassador. Thus he found means of access to the hostages from Tarentum and Thurii. They were kept under guard in the Atrium Libertatis, with less watchfulness because it was to the interest neither of the hostages themselves nor of their states to outwit the Romans. Phileas worked upon them by frequent conferences, and after bribing two temple-wardens brought them out of confinement at nightfall. Then he himself fled, sharing their secret journey. At daybreak their flight was reported everywhere in the city, and the men sent to pursue them arrested and brought them all back from Tarracina. They were led into the Comitium, scourged with rods with the approval of the people, and thrown down from the Rock.[1] B.C. 212

VIII. The relentlessness of this punishment outraged two of the most important Greek cities in Italy, both as states and personally as well, whenever individuals were connected either by relationship or friendship with those who were so cruelly executed. Of those so connected some thirteen noble youths of Tarentum formed a conspiracy, and Nico and Philemenus were the leaders. Thinking that they ought to confer with Hannibal before taking any step, these men left the city by night under pretext of hunting and set out to go to him. And when they were not far from his camp, the rest concealed themselves in the woods near the road; but Nico

A.U.C. 542 Philemenus progressi ad stationes comprehensique, ultro id petentes, ad Hannibalem deducti sunt.
6 Qui cum et causas consilii sui et quid pararent exposuissent, conlaudati oneratique promissis iubentur, ut fidem popularibus facerent praedandi causa se urbe egressos, pecora Carthaginiensium, quae pastum propulsa essent, ad urbem agere; tuto ac
7 sine certamine id facturos promissum est. Conspecta ea praeda iuvenum est, minusque iterum ac
8 saepius id eos audere miraculo fuit. Congressi cum Hannibale rursus fide sanxerunt liberos Tarentinos leges suas[1] suaque omnia habituros neque ullum vectigal Poeno pensuros praesidiumve invitos recepturos; prodita hospitia Romanorum cum[2] prae-
9 sidio Carthaginiensium fore. Haec ubi convenerunt, tunc vero Philemenus consuetudinem nocte egrediundi redeundique in urbem frequentiorem facere. Et erat venandi studio insignis, canesque et alius
10 apparatus sequebatur; captumque ferme aliquid aut ab hoste ex praeparato adlatum reportans donabat aut praefecto aut custodibus portarum. Nocte maxime commeare propter metum hostium credebant.

11 Ubi iam eo consuetudinis adducta res est ut, quocumque noctis tempore sibilo dedisset signum, porta aperiretur, tempus agendae rei Hannibali
12 visum est. Tridui viam aberat; ubi, quo minus

[1] suas *Wesenberg*: *om.* *P*(1).

[2] hospitia Romanorum cum *Weissenborn, Conway*: *om.* *P*(1), *a lost line*: *various emendations.*

and Philemenus advanced to the outposts, were seized and at their own request brought before Hannibal. After explaining the reasons for their plan and what they were plotting, they were warmly commended and loaded with promises. In order to make their fellow-citizens believe they had left the city to forage, they were bidden to drive to the city cattle belonging to the Carthaginians which had been turned out to graze. Promise was given that they would do so in safety and without a conflict. The young men's booty attracted attention, and less astonishment was caused by their making the same venture again and again. On meeting Hannibal again they had his formal assurance that the Tarentines as free men should have their own laws and all their possessions, and pay no tribute to the Carthaginians nor admit a garrison against their own wish; that houses occupied by Romans should be handed over, together with the garrison, and be assigned to the Carthaginians. So much agreed upon, Philemenus thereafter made it his more constant habit to leave the city and return to it by night. In fact he was noted for his devotion to the chase, and his hounds and other equipment would follow him. Usually he carried back something he had taken or that the enemy had brought him by agreement, and he would give it either to the commandant or to the gate-guards. They believed that he came and went preferably by night for fear of the enemy. B.C. 212

When the thing had become so habitual that the gate was opened at whatever hour of the night he gave the signal by a whistle, it seemed to Hannibal to be the time for action. He was at a distance of three days' march, and there he played the invalid, that his

A.U.C. mirum esset uno eodemque loco stativa eum tam diu
542 13 habere, aegrum simulabat. Romanis quoque qui in
praesidio Tarenti erant suspecta esse tam[1] segnis
mora eius desierat. IX. Ceterum postquam Tarentum ire constituit, decem milibus peditum atque
equitum, quos in expeditionem velocitate corporum
ac levitate armorum aptissimos esse ratus est,
2 electis, quarta vigilia noctis signa movit, prae-
missisque octoginta fere Numidis equitibus praecepit
ut discurrerent circa vias perlustrarentque omnia
oculis, ne quis agrestium procul spectator agminis
3 falleret; praegressos retraherent, obvios occiderent,
ut praedonum magis quam exercitus accolis species
esset. Ipse raptim agmine acto quindecim ferme
4 milium spatio castra ab Tarento posuit, et ne ibi
quidem denuntiato[2] quo pergerent, tantum convo-
catos milites monuit via omnes irent nec deverti
quemquam aut excedere ordine agminis paterentur,
et in primis intenti ad imperia accipienda essent neu
quid nisi ducum iussu facerent; se in tempore editu-
5 rum quae vellet agi. Eadem ferme hora Tarentum
fama praevenerat Numidas equites paucos populari
6 agros terroremque late agrestibus iniecisse. Ad
quem nuntium nihil ultra motus praefectus Romanus
quam ut partem equitum postero die luce prima
iuberet exire ad arcendum populationibus hostem;
7 in cetera adeo nihil ab eo intenta cura est ut contra

[1] tam *Madvig*: iam *P*(2): *om. Ax.*
[2] denuntiato *Madvig*: nuntiato *P*(1).

keeping a fixed camp so long in one and the same place might cause less wonder. The Romans also on garrison duty at Tarentum had ceased to find such prolonged inaction suspicious. IX. Once he had determined, however, to go to Tarentum, he picked ten thousand infantry and cavalry—the men whom he thought best suited to the enterprise on account of swiftness of foot and lightness of arms —and at the fourth watch of the night got in motion. And he ordered some eighty Numidian horsemen, who were sent in advance, to scour the country near the roads and keep an eye in every direction, that no farmer in the distance might observe the column without being noticed. They were to hold up those ahead of them and slay those they met, so that people living near by might have the impression of foragers rather than of an army. He himself, after a forced march, pitched camp at a distance of about fifteen miles from Tarentum. And not even there did he announce whither they were going. He merely summoned the soldiers and bade them all to keep to the road and not allow anyone to turn aside or leave his place in the column; and to be especially alert to hear commands and not to do anything without orders from their officers. He would in due time inform them what he wished to have done. About the same hour a rumour had preceded him to Tarentum that a few Numidian horsemen were ravaging the farms and had inspired widespread alarm among the rustics. On receiving this news the Roman commandant was only so far aroused as to command part of the cavalry to go out the next day at dawn, in order to prevent depredations of the enemy. For the rest his attention was so little aroused that B.C. 212

A.U.C. 542 pro argumento fuerit illa procursatio Numidarum
Hannibalem exercitumque e castris non movisse.
8 Hannibal concubia nocte movit. Dux Philemenus
erat cum solito captae venationis onere; ceteri
proditores ea quae composita erant expectabant.
9 Convenerat autem ut Philemenus portula adsueta
venationem inferens armatos induceret, parte alia
10 portam Temenitida adiret Hannibal. Ea medi-
terranea regio est orientem spectans; busta [1] aliquantum intra moenia includunt. Cum portae
adpropinquaret, editus ex composito ignis ab Hannibale est refulsitque idem redditum ab Nicone signum;
11 extinctae deinde utrimque flammae sunt. Hannibal
silentio ducebat ad portam. Nico ex improviso
adortus sopitos vigiles in cubilibus suis obtruncat
12 portamque aperit. Hannibal cum peditum agmine
ingreditur, equites subsistere iubet, ut quo res
13 postulet occurrere libero campo possent. Et Philemenus portulae parte alia, qua commeare adsuerat,
adpropinquabat. Nota vox eius et familiare iam
signum cum excitasset vigilem, dicenti [2] vix sustineri
14 grandis bestiae onus portula aperitur. Inferentes
aprum duos invenes secutus ipse cum expedito
venatore vigilem, incautius miraculo magnitudinis in
15 eos qui ferebant versum venabulo traicit. Ingressi
deinde triginta fere armati ceteros vigiles obtruncant

[1] spectans; busta *Ussing*: spectabest *P* (-bast *P*[1]*?*): spectabat (1).
[2] dicenti *x*: dicente *P*(1).

---

[1] *I.e.* at the time of the first sound sleep, not yet *intempesta nocte* (toward midnight); Cicero *de Div.* I. 57; Macrobius I. iii. 15.

on the contrary the raid of the Numidians was to him a proof that Hannibal and the army had not stirred from their camp. B.C. 212

Hannibal broke camp early in the night.[1] His guide was Philemenus with his usual load of game. The rest of the traitors were waiting for acts previously arranged. It had been agreed, namely, that Philemenus, as he brought in his game by the usual postern, should lead in armed men, while on another side Hannibal should approach the Temenitis Gate. That quarter is toward the inland, facing east; tombs occupy a considerable space inside the walls. As he approached the gate the fire signal was given by Hannibal according to agreement, and in reply from Nico the same signal blazed; then on both sides the flames were extinguished. Hannibal was leading his men silently to the gate. Nico unexpectedly attacks the sleeping sentries in their beds, slays them and opens the gate. Hannibal with his infantry column enters, orders the cavalry to halt, so that they can meet the enemy in the open, in whatever direction the situation may require. And Philemenus on another side of the city was approaching the postern by which he was accustomed to come and go. His well-known voice and the now familiar signal having aroused a sentry, the little gate was opened for Philemenus, just as he was saying they could scarcely carry the weight of a huge beast. While two young men were carrying in the boar, he himself followed them with a huntsman who was unencumbered, and as the sentry, thrown off his guard by its marvellous size, faced the men who were carrying it, Philemenus ran him through with a hunting spear. Then about thirty armed men

A.U.C. 542 refringuntque portam proximam, et agmen sub
signis confestim inrupit. Inde cum silentio in forum
16 ducti Hannibali sese coniunxerunt. Tum duo milia
Gallorum Poenus in tres divisa partis per urbem
dimittit; Tarentinos iis addit duces binos [1]; itinera
17 quam maxume frequentia occupari iubet, tumultu
orto Romanos passim caedi, oppidanis parci. Sed
ut fieri id posset, praecipit iuvenibus Tarentinis ut,
ubi quem suorum procul vidissent, quiescere ac silere
ac bono animo esse iuberent.

X. Iam tumultus erat clamorque qualis esse in
capta urbe solet; sed quid rei esset nemo satis pro
2 certo scire. Tarentini Romanos ad diripiendam
urbem credere coortos; Romanis seditio aliqua cum
3 fraude videri ab oppidanis mota. Praefectus primo
excitatus tumultu in portum effugit; inde acceptus
4 scapha in arcem circumvehitur. Errorem et tuba
audita ex theatro faciebat; nam et Romana erat, a
proditoribus ad hoc ipsum praeparata, et inscienter a
Graeco inflata quis aut quibus signum daret incertum
5 efficiebat. Ubi inluxit, et Romanis Punica et Gallica
arma cognita dubitationem exemerunt, et Graeci
Romanos passim caede stratos cernentes, ab Hanni-
6 bale captam urbem senserunt. Postquam lux certior
erat et Romani qui caedibus superfuerant in arcem

[1] iis addit duces binos *Böttcher* : *om.* *P*(1), *a lost line restored from Polybius* VIII. xxx (xxxii). 1.

entered, cut down the rest of the sentries and broke open the neighbouring gate; and the column with its standards at once rushed in. Thence they were marched in silence to the market-place and joined Hannibal. The Carthaginian then sent two thousand Gauls, divided into three units, through the city, and to each he attached two Tarentines as guides. He ordered them to occupy the most frequented streets, and when the uproar had begun, to slay the Romans everywhere, to spare the townspeople. But to make this possible he instructed the young Tarentines, whenever they saw one of their own people in the distance, to bid him be quiet and say nothing and be of good cheer. B.C. 212

X. Already there was such uproar and shouting as is usual in a captured city, but what it was about no one quite knew for certain. The Tarentines believed the Romans had surprised them, in order to plunder the city; the Romans thought it was some kind of uprising treacherously started by the townspeople. The commandant, aroused by the first uproar, escaped to the harbour; picked up by a skiff, he was rowed around from there to the citadel. Confusion was caused also by the sound of a trumpet from the theatre. For it was a Roman trumpet, furnished by the traitors for this very purpose; and in addition, being unskillfully sounded by a Greek, it left it uncertain who was giving the signal and to whom. When day broke the Punic and Gallic arms, now recognized, relieved the Romans of their uncertainty, and at the same time the Greeks, seeing slain Romans everywhere, were aware that the city had been captured by Hannibal. When it was no longer twilight and the Romans who survived the slaughter

A.U.C. 542 confugerant conticiscebatque paulatim tumultus,
tum Hannibal Tarentinos sine armis convocare iubet.
7 Convenere omnes, praeterquam qui cedentis in
arcem Romanos ad omnem adeundam simul fortu-
8 nam persecuti fuerant. Ibi Hannibal benigne
adlocutus Tarentinos testatusque quae praestitisset
civibus eorum quos ad Trasumennum aut ad Cannas
9 cepisset, simul in dominationem superbam Romanorum invectus, recipere se in domos suas quemque
iussit et foribus nomen suum inscribere; se domos
eas quae inscriptae non essent signo extemplo dato
diripi iussurum; si quis in hospitio civis Romani—
vacuas autem tenebant domos—nomen inscripsisset,
10 eum se pro hoste habiturum. Contione dimissa cum
titulis notatae fores discrimen pacatae ab hostili
domo fecissent, signo dato ad diripienda hospitia
Romana passim discursum est; et fuit praedae
aliquantum.

XI. Postero die ad oppugnandam arcem ducit;
quam cum et a mari, quo in paene insulae modum
pars maior circumluitur, praealtis rupibus et ab ipsa
urbe muro et fossa ingenti saeptam videret eoque
2 nec vi nec operibus expugnabilem esse, ne aut se
ipsum cura tuendi Tarentinos a maioribus rebus
moraretur, aut in relictos sine valido praesidio
Tarentinos impetum ex arce, cum vellent, Romani
facerent, vallo urbem ab arce intersaepire statuit,

---

[1] According to Polybius the legend was to be simply Ταραντίνου; VIII. xxxi. 4.

had fled to the citadel, and the uproar was gradually being stilled, Hannibal then gave orders to summon the Tarentines without arms. They all assembled, except those who had followed the Romans in their retreat to the citadel, to share with them any outcome. Thereupon Hannibal had kind words for the Tarentines and called to mind what he had done for their fellow-citizens whom he had captured at Lake Trasumennus or at Cannae. At the same time he inveighed against the haughty rule of the Romans and ordered them to go each to his own house and to write his name on the door.[1] He would order that at a given signal such houses as were not marked should at once be plundered. If any one should write his name on the quarters of a Roman citizen —now they were occupying vacant houses—he would regard such a man as an enemy. After the assembly had been dismissed and the marking of doors had distinguished the house of a citizen from that of an enemy, the signal was given and they scattered in all directions to plunder the Roman dwellings; and the booty was considerable. B.C. 212

XI. On the next day he led his men to an attack upon the citadel. He saw that not only was this defended by very high cliffs on the side towards the sea, which surrounds the larger part of it as a peninsula, but on the side toward the city itself by a wall and a great fosse, and hence could not be taken by assault nor by siege-works. Accordingly, to avoid either keeping himself from larger operations in his effort to protect the Tarentines, or else letting the Romans, whenever they pleased, make an attack from the citadel upon the Tarentines if he left them without a strong garrison, he decided to wall off

A.U.C. 542

3 non sine illa etiam spe, cum prohibentibus opus
Romanis manum posse conseri et, si ferocius procu-
currissent, magna caede ita attenuari praesidii vires,
ut facile per se ipsi Tarentini urbem ab iis tueri
4 possent. Ubi coeptum opus est, patefacta repente
porta impetum in munientis fecerunt Romani pellique
se statio passa est quae pro opere erat, ut successu
cresceret audacia pluresque et longius pulsos perse-
5 querentur. Tum signo dato coorti undique Poeni
sunt, quos instructos ad hoc Hannibal tenuerat.
Nec sustinuere impetum Romani, sed ab effusa fuga
loci angustiae eos impeditaque alia opere iam coepto,
6 alia apparatu operis morabantur. Plurimi in fossam
praecipitavere, occisique sunt plures in fuga quam in
7 pugna. Inde et [1] opus nullo prohibente fieri coeptum: fossa ingens ducta, et vallum intra eam erigi-
tur, modicoque post intervallo murum etiam eadem
regione addere parat, ut vel sine praesidio tueri se
8 adversus Romanos possent. Reliquit tamen modi-
cum praesidium, simul ut in perficiendo muro adiu-
varet. Ipse profectus cum ceteris copiis ad Galae-
sum flumen—quinque milia ab urbe abest—posuit
castra.

9 Ex his stativis regressus ad inspiciendum, quod
opus aliquantum opinione eius celerius creverat,

[1] Inde et *P*(1): inde *Madvig*.

the city from the citadel by an earthwork. He was B.C. 212 not without the hope also that he could engage the Romans if they tried to prevent the work, and that, if they should make a furious sally, the strength of the garrison would be so reduced by serious losses that the Tarentines by themselves could easily defend the city against them. After fortification began, a gate was suddenly opened and the Romans made an attack upon the men at work. And the outpost stationed in advance of the work allowed itself to be driven back, that boldness might grow with success and a larger number might pursue the repulsed and to a greater distance. Then at a given signal the Carthaginians, whom Hannibal had kept drawn up for this purpose, rose up on all sides. And the Romans did not withstand the attack, but limited space and ground obstructed partly by the work already begun, partly by preparations for the work, kept them from a disorderly flight. Very many leaped into the fosse, and more were slain in flight than in battle. Then even fortification began to proceed, with no one attempting to prevent. A great fosse was carried along, and inside of it an earthwork was raised; and at a short distance he prepared to add a stone wall likewise in the same direction, so that even without a garrison they could protect themselves against the Romans. He did, however, leave a garrison of moderate size, to aid as well in the completion of the wall. He himself set out with the rest of his forces and pitched camp at the river Galaesus, which is five miles from the city.

On returning from this permanent camp to inspect, inasmuch as the work had progressed with considerably more speed than he had anticipated, he

A.U.C. 542 spem cepit etiam arcem expugnari posse. Et est
non altitudine, ut ceterae,[1] tuta, sed loco plano posita
10 et ab urbe muro tantum ac fossa divisa. Cum iam
machinationum omni genere et operibus oppugnaretur, missum a Metaponto praesidium Romanis
fecit animum ut nocte ex inproviso opera hostium
invaderent. Alia disiecerunt, alia igni corruperunt,
isque finis Hannibali fuit ea parte arcem oppugnandi.
11 Reliqua erat in obsidione spes, nec ea satis efficax,
quia arcem tenentes, quae in paene insula posita imminet faucibus portus, mare liberum habebant, urbs
contra exclusa maritimis commeatibus propiusque in-
12 opiam erant obsidentes quam obsessi. Hannibal
convocatis principibus Tarentinis omnes praesentis
difficultates exposuit: neque arcis tam munitae
expugnandae cernere viam neque in obsidione
quicquam habere spei, donec mari hostes potiantur;
13 quod si naves sint, quibus commeatus invehi prohibeat, extemplo aut arce cessuros [2] aut dedituros se
14 hostis. Adsentiebantur Tarentini; ceterum ei qui
consilium adferret opem quoque in eam rem adferen-
15 dam censebant esse. Punicas enim naves ex Sicilia
accitas id posse facere; suas, quae sinu exiguo intus
inclusae essent, cum claustra portus hostis haberet,
quem ad modum inde in apertum mare evasuras?
16 "Evadent" inquit Hannibal; "multa quae inpedita
natura sunt consilio expediuntur. Urbem in campo

[1] ceterae *Crévier*: cetera *P*(1).
[2] arce cessuros *Gronovius*: arcessuros *P*(1): abscessuros *A*[2].

---

[1] According to Strabo VI. iii. 1 the only elevation of any consequence was the citadel.
[2] The mouth of the harbour was closed, as Strabo (*l.c.*) says, by a large bridge.

hoped that the citadel also could be taken by storm. B.C. 212
And it is not defended by height,[1] as other citadels are, but is on level ground and separated from the city merely by a wall and a fosse. While the attack was now in progress with engines of every kind and with siege-works, a garrison sent from Metapontum encouraged the Romans to make a surprise attack by night upon the works of the enemy. Some of these they pulled apart, others they ruined by fire; and this was the end of Hannibal's attack upon the citadel from that side. His remaining hope was in a blockade, and that was not very effectual, because the occupants of the citadel, which is situated on a peninsula and commands the harbour mouth, had the sea at their disposal, while the city on the other hand was shut off from supplies by sea and the besiegers were nearer to starvation than the besieged. Hannibal summoned the leading men of Tarentum and laid before them all the difficulties of the situation, saying that he neither saw a way to take so well fortified a citadel by storm, nor had any hope in a blockade, so long as the enemy had command of the sea. But if he should have ships with which to prevent the bringing in of supplies, the enemy would at once either withdraw from the citadel or surrender. The Tarentines assented, but thought that the giver of advice must give aid also to carry it out. For Carthaginian ships, summoned from Sicily, they said, could do it. As for their own ships, which were shut up inside a very small bay, while the enemy held the key to the harbour,[2] how were they to get out into the open sea? "They will get out", said Hannibal; "many things which are naturally difficult are solved by ingenuity. You have a city

A.U.C. 542 sitam habetis; planae et satis latae viae patent in
17 omnis partis. Via quae e portu per mediam urbem
ad mare transmissa est plaustris transveham naves
haud magna mole, et mare nostrum erit, quo nunc
hostes potiuntur, et illinc mari, hinc terra circumsede-
bimus arcem; immo brevi aut relictam ab hostibus
18 aut cum ipsis hostibus capiemus." Haec oratio non
spem modo effectus sed ingentem etiam ducis
admirationem fecit. Contracta extemplo undique
plaustra iunctaque inter se, et machinae ad subdu-
cendas naves admotae, munitumque iter, quo faci-
liora plaustra minorque moles in transitu esset.
19 Iumenta inde et homines contracti et opus inpigre
coeptum; paucosque post dies classis instructa ac
parata circumvehitur arcem et ante os ipsum portus
20 ancoras iacit. Hunc statum rerum Hannibal Tarenti
relinquit regressus ipse in hiberna. Ceterum defectio
Tarentinorum utrum priore anno an hoc facta sit, in
diversum auctores trahunt; plures propioresque
aetate memoriae rerum hoc anno factam tradunt.

XII. Romae consules praetoresque usque ad ante
2 diem quintum kal. Maias Latinae tenuerunt. Eo die
perpetrato sacro in monte in suas quisque provincias
proficiscuntur. Religio deinde nova obiecta est ex
3 carminibus Marcianis. Vates hic Marcius inlustris
fuerat, et cum conquisitio priore anno ex senatus con-

---

[1] That 213 B.C. was the correct date for their defection is shown by XXVII. xxv. 4.

[2] Mons Albanus (Monte Cavo), where a sacrifice on the fourth day brought the festival to an end.

situated in a plain. Level streets of ample breadth lead in all directions. Along the street that is carried across from the harbour through the centre of the city to the sea I shall transport ships on wagons with no great difficulty, and the sea, which the enemy now possess, will be ours, and we shall besiege the citadel on that side by sea, on this side by land; or rather we shall soon either take it, abandoned by the enemy, or take it enemy and all." This speech produced not merely the hope of success, but great admiration for the general as well. At once wagons were assembled from everywhere and joined together, and the tackle brought to draw up the ships, and the roadway paved, that the wagons might be easier to move, and the difficulty of transport lessened. Then mules and men were brought together and the work was begun with energy. And so a few days later a fleet furnished and equipped sailed around the citadel and cast anchor at the very mouth of the harbour. Such was the state of things which Hannibal left at Tarentum when he himself returned to his winter quarters. But whether the rebellion of the Tarentines took place in the previous year or in this year, authorities differ.[1] More of them and those nearer in time to men who remembered the events relate that it occurred in this year. B.C. 212

XII. At Rome the consuls and praetors were detained by the Latin festival until the 26th of April. After performing the rites on that day on the Mount,[2] each set out for his assignment. Then fresh religious scruples were aroused by the verses of Marcius. A noted seer had been this Marcius, and when in the preceding year search was being made by decree of the senate for such books, they had come

A.U.C. 542 sulto talium librorum fieret, in M. Aemili praetoris
4 urbani,[1] qui eam rem agebat, manus venerant. Is protinus novo praetori Sullae tradiderat. Ex huius Marcii duobus carminibus alterius post rem actam[2] editi comprobata[3] auctoritas eventu alteri quoque, cuius nondum tempus venerat, adferebat fidem.
5 Priore carmine Cannensis praedicta clades in haec fere verba erat: "Amnem, Troiugena,[4] fuge Cannam, ne te alienigenae cogant in campo Diomedis
6 conserere manus. Sed neque credes tu mihi, donec compleris sanguine campum, multaque milia occisa tua deferet amnis in pontum magnum ex terra frugifera; piscibus atque avibus ferisque quae incolunt terras iis fuat esca caro tua. Nam mihi ita
7 Iuppiter fatus est." Et Diomedis Argivi campos et Cannam flumen ii qui militaverant in iis locis iuxta
8 atque ipsam cladem agnoscebant. Tum alterum carmen recitatum, non eo tantum obscurius quia incertiora futura praeteritis sunt, sed perplexius
9 etiam scripturae genere. "Hostis, Romani, si expellere[5] vultis, vomicam[6] quae gentium venit longe, Apollini vovendos censeo ludos, qui quotannis comiter Apollini fiant; cum populus dederit ex publico partem, privati uti conferant pro se atque
10 suis; iis ludis faciendis praeerit[7] praetor is qui ius

[1] urbani *Sigonius*: urbem *P*(4): urb' (*or* -bis) C^4M^1?*BDA*: *rejected by Walters.*

[2] actam CA^y: acta *P*(10): factam *Madvig.*

[3] comprobata *Ussing*: cumrato *P*(4): curato *BDA*: comperto *Walters.*

[4] Troiugena *G. Hermann*: -nam *P*(1), *adding* romanae, *probably a gloss.*

[5] expellere *P*(1): ex agro expellere *Macrobius* I. xvii. 28.

[6] vomicam *A Macrobius*: vomica *P*(2).

[7] praeerit $CM^1B^xA^x$: praeterit *P*(10): praesit *Macrobius.*

into the hands of Marcus Aemilius,[1] the praetor B.C. 212
urbanus, who was in charge of the matter. He had immediately turned them over to the new praetor, Sulla. Of the two prophecies[2] of this Marcius the authority of one, made known after the event, was confirmed by the outcome and lent credibility to the other also, whose time had not yet come. In the earlier prophecy the disaster at Cannae had been predicted in such terms as these: "Flee the river Canna, thou descendant of Troy, that foreigners may not compel thee to do battle in the Plain of Diomed. But thou wilt not believe me until thou hast filled the plain with blood, and many thousands of thy slain will the river bear from the fruitful land down to the great sea. To fishes and birds and beasts that dwell on the land thy flesh shall be meat. For thus hath Jupiter declared to me." And those who had fought in that region recognized the plains of the Argive Diomed and the river Canna no less than the disaster itself. Then the second prophecy was read, being not only more obscure because the future is more uncertain than the past, but more difficult also in the way it was written. "If you wish, Romans, to drive out enemies, the sore which has come from afar, I propose that a festival be vowed to Apollo, to be observed with good cheer in honour of Apollo every year. When the people shall have given a part out of the treasury, private citizens shall contribute on their own behalf and that of their families. In charge of the conduct of that festival shall be the praetor who is then chief judge for the people and

[1] For the error cf. note on i. 11.

[2] The rough hexameters (probably translated from the Greek) had been reduced to prose.

A.U.C. 542 populo plebeique dabit summum; decemviri Graeco ritu hostiis sacra faciant. Hoc si recte facietis, gaudebitis semper fietque res vestra melior; nam is deum[1] extinguet perduellis vestros qui vestros
11 campos pascit placide." Ad id carmen explanandum[2] diem unum sumpserunt; postero die senatus consultum factum est ut decemviri[3] de ludis Apollini
12 reque divina facienda inspicerent. Ea cum inspecta relataque ad senatum essent, censuerunt patres Apollini ludos vovendos faciendosque et, quando ludi facti essent, duodecim milia aeris praetori ad
13 rem divinam et duas hostias maiores dandas. Alterum senatus consultum factum est ut decemviri sacrum Graeco ritu facerent hisque hostiis, Apollini bove aurato et capris duabus albis auratis, Latonae
14 bove femina aurata. Ludos praetor in circo maximo cum facturus esset, edixit ut populus per eos ludos stipem Apollini, quantam commodum esset, con-
15 ferret. Haec est origo ludorum Apollinarium, victoriae, non valetudinis ergo, ut plerique rentur, votorum factorumque. Populus coronatus spectavit, matronae supplicavere; vulgo apertis ianuis in propatulo[4] epulati sunt, celeberque dies omni caerimoniarum genere fuit.

XIII. Cum Hannibal circa Tarentum, consules

[1] deum *Riemann* (*or* divum): dium *P*(1): divus *x Macrobius*.
[2] explanandum *P*[2](1) *Madvig*: expiandum *P Walters*.
[3] decemviri *P*(1): decemviri libros *z Macrobius*.
[4] propatulo *A*: -lis *P*(2).

---

[1] '*I.e.* the *decemviri sacris faciundis*, charged with the oversight of sacrifices.
[2] The *libri Sibyllini*, of which the decemvirs were the custodians and authorized interpreters, but could not refer to them unless empowered by a decree of the senate.

the commons. The decemvirs[1] shall offer the victims according to Greek rite. If ye will do this rightly ye shall forever rejoice, and your state will change for the better. For that god who graciously nurtures your meadows will destroy your enemies." For the interpretation of the prophecy they took one day. On the next day the senate made a decree that in regard to the festival to be held and the sacrifices in honour of Apollo the decemvirs should consult the books.[2] Those passages having been consulted and reported to the senate, the fathers voted that a festival should be vowed and held in honour of Apollo, and after the festival had been held the sum of twelve thousand asses should be given to the praetor for the ceremonies, and two full-grown victims. A second decree of the senate was made, that the decemvirs should offer sacrifice according to Greek rite and with these victims: to Apollo an ox with gilded horns and two white she-goats[3] with gilded horns, to Latona a cow with gilded horns. When the praetor was about to open the festival in the Circus Maximus, he ordered by edict that during that feast the people should make their contribution to Apollo according to their means. Such is the origin of the festival of Apollo, vowed and kept to secure victory, not health, as most think. The people wore garlands at the spectacles, the matrons offered prayers, everybody feasted in the atrium with open doors, and the day was kept with every kind of ceremony. B.C. 212

XIII. While Hannibal was near Tarentum, and

[3] As she-goats would surely be offered to Diana, not to Apollo, there is good reason to believe that her name has been lost from the text, and before Macrobius' time, since he has the same statement; *Saturnalia* I. xvii. 29.

A.U.C. 542 ambo in Samnio essent, sed circumsessuri Capuam viderentur, quod malum diuturnae obsidionis esse solet, iam famem Campani sentiebant, quia sementem
2 facere prohibuerant eos Romani exercitus. Itaque legatos ad Hannibalem miserunt orantes ut, priusquam consules in agros suos educerent legiones viaeque omnes hostium praesidiis insiderentur, frumentum ex propinquis locis convehi iuberet
3 Capuam. Hannibal Hannonem ex Bruttiis cum exercitu in Campaniam transire et dare operam ut
4 frumenti copia fieret Campanis iussit. Hanno ex Bruttiis profectus cum exercitu, vitabundus castra hostium consulesque, qui in Samnio erant, cum Benevento iam adpropinquaret, tria milia passuum
5 ab ipsa urbe loco edito castra posuit; inde ex sociis circa populis, quo aestate comportatum erat, devehi frumentum in castra iussit praesidiis datis quae
6 commeatus eos prosequerentur. Capuam inde nuntium misit qua die in castris ad accipiendum frumentum praesto essent omni undique genere vehiculorum
7 iumentorumque ex agris contracto. Id pro cetera socordia neglegentiaque a Campanis actum: paulo plus quadringenta vehicula missa et pauca praeterea iumenta. Ob id castigatis ab Hannone quod ne fames quidem, quae mutas accenderet bestias, curam eorum stimulare posset, alia prodicta dies ad frumen-
8 tum maiore apparatu petendum. Ea omnia, sicut acta erant, cum enuntiata Beneventanis essent,

both consuls were in Samnium but seemed about to invest Capua, already the Campanians were suffering hunger (the usual hardship of a long investment), because the Roman armies had prevented them from sowing. And so they sent legates to Hannibal, praying that, before the consuls should lead the legions into their lands and all the roads should be blocked by forces of the enemy, he should order grain to be brought from neighbouring places to Capua. Hannibal ordered Hanno to march with his army from the land of the Bruttii over into Campania, and to see to it that the Campanians should have a supply of grain. Hanno set out from the land of the Bruttii with his army, avoided camps of the enemy and the consuls, who were in Samnium, and when he was now nearing Beneventum, pitched camp on high ground three miles from the city itself. Then he ordered grain to be brought into camp from allied peoples of the neighbourhood, among whom it had been garnered in the summer; and he furnished troops to escort the supplies. Then he sent word to Capua, naming a day on which they should appear at the camp to get their grain, after bringing together from the farms on all sides every kind of vehicle and beast of burden. This order was carried out by the Campanians with their usual carelessness and indifference. Little more than four hundred vehicles were sent, and a few beasts of burden besides. For this they were censured by Hanno, that not even hunger, which, as he said, inflames even dumb brutes, could spur their diligence; and another day was assigned for getting their grain with ampler means of transport. When all this was reported, just as it happened, to the Beneventans, they at once B.C. 212

A.U.C. 542 legatos decem extemplo ad consules—circa Bovianum
9 castra Romanorum erant—miserunt. Qui cum auditis quae ad Capuam agerentur inter se comparassent
ut alter in Campaniam exercitum duceret, Fulvius,
cui ea provincia obvenerat, profectus nocte Bene-
10 venti moenia est ingressus. Ex propinquo cognoscit
Hannonem cum exercitus parte profectum frumen-
tatum; per quaestorem Campanis datum frumentum; duo milia plaustrorum, inconditam inermem-
que aliam turbam advenisse; per tumultum ac
trepidationem omnia agi, castrorumque formam et
militarem ordinem inmixtis agrestibus et [1] iis externis sublatum.
11 His satis compertis, consul militibus edicit, signa
tantum armaque in proximam noctem expedirent;
12 castra Punica oppugnanda esse. Quarta vigilia
profecti sarcinis omnibus impedimentisque Beneventi
relictis, paulo ante lucem cum ad castra pervenissent,
tantum pavoris iniecerunt ut, si in plano castra posita
essent, haud dubie primo impetu capi potuerint.
13 Altitudo loci et munimenta defendere,[2] quae nulla
ex parte adiri nisi arduo ac difficili ascensu poterant.
14 Luce prima proelium ingens accensum est. Nec vallum modo tutantur Poeni, sed, ut quibus locus aequior
esset, deturbant nitentis per ardua hostes. XIV.
Vincit tamen omnia pertinax virtus, et aliquot simul
partibus ad vallum ac fossas perventum est, sed cum
2 multis vulneribus ac militum pernicie. Itaque

[1] et *Madvig*: *om.* *P*(1).
[2] defendere *Alschefski*: -erent $PCRMB^x$: -erunt *DA*: -erant C^4B.

---

[1] *I.e.* not Campanians.

sent ten legates to the consuls, the camp of the Romans being near Bovianum. The consuls, on hearing what was going on near Capua, mutually arranged that one of them should lead his army into Campania, and Fulvius, to whom that assignment had fallen, set out and entered the walls of Beneventum at night. Being near now, he learned that Hanno had gone with a part of his army to procure grain; that through his quaestor grain had been furnished to the Campanians; that two thousand wagons and in addition a mixed and unarmed multitude had arrived; that everything was being done in confusion and excitement, and that the arrangement of the camp and military routine had been broken down by the influx of rustics, foreigners [1] at that. B.C. 212

These facts being sufficiently established, the consul ordered the soldiers to make ready their standards and arms, and nothing else, for the following night; they must attack the Carthaginian camp. Setting out at the fourth watch, leaving all their packs and baggage at Beneventum, they reached the camp shortly before daylight and inspired such panic that, if the camp had been placed on level ground, it could undoubtedly have been taken by the first assault. The lofty situation protected it, also the fortifications, which could not be approached from any side except by a steep and difficult slope. At daybreak a great battle blazed up. And the Carthaginians not only defended the earthwork but, as they had the more favourable situation, pushed down the enemy struggling up the steep slope. XIV. Nevertheless obstinate courage surmounted everything, and so the earthwork and the trenches were reached in several places at once, but with many wounds and heavy loss of

A.U.C. 542 convocatis legatis [1] tribunisque militum consul absistendum temerario incepto ait; tutius sibi videri reduci eo die exercitum Beneventum, dein postero castra [2] castris hostium iungi, ne exire inde Campani
3 neve Hanno regredi posset; id quo facilius obtineatur, collegam quoque et exercitum eius se acciturum totumque eo versuros bellum. Haec consilia ducis, cum iam receptui caneret, clamor militum aspernan-
4 tium tam segne imperium disiecit. Proxima forte hosti [3] erat cohors Paeligna, cuius praefectus Vibius Accaus arreptum vexillum trans vallum hostium
5 traiecit. Execratus inde seque et cohortem, si eius vexilli hostes potiti essent, princeps ipse per fossam
6 vallumque in castra inrupit. Iamque intra vallum Paeligni pugnabant, cum altera parte, Valerio Flacco tribuno militum tertiae legionis exprobrante Romanis ignaviam, qui sociis captorum castrorum concederent
7 decus, T. Pedanius princeps primus centurio, cum signifero signum ademisset, "Iam hoc signum et hic centurio" inquit "intra vallum hostium erit: sequantur qui capi signum ab hoste prohibituri sunt." Manipulares sui primum transcendentem fossam,
8 dein legio tota secuta est. Iam et consul, ad conspectum transgredientium vallum mutato consilio, ab revocando ad incitandos hortandosque versus

[1] legatis *Alschefski* : *om. P*(1).
[2] castra *Crévier* : *om. P*(1).
[3] forte hosti *Madvig, Emend.* : portae (-e) hostium *P*(1).

men. Accordingly the consul called together his lieutenants and tribunes of the soldiers and told them he must give up his rash undertaking; that it seemed to him safer to lead the army back that day to Beneventum, and then on the following day to pitch camp close to that of the enemy, so that the Campanians might not be able to leave it nor Hanno to return. To accomplish that more readily, he would summon his colleague also and his army, and they would focus the entire war upon that point. These plans of the general were disrupted, when he was already sounding the recall, by the shouts of the soldiers rejecting an order so lacking in spirit. Nearest to the enemy happened to be a Paelignian cohort, whose prefect Vibius Accaus seized the banner and threw it over the enemy's earthwork. Then, with a curse upon himself and the cohort if the enemy should get possession of that banner, he was himself the first to dash over the trench and wall into the camp. And already the Paelignians were fighting inside the wall, when from the other side of the camp, while Valerius Flaccus, tribune of the soldiers of the third legion, was reproaching the Romans for their cowardice in yielding to allies the honour of capturing the camp, Titus Pedanius, first centurion of the *principes*, took a standard away from the standard-bearer and said "This standard and this centurion will in a moment be inside the enemy's wall. Let those follow who are to prevent the standard from being captured by the enemy." First the men of his own maniple followed him as he crossed the trench, then the whole legion. And now the consul at the sight of men crossing the wall changed his plan, turned from recalling his soldiers to arousing B.C. 212

A.U.C. 542 milites, ostendere in quanto discrimine ac periculo fortissima cohors sociorum et civium legio esset.
9 Itaque pro se quisque omnes per aequa atque iniqua loca, cum undique tela conicerentur armaque et corpora hostes obicerent, pervadunt inrumpuntque; multi volnerati etiam quos vires et sanguis desereret, ut intra vallum hostium caderent nite-
10 bantur. Capta itaque momento temporis velut in plano sita nec permunita castra. Caedes inde, non iam pugna erat omnibus intra vallum permixtis.
11 Supra sex[1] milia hostium occisa, supra septem milia capitum cum frumentatoribus Campanis omnique plaustrorum et iumentorum apparatu capta; et alia ingens praeda fuit quam Hanno, populabundus passim cum isset, ex sociorum populi
12 Romani agris traxerat. Inde deletis hostium castris Beneventum reditum, praedamque ibi ambo consules—nam et Ap. Claudius eo post paucos dies
13 venit—vendiderunt diviseruntque. Et donati quorum opera castra hostium capta erant, ante alios Accaus Paelignus et T. Pedanius, princeps tertiae
14 legionis. Hanno ab Cominio Ocrito, quo nuntiata castrorum clades est, cum paucis frumentatoribus quos forte secum habuerat fugae magis quam itineris modo in Bruttios rediit. XV. Et Campani, audita sua pariter sociorumque clade, legatos ad

[1] sex $R^2(7)$: ex PR : x P^x : decem *vulgate.*

and encouraging them, and pointed out to them in what a critical and perilous situation were the bravest cohort of the allies and a legion of their fellow-citizens. And so, each doing his best, over ground favourable and unfavourable, while javelins were being hurled from every side and the enemy were interposing weapons and their bodies, they made their way and burst in. Many wounded men, even those whose strength and blood were ebbing, strove to fall inside the enemy's wall. And so in a moment's time the camp was captured, just as if pitched on level ground and not strongly fortified. Then came slaughter, no longer mere battle, since everything inside the wall was in confusion. B.C. 212

Over six thousand of the enemy were slain, over seven thousand men captured, including the Campanians who came for grain, and the entire train of wagons and mules. In addition there was the immense booty which Hanno, having set out to plunder far and wide, had taken from farms of allies of the Roman people. Then after destroying the enemy's camp they returned to Beneventum, and there the two consuls—for Appius Claudius came there a few days later—sold and divided the booty. And the men by whose efforts the camp of the enemy had been captured, were rewarded, first of all Accaus the Paelignian and Titus Pedanius, first centurion of the third legion. Hanno, leaving Cominium Ocritum, where he received news of the disaster at the camp, with the few men he happened to have with him to get grain, returned in what resembled a flight rather than a march to the land of the Bruttii. XV. And the Campanians, hearing of what was a disaster as much to themselves as to their allies, sent legates to

A.U.C. 542 Hannibalem miserunt, qui nuntiarent duos consules ad Beneventum esse, diei iter a Capua; tantum non ad portas et muros bellum esse; ni propere subveniat, celerius Capuam quam Arpos in potesta-
2 tem hostium venturam. Ne Tarentum quidem, non modo arcem, tanti debere esse ut Capuam, quam Carthagini aequare sit solitus, desertam inde-
3 fensamque populo Romano tradat. Hannibal, curae sibi fore rem Campanam pollicitus, in praesentia duo milia equitum cum legatis mittit, quo praesidio agros populationibus possent prohibere.

4 Romanis interim, sicut aliarum rerum, arcis Tarentinae praesidiique quod ibi obsideretur cura est. C. Servilius legatus, ex auctoritate patrum a P. Cornelio praetore in Etruriam ad frumentum coemendum missus, cum aliquot navibus onustis in portum
5 Tarentinum inter hostium custodias pervenit. Cuius adventu qui ante in exigua spe vocati saepe ad transitionem ab hostibus per conloquia erant ultro ad transeundum hostis vocabant sollicitabantque. Et erat satis validum praesidium traductis ad arcem Tarenti tuendam qui Metaponti erant[1] militibus.
6 Itaque Metapontini extemplo metu quo tenebantur liberati ad Hannibalem defecere.

7 Hoc idem eadem ora maris et Thurini fecerunt. Movit eos non Tarentinorum magis defectio Meta-

[1] qui Metaponti erant *z* : *om.* *P*(1), *a lost line.*

---

[1] Cf. XXIV. xlvi f.

Hannibal to report that the two consuls were at Beneventum, a day's march from Capua; that the war was all but at their gates and walls; and that, if he did not come to their aid in haste, Capua would fall into the power of the enemy more promptly than Arpi.[1] They said that not even Tarentum, to say nothing of its citadel, ought to be of such importance that he should hand over to the Roman people the deserted and undefended Capua, which he had usually compared with Carthage. Hannibal, promising that the Campanian cause would be his concern, for the present sent two thousand horsemen with his lieutenants, that with this force they might be able to protect their farms from devastation. B.C. 212

The Romans meantime were concerned among other things for the citadel of Tarentum and the garrison there besieged. Gaius Servilius, who as lieutenant had been sent by Publius Cornelius, the praetor, into Etruria by authority of the senate to purchase grain, made his way through the enemy's blockade into the harbour of Tarentum with a number of shiploads. Thanks to his coming, the men who until then in their faint hope had often been invited by the enemy in parleys to change sides were actually inviting and urging the enemy to change sides. And the garrison was in fact strong enough, now that soldiers who were at Metapontum had been transferred to defend the citadel of Tarentum. Accordingly the Metapontines were at once relieved of the fear by which they were restrained, and went over to Hannibal.

The Thurians also, on the same coast, did the same. What impelled them was not more the

A.U.C. 542 pontinorumque, quibus indidem ex Achaia oriundi etiam cognatione iuncti erant, quam ira in Romanos
8 propter obsides nuper interfectos. Eorum amici cognatique litteras ac nuntios ad Hannonem Magonemque, qui in propinquo in Bruttiis erant, miserunt, si exercitum ad moenia admovissent, se in potestatem
9 eorum urbem tradituros esse. M. Atinius Thuriis cum modico praesidio praeerat, quem facile elici ad certamen temere ineundum rebantur posse, non tam[1] militum, quos perpaucos habebat, fiducia quam iuventutis Thurinae; eam ex industria centuria-
10 verat armaveratque ad talis casus. Divisis copiis inter se duces Poeni cum agrum Thurinum ingressi essent, Hanno cum peditum agmine infestis signis ire ad urbem pergit, Mago cum equitatu tectus collibus
11 apte ad tegendas insidias oppositis subsistit. Atinius peditum tantum agmine per exploratores comperto in aciem copias educit, et fraudis intestinae et hostium
12 insidiarum ignarus. Pedestre proelium fuit persegne paucis in prima acie pugnantibus Romanis, Thurinis expectantibus magis quam adiuvantibus eventum; et Carthaginiensium acies de industria pedem referebat, ut ad terga collis ab equite suo
13 insessi hostem incautum pertraheret. Quo ubi est ventum, coorti cum clamore equites prope inconditam Thurinorum turbam nec satis fido animo unde

[1] tam *z*: *om. P*(1).

---

[1] Not the brother of Hannibal; xvi. 7 f., 24; xviii. 1; xxi. 4.

[2] So in mustering old men into the service in VI. ii. 6, and freedmen in X. xxi. 4.

revolt of the Tarentines and that of the Metapontines, with whom they were linked by blood as well, being sprung from the same Achaia than anger against the Romans on account of the recent execution of the hostages. Friends and relatives of these sent a letter and messengers to Hanno and Mago,[1] who were not far away in the land of the Bruttii, saying that, if they should bring up an army to their walls, they would themselves deliver the city into their power. Marcus Atinius was in command at Thurii with a garrison of moderate size, and they thought that he could easily be tempted to dash rashly into battle, from his confidence not so much in his soldiers, of whom he had very few, as in the young men of Thurii. He had purposely organized them in centuries[2] and armed them with a view to such emergencies. The Carthaginian generals divided their forces between them and, on entering the territory of Thurii, Hanno, with the infantry column ready to attack, proceeded to the city. Mago with the cavalry halted under cover of hills conveniently interposed to conceal an ambuscade. Atinius, informed of the infantry column alone by scouts, led his troops out into line, he being unaware both of the conspiracy within and of the enemy's ambuscade. The infantry battle was very lacking in spirit, for only a few Romans were fighting in the front line, and the men of Thurii were awaiting the outcome, rather than contributing to it. And the Carthaginian line purposely retreated, in order to draw the heedless enemy to the other side of the hill occupied by their own cavalry. When they reached the place, the cavalry, suddenly attacking with a shout, at once put to flight the mass of the Thurians, which was B.C. 212

A.U.C. 542 pugnabat stantem extemplo in fugam averterunt.
14 Romani, quamquam circumventos hinc pedes, hinc
eques urgebat, tamen aliquamdiu pugnam traxere;
postremo et ipsi terga vertunt atque ad urbem
15 fugiunt. Ibi proditores conglobati cum popularium
agmen patentibus portis accepissent, ubi Romanos
fusos ad urbem ferri viderunt, conclamant instare
Poenum, permixtosque et hostis urbem invasuros,
ni propere portas claudant. Ita exclusos Romanos
praebuere hosti ad caedem; Atinius tamen cum
16 paucis receptus. Seditio inde paulisper tenuit,
cum [1] alii cedendum fortunae et tradendam urbem
17 victoribus censerent. Ceterum, ut plerumque, fortuna et consilia mala vicerunt: Atinio cum suis ad
mare ac naves deducto, magis quia ipsi ob imperium
in se mite ac iustum consultum volebant quam
respectu Romanorum, Carthaginienses in urbem
accipiunt.

18 Consules a Benevento in Campanum agrum legiones ducunt non ad frumenta modo, quae iam in
herbis erant, corrumpenda, sed ad Capuam oppug-
19 nandam, nobilem se consulatum tam opulentae
urbis excidio rati facturos, simul et ingens flagitium
imperio dempturos, quod urbi tam propinquae
20 tertium annum inpunita defectio esset. Ceterum
ne Beneventum sine praesidio esset, et ut ad subita

[1] cum, *P*(1) *add another* inde, *variously emended by those who require* alii . . . alii.

---

[1] In contrast with those who by admitting Atinius showed their preference for the Romans.

almost undisciplined and not entirely loyal to the side on which they were fighting. The Romans, though surrounded and hard pressed on one side by the infantry, on the other by the cavalry, nevertheless kept on fighting for some time. Finally they also faced about and fled to the city. There the traitors massed together and admitted the column of their citizens through wide-open gates; but when they saw the routed Romans moving toward the city, they shouted that the Carthaginian was upon them, and unless they hastily closed the gates the enemy also, mingling with them, would make their way into the city. Thus they shut out the Romans and left them to be slain by the enemy. Atinius, however, with a few men was admitted. Then for a short time dissension continued, the other party[1] being of the opinion that they must yield to destiny and surrender the city to the victors. But, as usual, chance and bad advice prevailed. Atinius and his men were brought down to the sea and ships, more because they wished his personal safety, on account of his mild and just rule over them, than out of regard for the Romans, and then they admitted the Carthaginians to the city. B.C. 212

The consuls led their legions from Beneventum into the Campanian territory, not merely to ruin the grain, which was by now green, but also to besiege Capua. They thought to make theirs a notable consulship by the destruction of so rich a city, and at the same time to remove a great disgrace from the empire, in that the revolt of a city so near had been unpunished for three years.[2] But, not to leave Beneventum without a garrison, and, with a view to

[2] It was really over three years, from 216 B.C.

A.U.C. 542 belli, si Hannibal, quod facturum haud dubitabant, ad opem ferendam sociis Capuam venisset, equitis vim sustinere possent, Ti. Gracchum ex Lucanis cum equitatu ac levi armatura Beneventum venire iubent; legionibus stativisque ad obtinendas res in Lucanis aliquem praeficeret.

XVI. Gracccho, priusquam ex Lucanis moveret,
2 sacrificanti triste prodigium factum est: ad exta sacrificio perpetrato angues duo ex occulto adlapsi adedere iocur conspectique repente ex oculis abierunt.
3 Ideo[1] cum haruspicum monitu sacrificium instauraretur atque intentius exta reservarentur, iterum ac tertium tradunt adlapsos[2] libatoque iocinere intactos
4 angues abisse. Cum haruspices ad imperatorem id pertinere prodigium praemonuissent et ab occultis cavendum hominibus consultisque, nulla tamen
5 providentia fatum imminens moveri potuit. Flavus Lucanus fuit, caput partis eius Lucanorum, cum pars ad Hannibalem defecisset, quae cum Romanis stabat; et iam altero[3] anno[4] in magistratu erat, ab iisdem
6 illis creatus praetor. Is mutata repente voluntate locum gratiae apud Poenum quaerens neque transire ipse neque trahere ad defectionem Lucanos satis habuit, nisi imperatoris et eiusdem hospitis proditi capite ac sanguine foedus cum hostibus sanxisset.

[1] Ideo *Köhler*: id *P*(1): ob id *Weissenborn*: et *Crévier*.
[2] adlapsos *Weissenborn*: *om. P*(1).
[3] altero *Weissenborn*: *om. P*(1).
[4] anno *PCR*: hanno *R*[1]*MBDA*: annuo *Jac. Gronovius*: altero anno *Weissenborn*.

emergencies, if Hannibal should come to Capua, as they had no doubt he would do, to lend aid to his allies, in order that they might be able to withstand the attack of his cavalry, they ordered Tiberius Gracchus to come from Lucania with his cavalry and light-armed troops to Beneventum. He was to put some one in command of the legions and permanent camps, in order to control the situation in Lucania. B.C. 212

XVI. As Gracchus was sacrificing before leaving Lucania, an unfavourable portent occurred. After the slaying of the victim two snakes gliding stealthily up to the entrails ate part of the liver, and on being noticed vanished suddenly from sight. When for that reason the sacrifice was repeated on the advice of the soothsayers, and while the entrails were being kept with greater care, they relate that the snakes for the second and the third time gliding up tasted the liver and went away unharmed. Although the soothsayers had warned in advance that that portent applied to the general, and that he must beware of men in hiding and of covert plans, still the impending fate could not be averted by any foresight. There was a Lucanian, Flavus, head of that party of the Lucanians which remained on the Roman side, although the other party had revolted to Hannibal. And he was now in the second year of his office, having been elected praetor by that same party. He suddenly changed his intention and, seeking to find favour with the Carthaginian, was not satisfied to change sides himself nor to draw the Lucanians into revolt without ratifying his agreement with the enemy by the life-blood of the general, betrayed though at the same time his guest-friend. He came

A.U.C. 542 7 Ad Magonem, qui in Bruttiis praeerat, clam in collo-
quium venit fideque ab eo accepta, si Romanum iis
imperatorem tradidisset, liberos cum suis legibus
venturos in amicitiam Lucanos, deducit Poenum in
locum quo cum[1] paucis Gracchum adducturum
8 ait: Mago ibi pedites equitesque armatos—et
capere eas latebras ingentem numerum—occuleret.
9 Loco satis inspecto atque undique explorato dies
composita gerendae rei est. Flavus ad Romanum
10 imperatorem venit. Rem se ait magnam incohasse,
ad quam perficiendam ipsius Gracchi opera opus
esse: omnium populorum praetoribus qui ad
Poenum in illo communi Italiae motu descissent,
persuasisse ut redirent in amicitiam Romanorum,
11 quando res quoque Romana, quae prope exitium
clade Cannensi venisset, in dies melior atque auctior
fieret, Hannibalis vis senesceret ac prope ad nihilum
12 venisset; veteri delicto haud inplacabilis fore
Romanos; nullam umquam gentem magis exorabilem
promptioremque veniae dandae fuisse; quotiens re-
13 bellioni etiam maiorum suorum ignotum! Haec ab
sese dicta; ceterum ab ipso Gracchо eadem haec
audire malle eos praesentisque contingere dextram
14 et id pignus fidei secum ferre. Locum se concilio
iis dixisse a conspectu amotum, haud procul castris
Romanis; ibi paucis verbis transigi rem posse ut

[1] quo cum *Gronovius, Madvig* : *om.* *P*(1) : illo cum A^{v}.

to Mago, who was in command in the country of the B.C. 212
Bruttii, for a secret conference, and received his promise that, if he should surrender the Roman commander into their hands, the Lucanians as free men with their own laws would be accepted as friends. He then led the Carthaginian to a place to which he said he would bring Gracchus with a few men; there Mago should conceal armed infantry and cavalry; and the hiding-place had room, he said, for a very large number. After they had sufficiently examined the spot and reconnoitred all around, a day was settled upon for the execution of the plan. Flavus came to the Roman commander, saying that he had begun an important business for the completion of which he needed Gracchus' own help; that he had persuaded the magistrates of all the peoples which in that general commotion in Italy had gone over to the Carthaginians, to return to the friendship of the Romans, since the Roman state also, which had been nearly destroyed by the disaster at Cannae, was daily improving and increasing, while Hannibal's power was growing feebler and had been reduced almost to nothing. To their old offence, he said, the Romans would not be implacable; no people had ever been more easily entreated and readier to grant forgiveness. How often had a rebellion even of their own ancestors been pardoned! These things he said he had told them; but that they preferred to hear these same statements from Gracchus himself, and to take hold of his right hand there before them, and to carry with them that pledge of his honour. He had appointed for their council a place out of sight, not far from the Roman camp; there in a few words it could be

A.U.C. 542 omne nomen Lucanum in fide ac societate Romana
15 sit. Gracchus fraudem et sermoni et rei abesse ratus ac similitudine veri captus cum lictoribus ac turma equitum e castris profectus duce hospite in
16 insidias praecipitat.[1] Hostes subito exorti, et, ne dubia proditio esset, Flavus iis se adiungit. Tela undique in Gracchum atque equites coniciuntur.
17 Gracchus ex equo desilit; idem ceteros facere iubet hortaturque ut, quod unum reliquum fortuna
18 fecerit, id cohonestent virtute: reliquum autem quid esse paucis a multitudine in valle silva ac montibus saepta circumventis praeter mortem?
19 Id referre, utrum praebentes corpora pecorum modo inulti trucidentur, an toti a patiendo expectandoque eventu in impetum atque iram versi, agentes audentesque, perfusi hostium cruore, inter exspirantium inimicorum cumulata armaque et corpora cadant.
20 Lucanum proditorem ac transfugam omnes peterent; qui eam victimam prae se ad inferos misisset, eum decus eximium, egregium solacium suae morti
21 inventurum. Inter haec dicta paludamento circa laevum brachium intorto—nam ne scuta quidem
22 secum extulerant—in hostis impetum fecit. Maior quam pro numero hominum editur pugna. Iaculis maxime aperta corpora Romanorum, cum [2] undique ex altioribus locis in cavam vallem coniectus esset,

[1] praecipitat *Madvig* (*possibly* P^x): -tatus *P*(1): -tatur *B marg. Gronovius*.
[2] cum *Madvig, Conway*: et cum *P*(1).

settled that the whole Lucanian people should be under the protection of the Romans and in alliance with them. Gracchus, thinking that both speech and proposal were free from guile, and misled by the plausibility of it, set out from the camp with his lictors and a troop of cavalry, and with a guest-friend as his guide fell into the ambush. The enemy suddenly came out, and, to leave no doubt about his treachery, Flavus joined them. Javelins assail Gracchus and his horsemen from every side. He springs from his horse, bids the rest to do the same and urges them to ennoble by courage the one thing fortune has left open to them. But to a few men surrounded by a multitude, in a valley hedged about by forest and mountains, what was left, he asked, but death? The one thing that mattered was whether they were to submit themselves like sheep to be slaughtered unavenged, or, far from calmly awaiting the outcome, were to be altogether bent on angry attack, and then, daring and doing, drenched by the blood of the enemy, among the heaps of arms and bodies of their dying foes, were to fall. They must all attack the Lucanian traitor and deserter. The man who sent that victim before him to the lower world would find great distinction and for his own death an extraordinary consolation. While thus speaking he wound his general's cloak around his left arm—for they had not taken even shields with them—and attacked the enemy. The battle was out of all proportion to the number of men engaged. The bodies of the Romans were especially unprotected against javelins, and were pierced by them, as they could be thrown from higher ground all around into the hollow valley. Gracchus, who B.C. 212

A.U.C. 542 23 transfiguntur. Gracchum iam nudatum praesidio vivum capere Poeni nituntur; ceterum conspicatus Lucanum hospitem inter hostis, adeo infestus confertos invasit ut parci ei sine multorum pernicie
24 non posset. Exanimem eum Mago extemplo ad Hannibalem misit ponique cum captis simul fascibus ante tribunal imperatoris iussit.

Haec si [1] vera fama est, Gracchus in Lucanis ad campos qui Veteres vocantur periit. XVII. Sunt qui in agro Beneventano prope Calorem fluvium contendant a castris cum lictoribus ac tribus servis
2 lavandi causa progressum, cum forte inter salicta innata ripis laterent hostes, nudum atque inermem saxisque quae volvit amnis propugnantem inter-
3 fectum. Sunt qui haruspicum monitu quingentos passus a castris progressum, uti loco puro ea quae ante dicta prodigia sunt procuraret, ab insidentibus forte locum duabus turmis Numidarum circumventum scribant. Adeo nec locus nec ratio mortis in viro
4 tam claro et insigni constat. Funeris quoque Gracchi varia est fama. Alii in castris Romanis sepultum ab suis, alii ab Hannibale—et ea vulgatior fama est—tradunt in vestibulo Punicorum castrorum
5 rogum extructum esse, armatum exercitum decucurrisse cum tripudiis Hispanorum motibusque armorum et corporum suae cuique genti adsuetis, ipso Hannibale

[1] si *Madvig* : *om.* *P*(1).

was by this time stripped of his defenders, the B.C. 212 Carthaginians strove to capture alive. But catching sight of his Lucanian guest-friend among the enemy, he dashed into the dense ranks with such animosity that he could not be spared without the loss of many lives. Mago at once sent the corpse to Hannibal and ordered it to be placed before the general's tribune together with the captured fasces.

If this is the true report, Gracchus perished in Lucania, on the Old Plains, as they are called. XVII. There are some who maintain that in the region of Beneventum, by the river Calor, he had gone out of the camp with his lictors and three slaves to bathe, while enemies, as it happened, were hiding among the willows growing on the banks, and was slain, naked and unarmed and defending himself with stones which the river rolls along. There are some writers who say that on the advice of the soothsayers he had gone five hundred paces from the camp to make atonement on an uncontaminated spot for the prodigies mentioned above, and was overpowered by two troops of Numidians who chanced to be in ambush there. So far are both the place and the manner of his death from being established, in spite of his eminence and distinction. In regard to Gracchus's funeral also reports vary. Some relate that he was buried in the Roman camp by his own men, others—and this is the prevalent report —that by Hannibal's order a pyre was erected directly outside the gate of the Carthaginian camp, and that the army defiled under arms, with dances by the Spanish troops and such movements of weapons and bodies as were customary for each tribe, while Hannibal himself

A.U.C. 542 omni rerum verborumque honore exequias celebrante.
6 Haec tradunt qui in Lucanis rei gestae auctores sunt. Si illis qui ad Calorem fluvium interfectum memorant credere velis, capitis tantum Gracchi
7 hostes potiti sunt; eo delato ad Hannibalem, missus ab eo confestim Carthalo, qui in castra Romana ad Cn. Cornelium quaestorem deferret; is funus imperatoris in castris celebrantibus cum exercitu Beneventanis fecit.

XVIII. Consules agrum Campanum ingressi cum passim popularentur, eruptione oppidanorum et Magonis cum equitatu territi et trepidi ad signa milites palatos passim revocarunt, et vixdum instructa acie fusi supra mille et quingentos milites
2 amiserunt. Inde ingens ferocia superbae suopte ingenio genti crevit, multisque proeliis lacessebant Romanos; sed intentiores ad cavendum consules una pugna fecerat incaute atque inconsulte inita.
3 Restituit tamen his animos et illis minuit audaciam parva una res; sed in bello nihil tam leve est quod non magnae interdum rei momentum faciat.
4 T. Quinctio Crispino Badius Campanus hospes erat, perfamiliari hospitio iunctus. Creverat consuetudo, quod aeger Romae apud Crispinum Badius ante defectionem Campanam liberaliter comiterque curatus
5 fuerat. Is tum[1] Badius, progressus ante stationes quae pro porta stabant, vocari Crispinum iussit.

[1] Is tum *Crévier* : stu *P* : tum P^2(1).

---

[1] Not to be confused with another man of the same name in xxvi. 4; XXIV. xxxix. 12; and frequently in XXVII.

honoured the obsequies with every tribute in act and word. These are the statements of those who vouch for its occurrence in Lucania. If you incline to believe those who state that he was slain at the river Calor, the enemy gained possession of Gracchus' head only. This being brought to Hannibal, Carthalo was at once sent by him to bring it to the Roman camp and Gnaeus Cornelius the quaestor. He conducted the funeral of the general in the camp, while the people of Beneventum joined with the army in doing him honour. B.C. 212

XVIII. While the consuls, on entering the Campanian region, were devastating it far and wide, being alarmed and dismayed by a sally of the Capuans and of Mago with his cavalry, they recalled their widely scattered soldiers to the standards, and being routed almost before their line was formed, lost over fifteen hundred men. Upon this the great overconfidence of a people naturally proud was greatly increased, and they sought to provoke the Romans by many battles. But a single engagement incautiously and imprudently begun had made the consuls more careful to be on their guard. One small occurrence, however, restored the courage of one army and lessened the boldness of the other. But in war nothing is so slight as not at times to bring about a great result. Titus Quinctius Crispinus[1] had one Badius, a Campanian, as his guest-friend, linked to him by intimate hospitality. Friendship had grown because in an illness Badius had been generously and kindly nursed at the house of Crispinus at Rome before the rebellion of Campania. This Badius at the time came up to the outposts stationed before the gate and bade them call

A.U.C. 542 Quod ubi est Crispino nuntiatum, ratus conloquium
amicum ac familiare quaeri, manente memoria etiam
in discidio publicorum foederum privati iuris, paulum
6 a ceteris processit. Postquam in conspectum venere,
"Provoco te" inquit "ad pugnam, Crispine,"
Badius; "conscendamus equos summotisque aliis
7 uter bello melior sit decernamus." Ad ea Crispinus
nec sibi nec illi ait hostes deesse in quibus virtutem
ostendant; se, etiamsi in acie occurrerit, declina-
turum, ne hospitali caede dextram violet; con-
8 versusque abibat. Enimvero ferocius tum Campanus
increpare mollitiam ignaviamque et se digna probra
in insontem iacere, hospitalem hostem appellans
simulantemque parcere cui sciat parem se non esse.
9 Si parum publicis foederibus ruptis dirempta simul
et privata iura esse putet, Badium Campanum
T. Quinctio Crispino Romano palam duobus exerciti-
10 bus audientibus renuntiare hospitium. Nihil sibi
cum eo consociatum, nihil foederatum, hosti cum
hoste, cuius patriam ac penates publicos privatosque
oppugnatum venisset. Si vir esset, congrederetur.
11 Diu cunctantem Crispinum perpulere turmales ne
12 impune insultare Campanum pateretur. Itaque
tantum moratus dum imperatores consuleret per-
mitterentne sibi extra ordinem in provocantem

Crispinus. When this was reported to Crispinus, he went a little beyond the others, thinking a friendly and intimate conversation was wanted, since the memory of a personal tie lingered in spite of the rupture of public treaties. When they had come in sight of each other, "I challenge you to battle, Crispinus," said Badius. "Let us mount our horses and, with others kept at a distance, decide which is the better warrior." In reply Crispinus said that neither he nor Badius lacked enemies on whom to show his courage. For himself, even if he should meet the other in battle-line, he would avoid him, lest he stain his right hand with the blood of a guest-friend. And he turned and was walking away. Then in truth the Campanian more fiercely reviled the effeminacy and cowardice of Crispinus and hurled reproaches which he himself deserved against an innocent man, calling him a guest-enemy and a man who pretended to spare one to whom he knew he was not equal. If he thought that with the rupture of public treaties private ties had not also been broken, then, he said, Badius the Campanian, openly in the hearing of two armies, renounced the guest-friendship of Titus Quinctius Crispinus the Roman. For himself, an enemy, nothing was hallowed by association, nothing by compact, with him, an enemy, since he had come to attack his native city and the Penates of the state and of the household. If he was a man, let him come on. Crispinus, after long hesitation, was prevailed upon by his comrades not to allow the Campanian to revile him with impunity. And so he delayed only long enough to consult the generals as to whether they permitted him to fight out of ranks against an enemy who challenged him.

B.C. 212

A.U.C. 542 hostem pugnare, permissu eorum arma cepit equum-
que conscendit et Badium nomine compellans ad
13 pugnam evocavit. Nulla mora a Campano facta est;
infestis equis concurrerunt. Crispinus supra scutum
sinistrum umerum Badio hasta transfixit, superque
delapsum cum vulnere ex equo desiluit, ut pedes
14 iacentem conficeret. Badius, priusquam opprimere-
tur, parma atque equo relicto ad suos aufugit;
15 Crispinus equum armaque capta et cruentam cuspi-
dem insignis spoliis ostentans cum magna laude et
gratulatione militum ad consules est deductus
laudatusque ibi magnifice et donis donatus.

XIX. Hannibal ex agro Beneventano castra ad
Capuam cum movisset, tertio post die quam venit
2 copias in aciem eduxit, haudquaquam dubius, quod
Campanis absente se paucos ante dies secunda
fuisset pugna, quin multo minus se suumque totiens
3 victorem exercitum sustinere Romani possent. Ceterum postquam pugnari coeptum est, equitum
maxime incursu, cum iaculis obrueretur, laborabat
Romana acies, donec signum equitibus datum est
4 ut in hostem admitterent equos. Ita equestre
proelium erat, cum procul visus Sempronianus exercitus, cui Cn. Cornelius quaestor praeerat, utrique
parti parem metum praebuit ne hostes novi adven-
5 tarent. Velut ex composito utrimque signum receptui datum, reductique in castra prope aequo
Marte discesserunt; plures tamen ab Romanis primo

[1] For the forces Gracchus had commanded cf. xv. 20.

With their permission he took his arms and mounted his horse, and addressing Badius by name called him out to battle. The Campanian made no delay; riding directly at each other they clashed. Crispinus with his spear pierced Badius' left shoulder above the shield; and after he fell wounded, leaped upon him from his horse, that, now dismounted, he might despatch the fallen. Badius, not to be overpowered, left shield and horse and fled to his own men. Crispinus, decked with spoils and displaying the horse and captured arms and his bloody spear, was conducted with much praise and congratulation on the part of the soldiers to the consuls, and there he was highly praised and rewarded with gifts. B.C. 212

XIX. Hannibal, having moved his camp from the region of Beneventum to the vicinity of Capua, led his troops out into battle-line on the third day after his arrival. Since in his absence the Campanians had had a successful battle a few days before, he had no doubt whatever that the Romans would be much less able to withstand himself and his repeatedly victorious army. But once the battle had begun, the Roman line was hard pressed, especially by the cavalry charge, being overwhelmed by their darts, until the signal was given to the cavalry to urge their horses against the enemy. Thus a cavalry battle was in progress when the distant sight of the Sempronian army,[1] commanded by Gnaeus Cornelius, the quaestor, inspired in both armies the same fear that fresh enemies were approaching. As if by agreement the signal for recall was given on both sides, and marching back to the camp they separated on almost even terms. Yet a larger number fell on the

A.U.C. 542 6 incursu equitum ceciderunt. Inde consules, ut
averterent Capua Hannibalem, nocte quae secuta
est diversi, Fulvius in agrum Cumanum, Claudius
7 in Lucanos abit. Postero die, cum vacua castra
Romanorum esse nuntiatum Hannibali esset et
duobus agminibus diversos abisse, incertus primo
8 utrum sequeretur, Appium institit sequi. Ille circumducto hoste qua voluit alio itinere ad Capuam
redit.

Hannibali alia in his locis bene gerendae rei for-
9 tuna oblata est. M. Centenius fuit cognomine
Paenula, insignis inter primi pili centuriones et
10 magnitudine corporis et animo. Is, perfunctus
militia, per P. Cornelium Sullam praetorem in senatum introductus petit a patribus uti sibi quinque milia
11 militum darentur: se peritum et hostis et regionum
brevi operae pretium facturum et, quibus artibus
ad id locorum nostri et duces et exercitus capti forent,
12 iis adversus inventorem usurum. Id non promissum
magis stolide quam stolide creditum, tamquam
13 eaedem militares et imperatoriae artes essent. Data
pro quinque octo milia militum, pars dimidia cives,
pars socii. Et ipse aliquantum voluntariorum in
itinere ex [1] agris concivit ac prope duplicato exercitu
in Lucanos pervenit, ubi Hannibal nequiquam
14 secutus Claudium substiterat. Haud dubia res

[1] ex *Madvig*: in *P*(1).

---

[1] A *primi pili centurio* (or *primus pilus*) was the ranking centurion of his legion, commanding the first century of the first maniple of the *triarii*.

Roman side because of the first charge of the horsemen. Thereupon the consuls, in order to draw Hannibal away from Capua, marched off the following night in different directions, Fulvius into the region of Cumae, Claudius into Lucania. The next day Hannibal, on being informed that the Roman camp was empty and that they had marched away in different directions in two columns, was at first uncertain which to follow, but pushed on in pursuit of Appius, who after leading the enemy around wherever he pleased, returned by a different road to Capua. B.C. 212

Hannibal had another opportunity for success presented to him in this region. There was one Marcus Centenius, with the cognomen Paenula, conspicuous among the centurions of the highest rank [1] for his huge body and his courage. Having finished his military service, he was brought into the senate by Publius Cornelius Sulla, a praetor, and begged the fathers to give him five thousand soldiers. He, being well-acquainted, he said, both with the enemy and the country, would soon accomplish something worth while, and as for the arts by which both our generals and our armies had till then been ensnared, he would use them against their inventor. This was not more stupidly promised than stupidly believed, as if the qualities of soldier and general were the same. Instead of five thousand, eight thousand soldiers were given him, half of them citizens, half allies. And he himself on his march raised a considerable number of volunteers from the farms, and with his army nearly doubled reached Lucania, where Hannibal had halted after vainly pursuing Claudius. The result was never in doubt,

A.U.C. 542

erat, quippe inter Hannibalem ducem et centurionem,
exercitusque alterum vincendo veteranum, alterum
novum totum, magna ex parte etiam tumultuarium
15 ac semermem. Ut conspecta inter se agmina sunt
et neutra pars detrectavit pugnam, extemplo instructae acies. Pugnatum tamen ut in nulla pari
re; duas amplius horas constitit pugna spe [1] con-
16 citante,[2] donec dux stetit, Romanam aciem.[3] Postquam is non pro vetere fama solum, sed etiam metu
futuri dedecoris, si sua temeritate contractae cladi
superesset, obiectans se hostium telis cecidit, fusa
17 extemplo est Romana acies; sed adeo ne fugae
quidem iter patuit omnibus viis ab equite insessis,
ut ex tanta multitudine vix mille evaserint, ceteri
passim alii alia peste absumpti sint.

XX. Capua a consulibus iterum summa vi obsideri
coepta est, quaeque in eam rem opus erant compor-
2 tabantur parabanturque. Casilinum frumentum convectum; ad Volturni ostium, ubi nunc urbs est,
castellum communitum ibique et Puteolis, quos iam [4]
ante Fabius Maximus munierat, praesidium impositum,
3 ut mare proximum et flumen in potestate essent. In ea
duo maritima castella frumentum, quod ex Sardinia
nuper missum erat quodque M. Iunius praetor ex
Etruria coemerat, ab Ostia convectum est, ut exerci-
4 tui per hiemem copia esset. Ceterum super eam
cladem quae in Lucanis accepta erat volonum quo-

[1] -stitit pugna spe con- *M. Müller*: *om.* *P*(1), *a lost line.*
[2] concitante *Madvig*: concitata et *P*(1): -atae *P*[1] *?*: -ata *Sigonius, Walters.*
[3] Romanam aciem *P*(1): -a acie *A*[y] *Valla.*
[4] ibique . . . iam *Conway, a line om. by* *P*(1).

---

[1] Cf. XXIV. vii. 10.

as between Hannibal as commander and a centurion, B.C. 212
and between armies one of which was a veteran in victory and the other altogether raw, in large part also irregular and half-armed. When the columns were in sight of each other and neither side refused battle, the lines were immediately drawn up. They fought, however, as was to be expected where nothing was fairly matched. For more than two hours the battle continued, since hope inspired the Roman line so long as their commander held his ground. Not only in keeping with his old reputation, but also for fear of future disgrace, if he should survive a disaster brought on by his own rashness, he threw himself upon the weapons of the enemy and fell, whereupon the Roman line was at once routed. But, as all the roads were occupied by cavalry, so far were they from having any route open even for flight that out of so great a multitude barely a thousand escaped, while the rest scattering met death in various forms.

XX. The siege of Capua was resumed with intensity by the consuls, and all that was needed for the purpose was being brought together and made ready. Casilinum was the depot for grain. At the mouth of the Volturnus, where there is now a city, a stronghold was fortified, and there and at Puteoli,[1] which Fabius Maximus had previously fortified, a garrison was placed, that the sea in that neighbourhood and the river might be in their power. To these two strongholds by the sea the grain which had been sent recently from Sardinia and that which the praetor Marcus Junius had purchased in Etruria was transported from Ostia, so that the army might have a supply through the winter. But in addition to the disaster incurred in Lucania, the army of slave-

A.U.C. 542 que exercitus, qui vivo Graccho summa fide stipendia
fecerat, velut exauctoratus morte ducis ab signis
discessit.

5 Hannibal non Capuam neglectam neque in tanto
discrimine desertos volebat socios; sed prospero ex
temeritate unius Romani ducis successu in alterius
ducis exercitusque opprimendi occasionem immine-
6 bat. Cn. Fulvium praetorem Apuli legati nuntiabant
primo, dum urbes quasdam Apulorum quae ad Hannibalem descivissent oppugnaret, intentius rem egisse:
postea nimio successu et ipsum et milites praeda
impletos in tantam licentiam socordiamque effusos
7 ut nulla disciplina militiae esset. Cum saepe alias,
tum paucis diebus ante expertus qualis sub inscio
duce exercitus esset, in Apuliam castra movit.
XXI. Circa Herdoneam Romanae legiones et praetor
Fulvius erat. Quo ubi allatum est hostis adventare,
prope est factum ut iniussu praetoris signis convulsis
in aciem exirent; nec res magis ulla tenuit quam
spes haud dubia suo id arbitrio ubi vellent facturos.
2 Nocte insequenti Hannibal, cum tumultuatum in
castris et plerosque ferociter, signum ut daret,
3 institisse duci ad arma vocantis sciret, haud dubius
prosperae pugnae occasionem dari, tria milia expedi-
torum militum in villis circa vepribusque et silvis
disponit, qui signo dato simul omnes e latebris

[1] Cf. XXIV. xx. 8.

volunteers also, which had served with the utmost B.C. 212
loyalty while Gracchus lived, abandoned its standards, as if discharged by the death of the general.

Hannibal did not wish that Capua should be neglected nor his allies abandoned in such a crisis. But in view of a success due to the rashness of one Roman general he was eager for an opportunity to surprise a second general and army. Apulian legates were informing him that the praetor Gnaeus Fulvius had at first been very active while besieging some Apulian cities which had revolted to Hannibal; but that later, owing to unmerited success, both he himself and his soldiers, who were loaded with booty, had gone to such lengths in licence and indifference that there was no military discipline. Hannibal, who frequently at other times, and particularly within a few days, had discovered what an army is under an incompetent general, moved his camp into Apulia. XXI. Near Herdonea [1] were Roman legions and the praetor Fulvius. When the news reached them there that the enemy were approaching, they barely refrained from catching up their standards and going out into battle-line without orders from the praetor. And nothing restrained them more than the hope, now beyond question, that they would do so at their own discretion whenever they pleased. The following night Hannibal, knowing that there had been an uproar in the camp and that many, calling to arms, had over-confidently pressed the commander to give the signal, had no doubt that an opportunity for a victory was offered. He accordingly posted three thousand lightly equipped soldiers in farmhouses near by and in the thickets and the woods, to come out of their hiding-places all at once,

A.U.C. 542

4 existerent, et Magonem ac duo ferme milia equitum,
qua fugam inclinaturam credebat, omnia itinera
insidere iubet. His nocte praeparatis, prima luce
5 in aciem copias educit; nec Fulvius est cunctatus,
non tam sua ulla spe quam militum impetu fortuito
tractus. Itaque eadem temeritate qua processum
in aciem est instruitur ipsa acies ad libidinem militum
forte procurrentium consistentiumque quo loco
ipsorum tulisset animus, deinde per libidinem aut
6 metum deserentium locum. Prima legio et sinistra
ala in primo instructae et in longitudinem porrecta
7 acies. Clamantibus tribunis nihil introrsus roboris
ac virium esse et, quacumque impetum fecisset
hostis, perrupturos, nihil quod salutare esset non
modo ad animum sed ne ad aures quidem admittebat.
8 Et Hannibal haudquaquam similis dux neque
simili exercitu neque ita instructo aderat. Ergo
ne clamorem quidem atque impetum primum eorum
9 Romani sustinuere. Dux, stultitia et temeritate
Centenio par, animo haudquaquam comparandus,
ubi rem inclinatam ac trepidantis suos videt, equo
arrepto cum ducentis ferme equitibus effugit;
10 cetera a fronte pulsa, inde a[1] tergo atque alis circumventa acies eo usque est caesa ut ex duodeviginti
milibus hominum duo milia haud amplius evaserint.
Castris hostes potiti sunt.

[1] inde a *Weissenborn*: in *P*(1).

---

[1] The *alae* were auxiliaries of the allies, each *ala* equal in strength to a legion (4200 men). When drawn up as here the second line would be made up of the other legion and the *ala dextra*. Such a formation was at times employed instead of the usual three lines, *hastati, principes, triarii,* of the legionaries. Cf. XXVII. i. 8; ii. 6.

when the signal was given. And he ordered Mago B.C. 212 and about two thousand horsemen to lie in wait along all the roads in the direction which he believed the flight would take. After making these preparations at night, he led his troops out into line at daybreak. Nor did Fulvius hesitate, dragged into it not so much by any hope of his own as by the haphazard impulse of the soldiers. And so, with the same recklessness with which they went out to form, they drew up even the line of battle according to the whim of soldiers who happened to dash forward and take their stand wherever their own fancy had carried them, and then capriciously or in fear abandoned their positions. The first legion and the left *ala* were placed in front,[1] and the line was made very long. Although the tribunes shouted that in depth it had no power to resist, and that wherever the enemy should make their attack they would pierce it, the men in line allowed no advice that was helpful to reach even their ears, not to say their attention. And there was Hannibal, surely not that sort of a general, nor with that sort of an army, drawn up in that fashion. Consequently the Romans did not withstand even their shout and the first onset. The general, a match for Centenius in folly and recklessness, but in courage by no means to be compared with him, seeing that the line was giving way and his own men in confusion, seized a horse and with about two hundred horsemen made his escape. The rest of the line, beaten back in front and then surrounded in the rear and on the wings, was so cut to pieces that out of eighteen thousand men not more than two thousand escaped. The camp was occupied by the enemy.

A.U.C. 542 XXII. Hae clades super aliam alia Romam cum essent nuntiatae, ingens quidem et luctus et pavor civitatem cepit; sed tamen quia consules, ubi summa rerum esset, ad id locorum prospere rem
2 gererent, minus his cladibus commovebantur. Legatos ad consules mittunt C. Laetorium M. Metilium qui nuntiarent ut reliquias duorum exercituum cum
3 cura colligerent darentque operam ne per metum ac desperationem hosti se dederent, id quod post Cannensem accidisset cladem, et ut desertores de
4 exercitu volonum conquirerent. Idem negotii P. Cornelio datum, cui et dilectus mandatus erat; isque per fora conciliabulaque edixit ut conquisitio volonum fieret iique ad signa reducerentur. Haec omnia intentissima cura acta.

5 Ap. Claudius consul D. Iunio ad ostium Volturni, M. Aurelio Cotta Puteolis praeposito, qui, ut quaeque naves ex Etruria ac Sardinia accessissent,
6 extemplo in castra mitterent frumentum, ipse ad Capuam regressus Q. Fulvium collegam invenit Casilino omnia deportantem molientemque ad
7 oppugnandam Capuam. Tum ambo circumsederunt urbem et Claudium Neronem praetorem ab Suessula
8 ex Claudianis castris exciverunt. Is quoque modico ibi praesidio ad tenendum locum relicto ceteris omnibus copiis ad Capuam descendit. Ita tria praetoria circa Capuam erecta; tres et [1] exercitus

[1] et *P*(2) *Conway*: *om. A Weissenborn, Walters.*

---

[1] *I.e.* the senate.
[2] In XXII. xxv. 3 he was *tribunus plebis.*
[3] Cf. above, note on v. 6.

XXII. When the news of these disasters one after another had reached Rome, great sorrow and alarm, it is true, took possession of the state. Nevertheless because the consuls, to whom fell the supreme command, were up to that time successful, they were less disturbed by these disasters. They[1] sent Gaius Laetorius and Marcus Metilius[2] as legates to the consuls, to inform them that they should carefully gather up the remnants of the two armies, and see to it that in fear and despair they did not surrender to the enemy, as had happened after the disaster at Cannae; also that they should search for the deserters from the army of slave-volunteers. The same duty was given to Publius Cornelius, to whom the levy also had been assigned. And he issued an edict in the market-towns and local centres,[3] that search should be made for the slave-volunteers, and that they be brought back to their standards. All these things were done with the utmost diligence. B.C. 212

Appius Claudius, the consul, placed Decimus Junius in command at the mouth of the Volturnus and Marcus Aurelius Cotta at Puteoli, in order that, as fast as ships came in from Etruria and Sardinia, they should send the grain at once to the camps. He himself, on returning to Capua, found his colleague Quintus Fulvius transporting everything from Casilinum and making every preparation for the siege of Capua. Then they both invested the city and summoned the praetor, Claudius Nero, from the Claudian camp at Suessula. He, leaving there only a garrison of moderate size to hold the place, likewise came down with all the rest of his forces to Capua. Thus three headquarters were set up around Capua. There were three armies too that,

A.U.C. 542 diversis partibus opus adgressi fossa valloque circumdare urbem parant et castella excitant modicis
9 intervallis multisque simul locis cum prohibentibus opera Campanis eo eventu pugnant ut postremo
10 portis muroque se contineret Campanus. Prius tamen quam haec continuarentur opera, legati ad Hannibalem missi qui quererentur desertam ab eo Capuam ac prope redditam Romanis obtestarenturque ut tunc saltem opem non circumsessis modo sed
11 etiam circumvallatis ferret. Consulibus litterae a P. Cornelio praetore missae ut, priusquam clauderent Capuam operibus, potestatem Campanis facerent ut qui eorum vellent exirent a Capua suasque res
12 secum ferrent:[1] liberos fore suaque omnia habituros qui ante idus Martias exissent; post eam diem quique exissent quique ibi mansissent, hostium
13 futuros numero. Ea pronuntiata Campanis atque ita spreta ut ultro contumelias dicerent minarenturque.

14 Hannibal ab Herdonea Tarentum duxerat legiones, spe aut vi aut dolo arcis Tarentinae potiundae; quod ubi parum processit, ad Brundisium flexit
15 iter, prodi id oppidum ratus. Ibi quoque cum frustra tereret tempus, legati Campani ad eum venerunt querentes simul orantesque; quibus Hannibal magnifice respondit et antea se solvisse obsidionem et nunc adventum suum consules non laturos.

[1] ferrent *M*^{4}*?* *Madvig*: inferrent *P*(6)*M?*: au- *M?Ax*: inde ferrent *Weissenborn*.

[1] In the name of the senate.

fell to work on different sides, made ready to encircle B.C. 212
the city with a ditch and an earthwork, and erected redoubts at moderate intervals; and at many points at the same time they fought with such success against the Campanians who endeavoured to hinder the works that finally the Campanians remained inside the gates and the wall. But before these siege-works could be made continuous, legates were sent to Hannibal, to complain that Capua had been deserted by him and almost given back to the Romans, and to implore him to bring aid, then at least, to men not only besieged but also encircled by entrenchments. The consuls received a letter from Publius Cornelius, the praetor, ordering[1] that, before enclosing Capua with their works, they should permit such of the Campanians as wished to do so to leave Capua and carry their possessions with them. Those who should leave before the fifteenth of March were to be free men and to keep all their property; those who left after that date and those who remained there were to be reckoned enemies. These terms were published to the Campanians, and were received with such contempt by them that they were actually insulting and made threats.

Hannibal had led his legions from Herdonea to Tarentum in the hope of getting possession of the citadel of Tarentum either by force or by ruse. When this did not succeed, he turned aside to Brundisium, thinking that town would certainly be betrayed. While there also he was wasting time, the Campanian legates came to him with complaints and at the same time entreaties. Hannibal replied to them grandly that he had previously raised a siege, and that now also the consuls would not with-

A.U.C. 542

16 Cum hac spe dimissi legati vix regredi Capuam iam duplici fossa valloque cinctam potuerunt.

XXIII. Cum maxume Capua circumvallaretur, Syracusarum oppugnatio ad finem venit, praeterquam vi ac virtute ducis exercitusque, intestina
2 etiam proditione adiuta. Namque Marcellus initio veris incertus utrum Agrigentum ad Himilconem et Hippocraten verteret bellum an obsidione Syra-
3 cusas premeret, quamquam nec vi capi videbat posse inexpugnabilem terrestri ac maritimo situ urbem nec fame, ut quam prope liberi a Carthagine com-
4 meatus alerent, tamen, ne quid inexpertum relinqueret, transfugas Syracusanos—erant autem apud Romanos aliqui nobilissimi viri, inter defectionem ab Romanis, quia ab novis consiliis abhorrebant, pulsi—conloquiis suae partis temptare hominum animos iussit et fidem dare, si traditae forent Syra-
5 cusae, liberos eos ac suis legibus victuros esse. Non erat conloquii copia, quia multorum animi suspecti omnium curam oculosque eo [1] converterant ne quid
6 falleret tale admissum. Servus unus exulum, pro transfuga intromissus in urbem, conventis paucis initium conloquendi de tali re fecit. Deinde in [2] piscatoria quidam nave retibus operti circumvectique ita ad castra Romana conlocutique cum transfugis,

[1] eo *B Riemann* : *om. P*(1).
[2] Deinde in *z* : dein *P*(1) : deinde *A*[2].

[1] Beyond the northern Wall of Dionysius, not far from the Hexapylon.

stand his coming. With this hope the legates were sent away, and it was with difficulty that they were able to return to Capua, now surrounded by two trenches and a double earthwork. B.C. 212

XXIII. Just as Capua was being encircled the siege of Syracuse came to an end, expedited not only by the vigour and valour of the general and the army but also by treachery within. For Marcellus, who at the beginning of the spring had been uncertain whether to shift the war to Agrigentum against Himilco and Hippocrates, or to press the siege of Syracuse, saw indeed that the city, impregnable in its position both on the landward and the seaward side, could not be taken by assault, nor by starvation, inasmuch as it was sustained by almost unhampered supplies from Carthage. Nevertheless, to leave nothing untried, deserters from Syracuse—and there were in the Roman lines some men of highest rank who during the estrangement from the Romans had been driven out because they were averse to a change of policy—were ordered by him to sound men of their faction in conferences, and to give them a pledge that, if Syracuse should be surrendered, they should live as free men and under their own laws. For a conference there was no opportunity, because the suspicious attitude of many men had attracted the attention and the eyes of all, to prevent such an offence from passing unnoticed. A single slave belonging to the exiles was admitted to the city as a deserter and by meeting a few men made a beginning of parleys on a matter of such moment. Then some men were hidden under nets on a fishing vessel, and thus sailed around to the Roman camp[1] and talked with the deserters. And

A.U.C. 542 et iidem saepius eodem modo et alii atque alii;
7 postremo ad octoginta facti. Et cum iam composita
omnia ad proditionem essent, indicio delato ad Epicyden per Attalum quendam, indignantem sibi
rem creditam non esse, necati omnes cum cruciatu
sunt.

8 Alia subinde spes, postquam haec vana evaserat,
excepit. Damippus quidam Lacedaemonius, missus
ab Syracusis ad Philippum regem, captus ab Romanis
9 navibus erat. Huius utique redimendi et Epicydae
cura erat ingens, nec abnuit Marcellus, iam tum
Aetolorum, quibus socii Lacedaemonii erant, amicitiam
10 adfectantibus Romanis. Ad conloquium de redemptione eius missis medius maxime atque utrisque
opportunus locus ad portum Trogilorum, propter
11 turrim quam vocant Galeagram, est visus. Quo
cum saepius commearent, unus ex Romanis ex
propinquo murum contemplans, numerando lapides
aestimandoque ipse secum quid in fronte paterent
12 singuli, altitudinem muri, quantum proxime coniectura
poterat, permensus humilioremquc aliquanto pristina
opinione sua et ceterorum omnium ratus esse et vel
mediocribus scalis superabilem, ad Marcellum rem
13 defert. Haud spernenda visa; sed cum adiri locus,
quia ob id ipsum intentius custodiebatur, non posset,
14 occasio quaerebatur; quam obtulit transfuga nun-
tians diem festum Dianae per triduum agi et, quia
alia in obsidione desint, vino largius epulas celebrari

---

[1] Merely a small bay, of no value for large vessels.

[2] The tower was probably beyond the wall in the open country.

the same men did this repeatedly in the same way, also others and again others. Finally they amounted to about eighty. And when now everything had been arranged for the betrayal, information was brought to Epicydes by one Attalus, who was outraged that the matter had not been confided to him, and they were all put to death with torture. B.C. 212

This hope having proved false, another at once took its place. Damippus a Lacedaemonian, who had been sent from Syracuse to King Philip, had been captured by Roman ships. Epicydes was very much concerned to ransom him at any cost, and Marcellus also was not averse, since the Romans were already courting the friendship of the Aetolians, whose allies the Lacedaemonians were. The men sent to confer in regard to the man's ransom thought that the most convenient place for both sides, and just half-way, was at the Trogili Harbour,[1] near the tower called Galeagra.[2] As they came there repeatedly, one of the Romans, observing the wall from near at hand, by counting the courses and making his own estimate of the height of each on its face, measured the height of the wall as nearly as he could by guesswork. And thinking it considerably lower than his own previous estimate of it and that of all the rest, and that it could be scaled by ladders even of moderate length, he reported to Marcellus. It did not seem a matter to be despised. But since the place, being more closely guarded for the very reason mentioned, could not be approached, they cast about for an opportunity. And this was offered by a deserter, reporting that the feast of Diana was being observed for three days, and that, since other things were lacking during the siege, it was with wine that the

A.U.C. 542 et ab Epicyde praebito universae plebei et per
tribus a principibus diviso.
15 Quod ubi[1] accepit Marcellus, cum paucis tribunorum militum conlocutus, electisque per eos ad
rem tantam agendam audendamque idoneis centurionibus militibusque et scalis in occulto comparatis,
ceteris signum dari iubet ut mature corpora curarent
quietique darent: nocte in expeditionem eundum
16 esse. Inde ubi id temporis visum quo de die epulatis
iam vini satias principiumque somni esset, signi
unius milites ferre scalas iussit; et ad mille fere
17 armati tenui agmine per silentium eo deducti. Ubi
sine strepitu ac tumultu primi evaserunt in murum,
secuti ordine alii, cum priorum audacia dubiis etiam
animum faceret. XXIV. Iam mille armatorum muri[2]
ceperant partem, cum ceterae admotae sunt copiae[3]
pluribusque scalis in murum evadebant signo ab
2 Hexapylo dato, quo per ingentem solitudinem
erat perventum, quia magna pars in turribus epulati
aut sopiti vino erant aut semigraves potabant;
paucos tamen eorum inproviso oppressos[4] in cubilibus
3 interfecerunt. Prope Hexapylon est portula; ea
magna vi refringi coepta et e muro ex composito
tuba datum signum erat et iam undique non furtim,
4 sed vi aperta[5] gerebatur res. Quippe ad Epipolas,

[1] quod ubi *M*[1] : id ubi *A*[2] : dubia *P*(1).
[2] muri *Madvig* : om. *P*(1) : eam *Harant*.
[3] sunt copiae *Weissenborn* : *om.* *P*(1).
[4] inproviso oppressos *Hertz* : inpressos *P*(1) : oppressos *xz*.
[5] aperta *Gronovius* : aperte *P*(1).

---

[1] *I.e.* the φυλαί, corresponding in a way to the Roman tribes.
[2] For this, the most important gate to the north, cf. XXIV. xxi. 7; xxxii. 5, etc.

banquets were more lavishly provided, this being furnished to the entire populace by Epicydes and distributed among the tribes [1] by leading citizens. B.C. 212

On learning of this, Marcellus conferred with a few tribunes of the soldiers, and after these had chosen centurions and soldiers able to dare and do a thing of such importance, and after ladders had been secretly made ready, he ordered the signal to be given to the others to eat early and then rest. In the night, he said, they must go on a raid. Then, when it seemed to be late enough for those who had begun their feast during the day to be sated, he thought, with their wine and now to be falling asleep, he ordered the soldiers of one maniple to carry the ladders. And about a thousand armed men were led in a thin column to the place in silence. When the first men without noise and confusion had made their way to the top of the wall, the others followed one after another, since the boldness of those ahead of them gave courage even to the wavering. XXIV. The thousand armed men had already taken a part of the wall, when the rest of the forces were brought up, and on more ladders they were making their way to the top of the wall, a signal having been given from the Hexapylon.[2] To that point they had advanced without encountering a soul, since many of the enemy, after feasting in the towers, either had been put to sleep by their wine or, while half-intoxicated, were still drinking. A few of them, however, they surprised and slew in their beds. Near the Hexapylon there is a postern. This they had begun to break open with great force, and from the wall the signal had been given by a trumpet, as agreed; and now the fighting was from every side, no longer by stealth, but with open violence. For

A.U.C. 542 frequentem custodiis locum, perventum erat, terrendique magis hostes erant quam fallendi, sicut territi
5 sunt. Nam simulac tubarum est auditus cantus clamorque tenentium muros partemque urbis, omnia teneri custodes rati[1] alii per murum fugere, alii salire de muro praecipitarique turba paventium.
6 Magna pars tamen ignara tanti mali erat et gravatis omnibus vino somnoque et in vastae magnitudinis urbe partium sensu non satis pertinente in omnia.
7 Sub lucem Hexapylo effracto Marcellus omnibus copiis urbem ingressus excitavit convertitque omnes ad arma capienda opemque, si quam possent, iam captae prope urbi ferendam.

8 Epicydes ab Insula, quam ipsi Nason vocant, citato profectus agmine, haud dubius quin paucos, per neglegentiam custodum transgressos murum,
9 expulsurus foret, occurrentibus pavidis tumultum augere eos dictitans et maiora ac terribiliora vero adferre, postquam conspexit omnia circa Epipolas armis conpleta, lacessito tantum hoste paucis missili-
10 bus retro in Achradinam agmen convertit, non tam vim multitudinemque hostium metuens quam ne qua intestina fraus per occasionem oreretur clausasque inter tumultum Achradinae atque Insulae inveniret
11 portas. Marcellus ut moenia ingressus ex superioribus locis urbem omnium ferme illa tempestate

[1] rati A^2 : *om.* $P(1)N$.

---

[1] Doric for Νῆσος, Insula.

[2] Timaeus, the historian of Sicily, had called Syracuse the greatest of Greek cities, the most beautiful of all cities; Cicero, *de Re Publica* III. 43; *in Verrem* IV. 117.

they had reached Epipolae, a well-guarded region, and the enemy had rather to be terrified than deceived, as they were in fact terrified. For as soon as they heard the notes of the trumpet and the shouting of the men holding the walls and a part of the city, the guards, thinking the whole city was occupied, fled, some of them along the wall; others leaped from the wall or were pushed over by the panic-stricken crowd. A large part of the people, however, were unaware of the great danger; for all were heavy with wine and sleep, and in a city of immense size knowledge concerning its quarters failed to reach the whole. At daybreak Marcellus burst open the Hexapylon, and entering the city with his entire force awakened everybody and set them to arming themselves and bringing aid, if possible, to a city now all but captured. B.C. 212

Epicydes came out from the Island, which they themselves call Nasos,[1] with a quickly moving column, not doubting that he would drive out a few men who, owing to the carelessness of the guards had got over the wall. When men met him in alarm, he would say that they were adding to the confusion and bringing exaggerated and unduly alarming news. On discovering that in and near Epipolae armed men were everywhere, he merely challenged the enemy by a few missiles and then marched his column back into Achradina. He feared, not so much the attack of the enemy and their great numbers, as that some treachery within the city might have opportunity to break out, and he might find the gates of Achradina and the Island closed during the disturbance. Marcellus, on entering the walls and from the higher ground viewing one of the most beautiful of all cities[2] in

A.U.C. 542 pulcherrimam subiectam oculis vidit, inlacrimasse dicitur partim gaudio tantae perpetratae rei, partim
12 vetusta gloria urbis. Atheniensium classes demersae et duo ingentes exercitus cum duobus clarissimis ducibus deleti occurrebant et tot bella cum Cartha-
13 giniensibus tanto cum discrimine gesta, tot tam opulenti tyranni regesque, praeter ceteros Hiero cum recentissimae memoriae rex, tum ante omnia quae virtus ei fortunaque sua dederat beneficiis
14 in populum Romanum insignis. Ea cum universa occurrerent animo subiretque cogitatio, iam illa momento horae arsura omnia et ad cineres reditura,
15 priusquam signa Achradinam admoveret, praemittit Syracusanos qui intra praesidia Romana, ut ante dictum est, fuerant, ut adloquio leni pellicerent[1] hostis ad dedendam urbem.

XXV. Tenebant Achradinae portas murosque maxume transfugae, quibus nulla erat per condiciones veniae spes; ei nec adire muros nec adloqui quem-
2 quam passi. Itaque Marcellus, postquam id inceptum inritum fuit, ad Euryalum signa referri iussit. Tumulus est in extrema parte urbis aversus a mari viaeque imminens ferenti in agros mediterraneaque insulae, percommode situs ad commeatus excipiendos.
3 Praeerat huic arci Philodemus Argivus ab Epicyde impositus; ad quem missus a Marcello Sosis, unus

[1] pellicerent $M^1?A^2$: pellerent $P(1)$: im- *Weissenborn.*

---

[1] *I.e.* Nicias and Demosthenes.

[2] At the western apex of the triangle; a narrow ridge nearly 500 feet above the sea, with a commanding view.

that age lying before his eyes, is said to have wept, B.C. 212 partly for joy over his great achievement, partly for the ancient glory of the city. The sinking of the fleets of the Athenians and the destruction of two mighty armies along with two very distinguished generals[1] came to his mind, and so many wars waged with so great a risk against the Carthaginians; tyrants and kings, so many and so wealthy, above all Hiero, a king vividly remembered and also, above all that his own merit and success had given him, conspicuous for his favours to the Roman people. Since all that came to mind and the thought suggested itself that now in the course of an hour everything there would be in flames and reduced to ashes, before advancing his standards into Achradina, he sent forward the Syracusans who had been within the Roman lines, as has been said before, in order to entice the enemy by mild words to surrender the city.

XXV. Holding the gates and walls of Achradina were chiefly deserters, who had no hope of pardon if terms were made. They did not allow the men either to approach the walls or to speak to any one. And so Marcellus, now that this attempt was fruitless, ordered the standards to be carried back to Euryalus. This is a hill[2] in the most distant part of the city, facing away from the sea, and commanding the road which leads to the country and the interior of the island, very conveniently placed for receiving supplies. In command of this citadel[3] was Philodemus the Argive, posted there by Epicydes. Sosis, one of the slayers

[3] The crowning point of Dionysius' great fortifications, and still accounted the strongest of Greek fortresses, with its three fosses, its towers, and a complicated system of tunnels cut through solid rock.

A.U.C. 542 ex interfectoribus tyranni, cum longo sermone habito dilatus per frustrationem esset, rettulit Marcello tempus eum ad deliberandum sumpsisse.
4 Cum is diem de die differret, dum Hippocrates atque Himilco admoverent castra legionesque,[1] haud dubius, si in arcem accepisset eos, deleri
5 Romanum exercitum inclusum muris posse, Marcellus, ut Euryalum neque tradi neque capi vidit posse, inter Neapolim et Tycham—nomina ea partium urbis et instar urbium sunt—posuit castra, timens ne, si frequentia intrasset loca, contineri ab discursu miles
6 avidus praedae non posset. Legati eo ab Tycha et Neapoli cum infulis et velamentis venerunt, precantes
7 ut a caedibus et ab incendiis parceretur. De quorum precibus quam postulatis magis consilio habito Marcellus ex omnium sententia edixit militibus ne quis liberum corpus violaret: cetera praedae
8 futura. Castra testis [2] parietum pro muro saepta; portis regione platearum patentibus stationes praesidiaque disposuit, ne quis in discursu militum
9 impetus in castra fieri posset. Inde signo dato milites discurrerunt; refractisque foribus cum omnia terrore ac tumultu streperent, a caedibus tamen temperatum est; rapinis nullus ante modus fuit quam omnia diuturna felicitate cumulata bona

[1] -que C^4A^2 : *om.* $P(1)$.
[2] testis *M. Müller* (*after* -que testis *Röhl, Riemann*) : -que tectis $P(1)$: obiectu *Stroth, Madvig*^{3}, *Walters* : contextu *Madvig*^{4} (*praef.*), *Luchs* : contextis *Heusinger*.

---

[1] Cf. XXIV. xxx. 14.
[2] Here the text is very uncertain, but most of the emendations are open to serious objections, as involving Marcellus' use of more or less continuous house-walls—a feeble defence, and not easily to be reconciled with the idea of an open space lying between two built-up quarters of the city.

of the tyrant, was sent to him by Marcellus, and after B.C. 212
being balked and put off by the delivery of a long speech, he reported to Marcellus that Philodemus had taken time to consider. Philodemus was postponing from day to day, waiting for Hippocrates and Himilco to move up their camp and legions, and not doubting that, if he should get them into the citadel, the Roman army, shut up within the city walls, could be destroyed. Consequently Marcellus, seeing that Euryalus could neither be won by surrender nor by assault, pitched his camp between Neapolis and Tycha, these being the names of quarters of the city, virtually cities in themselves. For he feared that, if he should enter thickly settled parts, the soldiers in their eagerness for booty could not be restrained from scattering. To this camp came legates from Tycha and Neapolis with fillets and woollen bands,[1] praying that they be spared bloodshed and fires. Marcellus held a council in regard to their prayers—such they were rather than demands—and with the approval of all gave an order to the soldiers that no one should injure a free person; everything else would be spoil. The camp was enclosed by bricks from house-walls [2] to serve as a wall of defence. At those camp gates which opened toward the streets outposts and detachments were stationed by Marcellus, that no attack upon the camp might occur while the soldiers were dispersed. Then at a given signal the soldiers scattered. And although doors were forced and everywhere were the sounds of panic and uproar, they nevertheless refrained from bloodshed. To plundering there was no limit until they had carried away all the possessions accumulated in a long-continued

A.U.C. 542

10 egesserunt. Inter haec et Philodemus, cum spes
auxilii nulla esset, fide accepta ut inviolatus ad
Epicyden rediret, deducto praesidio tradidit tumulum
11 Romanis. Aversis omnibus ad tumultum ex parte
captae urbis Bomilcar noctem eam nactus qua propter
vim tempestatis stare ad ancoram in salo Romana
12 classis non posset, cum triginta quinque navibus ex
portu Syracusano profectus libero mari vela in altum
dedit quinque et quinquaginta navibus Epicydae
13 et Syracusanis relictis; edoctisque Carthaginiensibus
in quanto res Syracusana discrimine esset, cum centum
navibus post paucos dies redit, multis, ut fama est,
donis ex Hieronis gaza ab Epicyde donatus.

XXVI. Marcellus Euryalo recepto praesidioque
addito una cura erat liber, ne qua ab tergo vis
hostium in arcem accepta inclusos impeditosque moe-
2 nibus suos turbaret. Achradinam inde trinis castris
per idonea dispositis loca spe ad inopiam omnium
3 rerum inclusos redacturum, circumsedit. Cum per
aliquot dies quietae stationes utrimque fuissent,
repente adventus Hippocratis et Himilconis ut ultro
4 undique oppugnarentur Romani fecit. Nam et
Hippocrates castris ad magnum portum communitis
signoque iis dato qui Achradinam tenebant castra
vetera Romanorum adortus est, quibus Crispinus
praeerat, et Epicydes eruptionem in stationes Marcelli fecit, et classis Punica litori quod inter urbem

---

[1] Cf. XXIV. xxxiii. 3; xxxix. 12.

prosperity. Meanwhile even Philodemus, having B.C. 212 no hope of assistance and receiving assurance that he might return unharmed to Epicydes, led his garrison out and surrendered the hill to the Romans. While the attention of all was diverted in the direction of the uproar of a city in part captured, Bomilcar, favoured by such a night that on account of a violent storm the Roman fleet could not ride at anchor in open water, came out of the harbour of Syracuse with thirty-five ships, and with no enemy to prevent, put to sea, leaving fifty-five ships to Epicydes and the Syracusans. And after informing the Carthaginians how critical was the situation at Syracuse, he returned after a few days with a hundred ships. He was presented with many gifts, it is reported, by Epicydes out of the royal treasures of Hiero.

XXVI. Marcellus, after getting possession of Euryalus and garrisoning it, was relieved of one fear, that some troops of the enemy in the rear might be admitted to the citadel and embarrass his men, hemmed in and hampered by the walls. He thereupon laid siege to Achradina with three camps placed in suitable positions, in the hope of reducing the beleaguered to absolute want. When the outposts on both sides had been inactive for some days, suddenly the arrival of Hippocrates and Himilco had the effect that the Romans were actually besieged on all sides. For Hippocrates, after fortifying a camp by the Great Harbour and giving the signal to the forces occupying Achradina, attacked the old Roman camp,[1] which was commanded by Crispinus, at the same time that Epicydes made a sally against Marcellus' outposts, and just when the Carthaginian fleet put in to the shore lying between the city and

A.U.C. 542
et castra Romana erat adpulsa est, ne quid praesidii
5 Crispino submitti a Marcello posset. Tumultum
tamen maiorem hostes praebuerunt quam certamen;
nam et Crispinus Hippocraten non reppulit tantum
munimentis, sed insecutus etiam est trepide fugien-
6 tem, et Epicyden Marcellus in urbem compulit; satis-
que iam etiam in posterum videbatur provisum ne quid
ab repentinis eorum excursionibus periculi foret.
7 Accessit et ab [1] pestilentia commune malum quod
facile utrorumque animos averteret a belli consiliis.
Nam tempore autumni et locis natura gravibus,
multo tamen magis extra urbem quam in urbe, in-
toleranda vis aestus per utraque castra omnium
8 ferme corpora movit. Ac primo temporis ac loci
vitio et aegri erant et moriebantur; postea curatio
ipsa et contactus aegrorum volgabat morbos, ut aut
neglecti desertique qui incidissent morerentur, aut
adsidentis curantisque eadem vi morbi repletos
9 secum traherent, cotidianaque funera et mors ob
oculos esset et undique dies noctesque ploratus
10 audirentur. Postremo ita adsuetudine mali effera-
verant animos ut non modo lacrimis iustoque conplora-
tu prosequerentur mortuos, sed ne efferrent quidem
aut sepelirent, iacerentque strata exanima corpora
11 in conspectu similem mortem expectantium, mortuique
aegros, aegri validos cum metu, tum tabe ac pestifero
odore corporum conficerent; et ut ferro potius morerentur, quidam invadebant soli hostium stationes.

[1] ab *Salvinius*: ad *P*(1): ad haec A^y *Walters*: *om.* C^x *Conway*.

the Roman camp, to make it impossible for any force B.C. 212 to be sent to the aid of Crispinus by Marcellus. However, it was more of an uproar than a battle that the enemy offered. For Crispinus not only drove Hippocrates back from his fortifications, but also pursued him as he fled in disorder, and Marcellus likewise forced Epicydes into the city. And now, even for the future, he seemed to have sufficiently insured that there should be no danger from their sudden raids. Then in addition pestilence brought to both sides a calamity which forthwith diverted the attention of the two armies from strategy. For owing to the autumn season and places naturally unhealthy, unendurable heat affected the health of nearly all the men in both camps, but much more outside the city than within. And at first they sickened and died owing to the season and their position. Later the mere care of the ill and contagion spread the disease, so that those who had fallen ill died neglected and abandoned, or else they carried off with them those who sat by them and those who nursed, having caught the same malignant disease. And so every day funerals and death were before their eyes, and wailings were heard on all sides day and night. Finally, from habituation to misery they had so lost their humane feelings that, so far from escorting the dead with tears and the wailing that was their due, they did not even carry them out and bury them; and dead bodies lay strewn about before the eyes of men awaiting a like death, and the dead seriously affected the ill, the ill the sound, not only through fear, but also by putrefaction and the pestilent odour of corpses. And some choosing to die by the sword, dashed into the outposts of

A.U.C. 542 12 Multo tamen vis maior pestis Poenorum castra quam Romana invaserat; nam Romani [1] diu circumsedendo
13 Syracusas caelo aquisque adsuerant magis. Ex hostium exercitu Siculi, ut primum videre ex gravitate loci volgari morbos, in suas quisque propinquas
14 urbes dilapsi sunt; et Carthaginienses, quibus nusquam receptus erat, cum ipsis ducibus Hippocrate atque Himilcone ad internecionem omnes
15 perierunt. Marcellus, ut tanta vis ingruebat mali, traduxerat in urbem suos infirmaque corpora tecta et umbrae recreaverant; multi tamen ex Romano exercitu eadem peste absumpti sunt.

XXVII. Deleto terrestri Punico exercitu Siculi qui Hippocratis milites fuerant . . . ,[2] haud magna oppida, ceterum et situ et munimentis tuta; tria milia alterum ab Syracusis, alterum quindecim abest; eo et commeatus e civitatibus suis comporta-
2 bant et auxilia accersebant. Interea Bomilcar iterum cum classe profectus Carthaginem, ita exposita fortuna sociorum ut spem faceret non ipsis modo salutarem opem ferri posse, sed Romanos quoque in
3 capta quodam modo urbe capi, perpulit ut onerarias naves quam plurumas omni copia rerum onustas
4 secum mitterent classemque suam augerent. Igitur centum triginta navibus longis, septingentis onerariis profectus a Carthagine satis prosperos

[1] invaserat; nam Romani *H. J. Müller*: *om. P*(1), *a lost line.*

[2] *Missing are two town names and perhaps* ceperant, *in an omitted line.*

---

[1] One of the two omitted towns was perhaps Bidis, mentioned by Cicero *in Verrem* II. 53. Rossbach and Conway thought that the other might be Dascon (Thucydides and Diodorus).

the enemy single-handed. A much more violent epidemic, however, had attacked the Carthaginian camp than the Roman. For the Romans in their long blockade of Syracuse had grown more accustomed to the climate and the water. Of the enemy's army, the Sicilians scattered, each to his own neighbouring city, as soon as they saw that the disease was spreading owing to the unwholesomeness of the place, while the Carthaginians, who had no refuge anywhere, with even their generals, Hippocrates and Himilco, perished to the last man. Marcellus, as soon as the pestilence began to be so serious, had transferred his soldiers into the city, and shelter and shade had revived the invalids. Nevertheless many in the Roman army were carried off by the same pestilence. B.C. 212

XXVII. The Carthaginian land-army having been destroyed, the Sicilians who had been Hippocrates' soldiers had occupied . . .,[1] not large towns, but defended both by situation and fortifications. One of them is three miles from Syracuse, the other fifteen miles. To these they were bringing supplies from their own communities and also summoning auxiliaries. Meanwhile Bomilcar left for Carthage a second time with his fleet, and he set forth the situation of their allies in such terms as to inspire hope, not only that effectual aid could be lent to them, but also that the Romans could be captured in the virtually captured city. He thus prevailed upon them to send with him as many transports as possible, laden with all kinds of supplies, and to enlarge his fleet. Accordingly, setting out from Carthage with a hundred and thirty warships and seven hundred transports, he had winds quite favourable for the

A.U.C. 542 ventos ad traiciendum in Siciliam habuit; sed iidem
5 venti superare eum Pachynum prohibebant. Bomilcaris adventus fama primo, dein praeter spem mora
cum gaudium et metum in vicem Romanis Syra-
6 cusanisque praebuisset, Epicydes metuens ne, si
pergerent iidem qui tum tenebant ab ortu solis
flare per dies plures venti, classis Punica Africam
7 repeteret, tradita Achradina mercennariorum mili-
8 tum ducibus ad Bomilcarem navigat. Classem in
statione versa in Africam habentem atque timentem
navale proelium, non tam quod impar viribus aut
numero navium esset—quippe etiam plures habebat
—quam quod venti aptiores Romanae quam suae
classi flarent, perpulit tamen ut fortunam navalis
9 certaminis experiri vellet. Et Marcellus, cum et
Siculum exercitum ex tota insula conciri videret et
cum ingenti commeatu classem Punicam adventare,
ne simul terra marique inclusus urbe hostium urgere-
tur, quamquam impar numero navium erat, prohibere aditu Syracusarum Bomilcarem constituit.
10 Duae classes infestae circa promunturium Pachynum
stabant, ubi prima tranquillitas maris in altum
11 evexisset, concursurae. Itaque cadente iam Euro,
qui per dies aliquot saevierat, prior Bomilcar movit;
cuius primo classis petere altum visa est, quo facilius
12 superaret promunturium; ceterum postquam tendere
ad se Romanas naves vidit, incertum qua subita

crossing to Sicily. But the same winds did not allow B.C. 212 him to round Pachynum. The report at first of Bomilcar's coming, and then its unexpected delay, brought rejoicing and fear by turns to Romans and Syracusans. Upon that Epicydes, fearing that, if the same winds which were then holding should continue to blow from the east for several days, the Carthaginian fleet would make for Africa again, turned over Achradina to the commanders of the mercenaries and sailed to meet Bomilcar, who was keeping his fleet in a roadstead facing Africa. He feared a naval battle, not so much because he was inferior in his forces and the number of his ships—in fact he had even more—as because the winds then blowing were more favourable to the Roman fleet than to his own. Nevertheless Epicydes gained his consent to try the fortune of a naval engagement. And Marcellus too, seeing that a Sicilian army was being brought together from the entire island and at the same time a Carthaginian fleet was approaching with unlimited supplies, and fearing that he might be hard pressed by land and sea, being shut up within the enemies' city, decided, although he was inferior in the number of his ships, to prevent Bomilcar from reaching Syracuse. The two opposing fleets lay on this side and that of the promontory of Pachynum, ready to engage as soon as calm weather should enable them to put to sea. And so, as the southeast wind, which had been blowing hard for some days, was now dropping, Bomilcar was the first to get under weigh. And at first his fleet appeared to be heading out to sea, the more readily to round the promontory. But on seeing that the Roman ships were steering towards

A.U.C. 542 territus re, Bomilcar vela in altum dedit missisque
nuntiis Heracleam qui onerarias retro inde Africam
repetere iuberent, ipse Siciliam praetervectus Taren-
13 tum petit. Epicydes, a tanta repente destitutus
spe, ne in obsidionem magna ex parte captae urbis
rediret, Agrigentum navigat, expectaturus magis
eventum quam inde quicquam moturus.

XXVIII. Quae ubi in castra Siculorum sunt
nuntiata, Epicyden Syracusis excessisse, a Carthaginiensibus relictam insulam et prope iterum traditam
2 Romanis, legatos de condicionibus dedendae urbis
explorata prius per conloquia voluntate eorum qui
3 obsidebantur ad Marcellum mittunt. Cum haud
ferme discreparet quin quae ubique regum fuissent
Romanorum essent, Siculis cetera cum libertate ac
legibus suis servarentur, evocatis ad conloquium iis
4 quibus ab Epicyde creditae res erant, missos se simul
ad Marcellum, simul ad eos ab exercitu Siculorum
aiunt, ut una omnium qui obsiderentur quique extra
obsidionem fuissent fortuna esset neve alteri proprie
5 sibi paciscerentur quicquam. Recepti deinde ab iis,
ut necessarios hospitesque adloquerentur, expositis
quae pacta iam cum Marcello haberent, oblata spe
salutis perpulere eos ut secum praefectos Epicydis
Polyclitum et Philistionem et Epicyden, cui Sindon
6 cognomen erat, adgrederentur. Interfectis iis et

[1] Cf. XXIV. xxxv. 3.

him, Bomilcar, alarmed by something unforeseen, B.C. 212
made sail for open water, and after sending messengers to Heraclea [1] to command the transports to return thence to Africa, he himself sailed along the coast of Sicily and made for Tarentum. Epicydes, suddenly bereft of a hope so high, in order not to return, only to share the siege of a city in large part captured, sailed to Agrigentum, intending to await the outcome, rather than to set anything in motion from there.

XXVIII. When these things were reported to the camp of the Sicilians, that Epicydes had left Syracuse, that the island had been abandoned by the Carthaginians and almost handed over a second time to the Romans, after first ascertaining by conferences the wish of the besieged, they sent legates to Marcellus to make terms for the surrender of the city. It was virtually agreed that all that had anywhere belonged to the kings should belong to the Romans, that everything else should be secured to the Sicilians along with freedom and their own laws. Accordingly the legates summoned to a conference the men to whom power had been entrusted by Epicydes, and said that they had been sent by the army of the Sicilians at the same time to Marcellus and to them, in order that all, the besieged and those who had been outside of the operations, might share the same lot and neither party make any special terms for itself. And then, being admitted by them, that they might speak with their relatives and guest-friends, they explained the terms which they had already settled with Marcellus, and by holding out assurances of safety prevailed upon them to join with themselves in an attack upon Epicydes' prefects, Polyclitus and Philistion and an Epicydes surnamed Sindon. After slaying them and

A.U.C. 542 multitudine ad contionem vocata, inopiam quaeque ipsi inter se fremere occulti[1] soliti erant conquesti, quamquam tot mala urgerent, negarunt fortunam accusandam esse, quod in ipsorum esset potestate
7 quamdiu ea paterentur. Romanis causam oppugnandi Syracusas fuisse caritatem Syracusanorum, non odium; nam ut occupatas res ab satellitibus Hannibalis, deinde Hieronymi, Hippocrate atque Epicyde, audierint, tum bellum movisse et obsidere urbem coepisse, ut crudelis tyrannos eius, non ut
8 ipsam urbem expugnarent. Hippocrate vero interempto, Epicyde intercluso ab Syracusis et praefectis eius occisis, Carthaginiensibus omni possessione Siciliae terra marique pulsis, quam superesse causam Romanis cur non, perinde ac si Hiero ipse viveret, unicus Romanae amicitiae cultor, incolumis Syracusas
9 esse velint? Itaque nec urbi nec hominibus aliud periculum quam ab semet ipsis esse, si occasionem reconciliandi se Romanis praetermisissent; eam autem, qualis illo momento horae sit, nullam deinde fore, si simul liberatas ab impotentibus tyrannis . . .[2] apparuisset.

XXIX. Omnium ingenti adsensu audita ea oratio est. Praetores tamen prius creari quam legatos nominari placuit; ex ipsorum deinde praetorum

[1] occulti *P*(2): occulte *A*.
[2] *A lacuna variously supplied, e.g.* Syracusas esse et applicare se Romanis *Madvig* (*two lines*): accipere noluissent *Walters* (*one line after* apparuisset).

---

[1] Madvig's restoration is based upon the idea of an immediate return to their former friendship ("and was taking the Roman side"). Walters supplied the thought that the Romans might even reject such advances.

calling the populace to an assembly, they complained of privation and other things at which among themselves they had been in the habit of murmuring in secret. And they said that, although so many hardships were a burden to them, they ought not to blame fortune, because it was in their own power to say how long they would endure them. The Romans, they said, had had as their ground for besieging Syracuse their love, not hatred, of the Syracusans. For on learning that the power had been seized by Hippocrates and Epicydes, minions of Hannibal and later of Hieronymus, it was then that they had made war and had begun to besiege the city, in order to capture, not the city itself, but its cruel tyrants. But now that Hippocrates had perished, that Epicydes had been cut off from Syracuse and his prefects slain, now that the Carthaginians had everywhere been driven by land and sea from their occupation of Sicily, what reason remained for the Romans not to wish Syracuse to be preserved, just as if Hiero himself, who was unrivalled in maintaining friendship with Rome, were still alive? Accordingly both for the city and for individuals there was no other danger than from themselves, if they should let slip the opportunity of a reconciliation with the Romans. Moreover so favourable an opportunity as there was at that moment, if it should be evident that Syracuse, once it had been freed from insolent tyrants, . . . ,[1] would never come again. B.C. 212

XXIX. The speech was heard with great and unanimous approval. It was decided, however, to elect magistrates before naming legates. Then out of the number of these magistrates' representatives

A.U.C. 542

2 numero missi oratores ad Marcellum, quorum princeps "Neque primo" inquit "Syracusani a vobis defecimus, sed Hieronymus, nequaquam tam
3 in vos impius quam in nos, nec postea pacem tyranni caede compositam Syracusanus quisquam, sed satellites regii Hippocrates atque Epicydes oppressis nobis hinc metu, hinc fraude turbaverunt. Nec quisquam dicere potest aliquando nobis libertatis tempus fuisse quod pacis vobiscum non fuerit.
4 Nunc certe caede eorum qui oppressas tenebant Syracusas cum primum nostri arbitrii esse coepimus, extemplo venimus ad tradenda arma, dedendos nos, urbem, moenia, nullam recusandam fortunam quae
5 imposita a vobis fuerit. Gloriam captae nobilissimae pulcherrimaeque urbis Graecarum dei tibi dederunt, Marcelle. Quidquid umquam terra marique memorandum gessimus, id tui triumphi titulo
6 accedit. Famaene credi velis quanta urbs a te capta sit, quam posteris quoque eam spectaculo esse, quo quisquis terra, quisquis mari venerit, nunc nostra de Atheniensibus Carthaginiensibusque tropaea, nunc tua de nobis ostendat, incolumesque Syracusas familiae vestrae sub clientela nominis Marcellorum
7 tutelaque habendas tradas? Ne plus apud vos Hieronymi quam Hieronis memoria momenti faciat. Diutius ille multo amicus fuit quam hic hostis, et

were sent to Marcellus. The foremost of these said: B.C. 212
"In the beginning it was not we Syracusans who forsook your friendship, but Hieronymus, who was by no means so conscienceless toward you as toward us. And later the peace concluded on the assassination of the tyrant was broken, not by any Syracusan, but by the king's minions, Hippocrates and Epicydes, after they had subdued us, now by terrorizing, now by treason. Nor can any man say that there has ever been any time of freedom for us that was not a time of peace with you. Certain it is that now, when through the slaying of those who were holding Syracuse in subjection we have begun for the first time to be our own masters, we have come forthwith to give up our arms, to surrender ourselves, the city, the walls, to reject no lot which shall be imposed by you Romans. The glory of capturing the most notable and most beautiful of Greek cities the gods have given to you, Marcellus. All that we have ever accomplished on land and sea that is worthy of record is added to the distinction of your triumph. Would you wish men merely to believe tradition as to the greatness of the city you have captured, rather than that it be a sight even to posterity, a city which shall show to every man who comes by land or by sea, at one spot our trophies won from the Athenians and the Carthaginians, at another your trophies won from us, and that you hand over Syracuse intact to your house, to be kept under the clientship and tutelage of those who bear the name Marcellus? Let not the memory of Hieronymus have more weight with you Romans than that of Hiero. The latter was much longer your friend than the former your enemy; and you

A.U.C. 542

illius benefacta etiam re [1] sensistis, huius amentia
8 ad perniciem tantum ipsius valuit." Omnia et
impetrabilia et tuta erant apud Romanos: inter
ipsos plus belli ac periculi erat. Namque transfugae, tradi se Romanis rati, mercennariorum quoque
militum auxilia in eundem compulere metum;
9 arreptisque armis praetores primum obtruncant, inde
ad caedem Syracusanorum discurrunt quosque fors
obtulit irati interfecere atque omnia quae in promptu
10 erant diripuerunt. Tum, ne sine ducibus essent, sex
praefectos creavere, ut terni Achradinae ac Naso
praeessent. Sedato tandem tumultu exequentibus
sciscitando quae acta cum Romanis essent, dilucere
id quod erat coepit, aliam suam ac perfugarum
causam esse.

XXX. In tempore legati a Marcello redierunt,
falsa eos suspicione incitatos memorantes nec causam
expetendae poenae eorum ullam Romanis esse.
2 Erat e tribus Achradinae praefectis Hispanus,
Moericus nomine. Ad eum inter comites legatorum
de industria unus ex Hispanorum auxiliaribus est
missus, qui sine arbitris Moericum nanctus primum
quo in statu reliquisset Hispaniam—et nuper inde
venerat—exponit: omnia Romanis ibi obtineri armis.
3 Posse eum, si operae pretium faciat, principem
popularium esse, seu militare cum Romanis seu in
patriam reverti libeat; contra, si malle obsideri

[1] re *PC* : pre *P*²?(10) : recentia *M. Müller* : rebus adversis *Luchs.*

---

[1] *I.e.* the mercenaries.

[2] We learn from XXVI. xxi. 13 that his name was Belligenes.

have had positive experience of the good deeds of the one, while the other's folly resulted only in his own destruction." Everything could be obtained from the Romans and was already assured. It was among the Sicilians themselves that war and danger chiefly lay. For the deserters, thinking that they would surely be handed over to the Romans, aroused the mercenary auxiliaries also to the same fear. And seizing arms they[1] first slew the magistrates and then dispersed to massacre the Syracusans, and in anger they slew all whom chance threw in their way and carried off everything on which they could lay hands. Then, not to be without commanders, they chose six prefects, three to be in charge of Achradina and three of Nasus. When the uproar was at last stilled and they were diligently enquiring what terms had been made with the Romans, the truth began to dawn upon them, that their case was different from that of the deserters. B.C. 212

XXX. Just at the right moment the legates returned from Marcellus, stating that the mercenaries had been aroused by an unfounded suspicion, and that the Romans had no reason for demanding their punishment. One of the three prefects of Achradina was a Spaniard, Moericus by name. To him, among the retinue of the legates, one[2] of the Spanish auxiliaries was sent on purpose. Finding Moericus alone, he first explained the condition in which he had left Spain, from which he had recently come. The whole of that country, he said, was held by Roman arms. If he should do something worth while, he could be a chief among his own people, whether he preferred to serve on the Roman side or to return to his native town. On the other hand, if he

A.U.C. 542 pergat, quam spem esse terra marique clauso?
4 Motus his Moericus, cum legatos ad Marcellum mitti
placuisset, fratrem inter eos mittit, qui per eundem
illum Hispanum secretus ab aliis ad Marcellum
deductus, cum fidem accepisset composuissetque
5 agendae ordinem rei, Achradinam redit. Tum
Moericus, ut ab suspicione proditionis averteret
omnium animos, negat sibi placere legatos commeare ultro citroque: neque recipiendum quemquam neque mittendum et, quo intentius custodiae
serventur, opportuna dividenda praefectis esse, ut
suae quisque partis tutandae reus sit. Omnes
6 adsensi sunt. Partibus dividendis ipsi regio evenit
ab Arethusa fonte usque ad ostium magni portus;
7 id ut scirent Romani fecit. Itaque Marcellus nocte
navem onerariam cum armatis remulco quadriremis
trahi ad Achradinam [1] iussit exponique milites regione
8 portae quae prope fontem Arethusam est. Hoc
cum quarta vigilia factum esset expositosque milites
porta, ut convenerat, recepisset Moericus, luce prima
Marcellus omnibus copiis moenia Achradinae adgre-
9 ditur, ita ut non eos solum qui Achradinam tenebant
in se converteret, sed ab Naso etiam agmina armatorum concurrerent relictis stationibus suis ad vim
10 et impetum Romanorum arcendum. In hoc tumultu
actuariae naves instructae iam ante circumvectaeque
ad Nasum armatos exponunt, qui inproviso adorti

[1] Achradinam *P*(1) : Nasum *H. J. Müller*.

---

[1] An evident error for the Island (Nasus), due possibly to Livy's attempt to combine several different accounts. There is further confusion in the passage which follows.

continued to prefer to be besieged, what hope was there for a man shut in by land and sea? Moericus was impressed by these words, and when it was decided to send legates to Marcellus, sent his brother as one of them. He was escorted separately from the rest to Marcellus by that same Spaniard, and after receiving a promise and arranging the steps to be taken, returned to Achradina. Then Moericus, to divert the attention of everybody from the suspicion of treason, said he did not approve of having legates going back and forth; that none should be admitted or sent; and that, in order to keep a closer guard, suitable positions should be divided among the prefects, so that each should be responsible for the defence of his own section. All agreed. In the assignment of sections the region extending from the Fountain of Arethusa to the entrance of the Great Harbour fell to Moericus himself. He saw to it that the Romans knew that. Accordingly Marcellus ordered a transport with armed men to be towed at night by a four-banker to Achradina,[1] and the soldiers to be landed near the gate which is by the Fountain of Arethusa. This done at the fourth watch, and the soldiers landed there having been admitted according to agreement by Moericus through the gate, Marcellus at daybreak with all his forces assailed the walls of Achradina. The result was that not only did he turn the attention of the defenders of Achradina to himself, but from Nasus also columns of armed men, leaving their posts, united in haste, to ward off the violent attack of the Romans. During this confusion light vessels, previously equipped, sailed around to Nasus and landed their troops. These made an unexpected attack upon B.C. 212

A.U.C. 542 semiplenas stationes et adapertas fores portae, qua paulo ante excurrerant armati, haud magno certamine Nasum cepere desertam trepidatione et fuga
11 custodum. Neque in ullis minus praesidii aut pertinaciae ad manendum quam in transfugis fuit, quia ne suis quidem satis credentes e medio certa-
12 mine effugerunt. Marcellus, ut captam esse Nasum comperit[1] et Achradinae regionem unam teneri Moericumque cum praesidio suis adiunctum, receptui cecinit, ne regiae opes, quarum fama maior quam res erat, diriperentur.

XXXI. Suppresso impetu militum ut iis qui in Achradina erant transfugis spatium locusque fugae
2 datus est, Syracusani tandem liberi metu portis Achradinae apertis oratores ad Marcellum mittunt, nihil petentis aliud quam incolumitatem sibi liberis-
3 que suis. Marcellus consilio advocato et adhibitis etiam Syracusanis qui per seditiones pulsi ab domo
4 intra praesidia Romana fuerant, respondit non plura per annos quinquaginta benefacta Hieronis quam paucis his annis maleficia eorum qui Syracusas tenuerint erga populum Romanum esse; sed pleraque eorum quo debuerint reccidisse, foederumque ruptorum ipsos ab se graviores multo quam populus
5 Romanus voluerit poenas exegisse. Se quidem tertium annum circumsedere Syracusas, non ut populus Romanus servam[2] civitatem haberet, sed

[1] comperit *Weissenborn*: *om.* *P*(1): vidit (*after* ut) *Walters*.

[2] Romanus (*i.e.* R.) servam *x* *Sigonius*: reservatam *P*(10): -ta *C*.

the half-manned outposts and the open doors of the gate through which the armed men had dashed out a little while before, and with no great resistance captured Nasus, deserted by the excitement and flight of the guards. And no others showed less capacity to defend or determination to hold out than the deserters, since they did not quite trust even their own men and fled out of the midst of the conflict. Marcellus, on learning that Nasus had been captured and one section of Achradina occupied, also that Moericus with his force had joined the Romans, sounded the recall, to prevent the royal treasures, which were reported to be larger than they really were, from being plundered. B.C. 212

XXXI. The onslaught of the soldiers being checked and time and place for their flight given to the deserters who were in Achradina, the Syracusans, at last relieved of their fear, open the gates of Achradina and send representatives to Marcellus, asking nothing else than their own lives and those of their children. Marcellus, calling a council and admitting also those Syracusans who, after being driven from home during the uprisings, had been inside the Roman lines, replied that the good acts of Hiero toward the Roman people during fifty years had not been more numerous than the evil deeds done in the last few years by those who held Syracuse. But most of the misdeeds, he said, had reacted just as they should, and the men had exacted from themselves much more serious penalties for the broken treaties than the Roman people wished. For his part, he was besieging Syracuse for the third year, not that the Roman people might keep the city enslaved, but to prevent the commanders of deserters

A.U.C. 542 ne transfugarum alienigenarumque[1] duces captam
6 et oppressam tenerent. Quid potuerint Syracusani
facere, exemplo vel eos esse Syracusanorum qui intra
praesidia Romana fuerint, vel Hispanum ducem
Moericum, qui praesidium tradiderit, vel ipsorum
Syracusanorum postremo serum quidem, sed forte
7 consilium. Sibi omnium laborum periculorumque
circa moenia Syracusana terra marique tam diu
exhaustorum nequaquam tanti eum[2] fructum esse
8 quod capere Syracusas[3] potuisset. Inde quaestor
cum praesidio ab Naso[4] ad accipiendam pecuniam
regiam custodiendamque missus. Urbs[5] diripienda
militi data est custodibus divisis per domos eorum
9 qui intra praesidia Romana fuerant. Cum multa
irae, multa avaritiae foeda exempla ederentur,
Archimeden memoriae proditum est in tanto tumultu,
quantum captae terror[6] urbis in discursu diripientium
militum ciere poterat, intentum formis quas in
pulvere descripserat, ab ignaro milite quis esset
10 interfectum; aegre id Marcellum tulisse sepulturae-
que curam habitam, et propinquis etiam inquisitis
honori praesidioque nomen ac memoriam eius
11 fuisse. Hoc maxume modo Syracusae captae; in
quibus praedae tantum fuit, quantum vix capta

[1] alienigenarum *Hertz*: mercennariorum *Gerlach*: *om.* *P*(1) *Walters* (*also the* -que *of PC*).

[2] tanti eum *Harant* (*without assuming a lacuna below*): tantum *P*(1) *Madvig, Conway.*

[3] *Here Madvig inserted* potuerit, quantum, si servare: *Conway* (*after* capere), sibi contigerit, quantum si servare (*two lines*): *Gronovius conj.* quam si parcere Syracusis *for* quod capere Syracusas.

[4] ab Naso ad *Geyer*: ab nassum et *P*(4): ad nassum et C^4M^3BDA: ad Nassum ad *z Walters.*

[5] Urbs *x Walters*: *om.* *P*(1): Achradina *Weissenborn.*

and foreigners from holding it in captivity and subjection. What the Syracusans could have done was shown by the example either of those Syracusans inside the Roman lines, or of the Spanish commander Moericus, who surrendered his post, or finally of the belated but courageous resolution of the Syracusans themselves. To his mind it was by no means a sufficient reward for all the hardships and dangers, so long endured on land and sea about the Syracusan walls, that he had been able to capture Syracuse. Thereupon the quaestor was sent from Nasus with a force to receive and guard the royal funds. The city was given over to the soldiers to plunder, guards being first assigned to the houses of the men who had been inside the Roman lines. While many shameful examples of anger and many of greed were being given, the tradition is that Archimedes, in all the uproar which the alarm of a captured city could produce in the midst of plundering soldiers dashing about, was intent upon the figures which he had traced in the dust and was slain by a soldier, not knowing who he was;[1] that Marcellus was grieved at this, and his burial duly provided for; and that his name and memory were an honour and a protection to his relatives, search even being made for them. Such in the main was the capture of Syracuse,[2] in which there was booty in such quantity as there would scarcely have been B.C. 212

[1] Cf. Plutarch's account, *Marcellus* 19; Valerius Maximus VIII. 7. Ext. 7; Cicero *de Finibus* V. 50.

[2] Actually the fall of Syracuse appears to have taken place in the following year, 211 B.C.

[6] terror *Böttcher*: *om.* *P*(1): pavor *Weissenborn*.

A.U.C. 542 Carthagine tum fuisset, cum qua[1] viribus aequis certabatur.

12 Paucis ante diebus quam Syracusae caperentur, T. Otacilius cum quinqueremibus octoginta Uticam
13 ab Lilybaeo transmisit, et cum ante lucem portum intrasset, onerarias frumento onustas cepit, egressusque in terram depopulatus est aliquantum agri circa Uticam praedamque omnis generis retro ad navis
14 egit. Lilybaeum tertio die quam inde profectus erat cum centum triginta onerariis navibus frumento praedaque onustis rediit idque frumentum extemplo
15 Syracusas misit; quod ni tam in tempore subvenisset, victoribus victisque pariter perniciosa fames instabat.

XXXII. Eadem aestate in Hispania, cum biennio ferme nihil admodum memorabile factum esset consiliisque magis quam armis bellum gereretur, Romani imperatores egressi hibernis copias coniunxerunt.
2 Ibi consilium advocatum omniumque in unum congruerunt sententiae, quando ad id locorum id modo actum esset ut Hasdrubalem tendentem in Italiam retinerent, tempus esse id iam agi ut bellum in
3 Hispania finiretur. Et satis ad id virium credebant accessisse viginti milia Celtiberorum ea hieme ad arma excita. Hostium[2] tres exercitus erant:
4 Hasdrubal Gisgonis filius et Mago coniunctis castris quinque ferme dierum iter ab Romanis aberant;
5 propior erat Hamilcaris filius Hasdrubal, vetus in Hispania imperator; ad urbem nomine Amtorgim
6 exercitum habebat. Eum volebant prius opprimi

[1] cum qua *P*(1) : cum (quum) *Madvig*.

[2] excita. Hostium *Alschefski*: excitatum *PRM* : -ta *Cz*: -ti *DA* : excitorum *Gronovius*.

if Carthage, with which the conflict was on even terms, had at that time been captured. B.C. 212

A few days before Syracuse was taken, Titus Otacilius with eighty five-bankers crossed over from Lilybaeum to Utica. And having entered the harbour before daylight, he captured cargo-ships laden with grain, and disembarking ravaged a considerable area around Utica and drove booty of every kind back to the ships. On the third day after he had left Lilybaeum he returned thither with a hundred and thirty cargo-ships laden with grain and booty, and sent the grain at once to Syracuse. Had it not arrived so opportunely, a famine equally destructive to victors and vanquished was impending.

XXXII. In Spain in the same summer, when for about two years[1] nothing very notable had occurred and the war was being waged more by diplomacy than by arms, the Roman generals, on leaving their winter-quarters, united their forces. Thereupon a council was called and all were of one mind, that, since up to that time they had accomplished nothing except to hold Hasdrubal back from pushing on into Italy, it was time that their task should now be to end the war in Spain. And they believed they had sufficient reinforcements for that purpose in twenty thousand Celtiberians who had been called to arms that winter. The enemy had three armies. Hasdrubal, the son of Gisgo, and Mago with adjoining camps were about five days' march from the Romans. Nearer was Hasdrubal, the son of Hamilcar, a veteran commander in Spain. He had his army near a city called Amtorgis. It was he that the

[1] This apparently from a source which placed the defeat and death of the Scipios in 211 B.C.; cf. note on xxxvi. 14.

A.U.C. 542 duces Romani; et spes erat satis superque ad id virium esse; illa restabat cura, ne fuso eo perculsi alter Hasdrubal et Mago in avios saltus montesque
7 recipientes sese bellum extraherent. Optimum igitur rati divisis bifariam copiis totius simul Hispaniae amplecti bellum, ita inter se diviserunt ut P. Cornelius duas partes exercitus Romanorum sociorumque adversus Magonem duceret atque Hasdru-
8 balem, Cn. Cornelius cum tertia parte veteris exercitus Celtiberis adiunctis cum Hasdrubale Barcino
9 bellum gereret. Una profecti ambo duces exercitusque Celtiberis praegredientibus ad urbem Amtorgim in conspectu hostium dirimente amni ponunt castra.
10 Ibi Cn. Scipio cum quibus ante dictum est copiis substitit; P. Scipio profectus ad destinatam belli partem.

XXXIII. Hasdrubal postquam animadvertit exiguum Romanum exercitum in castris et spem omnem
2 in Celtiberorum auxiliis esse, peritus omnis barbaricae et praecipue earum[1] gentium in quibus per tot
3 annos militabat perfidiae, facili linguae commercio,[2] cum utraque castra plena Hispanorum essent, per occulta conloquia paciscitur magna mercede cum Celtiberorum principibus ut copias inde abducant.
4 Nec atrox visum facinus—non enim ut in Romanos verterent arma agebatur—et merces quanta vel

[1] earum *Gronovius*: omnium earum *P*(1).
[2] commercio *z Conway*: *om.* *P*(1).

---

[1] Probably the Baetis, as Iliturgi was not far away; cf. XXVIII. xix. 2.

Roman generals wished first to overpower; and they B.C. 212
hoped they had quite ample forces for that end. The one remaining concern was the fear that, if he was defeated, the other Hasdrubal and Mago might in alarm withdraw to pathless forests and mountains and prolong the war. They thought it best therefore to divide their forces into two armies and include the whole of Spain in their plan of operations. And they divided in such manner that Publius Cornelius should lead two-thirds of the army of Romans and allies against Mago and Hasdrubal, and that Gnaeus Cornelius with one-third of the old army and the Celtiberians in addition should carry on the war with Hasdrubal Barca. Setting out together, with the Celtiberians in the van, both generals and armies pitched camp near the city of Amtorgis, in sight of the enemy, but separated by a river.[1] There Gnaeus Scipio remained with the above-mentioned forces, while Publius Scipio set out for his previously appointed share of the war.

XXXIII. Hasdrubal first noted that there was only a small army of Romans in the camp and that all their hope was in the Celtiberian auxiliaries. Then, as he was well acquainted with every form of treachery practised by barbarians and particularly by those tribes among which he had been campaigning for so many years, and as oral communication was easy, since both camps were full of Spaniards, by means of secret conferences he made an agreement with the chief men of the Celtiberians at a high price that they should withdraw their troops. Nor did it seem an outrageous act—for it was not urged that they should turn their arms against the Romans—and a price which would have been ample even for engaging

A.U.C. 542 pro bello satis esset dabatur ne bellum gererent, et
cum quies ipsa, tum reditus domum fructusque
5 videndi suos suaque grata vulgo erant. Itaque non
ducibus facilius quam multitudini persuasum est.
Simul ne metus quidem ab Romanis erat, quippe
6 tam paucis, si vi retinerent. Id quidem cavendum
semper Romanis ducibus erit exemplaque haec vere
pro documentis habenda, ne ita externis credant
auxiliis ut non plus sui roboris suarumque proprie
7 virium in castris habeant. Signis repente sublatis
Celtiberi abeunt, nihil aliud quaerentibus causam
obtestantibusque ut manerent Romanis respondentes
8 quam domestico se avocari bello. Scipio, postquam
socii nec precibus nec vi retineri poterant, nec se aut
parem sine illis hosti esse aut fratri rursus coniungi
vidit posse, nec ullum aliud salutare consilium in
9 promptu esse, retro quantum posset cedere statuit,
in id omni cura intentus necubi hosti aequo se
committeret loco, qui transgressus flumen prope
vestigiis abeuntium insistebat.

XXXIV. Per eosdem dies P. Scipionem par terror,
2 periculum maius ab novo hoste urgebat. Masinissa
erat iuvenis, eo tempore socius Carthaginiensium,
quem deinde clarum potentemque Romana fecit
3 amicitia. Is tum cum equitatu Numidarum et
advenienti P. Scipioni occurrit et deinde adsidue

in the war was offered them not to wage war. Again, not only peace itself, but also a return home and the advantage of seeing their families and their property were attractions to the mass of them. Accordingly their leaders were not more easily persuaded than the rank and file. At the same time they had no fear from the Romans either, if they, being so few in number, should try to hold them by force. It will always be a necessary precaution for Roman generals, and these instances must really be accounted warnings, not so to trust their foreign auxiliaries as not to have in camp more of their own strength and of forces that are absolutely their own. The Celtiberians suddenly took up their standards and departed, and when Romans asked the reason and implored them to remain, they gave no other answer than that they were called away by a war at home. Scipio, now that his allies could not be held either by entreaties or by force, saw that he could neither be a match for the enemy without them nor rejoin his brother, and that no other promising plan was available. Thereupon he decided to retire as far as possible, taking every care and being on the alert not to expose himself anywhere on level ground to the enemy, who crossed the river and kept almost at their heels as they withdrew. B.C. 212

XXXIV. About the same time Publius Scipio was beset by a fear no less grave and a danger that was greater from a new enemy. There was the young Masinissa, at that time an ally of the Carthaginians, a man whom friendship with the Romans later made famous and powerful. With his Numidian cavalry he now encountered Publius Scipio on his advance, and also was continually at hand day and night, ready

A.U.C. 542
4 dies noctesque infestus aderat, ut non vagos tantum
procul a castris lignatum pabulatumque progressos
exciperet, sed ipsis obequitaret castris invectusque
in medias saepe stationes omnia ingenti tumultu
5 turbaret. Noctibus quoque saepe incursu repentino
in portis valloque trepidatum est, nec aut locus aut
tempus ullum vacuum a metu ac sollicitudine erat
6 Romanis, compulsique intra vallum adempto rerum
omnium usu. Cum prope iusta obsidio esset futuram-
que artiorem eam appareret, si se Indibilis, quem
cum septem milibus et quingentis Suessetanorum
7 adventare fama erat, Poenis coniunxisset, dux
cautus et providens Scipio victus necessitatibus
temerarium capit consilium, ut nocte Indibili
obviam iret et, quocumque occurrisset loco, proelium
8 consereret. Relicto igitur modico praesidio in castris
praepositoque Ti. Fonteio legato media nocte pro-
9 fectus cum obviis hostibus manus conseruit. Agmina
magis quam acies pugnabant; superior tamen, ut in
tumultuaria pugna, Romanus erat. Ceterum et
equites Numidae repente, quos fefellisse se dux ratus
erat, ab lateribus circumfusi magnum terrorem
10 intulere, et [1] contracto adversus Numidas certamine
novo tertius insuper advenit hostis, duces Poeni
adsecuti ab tergo iam pugnantis; ancepsque proelium Romanos circumsteterat incertos in quem
potissimum hostem quamve in partem conferti
11 eruptionem facerent. Pugnanti hortantique impera-

[1] et *Crévier* : *om.* *P*(1).

to attack, so that he not only captured soldiers B.C. 212 who had wandered far from the camp in search of wood and fodder, but also rode up to the camp itself, and often dashing into the midst of the outposts threw everything into great confusion. By night also there was often alarm at the gates and on the earthwork owing to a sudden attack, nor was any place or time free from fear and anxiety for the Romans, and they were confined within their earthwork, unable to obtain anything. It was almost a regular blockade, and this would evidently be stricter if Indibilis, who was reported as approaching with seven thousand five hundred Suessetani, should join the Carthaginians. Consequently Scipio, though a general marked by caution and foresight, being forced by his straits, adopted the rash plan of going by night to meet Indibilis and giving battle wherever he should encounter him. Therefore, leaving a moderate garrison at the camp and putting his lieutenant, Tiberius Fonteius, in command of it, he set out at midnight, and on meeting the enemy engaged them. It was a battle of columns rather than lines; yet, so far as could be in an engagement without order, the Roman had the advantage. But the Numidian cavalry, whose notice the general had thought he had escaped, by outflanking them inspired great alarm, and in addition, when they had entered a fresh battle with the Numidians, a third enemy also arrived, the Carthaginian generals, who from the rear overtook them when already engaged. And the Romans found themselves between two battles, uncertain against which enemy and in which direction they should choose to break through in a mass. As the general was fighting and exhorting,

A.U.C. 542 tori et offerenti se ubi plurimus labor erat latus dextrum lancea traicitur; cuneusque is hostium qui in confertos circa ducem impetum fecerat, ut exanimem labentem ex equo Scipionem vidit, alacres gaudio cum clamore per totam aciem nuntiantes
12 discurrunt imperatorem Romanum cecidisse. Ea pervagata passim vox ut et hostes haud dubie pro
13 victoribus et Romani pro victis essent fecit. Fuga confestim ex acie duce amisso fieri coepta est; ceterum ut ad erumpendum inter Numidas levium-
14 que armorum alia auxilia haud difficilis erat, ita effugere tantum equitum aequantiumque equos velocitate peditum vix poterant, caesique prope plures in fuga quam in pugna sunt; nec superfuisset quisquam, ni praecipiti iam ad vesperum die nox intervenisset.

XXXV. Haud segniter inde duces Poeni fortuna usi confestim e proelio vix necessaria quiete data militibus ad Hasdrubalem Hamilcaris citatum agmen rapiunt non dubia spe, cum[1] se[2] coniunxissent,
2 debellari posse. Quo ubi est ventum, inter exercitus ducesque victoria recenti laetos gratulatio ingens facta, imperatore tanto cum omni exercitu deleto et alteram pro haud dubia parem victoriam expectantes.
3 Ad Romanos nondum quidem fama tantae cladis pervenerat, sed maestum quoddam silentium erat et

[1] cum *Ax*: *om. P*(2).
[2] se *x*: *om. P*(1).

and exposing himself where there was most to be done, his right side was pierced by a lance. And those of the enemy who in a wedge had made an attack upon the men pressing close about the general, on seeing the dying Scipio slipping from his horse, dashed everywhere along the line, wild with delight, shouting and announcing that the Roman commander had fallen. The broadcasting of that announcement far and wide made the enemy as good as victors beyond a doubt and the Romans as good as vanquished. Flight directly from the battle-line began, once they had lost their general. But while, so far as bursting through the Numidians and the light-armed auxiliaries as well was concerned, flight was not difficult, yet it was hardly possible for them to escape such numbers of horsemen and infantry who by their speed kept up with the horses. And almost more were slain in flight than in battle, nor would anyone have survived but for the coming on of night, as the day was now rapidly drawing to a close. B.C. 212

XXXV. Then the Carthaginian generals directly after the battle, making no indifferent use of their success, barely allowed their soldiers necessary rest, and rushed their column with all speed in the direction of Hasdrubal, the son of Hamilcar, with the certain hope that, when they should unite with him, the war could be finished. Upon their arrival there was great congratulation between the armies and generals rejoicing in the recent victory, since so great a general and his entire army had been destroyed, and they were looking for just such another victory as beyond question. As for the Romans, not yet indeed had a report of the great disaster reached them, but there was a gloomy silence and an unexpressed foreboding,

A.U.C. 542 tacita divinatio, qualis iam praesagientibus animis
4 inminentis mali esse solet. Imperator ipse, praeterquam quod ab sociis se desertum, hostium tantum
auctas copias sentiebat, coniectura etiam et ratione
ad suspicionem acceptae cladis quam ad ullam bonam
5 spem pronior erat: quonam modo enim Hasdrubalem
ac Magonem, nisi defunctos suo bello, sine certamine
6 adducere exercitum potuisse? Quo modo autem
non obstitisse aut ab tergo secutum fratrem, ut, si
prohibere quo minus in unum coirent et duces et
exercitus hostium non posset, ipse certe cum fratre
7 coniungeret copias? His anxius curis id modo esse
salutare in praesens credebat, cedere inde quantum
posset; exinde [1] una nocte ignaris hostibus et ob
8 id quietis aliquantum emensus est iter. Luce ut
senserunt profectos, hostes praemissis Numidis quam
poterant maxime citato agmine sequi coeperunt.
Ante noctem adsecuti Numidae, nunc ab tergo, nunc
in latera incursantes, consistere coegerunt ac tutari
9 agmen; quantum possent tamen tuto, ut simul
pugnarent procederentque Scipio hortabatur, priusquam pedestres copiae adsequerentur. XXXVI.
Ceterum nunc agendo, nunc sustinendo agmen cum
aliquamdiu haud multum procederetur et nox iam
2 instaret, revocat e proelio suos Scipio et conlectos in
tumulum quendam non quidem satis tutum, prae-

[1] exinde *Conway*: et inde *P*(1): et *Gronovius*.

such as is usually the forecast of impending misfortune when men already have presentiments. The general himself, in addition to the knowledge that he had been deserted by his allies and that the enemy's forces had been so greatly increased, was more inclined by logical inference to suspect that a disaster had occurred than to entertain any good hope. For how, he thought, could Hasdrubal and Mago, unless they had quite finished their own war, have been able to bring up their army without an engagement? And how had his brother failed to confront them or to follow in their rear, so that, if unable to prevent the generals and armies of the enemy from uniting, he might himself at least combine his forces with those of his brother? Troubled by these anxieties, he believed that the one safe course at present was to retreat as far away as possible. Then in one night, while the enemy were unaware of it and hence made no move, he marched a considerable distance. In the morning the enemy, on discovering that they had gone, sent the Numidians in advance and began to follow them in a column at its utmost speed. Before night the Numidians had overtaken them, and charging now in the rear, now on the flanks, compelled them to halt and defend their column. Scipio kept encouraging them to fight and advance at the same time, so far, that is, as they could do so with safety, before the infantry forces should overtake them. XXXVI. But while he now urged his column forward, now ordered it to halt, for a long time little progress was being made and night was now at hand. Scipio therefore recalled his men from battle, concentrated them and led them up a hill that was not indeed quite safe, especially B.C. 212

A.U.C. 542 sertim agmini perculso, editiorem tamen quam
3 cetera circa erant, subducit. Ibi primo impedi-
mentis et equitatu in medium receptis circumdati
pedites haud difficulter impetus incursantium Numi-
4 darum arcebant; dein, postquam toto agmine tres
imperatores cum tribus iustis exercitibus aderant
apparebatque parum armis ad tuendum locum sine
5 munimento valituros esse, circumspectare atque agi-
tare dux coepit, si quo modo posset vallum circum-
icere. Sed erat adeo nudus tumulus et asperi soli ut
nec virgulta vallo caedendo nec terra caespiti faciendo
aut ducendae fossae aliive ulli operi apta inveniri
6 posset; nec natura quicquam satis arduum aut absci-
sum erat quod hosti aditum ascensumve difficilem
7 praeberet; omnia fastigio leni subvexa. Ut tamen
aliquam imaginem valli obicerent, clitellas inligatas
oneribus velut struentes ad altitudinem solitam cir-
cumdabant, cumulo sarcinarum omnis generis obiecto,
ubi ad moliendum clitellae defuerant.

8 Punici exercitus postquam advenere, in tumulum
quidem perfacile agmen erexere; munitionis facies
9 nova primo eos velut miraculo quodam tenuit, cum
duces undique vociferarentur quid starent et non
ludibrium illud, vix feminis puerisve morandis satis
validum, distraherent diriperentque? Captum
10 hostem teneri, latentem post sarcinas. Haec contemptim duces increpabant; ceterum neque transi-
lire nec moliri onera obiecta nec caedere stipatas
11 clitellas ipsisque obrutas sarcinis facile erat. At

for a terrified column, but still was higher than the B.C. 212
country around it. There the infantry, surrounding the baggage and cavalry placed in the centre, at first kept off the charges of the Numidians without difficulty. Then, when three generals arrived in full force with three regular armies, and it was evident that they would be unable by arms to defend an unfortified position, the general began to cast about and consider whether he could in some way surround it with an earthwork. But the hill was so bare and rocky that neither could thickets be found for the cutting of stakes nor ground such that they could get turf or carry a trench in it or any other earthwork. And yet no spot was naturally so elevated or rugged as to make approach or ascent difficult for the enemy. Everywhere the ground rose at a gentle slope. However, in order to interpose some semblance of an earthwork, they laid up, as it were, to the usual height all around them, pack-saddles still tied to their loads, while, wherever the pack-saddles failed to make a barricade, they piled on top lighter baggage of every kind.

The Carthaginian armies, on arriving, very easily marched in column up the hill; but the strange appearance of the defences at first checked them in a certain amazement, while their commanders kept shouting from all sides, asking why they stood still and did not pull apart and scatter that pretence, hardly strong enough to delay women or children. The enemy, they said, was held captive, lurking behind his baggage. Such were the scornful taunts of the commanders. But it was not easy to leap over or clear away the baggage in front of them, nor to cut apart the mass of pack-saddles, buried under

A.U.C. 542 trudibus[1] cum amoliti obiecta onera armatis dedissent viam pluribusque idem partibus fieret, capta iam
12 undique castra erant. Pauci a multis perculsique a victoribus passim caedebantur; magna pars tamen militum, cum in propinquas refugisset silvas, in castra P. Scipionis, quibus Ti. Fonteius legatus prae-
13 erat, perfugerunt. Cn. Scipionem alii in tumulo primo impetu hostium caesum tradunt, alii cum paucis in propinquam castris turrim perfugisse; hanc igni circumdatam atque ita exustis foribus, quas nulla moliri potuerant vi, captam omnisque intus cum ipso imperatore occisos.

14 Anno octavo postquam in Hispaniam venerat Cn. Scipio, undetricensimo die post fratris mortem, est interfectus. Luctus ex morte eorum non Romae
15 maior quam per totam Hispaniam fuit; quin apud civis partem doloris et exercitus amissi et alienata
16 provincia et publica trahebat clades; Hispaniae ipsos lugebant desiderabantque duces, Gnaeum magis, quod diutius praefuerat iis priorque et favorem occupaverat et specimen iustitiae temperantiaeque Romanae primus dederat.

XXXVII. Cum deleti exercitus amissaeque Hispa-
2 niae viderentur, vir unus res perditas restituit. Erat in exercitu L. Marcius Septimi filius, eques Romanus,

[1] At trudibus *W. Heraeus, Walters*: traditisdibi *PR* (divi *R^1*: ibi *CR^xM*: dibu *BD*: diu *A*): trudentes sudibus *Madvig.*

---

[1] Correct, though inconsistent with Livy's general chronology, which would make it the seventh year; cf. XXI. xxxii. 3. In xxxviii. 6 also Livy has followed an authority who placed the disasters in Spain in 211 B.C.; cf. note on xxxii. 1.

the added loads. But after they had cleared away B.C. 212
the baggage in front of them with hooked poles and made a way for the armed men, and the same thing was being done in different places, the camp had by this time been captured from all sides. Everywhere there was slaughter of the few by the many, of the panic-stricken by the victorious. A large part of the soldiers, however, after fleeing into the neighbouring forest, made their escape to Publius Scipio's camp, of which Tiberius Fonteius, his lieutenant, was commander. As for Gnaeus Scipio, some relate that he was slain on the hill in the first onset of the enemy, others that with a few men he made his escape to a tower near the camp; that fire was lighted around this, and so, by burning the doors which they had been unable to force in any way, they captured the tower and all were slain in it along with the commander himself.

In the eighth year[1] after his arrival in Spain Gnaeus Scipio was killed, on the twenty-ninth day after the death of his brother. Grief for their deaths was not greater in Rome than throughout Spain; in fact among the citizens the destruction of armies and the loss of a province and the national disaster claimed a part in their sorrow, while all Spain mourned for the generals themselves and missed them, Gnaeus more than Publius, because he had been longer in command and had earlier won their favour, and had given for the first time an example of Roman justice and self-control.

XXXVII. While it seemed that the armies had been wiped out and all Spain lost, a single man repaired their shattered fortunes. In the army was Lucius Marcius, son of Septimus, a Roman knight, an active

A.U.C. 542 impiger iuvenis animique et ingenii aliquanto quam
3 pro fortuna in qua erat natus maioris. Ad summam
indolem accesserat Cn. Scipionis disciplina, sub qua
4 per tot annos omnis militiae artis edoctus fuerat. Is [1]
et ex fuga collectis militibus et quibusdam de praesidiis deductis haud contemnendum exercitum fecerat
iunxeratque cum Ti. Fonteio, P. Scipionis legato.
5 Sed tantum praestitit eques Romanus auctoritate
inter milites atque honore ut, castris citra Hiberum
communitis, cum ducem exercitus comitiis militari-
6 bus creari placuisset, subeuntes alii aliis in custodiam valli stationesque, donec per omnis suffragium
iret, ad L. Marcium cuncti summam imperii detule-
7 rint. Omne inde tempus—exiguum id fuit—muniendis castris convehendisque commeatibus consumpsit, et omnia imperia milites cum inpigre, tum
8 haudquaquam abiecto animo exequebantur. Ceterum postquam Hasdrubalem Gisgonis venientem ad
reliquias belli delendas transisse Hiberum et adpropinquare adlatum est, signumque pugnae propositum
9 ab novo duce milites viderunt, recordati quos paulo
ante imperatores habuissent quibusque et ducibus
et copiis freti prodire in pugnam soliti essent, flere
omnes repente et offensare capita et alii manus ad
caelum tendere deos incusantes, alii strati humi
10 suum quisque nominatim ducem implorare. Neque

[1] Is *Weissenborn* : hic $M^x A^y$: *om.* P(1).

young man of much more spirit and talent than was B.C. 212 to be expected in the station in which he had been born. In addition to his high promise he had had the training of Gnaeus Scipio, in which during so many years he had mastered all the arts of the soldier. This man had made an army that was not to be despised out of soldiers gathered up from the flight and in part withdrawn from garrison towns, and he had united it with that of Tiberius Fonteius, the lieutenant of Publius Scipio. But so preëminent was a mere Roman knight in his personal influence with the soldiers and in the respect they paid him that, after they had fortified a camp on this side of the Hiberus and decided that a commander of the army should be chosen in an election by the soldiers, relieving each other as sentries on the wall and in outpost duty until all had cast their votes, they unanimously conferred the high command upon Lucius Marcius. He then spent the whole time—and it was very short—in fortifying the camp and bringing up supplies. And the soldiers carried out all his commands, not only with energy, but also in no dejected spirit. But when the news came that Hasdrubal the son of Gisgo, on his way to wipe out the last remains of the war, had crossed the Hiberus and was approaching, and the soldiers saw the signal for battle raised by a new general, they remembered what commanders they had had a short time before, and upon what generals and forces they had usually relied as they went into battle. Suddenly they all were weeping and dashing their heads against obstacles; and some raised their hands to heaven, blaming the gods, others lying on the ground invoked their respective generals by name. And the wailing

A.U.C. 542 sedari lamentatio poterat excitantibus centurionibus manipulares et ipso mulcente et increpante Marcio, quod in muliebris et inutiles se proiecissent fletus potius quam ad tutandos semet ipsos et rem publicam secum acuerent animos, et ne inultos
11 imperatores suos iacere sinerent, cum subito clamor tubarumque sonus—iam enim prope vallum hostes erant—exauditur. Inde verso repente in iram luctu discurrunt [1] ad arma ac velut accensi rabie discurrunt [2] ad portas et in hostem neglegenter atque incom-
12 posite venientem incurrunt. Extemplo inprovisa res pavorem incutit Poenis, mirabundique unde tot hostes subito exorti prope deleto exercitu forent, unde tanta audacia, tanta fiducia sui victis ac fugatis, quis imperator duobus Scipionibus caesis exstitisset, quis castris praeesset, quis signum dedisset pugnae—
13 ad haec tot tam necopinata primo omnium incerti stupentesque referunt pedem, dein valida inpressione
14 pulsi terga vertunt. Et aut fugientium caedes foeda fuisset aut temerarius periculosusque sequentium impetus, ni Marcius propere receptui dedisset signum obsistensque ad prima signa et quosdam ipse retinens concitatam repressisset aciem. Inde in castra avidos adhuc caedisque et sanguinis
15 reduxit. Carthaginienses trepide primo ab hostium vallo acti, postquam neminem insequi viderunt, metu

[1] discurrunt *P*(3) : *om. Crévier, Jac. Gronovius.*

[2] discurrunt *P*(1) *Conway* : concurrunt *Gronovius* : *Madvig rejected* discurrunt ad portas et.

could not be stilled, although the centurions tried to arouse the men of their maniples and Marcius himself to calm them and upbraided them for having given themselves up to womanish and useless weeping, instead of whetting their courage to defend themselves and with them the state, and begged them not to let their commanders lie unavenged, when suddenly—for the enemy were now near the earthwork—a shout and the sound of trumpets were heard. Upon that, their grief instantly changing to anger, they scatter to arms, and as if fired by frenzy, to the different gates, and dash into the enemy coming on carelessly and in disorder. At once the unexpected act inspired alarm among the Carthaginians, and they wondered whence so many enemies had suddenly appeared after the army had been almost wiped out, whence came such boldness and self-confidence so great in men beaten and put to flight, what commander had arisen after the two Scipios had been slain, who was in command of the camp, who had given the signal for battle. In the face of all that—so many things so unexpected—they at first retreated, completely at a loss and dumbfounded; then beaten back by the strength of the attack they took to flight. And there would have been either a terrible slaughter of the fleeing or a reckless and dangerous attack on the part of the pursuers, had not Marcius promptly given the signal for the recall and kept back his own excited line, facing his men in the front line and laying hold of some with his own hands. He then led them back to camp still thirsting for slaughter and bloodshed. The Carthaginians were at first forced away in confusion from the enemies' earthwork; then, when they saw that no one was pursuing, B.C. 212

A.U.C. 542 substitisse rati, contemptim rursus et sedato gradu in castra abeunt.

16 Par neglegentia in castris custodiendis fuit; nam etsi propinquus hostis erat, tamen reliquias eum esse duorum exercituum ante paucos dies deletorum suc-
17 currebat. Ob hoc cum omnia neglecta apud hostis essent, exploratis iis Marcius ad consilium prima specie temerarium magis quam audax animum adie-
18 cit, ut ultro castra hostium oppugnaret, facilius esse ratus unius Hasdrubalis expugnari castra quam, si se rursus tres exercitus ac tres duces iunxissent, sua
19 defendi; simul aut, si successisset coeptis, erecturum se adflictas res aut, si pulsus esset, tamen ultro inferendo arma contemptum sui dempturum.

XXXVIII. Ne tamen subita res et nocturnus terror et iam non suae fortunae consilium perturbaret, adloquendos adhortandosque sibi milites ratus,
2 contione advocata ita disseruit: "Vel mea erga imperatores nostros vivos mortuosque pietas vel praesens omnium nostrum, milites, fortuna fidem cuivis facere potest mihi hoc imperium, ut amplum iudicio vestro, ita re ipsa grave ac sollicitum esse.
3 Quo enim tempore, nisi metus maerorem obstupefaceret, vix ita compos mei essem ut aliqua solacia invenire aegro animo possem, cogor vestram omnium vicem, quod difficillimum in luctu est, unus consulere.
4 Et ne tum quidem, ubi quonam modo has reliquias duorum exercituum patriae conservare possim cogi-

they thought they had halted for fear, and with fresh contempt and at a slow pace they retired to their camp. B.C. 212

There was just as much carelessness in guarding the camp. For, although the enemy was near, still they kept reflecting that it was only a remnant of the two armies wiped out a few days before. Since for this reason every precaution had been omitted on the enemy's side, Marcius, informed of the facts, turned his attention to a plan at first sight reckless rather than bold, actually to attack the camp of the enemy, in the belief that it was easier to storm the camp of Hasdrubal alone than to defend his own, if the three armies and three generals should again unite. At the same time he thought that, if his efforts should prove successful, he would relieve his critical situation or, even if defeated, by venturing to attack he would at least take away their contempt for himself. XXXVIII. But for fear an unexpected action, and alarm in the night and a plan no longer in keeping with his present situation, might bring confusion, he thought he must address his soldiers and encourage them, called an assembly and spoke as follows: "Either my devotion to our commanders, living and dead, or the present situation of us all, soldiers, can convince any one that this high command, though a great honour as your tribute, is yet in fact a burden to me and an anxious care. For at a time when, if fear did not paralyse grief, I should scarcely have such self-control as would enable me to find some comfort for distress of mind, I am compelled —a most difficult thing in sorrow—alone to plan for all of you. And even when I must consider how I may be able to save these remnants of two armies

A.U.C. 542 tandum est, avertere animum ab assiduo maerore
5 licet.[1] Praesto est enim acerba memoria, et Scipiones me ambo dies noctesque curis insomniisque agitant
6 et excitant saepe somno, neu se neu invictos per octo annos in his terris milites suos, commilitones vestros, neu rem publicam patiar inultam, et suam discipli-
7 nam suaque instituta sequi iubent et, ut imperiis vivorum nemo oboedientior me uno fuerit, ita post mortem suam, quod in quaque re facturos illos fuisse
8 maxime censeam, id optimum ducere. Vos quoque velim, milites, non lamentis lacrimisque tamquam extinctos prosequi—vivunt vigentque fama rerum gestarum—, sed, quotienscumque occurret memoria illorum, velut si adhortantis signumque dantis
9 videatis eos, ita proelia inire. Nec alia profecto species hesterno die oblata oculis animisque vestris memorabile illud edidit proelium, quo documentum dedistis hostibus non cum Scipionibus extinctum esse
10 nomen Romanum et, cuius populi vis atque virtus non obruta sit Cannensi clade, ex omni profecto saevitia fortunae emersurum[2] esse.

11 "Nunc, quia tantum ausi estis sponte vestra, experiri libet quantum audeatis duce vestro auctore. Non enim hesterno die, cum signum receptui dedi sequentibus effuse vobis turbatum hostem, frangere audaciam vestram, sed differre in maiorem gloriam atque

[1] licet *Gronovius*: libet *P*(1) *Riemann*.
[2] emersurum *xz*: -am *P*(1) *Madvig*.

for our country, I may not turn my thoughts away B.C. 212
from unremitting grief. For a bitter memory is present with me, and both Scipios trouble me all day and all night with anxiety and loss of sleep, and often arouse me from slumber, bidding me not to allow either themselves or their soldiers, your comrades, undefeated in this land for eight years,[1] or the state, to go unavenged. And they command me to follow their teachings and their methods, and, just as while they lived not a man was more obedient to their orders than I, so after their death to hold that to be the best course which in each case I am confident they would have done. As for you, soldiers, I would have you also honour them, not with lamentations and tears as though dead. They live and work by the glory of their achievements. But whenever you shall remember them, just as if you saw them encouraging you and giving the signal,—in that spirit would I have you go into battle. It was surely no other image which presented itself yesterday to your eyes and minds and brought about that notable battle, by which you gave the enemy proof that the Roman name has not been extinguished with the Scipios, and that the people whose might and courage were not overwhelmed by the disaster at Cannae will surely survive any cruelty of Fortune.

"At present, because you have of your own accord shown such daring, I should like to find how much you have when your general gives the command. For yesterday, when I sounded the recall, as you in disorder were pursuing the routed enemy, it was not my wish to crush your boldness, but to reserve it for higher fame and a more favourable situation, that

[1] Cf. xxxvi. 14 and note.

A.U.C. 542 12 opportunitatem volui, ut postmodo praeparati incautos, armati inermes atque etiam sopitos per occasionem adgredi possetis. Nec huius occasionis spem, milites, forte temere, sed ex re ipsa conceptam
13 habeo. A vobis quoque profecto si quis quaerat quonam modo pauci a multis, victi a victoribus castra tutati sitis, nihil aliud respondeatis quam id ipsum timentis vos omnia et operibus firmata habuisse et
14 ipsos paratos instructosque fuisse. Et ita se res habet: ad id quod ne timeatur fortuna facit minime tuti sunt homines, quia quod neglexeris incautum
15 atque apertum habeas. Nihil omnium nunc minus metuunt hostes quam ne, obsessi modo ipsi atque oppugnati, castra sua ultro oppugnemus. Audeamus quod credi non potest ausuros nos; eo ipso quod
16 difficillimum videtur facilius erit. Tertia vigilia noctis silenti agmine ducam vos. Exploratum habeo non vigiliarum ordinem, non stationes iustas
17 esse. Clamor in portis auditus et primus impetus castra ceperit. Tum inter torpidos somno paventisque ad necopinatum tumultum et inermis in cubilibus suis oppressos illa caedes edatur a qua vos hesterno
18 die revocatos aegre ferebatis. Scio audax videri consilium; sed in rebus asperis et tenui spe fortissima quaeque consilia tutissima sunt, quia, si in occasionis momento cuius praetervolat opportunitas cunctatus paulum fueris, nequiquam mox omissam quaeras.
19 Unus exercitus in propinquo est, duo haud procul

later, being well prepared and armed, you might be able, as opportunity offered, to attack the unprepared and unarmed, and even the sleeping. And not haphazard or at random do I cherish a hope of this opportunity, soldiers, but from the actual situation. You too, if someone should ask how you, a few men, have defended your camp against many, the vanquished against the victors, would surely give no other answer than that, fearing just that, you had kept everything in a state of defence and also had been in readiness yourselves and in line. And the fact is this: men are least protected against the thing which success leads them not to fear, since what one has made light of remains unguarded and uncovered. There is nothing in the world which the enemy now fear less than that we, who have ourselves just been beset and attacked, may venture to attack their camp. Let us dare what it is incredible that we should dare; for the very reason that it appears most difficult it will be easier. In the third watch of the night I shall lead you in a silent column. I am assured that there is no relieving of sentries, no regular outposts. The sound of a shout at the gate and a first assault will at once capture the camp. Then, among men dazed with sleep and alarmed at the unexpected uproar and surprised unarmed in their beds, let there be the slaughter from which you were recalled yesterday under protest. I know it seems a bold plan. But in dangerous and desperate situations the bravest decisions are always the safest. For if at the opportune moment, whose advantage swiftly passes, one hesitates even a little, it is vain for one to look later for the neglected opportunity. One army is near, two not far away. If we attack now there is B.C. 212

A.U.C. 542 absunt. Nunc adgredientibus spes aliqua est, et
20 iam temptastis vestras atque illorum vires: si diem
proferimus et hesternae eruptionis fama contemni
desierimus, periculum est ne omnes duces, omnes
copiae conveniant. Tres deinde duces, tres exercitus
sustinebimus hostium quos Cn. Scipio incolumi
21 exercitu non sustinuit? Ut dividendo copias periere
duces nostri, ita separatim ac divisi opprimi possunt
hostes. Alia belli gerendi via nulla est. Proinde
nihil praeter noctis proximae opportunitatem
22 expectemus. Ite deis bene iuvantibus, corpora
curate, ut integri vigentesque eodem animo in castra
hostium inrumpatis quo vestra tutati estis."

23 Laeti et audiere ab novo duce novum consilium,
et quo audacius erat magis placebat. Reliquum diei
expediendis armis et curatione corporum con-
sumptum et maior pars noctis quieti data est.
Quarta vigilia movere. XXXIX. Erant ultra proxu-
ma castra sex milium intervallo distantes aliae copiae
Poenorum. Valles cava intererat, condensa arboribus; in huius silvae medio ferme spatio cohors
2 Romana arte Punica abditur et equites. Ita medio
itinere intercepto ceterae copiae silenti agmine ad
proximos hostis ductae et, cum statio nulla pro
portis neque in vallo custodiae essent, velut in sua
3 castra nullo usquam obsistente penetravere. Inde
signa canunt et tollitur clamor. Pars semisomnos

no little hope, and already you have tried your strength B.C. 212
and theirs. If we put off the day and owing to the report of yesterday's sally come to be no longer despised, there is danger that all the generals and all the forces may combine. Shall we then withstand the enemy's three generals, three armies, which Gnaeus Scipio with his army still undiminished did not withstand? Just as through dividing their forces our generals perished, so the enemy, if divided and in different places, can be overpowered. There is no other way of conducting the war. Therefore let us wait for nothing beyond the favourable moment to-night. Go with the kind aid of the gods, put yourselves in condition, that, sound and strong, you may burst into the camp of the enemy with the same spirit with which you defended yours."

With joy they heard of the new plan from their new commander, and the bolder it was the more it pleased them. The rest of the day was spent in putting their arms in order and themselves in condition; and the larger part of the night was given to rest. At the fourth watch they started. XXXIX. Beyond the nearest camp and at a distance of six miles from it were other forces of the Carthaginians. Between them there was a deep valley, densely wooded. About the middle of this wood a Roman cohort and cavalry were concealed after the Punic method. The road being thus cut off at the half-way, the rest of the forces were led in a silent column to the nearest enemy. And as there was no outpost before the gates nor sentinels on the earthwork, and no one anywhere opposed them, they made their way into the camp as if it were their own. Then the trumpets sound and a shout is raised. Some slay

A.U.C. 542 hostis caedunt, pars ignes casis stramento arido tectis
iniciunt, pars portas occupant, ut fugam intercludant.
4 Hostes simul ignis, clamor, caedes velut alienatos
sensibus nec audire nec providere quicquam sinunt.
5 Incidunt inermes inter catervas armatorum. Alii
ruunt ad portas, alii obsaeptis itineribus super vallum
6 saliunt; et, ut quisque evaserat, protinus ad castra
altera fugiunt, ubi ab cohorte et equitibus ex occulto
procurrentibus circumventi caesique ad unum omnes
7 sunt; quamquam, etiamsi quis ex ea caede effugisset,
adeo raptim a captis propioribus castris in altera
transcursum castra ab Romanis est, ut praevenire
8 nuntius cladis non posset. Ibi vero, quo longius
ab hoste aberant et quia sub lucem pabulatum
lignatumque et praedatum quidam dilapsi fuerant,
neglecta magis omnia ac soluta invenere, arma
tantum in stationibus posita, milites inermes aut
humi sedentes accubantesque aut obambulantes ante
9 vallum portasque. Cum his tam securis solutisque
Romani calentes adhuc ab recenti pugna ferocesque
victoria proelium ineunt. Itaque nequaquam resisti
in portis potuit; intra portas concursu ex totis castris
ad primum clamorem et tumultum facto atrox proe-
10 lium oritur; diuque tenuisset, ni cruenta scuta
Romanorum visa indicium alterius cladis Poenis
11 atque inde pavorem iniecissent. Hic terror in
fugam avertit omnis, effusique qua iter est, nisi quos

the enemy half-asleep, some throw firebrands on the dry, thatched huts, some seize the gates, to block escape. As for the enemy, fire, shouting and slaughter, all at once, make them virtually senseless and do not allow them to hear any orders or to look out for themselves. Unharmed they encounter bodies of armed men. Some rush to the gates, others, since the roads are blocked, leap over the earthwork. And everyone who escaped fled at once in the direction of the other camp; whereupon they were surrounded by the cohort and cavalry dashing out of their hiding-place and were slain to the last man. Yet, even if a man had escaped from that slaughter, so swiftly did the Romans hasten from the captured nearer camp to the other camp that news of the disaster could not anticipate them. But there, the farther it was from their enemy, and since some had scattered just before daylight to bring in fodder and firewood and booty, the more neglect and disorder did they find everywhere; only stacked arms at the outposts, the soldiers unarmed, either sitting and lying on the ground or strolling outside the wall and the gates. Against these men, so care-free and regardless of order, the Romans, who were still fired by their recent battle and made confident by victory, went into battle. And so no resistance whatever could be offered at the gates. Inside the gates there was a rush from every part of the camp at the first shouting and commotion, and a fierce battle began. It would have lasted long too, had not the sight of the Romans' bloody shields given the Carthaginians evidence of the other disaster and consequently inspired alarm. This terror made them all take to flight, and pouring out wherever a way could be found B.C. 212

A.U.C. 542 caedes oppressit, exuuntur castris. Ita nocte ac die bina castra hostium expugnata [1] ductu L. Marcii.
12 Ad triginta septem milia hostium caesa auctor est Claudius, qui annales Acilianos ex Graeco in Latinum sermonem vertit, captos ad mille octingentos triginta,
13 praedam ingentem partam; in ea fuisse clipeum argenteum pondo centum triginta septem cum
14 imagine Barcini Hasdrubalis. Valerius Antias una castra Magonis capta tradit, septem milia caesa hostium; altero proelio eruptione pugnatum cum Hasdrubale, decem milia occisa, quattuor milia
15 trecentos triginta captos. Piso quinque milia hominum, cum Mago cedentis nostros effuse sequeretur,
16 caesa ex insidiis scribit. Apud omnis magnum nomen Marcii ducis est; et verae gloriae eius etiam miracula addunt, flammam ei contionanti fusam e capite sine ipsius sensu cum magno pavore circum-
17 stantium militum; monimentumque victoriae eius de Poenis usque ad incensum Capitolium fuisse in templo clipeum, Marcium appellatum, cum imagine
18 Hasdrubalis.—Quietae deinde aliquamdiu in Hispania res fuere, utrisque post tantas in vicem acceptas

[1] expugnata *z Conway*: oppugnata *P*(1).

---

[1] *I.e.* Q. Claudius Quadrigarius, who wrote in the time of Sulla. His history, in at least 23 books, began with the capture of the city by the Gauls. Acilius' Greek history of Rome had begun with the founding of the city. In 155 B.C. Acilius acted as interpreter when the three Greek philosophers, Carneades among them, appeared before the senate.

[2] Valerius, a contemporary of Claudius, wrote a voluminous history from the founding of Rome in upwards of 75 books. Here by exception his figures for the enemy slain are very moderate.

[3] L. Calpurnius Piso Frugi, the annalist, was consul in 133 B.C. His work, here cited for the last time in the extant Livy,

—except those overtaken by the sword—they lost possession of the camp. Thus in a night and a day two camps of the enemy were taken by assault under the command of Lucius Marcius. That about thirty-seven thousand of the enemy were slain is the statement of Claudius,[1] who translated Acilius' annals out of Greek into the Latin language; that about one thousand eight hundred and thirty were captured and a vast amount of booty taken. And in this he says that there was a silver shield weighing a hundred and thirty-seven pounds, bearing the likeness of Hasdrubal Barca. Valerius of Antium[2] relates that one camp was captured, that of Mago, and seven thousand of the enemy slain; that in a second battle they sallied out and fought with Hasdrubal; that ten thousand were slain, four thousand three hundred and thirty captured. Piso[3] states that five thousand men were slain from an ambush, while Mago was pursuing in disorder our retreating men. In all of them great is the name of Marcius the general. And to his real fame they add even marvels: that as he was speaking a flame burst from his head without his knowledge, causing great alarm among the soldiers who stood around him. They say that as a memorial of his victory over the Carthaginians, down to the burning of the Capitol there was in the temple a shield called the Marcian, bearing a likeness of Hasdrubal.[4]—Thereafter the situation in Spain was quiet for a long time, since both sides, after receiving and inflicting such losses

B.C. 212

probably consisted of seven books, beginning with the founding of the city.

[4] Pliny (*N.H.* XXXV. 14) says this shield hung above the door of the Capitoline temple until the fire of 84 B.C.

A.U.C. 542 inlatasque clades cunctantibus periculum summae rerum facere.

XL. Dum haec in Hispania geruntur, Marcellus captis Syracusis, cum cetera in Sicilia tanta fide atque integritate composuisset ut non modo suam gloriam sed etiam maiestatem populi Romani augeret, ornamenta urbis, signa tabulasque quibus abundabant Syracusae, Romam devexit, hostium
2 quidem illa spolia et parta belli iure; ceterum inde primum initium mirandi Graecarum artium opera licentiaeque huius[1] sacra profanaque omnia vulgo spoliandi factum est, quae postremo in Romanos deos, templum id ipsum primum quod a Marcello
3 eximie ornatum est, vertit. Visebantur enim ab externis ad portam Capenam dedicata a M. Marcello templa propter excellentia eius generis ornamenta, quorum perexigua pars comparet.

4 Legationes omnium ferme civitatium Siciliae ad eum conveniebant. Dispar ut causa earum, ita condicio erat. Qui ante captas Syracusas aut non desciverant aut redierant in amicitiam, ut socii fideles accepti cultique; quos metus post captas Syracusas dediderat, ut victi a victore leges accepe-
5 runt. Erant tamen haud parvae reliquiae belli circa Agrigentum Romanis, Epicydes et Hanno, duces reliqui prioris belli, et tertius novus ab Hanni-

[1] huius *Ussing, Conway*: huic *P*(2): hinc *A Walters.*

---

[1] The Temples of Honos and Virtus were outside the gate, on the Appian Way; XXVI. xxxii. 4; XXVII. xxv. 7–9; Plutarch, *Marcellus* 28. Dedicated in 205 B.C. by Marcellus' son; XXIX. xi. 13. In the Temple of Virtus stood the famous *sphaera* (orrery) of Archimedes; Cicero *de Re Publica* I. 21.

upon each other, hesitated to risk a decisive engagement. B.C. 212

XL. While these things were being done in Spain, it is true that Marcellus, after the capture of Syracuse, had settled matters in general in Sicily with such conscientiousness and honesty that he added not only to his own fame, but also to the dignity of the Roman people. But as regards the adornments of the city, the statues and paintings which Syracuse possessed in abundance, he carried them away to Rome. They were spoils of the enemy, to be sure, and acquired by right of war. Yet from that came the very beginning of enthusiasm for Greek works of art and consequently of this general licence to despoil all kinds of buildings, sacred and profane, a licence which finally turned against Roman gods, and first of all against the very temple which was magnificently adorned by Marcellus. For temples dedicated by Marcus Marcellus near the Porta Capena [1] used to be visited by foreigners on account of their remarkable adornments of that kind; but of these a very small part is still to be seen.

Embassies from nearly all the states in Sicily kept coming to him. As their pleas were different, so was their status. Those who before the capture of Syracuse either had not rebelled or had returned to friendly relations were admitted and honoured as faithful allies. Those whom fear had led to surrender after the capture of Syracuse, as vanquished received terms from the victor. There was left to the Romans, however, no small remainder of the war around Agrigentum, namely, Epicydes and Hanno, the surviving commanders in the previous war, and a third new general sent by Hannibal in place of

A.U.C. 542 bale in locum Hippocratis missus, Libyphoenicum
generis Hippacritanus—Muttinen populares vocabant—, vir inpiger et sub Hannibale magistro omnis
6 belli artes edoctus. Huic ab Epicyde et Hannone
Numidae dati auxiliares, cum quibus ita pervagatus
est hostium agros, ita socios ad retinendos in fide
animos eorum ferendo in tempore cuique auxilium
7 adiit ut brevi tempore totam Siciliam impleret
nominis sui, nec spes alia maior apud faventis rebus
8 Carthaginiensium esset. Itaque inclusi ad id tempus moenibus Agrigenti dux Poenus Syraeusanus-
que, non consilio Muttinis quam fiducia magis ausi
egredi extra muros ad Himeram amnem posuerunt
9 castra. Quod ubi perlatum ad Marcellum est, extemplo copias movit et ab hoste quattuor ferme
milium intervallo consedit, quid agerent pararentve
10 expectaturus. Sed nullum neque locum neque
tempus cunctationi consiliove dedit Muttines, transgressus amnem ac stationibus hostium cum ingenti
11 terrore ac tumultu invectus. Postero die prope
iusto proelio compulit hostis intra munimenta. Inde
revocatus seditione Numidarum in castris facta, cum
trecenti ferme eorum Heracleam Minoam con-
cessissent, ad mitigandos revocandosque eos profectus magno opere monuisse duces dicitur ne
12 absente se cum hoste manus consererent. Id ambo
aegre passi duces, magis Hanno, iam ante anxius
gloria eius: Muttinem sibi modum facere, degene-

---

[1] *I.e.* Hippo Diarrhytus, northwest of Utica, on the coast.

Hippocrates. He was of Libyphoenician race, from Hippacra,[1] and called Muttines by his countrymen, a man of energy who under Hannibal's teaching had mastered all the arts of war. He was furnished by Epicydes and Hanno with Numidian auxiliaries, with which he so thoroughly scoured the enemy's lands and sought out allies, in order to retain their loyalty by lending aid to each man at the right moment, that in a short time he filled all Sicily with his name and was the highest hope of those supporting the Carthaginian cause. And so, after being confined until then within the walls of Agrigentum, the Carthaginian general and the Syracusan, emboldened not more by the advice of Muttines than by their confidence in him to go outside the walls, pitched their camp by the river Himera. When news of this reached Marcellus, he at once set his troops in motion and established himself at a distance of about four miles from the enemy, to wait and see what they were doing or intending. But Muttines gave no occasion or time for hesitation, or for a plan of action; for he crossed the river and attacked the outposts of the enemy, causing great alarm and confusion. The next day by an engagement almost in regular form he drove the enemy inside their fortifications. Then he was recalled by a mutiny of the Numidians breaking out in the camp, after about three hundred of them had retired to Heraclea Minoa. On leaving, to pacify and recall these men, he is said to have expressly warned the generals not to engage the enemy in his absence. At that both generals were indignant, especially Hanno, already uneasy because of the man's fame. To think that Muttines, a degenerate African, should set a limit

B.C. 212

A.U.C. 542 rem Afrum imperatori Carthaginiensi misso ab
13 senatu populoque! Is perpulit cunctantem Epicyden ut transgressi flumen in aciem exirent: nam si Muttinem opperirentur, et secunda pugnae fortuna evenisset, haud dubie Muttinis gloriam fore.

XLI. Enimvero indignum ratus Marcellus se, qui Hannibalem subnixum victoria Cannensi ab Nola reppulisset, his terra marique victis ab se hostibus cedere, arma propere capere milites et efferri signa
2 iubet. Instruenti[1] exercitum decem effusis equis advolant ex hostium acie Numidae nuntiantes populares suos, primum ea seditione motos qua
3 trecenti ex numero suo concesserint Heracleam, dein quod praefectum suum ab obtrectantibus ducibus gloriae eius sub ipsam certaminis diem ablegatum
4 videant, quieturos in pugna. Gens fallax promissi fidem praestitit. Itaque et Romanis crevit animus nuntio celeri per ordines misso, destitutum ab equite
5 hostem esse, quem maxime timuerant, et territi hostes, praeterquam quod maxima parte virium suarum non iuvabantur, timore etiam incusso, ne
6 ab suomet ipsi equite oppugnarentur. Itaque haud magni certaminis res[2] fuit; primus clamor atque inpetus rem decrevit. Numidae cum in concursu quieti stetissent in cornibus, ut terga dantis suos viderunt, fugae tantum parumper comites facti,

[1] instruenti *Gronovius*: -te *P*(1).
[2] res *Conway*: *om.* *P*(1): proelium *or* res (*after* fuit) *Weissenborn*.

for him, a Carthaginian commander, sent by senate and people! He prevailed upon the hesitating Epicydes to cross the river and form their battle-line. For if they should wait for Muttines and the fortune of battle should favour, the glory, he said, would unquestionably fall to Muttines. B.C. 212

XLI. Marcellus, thinking it was a veritable outrage for him, a man who had driven Hannibal, backed by his victory at Cannae, from Nola, to yield to these enemies whom he had himself defeated on land and sea, ordered his soldiers to take up their arms in haste and the standard-bearers to set out. As he was drawing up his army, ten Numidians rode out of the enemy's ranks and at full speed up to him, reporting that their countrymen were aroused, first by the mutiny in which three hundred of their number had retired to Heraclea, and then by seeing their commander sent away just on the eve of battle by generals who belittled his reputation, and that in the fight they would remain inactive. A deceitful race kept its promise faithfully. And so the Romans' spirits rose when the message was sent swiftly through the ranks that the enemy had been deserted by his cavalry, which they had particularly dreaded; at the same time the enemy were terrified not only because they were having no help from the largest part of their forces, but also by the fear thus aroused that they might themselves be attacked by their own cavalry. Accordingly it was no great struggle; the first shout, the first onset, decided the matter. The Numidians, having remained motionless on the wings at the beginning of the battle, seeing their men retreating, shared only the flight with them for a short time. When they saw them all making for

A.U.C. 542 7 postquam omnes Agrigentum trepido agmine petentes viderunt, ipsi metu obsidionis passim in civitatis proxumas dilapsi. Multa milia hominum caesa, capta . . .[1] et octo elephanti. Haec ultima in Sicilia Marcelli pugna fuit; victor inde Syracusas rediit.

8 Iam ferme in exitu annus erat; itaque senatus Romae decrevit ut P. Cornelius praetor litteras Ca-
9 puam ad consules mitteret, dum Hannibal procul abesset nec ulla magni discriminis res ad Capuam gereretur, alter eorum, si ita videretur, ad magistratus
10 subrogandos Romam veniret. Litteris acceptis inter se consules compararunt ut Claudius comitia per-
11 ficeret, Fulvius ad Capuam maneret. Consules Claudius creavit Cn. Fulvium Centumalum et P. Sulpicium Servii filium Galbam, qui nullum antea
12 curulem magistratum gessisset. Praetores deinde creati L. Cornelius Lentulus, M. Cornelius Cethegus,
13 C. Sulpicius, C. Calpurnius Piso.[2] Pisoni iuris dictio urbana, Sulpicio Sicilia, Cethego Apulia, Lentulo Sardinia evenit. Consulibus prorogatum in annum imperium est.

[1] *Perhaps* sex milia (*i.e.* $\overline{\text{vi}}$) *Madvig.*

[2] *Names in this sentence are in part restored by Aldus and Sigonius. P*(1) *omit* L. Cornelius Lentulus (13 *and* XXVI. i. 11) *and* M. (ii. 2), *also* C. Calpurnius (XXVI. iii. 9).

Agrigentum in a panic-stricken column, they themselves scattered in every direction to the neighbouring cities, fearing a siege. Many thousand men were slain . . . thousand captured, also eight elephants. This was Marcellus' last battle in Sicily; from it he returned as victor to Syracuse. B.C. 212

By this time the year was nearly at an end. Accordingly the senate at Rome decreed that Publius Cornelius, the praetor, should send a letter to the consuls at Capua, saying that, while Hannibal was far away and there was no decisive action around Capua, one of them, if they thought it best, should come to Rome for the replacement of magistrates. On receiving the letter the consuls arranged between them that Claudius should conduct the elections, and Fulvius remain near Capua. For the consulship Claudius announced the election of Gnaeus Fulvius Centumalus and Publius Sulpicius Galba, son of Servius, although he had previously held no curule office. As praetors the following were then elected: Lucius Cornelius Lentulus, Marcus Cornelius Cethegus, Gaius Sulpicius, Gaius Calpurnius Piso. The duties of the city praetor fell to Piso,[1] Sicily to Sulpicius, Apulia to Cethegus, Sardinia to Lentulus. As for the consuls, their military authority was continued for one year.

[1] Evidently the duties of the praetor peregrinus also were assigned to the praetor urbanus, as for the two preceding years; cf. notes on i. 11 and iii. 2.

LIBRI XXV PERIOCHA

P. Cornelius Scipio, postea Africanus, ante annos aedilis factus. Hannibal urbem Tarenton praeter arcem, in quam praesidium Romanorum fugerat, per Tarentinos iuvenes, qui se noctu venatum ire simulaverant, cepit. Ludi Apollinares ex Marcii carminibus, quibus Cannensis clades praedicta fuerat, instituti sunt. A Q. Fulvio et Ap. Claudio consulibus adversus Hannonem Poenorum ducem prospere pugnatum est. Tib. Sempronius Gracchus proconsul, ab hospite suo Lucano in insidias deductus, a Magone interfectus est. Centenius Paenula, qui centurio militaverat, cum petisset a senatu ut sibi exercitus daretur, pollicitusque esset, si hoc impetrasset, de Hannibale victoriam, $\overline{\text{VIII}}$ acceptis militum dux factus conflixit acie cum Hannibale et cum exercitu caesus est. Capua obsessa est a Q. Fulvio et Ap. Claudio consulibus. Cn. Fulvius praetor male adversus Hannibalem pugnavit, in quo proelio $\overline{\text{XX}}$[1] hominum ceciderunt; ipse cum equitibus ducentis effugit. Claudius Marcellus Syracusas expugnavit tertio anno et ingentem se virum gessit. In eo tumultu captae urbis Archimedes intentus formis quas in pulvere descripserat interfectus est. P. et Cn. Scipiones in Hispania tot rerum feliciter gestarum tristem exitum tulerunt, prope cum totis exercitibus caesi anno octavo quam in Hispaniam ierunt. Amissaque eius provinciae possessio foret, nisi L. Marcii equitis Romani virtute et industria contractis exercituum reliquiis eiusdem hortatu bina castra hostium expugnata essent. Ad $\overline{\text{XXVII}}$[2] caesa, ad[3] mille octingentos, praeda ingens capta. Dux Marcius appellatus est.

[1] *This should be* $\overline{\text{XVI}}$: *cf.* xxi. 10.

[2] *An error for* $\overline{\text{XXXVII}}$: *cf.* xxxix. 12.

[3] *For* ad (*Sigonius*) *the MSS. have* ex.

SUMMARY OF BOOK XXV

Publius Cornelius Scipio, later Africanus, was made aedile before the legal age. Hannibal, with the aid of young Tarentines who had pretended that they were going hunting at night, captured the city of Tarentum, except the citadel, to which the Roman garrison had fled. The Ludi Apollinares were established in accordance with the oracles of Marcius, in which the disaster at Cannae had been predicted. A successful battle was fought by Quintus Fulvius and Appius Claudius, the consuls, against Hanno, a general of the Carthaginians. Tiberius Sempronius Gracchus, the proconsul, was led into an ambuscade by his Lucanian guest-friend and slain by Mago. Centenius Paenula, who had served as a centurion, after begging the senate to give him an army and promising a victory over Hannibal if he gained his request, received eight thousand soldiers, was made commander, engaged Hannibal in battle-line, and with his army was slain. Capua was besieged by Quintus Fulvius and Appius Claudius, the consuls. Gnaeus Fulvius, a praetor, was defeated in a battle with Hannibal in which twenty thousand men fell. Fulvius himself escaped with two hundred horsemen. Claudius Marcellus took Syracuse after two years and bore himself as a great man. In that uproar of the captured city Archimedes, while intent upon the figures he had traced in the dust, was slain. Publius and Gnaeus Scipio in Spain met with an unhappy end of their many successes, being slain with almost their entire armies in the eighth year after they went to Spain. And possession of that province would have been lost, had not the remnants of the armies been brought together by the bravery and activity of Lucius Marcius, a Roman knight, and with his encouragement two camps of the enemy been taken by storm. About twenty-seven thousand were slain, about one thousand eight hundred men and vast booty captured. Marcius was named commander.

APPENDIX

THE TOPOGRAPHY OF SYRACUSE

Syracuse is the extreme example of a Greek city whose walls for military reasons, and probably for no other reasons, enclosed a vastly larger space than was required by the actual size of the city. Other examples are Priene, Ephesus, Samos, Tarentum, Croton; also a number of small and little-known cities in Aetolia and Acarnania.[1] In such cases the desire to include some commanding height or heights in dangerous proximity to the city led to a conspicuous enlargement of the walled circuit. For Syracuse no other motive accounts for the Wall of Dionysius, enclosing the great triangular plateau to the north and northwest of the city. Military operations on this elevation during the siege by the Athenian army (414–413 B.C.) had only confirmed the obvious, that it was essential to prevent any invader from establishing himself on heights so near the city. Dionysius accordingly extended the city walls so as to enclose the entire triangle, from its apex to the west, at his fortress of Euryalus, all the way to its wide base close to the Ionian Sea, *i.e.* a distance of 3½ miles.

[1] Cf. von Gerkan, *Griechische Städteanlagen*, 1924, p. 110; Noack, in *Archäologischer Anzeiger*, 1916, 215 f.

Thenceforward the entire circuit of the walls of Syracuse amounted to 17 miles (English) or 27 km., about 7 km. ($4\frac{1}{2}$ miles) more than the Walls of Aurelian at Rome, or about 9 km. ($5\frac{1}{2}$ miles) more than the walls of Alexandria. No one now believes that Syracuse at the height of its prosperity had so immense a population. The tendency of recent estimates is in the opposite direction, due account being taken of the agricultural basis on which that prosperity rested, and of the constant practice of employing mercenaries, so that previous estimates based upon the strength of the army are to be discarded.[1]

Maps produced at the beginning of the XVIIth century show the entire plateau occupied by streets, houses and other buildings, of which no trace can be found. They make Epipolae, the Heights, an inhabited quarter, though nowhere mentioned as such in our sources. They have Achradina stretching away to the northern Wall of Dionysius, quite three miles from the southern limit of the same quarter on the Porto Grande; and Tycha just inside the same north wall and near the Hexapylon. In these also they are unsupported by ancient authority. From these highly imaginative sheets of Mirabella and Cluver have descended the maps in all of our atlases, in histories (*e.g.* Freeman), in special works on Syracuse, in editions of Thucydides, Cicero's *Verrines* and Livy.

" There is no doubt that the population of Syracuse never filled up anything like the whole space enclosed by the walls of Dionysius." So wrote Haver-

[1] Cf. von Gerkan in *Deutsche Litteraturzeitung*, 1933, Sp. 1403.

field fifty years ago.[1] Visitors, more and more numerous, have had steadily increasing doubts with regard to the possibility that Epipolae could ever have been more than very sparsely inhabited. No one who stands on the ruins of Euryalus and looks down the length and breadth of that vast isosceles triangle, with its base (two miles long from north to south) almost reaching the sea, will be easily persuaded that even scattèred villas occupied so barren and rocky à soil.

This scepticism, shared by such a master as Orsi, has culminated in the studies of the historian, Professor Knud Fabricius, of the University of Copenhagen, published in his *Das antike Syrakus* (*Klio*, Beiheft XXVIII, 1932), with illustrations and a map. A model of clear-cut method, this work shows conclusively that Epipolae was never in ancient times reckoned one of the quarters of the city; that the real city lay to the south of the plateau; that the latter was fortified, not for its own sake, but to ensure the city against attack from higher ground dangerously near; that it becomes necessary to revise our maps, to show Tycha and Achradina on the lower level south of the quarries.

Epipolae, frequently mentioned by Thucydides, was to his mind simply a height (*e.g.* VI. xcvi f.; VII. iv), and his "outer city" (ἡ ἔξω, VI. iii) certainly did not extend so far from Ortygia. Livy mentions Epipolae in a single chapter (XXV. xxiv), calling it at first merely a *locus* (§ 4), then a *pars urbis* (§ 5); but this does not prove that he classed it with the quarters named, probably after Timaeus, by Cicero in his list of four *urbes* (Insula, Achradina,

[1] *Classical Review*, 1889, p. 111.

Tycha, Neapolis—*in Verrem* IV. 119).[1] For as the walls belong to Syracuse, any place inside the walls is in a loose sense a *pars urbis*.[2] To be sure, when Marcellus has forced the Hexapylon (xxiv. § 7), we read *omnibus copiis urbem ingressus*, but only the outer works can be meant, for it is from the high ground of Epipolae that he has an unobstructed view of the city itself in the distance (§ 11; cf. Plutarch, *Marcellus* 19. 1).

Fabricius's demonstration that the heights were almost unoccupied has been completely approved by such competent authorities as von Gerkan (in *Deutsche Litteraturzeitung*, 1933, Sp. 1404–07) and Ian Richmond (*Classical Review*, 1933, pp. 16 f.), both of whom are experts on city walls in ancient times; also by Libertini (*Il Mondo Classico*, 1934, pp. 29 ff.).

If, then, there were no inhabited quarters on the plateau it becomes necessary to remove Tycha from a position near the Hexapylon assigned to it by tradition since the Renaissance. The topographers have thought that that gate admitted one directly to this quarter, and hence placed Tycha just inside the northern Wall of Dionysius, adjoining Achradina, as they believed, on the east and Epipolae on the south and west. If Livy, however, is correct (XXV. xxiv. 4) the six-fold gate did not give entrance to Tycha but to Epipolae, and nothing proves that Tycha

[1] Strabo's πεντάπολις (VI. ii. 4) does not necessarily include Epipolae, for he may have listed Temenites in addition to Neapolis. If he did mean Epipolae it does not follow that he really thought of it as a built-up quarter.

[2] Cf. XXV. xxv. 2, where Euryalus is *in extrema parte urbis*—too literally interpreted by the mapmakers.

was anywhere near the gate. No archaeological evidence supports the supposition that this quarter (a populous section according to Cicero, *l.c.*, with several temples and a gymnasium) was more than two miles from the centre of the city, or even on the plateau at all. The most that we can be said to know is that those who entered Dionysius' Hexapylon came to Tycha before they could reach the gates of Achradina (XXIV. xxi. 7). No clue is given as to the distance, nor does Thucydides even mention Tycha.

A further consequence of Fabricius's demonstration that no quarters of the city were on the plateau is the necessary reduction—a great reduction—in the area assigned to Achradina. Haverfield seems to have been the first to suggest that Achradina was merely " the lower ground between Ortygia and Epipolae " (*l.c.*). This view abandoned " upper Achradina " (a modern term), extending northward to the sea near Livy's Portus Trogilorum (Trogilos), and no opinion was expressed as to the situation of a northern wall for the diminished quarter. Probably Haverfield would have looked for such a line of defence just above the series of quarries (Q, Q on our map).

Fabricius accepts this reduction in principle, but brings the northern limit of Achradina still further south. For it is to the *north* of Achradina, and extending only as far as the quarries, that he finds a place for Tycha, thus made to adjoin Neapolis on the west. Both of these quarters directly adjoined Achradina, which Plutarch describes as " the strongest, most beautiful and largest part," adding that " it had been fortified on the side towards the

outer city, one part of which they call Neapolis, and another Tyche" (*Marcellus*, L.C.L., by Perrin, 18. 4).

This wall separating the quarters just named has been understood to mean the so-called "Wall of Gelon" (this unwarranted name only since 1839). But Fabricius (p. 14) has shown that it is not a wall; that it shows no signs of ever having been prolonged to north or south of its 700 metres; that it was, in fact, a quarry. Hence nothing survives to indicate that Achradina was vastly larger than the three other quarters, or that Tycha lay to the *west* of any part of it.

The new position assigned by the Danish scholar to Tycha, *i.e.* directly north of a much-diminished Achradina, has been accepted on our map, not without some hesitation. Difficulties remain in accounting for the complete disappearance both of the north wall of Tycha, perhaps just above the *latomie*, and of another more or less parallel wall, still stronger, which separated these two quarters from each other, at a distance of perhaps half a mile south of the quarries. But any other position for Tycha involves greater difficulties. Further studies will probably bring confirmation of the main proposition, and it must be at once granted that a long step in advance has been taken by Professor Fabricius.[1]

[1] Hochholzer's *Zur Geographie des antiken Syrakus* (*Klio*, 1936, pp. 164 ff.) agrees substantially with Fabricius, not without some confusion, and adds little to our purpose.

INDEX OF NAMES

(The References are to Pages)

ACERRAE, 54, 56 (*bis*); Acerrani, 56, 64
Achaia, 398
Achradina (Syracuse), 242, 244 (*bis*), 246, 248, 256, 278 (*bis*), 282 (*bis*), 434 (*bis*), 436 (*bis*), 440 (*bis*), 446, 454 (*bis*), 456 (*ter*), 458 (*ter*)
Aciliani annales, 492
Acrae, 288
Acrillae, 288
Acuca, 238
Adranodorus, 186, 188 (*bis*), 190, 194, 242 (*bis*), 244 (*ter*), 246, 248, 252 (*bis*), 254 (*ter*), 256, 258, 260
Aecae, 236
Aegates insulae, 40
Aelius Paetus, Q. (*pontifex*), 72
Aemilius, M. (*praetor*, 216 B.C.), 68, 74
Aemilius Lepidus, M. (*consul*, 232 B.C. *and about* 220), 102; his sons, *ibid.*; Aemilius Lepidus, M. (*praetor*, 213 B.C.), 314 (*bis*), 342, 346, 348, 384
Aemilius Papus, L. (*consul*, 225 B.C.; *censor*, 220 B.C.), 72 (*bis*), 76 (*bis*), 210
Aemilius Paulus, L. (*consul*, 219 *and* 216 B.C.), 72, 76, 154
Aemilius Regillus, M., 196, 198
Aequimaelium, 328
Aetoli, 430
Africa, 14, 16 (*bis*), 46, 70, 86, 102, 140 (*bis*), 156, 200 (*bis*), 290, 324, 328, 332 (*bis*), 340, 446 (*bis*), 448; Afri, 96 (*bis*); Afer, 498; collective, 98; Africanus (Scipio), 344
Agrigentum, 288 (*bis*), 300, 428, 448, 494, 496, 500
Albanus mons, 364
Alexandria, 32, 258
Allia, 360 (*bis*)
Alpes, 94, 114, 152
Amiternum, 316
Amtorgis, 462, 464
Anapus, 290
Anicius, M., 68
Anio, 198; Aniensis tribus, 196, 202
Antistius, L., 134
Apollo, 384, 386 (*ter*); Pythius, 32; ara Apollinis, 34; ludi Apollinares, 386
Apollonia, 302 (*bis*), 306; Apolloniates (-tae), 304 (*bis*)
Apollonides, 264
Apulia, 2, 76, 84, 86, 112, 114, 156, 158, 162, 184, 206, 208, 240, 316, 326, 346, 420, 500; Apuli, 34, 236, 420
Apustius, L., 132 (*bis*)
Archimedes, 282, 284, 286, 460
Ardaneae, 238
Arethusa fons, 456 (*bis*)
Argivus, 384, 436
Aricia, 316
Ariminum, 314
Aristo, 252
Aristomachus, 180 (*bis*), 184 (*bis*)
Arpi, 156, 184, 212 (*bis*), 318 (*bis*), 320, 322, 326, 396; Arpini, 324 (*quinquies*); praetor Arpinus, 324
Ascua, 90
Atellanus, 232
Athenienses, 436, 452
Atilius, C., 72; Atilius, L., 176; Atilius, M., 72
Atilius Regulus, M. (*consul*, 227 *and* 217 B.C.; *censor* 214 B.C.), 72, 210, 312 (*bis*); Atilius Regulus, M. (*praetor*, 213 B.C.), 314 (*bis*)
Atinius, M, 398 (*bis*), 400 (*bis*)
Atrinum, 326
Attalus, 430
Aurelius, C., 54
Aurelius Cotta, M. (*aedile*, 216 B.C.), 102, 424

INDEX OF NAMES

Aurinx, 310
Austicula, 134
Aventinus, 226
Averni lacus, 212 (*bis*), 238

BADIUS, 410 (*ter*), 412 (*bis*), 414 (*ter*)
Baliares insulae, 120, 138, 140
Bantius, L., 48
Barcina factio, 36; familia, 42; Barcinus, 464, 492
Beneventum, 212, 216, 224, 226, 232, 234, 388, 390 (*bis*), 392, 394, 396, 400 (*bis*), 402; Beneventani, 224, 388, 410; Beneventanus ager, 408, 414
Bigerra, 308
Blanda, 236
Blossius, Marius, 20, 22
Boii, 82
Bomilcar, 142 (*bis*), 290 (*bis*), 440, 444, 446 (*quater*), 448
Bostar, 116
Bovianum, 390
Brundisium, 112, 162, 206, 208, 214, 238, 302, 426; Brundisinus portus, 114
Bruttii, 34 (*bis*), 68, 70, 100 (*ter*), 130, 142, 146, 156, 174 (*quater*), 176, 178 (*bis*), 180 (*ter*), 182 (*bis*), 184 (*bis*), 204, 216, 218, 236, 340, 388, 394, 404; Bruttius (collective), 178, 220; ager Bruttius, 340

CAECILIUS METELLUS, M. (*tribune*, 214 B.C.), 228, 312; Caecilius Metellus, Q. (*consul*, 206 B.C.), 72
Caiatia, 46
Caieta (*possibly*), 316
Calabria, 116, 210, 302
Calavius, Pacuvius, 4, 8, 10, 22, 24; his son, 24
Cales, 104 (*bis*), 126, 206, 216, 320; Caleni legati, 320
Callo, 190
Calor, 216, 408, 410
Calpurnius Piso, C. (*praetor*, 211 B.C.), 500; Calpurnius Piso Frugi, L. (*historian*; *consul*, 133 B.C.), 492
Campania, 16, 36, 48, 56, 106, 114, 118, 174, 212, 390; Campani, 6, 12 (*et passim*); Campanus (collective), 426; ager Campanus, 2, 158, 162, 400, 410; civis, 18, 20; exercitus, 122; populus, 12, 106; praetor, 20; senatus, 120; defectio Campana, 410; luxuria, 152; res, 396; equites Campani, 106; castra Campana, 124
Canna amnis, 384 (*bis*)
Cannae, 14, 34, 40, 48, 60, 104, 144, 146, 148, 154 (*ter*), 164, 192, 202, 212, 228, 312, 314, 358 (*ter*), 362, 364, 376; Cannensis acies, 62, 360; clades, 12, 14, 56, 102, 104, 318, 356, 384, 404, 424, 484; exercitus, 104, 230, 360; fuga, 84; pugna, 2, 36, 58, 72, 228; ruina, 84; victoria, 498; Cannense proelium, 50
Canusium, 12
Capena porta, 110, 494
Capitolium, 74, 104, 106, 112, 204, 206, 342, 350, 364, 492
Capua, 4, 6, 18, 22, 28 (*bis*), 30 (*ter*), 32 (*bis*), 34, 44, 48, 56, 58, 60, 62 (*bis*), 114, 126 (*quater*), 134, 136, 148, 154 (*bis*), 158, 198, 210 (*bis*), 212 (*bis*), 234, 236, 326 (*bis*), 388 (*ter*), 390, 396 (*ter*), 400, 402, 414, 416 (*bis*), 418, 420, 424 (*quater*), 426 (*ter*), 428 (*bis*), 500 (*ter*)
Carales, 136, 138 (*bis*), 140
Carmentalis porta, 326, 364
Carthago, 16, 30, 34, 92 (*bis*), 110, 120, 138, 142, 146, 192 (*bis*), 200, 286, 396, 428, 444 (*bis*), 462; Carthaginienses, 38, 68, 84, 88, 94 (*bis*), 116, 128, 166, 174, 188, 206, 264 (*bis*), 286, 288, 290, 296, 298, 306, 308 (*bis*), 312, 326, 328 (*bis*), 330 (*bis*), 332 (*bis*), 348, 368 (*bis*), 398, 400, 436, 440, 444, 448, 450, 452, 466, 480, 496; Carthaginiensis (collective), 326; ager Carthaginiensis, 140; hostis, 330; imperator, 498; populus, 192, 196; Carthaginienses legiones, 332; nobiles, 138
Carthalo, 42 (*possibly*), 410
Carvilius, L. (*tribune*, 212 B.C.), 350, 352; Carvilius, Sp. (*tribune*, 212 B.C.), 350, 352
Carvilius Maximus, Sp. (*consul*, 293 and 272 B.C.), 204; Carvilius Maximus, Sp. (*consul*, 234 and 228 B.C.), 74
Casilinum, 46 (*bis*), 56 (*quater*), 58 (*ter*), 62, 64 (*ter*), 66, 68 (*bis*), 74, 216, 232, 234 (*quater*), 236 (*bis*), 418, 424
Castrum Album, 306

INDEX OF NAMES

Castulo, 308
Caudinae Furculae, 360; Caudinae legiones, 360
Caudini, v. Samnites
Celtiberi, 334 (*bis*), 462, 464 (*quater*)
Centenius Paenula, M., 416, 422
Ceres, 296
Chalbus, 88
Claudiana Castra, 104 (*bis*), 136, 162, 424
Claudius Asellus, 158 (*ter*), 160 (*ter*), 198
Claudius Cento, C. (*consul*, 240 B.C.; *censor*, 225), 344
Claudius Marcellus, M. (*consul*, 222, 214, 210, 208 B.C.), 44, 46, 48, 50 (*bis*), 52 (*bis*), 54 (*bis*), 64, 78, 84 (*bis*), 104 (*bis*), 106 (*quater*), 108 (*ter*), 136, 142, 144, 148 (*bis*), 218, 228, 234 (*ter*), 236, 238, 240, 262 (*bis*), 266, 268, 274, 282, 286, 288, 290 (*bis*), 294, 300 (*bis*), 312, 314, 348, 356 (*ter*), 358, 362, 364, 428, 430 (*bis*), 432, 434 (*bis*), 436 (*bis*), 438 (*ter*), 440 (*bis*), 442 (*bis*), 444, 446, 448 (*ter*), 452 (*bis*), 454, 456 (*quater*), 458 (*ter*), 460, 494 (*ter*), 498, 500; Claudius Marcellus, M. (*aedile* 216 B.C.), 102
Claudius Nero, C. (*consul*, 207 B.C.; *censor*, 204), 226 (*bis*), 228, 344, 346 (*bis*), 424
Claudius Pulcher, Ap. (*consul*, 212 B.C.), 6, 80, 104 (*bis*), 142 (*bis*), 178, 192, 196, 262 (*ter*), 266, 270, 280, 290, 300, 344, 346, 394, 416 (*ter*), 424, 500 (*bis*)
Claudius Quadrigarius, Q. (*historian*), 492
Coelius Antipater (*historian*), 18
Combulteria, 134
Cominium Ocritum, 394
Compsa, 2, 236
Concordia, temple of (Rome, *in arce*), 72; altar of (Syracuse), 244, 246
Conpulteria, 236
Consentia, 100; Consentini, 340
Cornelius Calussa, P. (*pontifex maximus before* 304 B.C.), 354
Cornelius Cethegus, M. (*censor*, 209 B.C.; *consul*, 204), 344 (*bis*), 354, 500
Cornelius Lentulus, Cn. (*consul*, 201 B.C.), 410, 414; Cornelius Lentulus, L. (*pontifex maximus*), 344; Cornelius Lentulus, L. *praetor*, 211 B.C.), 344, 500; Cornelius Lentulus, P. (*praetor*, 214 B.C.), 202, 206, 212, 316, 348, 356 (*bis*)
Cornelius Mammula, A. (*propraetor*, 216 B.C.), 70, 72, 110, 118
Cornelius Scipio Calvus, Cn. (*consul*, 222 B.C.), 86, 100, 162, 306, 308 (*ter*), 310, 328, 348, 464 (*bis*), 466, 472 (*bis*), 476 (*ter*), 478, 488
Cornelius Scipio, P. (*consul*, 218 B.C.), 86, 100, 162, 306, 308, 328, 348, 464 (*bis*), 466 (*bis*), 468, 470, 476, 478; Cornelius Scipio (Africanus), P. (*consul*, 205, 194 B.C.; *censor*, 199), 344
Cornelius Sulla, P. (*praetor*, 212 B.C.), 344, 346, 384, 396, 416, 424, 426, 500
Cornus, 136, 140
Cretenses, 272, 274
Crito, 134
Croto(n), 100, 178 (*ter*), 180 (*bis*), 182, 184; Crotoniatae (-tes), 182 (*bis*), 184
Cumae, 48, 124, 126 (*quater*), 130 (*ter*), 152, 162, 364; Cumani, 106, 120 (*bis*), 122 (*bis*); ager Cumanus, 126, 214, 416; res Cumana, 120; Cumanus senatus, 120
Cyrenae, 30

DAMARATA, 246, 256
Damippus, 430
Dasius Altinius, 318, 320, 322
Decius, v. Magius
Decius Mus, P. (*consul* IV, 295 B.C.), 204
Delphi, 32
Diana, 430
Dinomenes, 194 (*ter*), 248, 270
Diomedis campus, 384 (*bis*)
Dionysius, tyrant of Syracuse, 182, 188, 246

EPICYDES, 190, 194, 250, 252, 260, 262, 266 (*bis*), 268, 270, 272 (*ter*), 276, 278 (*bis*), 280 (*bis*), 288, 430 (*bis*), 432, 434, 436, 440 (*quater*), 442, 446, 448 (*quater*), 450 (*bis*), 452, 494, 496; Epicydes Sindon, 448
Epipolae (Syracuse), 432, 434
Erycina, v. Venus
Etruria, 396, 418, 424; Etruscus, 14

INDEX OF NAMES

Eurus, 446
Euryalus (Syracuse), 436, 438, 440

FABIUS BUTEO, M. (*consul*, 245 B.C.; *censor*, 241), 76
Fabius Maximus Rullus, Q. (*consul* V, 295 B.C.), 204
Fabius Maximus Verrucosus, Q, (*consul*, 233, 228, 215, 214, 209 B.C.; *dictator*, 217), 72, 74, 102 (*bis*), 106, 108, 112, 126, 128, 134 (*bis*), 136; 156, 196 (*bis*), 202, 204 (*bis*), 210, 212, 216, 232, 234 (*ter*), 236 (*bis*), 238, 312 (*bis*), 314, 318, 320, 418; his son Q. (*consul*, 213 B.C.), 202, 208, 212, 238, 312, 314, 316, 318, 322, 346
Fabius Pictor, Q. (*historian*), 32
Falerii, 318
Flaminius, C. (*consul*, 223, 217 B.C.; *censor*, 220), 44, 72, 76 (*bis*), 154, 210
Flavus, 402, 404, 406
Fonteius, Ti., 468, 476, 478
Fortuna (Praeneste), 68; (Rome), 328, 364
Fugifulae, 236
Fulvius Centumalus, Cn. (*consul*, 211 B.C.), 314 (*bis*), 326, 346, 500
Fulvius Flaccus, Cn. (*praetor*, 212 B.C.), 344, 346 (*bis*), 420 (*bis*), 422; Fulvius Flaccus, Q. (*consul*, 237, 224, 212, 209 B.C.), 72, 80, 104, 112, 118, 140, 164, 202, 344, 346, 350, 354, 390, 416, 424, 500
Fundanius Fundulus, M. (*aedile*, 213 B.C.), 346
Furculae Caudinae, 360
Furius Camillus, M. (*censor*, 403 B.C.; *dictator*, 396), 352
Furius Philus, P. (*consul*, 223 B.C.; *censor*, 214), 70, 210, 312 (*bis*), 344

GABII, 206
Gades, 332
Gaetuli, 58
Gala, 332 (*quater*)
Galaesus, 378
Galeagra turris, 430
Gallia, 80, 84, 208, 348; Galli, 80 (*ter*), 82 (*bis*), 242, 310 (*bis*), 374; Gallus, 198 (*bis*); Gallicus ager, 42, 206; Gallicum bellum, 84, 204; Gallica arma, 374; auxilia, 94; spolia, 44, 310
Gelo, 102, 188, 252 (*bis*) 256 (*bis*), 258
Gisgo, 116 (v. Hasdrubal)
Graecia, 116, 316, 348; Graeci, 252, 374; Graecus, 374; ritus, 386 (*bis*); sermo, 492; Graecum carmen, 32; Graeca urbs, 100, 178, 452; Graecae artes, 494
Grumentum, 130

HADRIA, 208
Hamae, 120, 124 (*bis*), 126 (*bis*)
Hamilcar, 174, 176
Hamilcar Barca, 34, 306, 462, 470
Hampsicora, 110, 136, 138 (*bis*), 140 (*ter*)
Hannibal, 2 (*bis*), 4 (*et passim*); is wife, 308; the son of Bomilcar, 166; another Hannibal, 190
Hanno (opponent of Hannibal), 36, 38, 42; a general, 130 (*bis*), 138 (*bis*), 142, 146, 148, 156, 174, 178, 182, 184, 216 (*bis*), 236, 340, 348, 388 (*ter*), 390, 392, 394 (*bis*), 398 (*bis*); another Hanno, 494, 496 (*bis*)
Harmonia, 252, 256
Hasdrubal (brother of Hannibal), 86, 88 (*bis*), 90 (*bis*), 92 (*ter*), 94 (*quinquies*), 96 (*bis*), 98 (*bis*), 100, 166 (*bis*), 306, 462 (*bis*), 464 (*bis*), 470, 492 (*ter*); the son of Gisgo, 306, 462, 464 (*bis*), 472, 478, 482; Hasdrubal Calvus, 112, 120, 138 (*ter*), 140
Hegeas, 4
Helorus, 286
Henna, 292, 296 (*bis*), 300 (*bis*); Hennenses, 292, 294, 296, 298, 300
Heraclea (Lucania), 358; ager Heracleensis, 240
Heraclea Minoa, 286, 288, 448, 496, 498
Heraclia, 256
Heraclitus, 134
Herbesus, 270, 272 (*bis*), 286
Herculis columnae, 14
Herdonea, 420, 426
Herennius Bassus, 148, 150
Herius, v. Pettius
Hexapylon (Syracuse), 242, 276, 278 (*bis*), 282, 300, 432 (*bis*), 434
Hibera, 94
Hiberus, 86, 92, 94 (*bis*), 306 (*bis*), 478 (*bis*)
Hiero II, king of Syracuse, 72, 102, 134

(*bis*), 184, 186, 188 (*ter*), 192, 242. 244, 246, 254, 256 (*ter*), 264, 286, 316, 348, 436, 440, 450, 452, 458
Hieronymus, do., 184, 188, 190, 192 (*ter*), 240, 244, 250, 254 (*quater*), 256, 258 (*ter*), 264, 272, 450, 452
Himera (the southern), 192, 496
Himilco, 36, 38 (*bis*), 40; another, 92; another, 100; another (a general) 286, 288 (*bis*), 290 (*ter*), 292, 298, 300, 428, 438, 440, 444
Hippacritanus, 496
Hippocrates, 190, 194, 250, 260, 262, 266 (*ter*), 268, 270, 272 (*ter*), 274 (*bis*), 276 (*bis*), 278, 280, 286 (*bis*), 288 (*bis*), 290, 300, 428, 438, 440 (*bis*), 442, 444 (*bis*), 450 (*bis*), 452, 496
Hirpini, 2, 130 (*bis*), 146; ager Hirpinus, 142, 146
Hispania, 42 (*bis*), 86, 92 (*quater*), 94, 98 (*ter*), 100, 102, 110 (*bis*), 112, 156, 162, 168, 306 (*bis*), 308, 312 (*bis*), 328, 330 (*bis*), 332 (*bis*), 334 (*bis*), 340, 454, 462 (*ter*), 464, 476 (*bis*), 492, 494; Hispaniae, 348, 476 (*bis*); Hispani, 96, 98 (*bis*), 156 (*bis*), 162, 212, 252, 306, 326 (*bis*), 334, 408, 454, 464; Hispanus, 454, 456; dux, 460; eques, 88; Hispaniensis exercitus, 94, 164
Hostus, 136, 140

IANICULUM, 208
Iliturgi(s), 166 (*bis*), 308 (*bis*)
Illyrii, 242
Indibilis, 468 (*bis*)
Insteius vicus, 206
Insula (Syracuse), 242, 244, 246 (*bis*), 248, 254 (*ter*), 434 (*bis*); v. Nasos
Intibili, 166
Ionium mare, 114
Isalcas, 58
Italia, 14, 16 (*et passim*); Italici, 46, 218, 324; Italicum nomen, 148
Iugarius vicus, 328
Iunius, D., 424
Iunius Pera, M. (*consul*, 230 B.C.; *dictator*, 216), 42, 108
Iunius Silanus, M. (*praetor*, 212 B.C.), 46, 344, 346 (*bis*), 418
Iuno Lacinia, temple of, 114, 116, 182; Sospita (Lanuvium), 108, 206
Iuppiter, 384; temple at Aricia; 316; Olympius, temples at and near Syracuse, 242, 280; Vicilinus, 316

LACEDAEMONII, 430
Lacinia, v. Iuno
Laetorius, C. (*aedile*, 216 B.C.), 102, 424
Lanuvium, 108, 206
Latini, 18, 74 (*bis*), 350; Latinus, 74; Latinum nomen, 40, 56, 74; Latinae (feriae), 382; Latinus sermo, 492
Latona, 386
Leon, 300
Leontini, 194, 240, 246, 248, 266 (*bis*), 268 (*bis*), 270 (*ter*), 274, 276 (*bis*), 278, 282 (*bis*), 300
Libertas, temple of, 226; atrium of, 366
Libyphoenices, 496
Licinius Crassus, P. (*consul*, 205 B.C.), 354
Lilybaeum, 70, 140, 462 (*bis*)
Litana silva, 80
Liternum, 122
Livius Macatus, M., 238
Livius Salinator, M. (*consul*, 219, 207 B.C.; *censor*, 204), 6
Locri, 142 (*bis*), 178 (*bis*), 184 (*bis*), 250, 268; Locrenses, 100, 142, 174, 176 (*bis*), 178 (*ter*), 184
Lucani, 34, 130 (*bis*), 218, 236 (*bis*), 316, 326, 340 (*bis*), 348 (*bis*), 402 (*quinquies*), 410, 416 (*bis*), 418; Lucanus (collective), 220; hospes, 408; populus, 204; proditor, 406; nomen Lucanum, 406; Lucani fines, 130
Luceria, 114, 130, 162, 184, 208, 212, 216, 238, 314, 346
Lutatius Catulus, C. (*consul*, 241 B.C.), 40

MACEDONIA, 116, 132, 214, 306, 316; Macedones, 114, 116, 118, 130, 206, 302; Macedonicum bellum, 132 (*ter*), 162, 164
Maecilius Croto, Ti., 104
Maesuli, 332
Magius, Cn., 232; Magius, Decius, 20 (*bis*), 22 (*bis*), 28, 30 (*bis*), 32
Mago, brother of Hannibal, 2, 34, 36, 38, 40 (*quater*), 110 (*bis*), 112 (*bis*); 166, 306, 310, 462, 464 (*bis*), 472, 492 (*bis*); a relative of Hannibal, 138; a general, 398 (*bis*), 404 (*bis*), 408, 410, 422; another, 116
Maharbal, 58

INDEX OF NAMES

Manlius Torquatus, T. (*consul*, 347 344, 340 B.C.), 198; Manlius Torquatus, T. (*consul*, 235, 224 B.C.; *censor*, 231), 74, 120, 136 (*bis*), 138 (*bis*), 140, 354
Manlius Volso, L. (*praetor*, 218 B.C.), 72
Mantua, 206
Marcelli, 452
Marcius, 382, 384; Marciana carmina, 382
Marcius Septimus, L., 476, 478, 480 (*bis*), 482, 492 (*bis*); Marcius clipeus, 492
Marius, v. Blossius
Marius Alfius, 124 (*bis*)
Marrucini, 208
Mars, 208; (= *proelium*), 330, 414
Masinissa, 332 (*bis*), 466
Matuta, temple of, 328, 364
Mauri, 16, 98, 220, 240; Maurus, 90
Maurusii, 332
Megara, 270, 272, 274 (*bis*), 286
Mens, temple of, 106, 112
Messana, 142 (*bis*), 176
Metapontum, 380, 396; Metapontini, 396 (*bis*); Metapontinus ager, 240
Metilius, M., 424
Mincius, 206
Minucius, M. (*tribune*, 216 B.C.), 72
Miseni promunturium, 214
Moeniacoeptus, 310
Moericus, 454, 456 (*ter*), 458
Mopsii, 2
Mucius Scaevola, Q. (*praetor*, 215 B.C.), 80, 104, 118, 120, 136, 206, 316, 348
Munda, 308
Murgantia, 262, 292, 296, 300
Muttines, 496 (*quater*), 498
Mylas, 270, 276

NAEVIUS CRISTA, Q., 304
Nasos (= Insula, Syracuse), 434, 454, 456 (*bis*), 458 (*bis*), 460
Neapolis, 2, 46 (*ter*), 48, 126, 158; Neapolitani, 2, 44, 46; ager Neapolitanus, 214, 226
Neapolis (quarter of Syracuse), 438 (*bis*)
Nico, 366 (*bis*), 372 (*bis*)
Ninnius Celer, Pacuvius, 22; Sthenius, *ibid.*
Nola, 46 (*bis*), 48 (*bis*), 50 (*bis*), 54, 108, 134, 136, 142, 144, 146 (*bis*), 148 (*ter*), 150 (*bis*), 152 (*bis*), 154, 156 (*bis*), 158, 162, 216 (*bis*), 226, 228, 234 (*quater*), 236, 238, 498; Nolani, 46, 52 (*ter*), 64, 150, 152, 156, 216; ager Nolanus, 44, 46, 152; civis, 48; populus, 150; senatores, 148; Nolana res, 46, 48; plebes, 50, 214; subsidia, 154
Nuceria, 46, 48, 50, 148, 150
Numidae, 4, 16, 42, 96 (*bis*), 98, 146, 156 (*bis*), 212, 218, 220, 240, 328 (*bis*), 330 (*ter*), 332, 370 (*bis*), 372, 408, 466, 468, 470, 472 (*bis*), 474, 496 (*bis*), 498 (*bis*); Numida eques, 88, 468
Numidia, 332

OCEANUS, 14, 332
Olympium (Syracuse), 280
Orbitanium, 236
Oricum, 302 (*ter*), 304, 306 (*bis*)
Ostia, 132, 418
Otacilius Crassus, T. (*praetor*, 217, 214 B.C.), 70, 72, 106, 112, 140, 196, 198, 200 (*ter*), 202 (*bis*), 206, 210, 212, 316, 348, 462

PACHYNUM PROMUNTURIUM, 262, 286 (*bis*), 290, 446 (*bis*)
Pacuvius, v. Calavius
Paeligni, 392; Paelignus, 394; Paeligna cohors, 392
Panormus, 290 (*bis*)
Papirius Cursor, L. (*consul* II, 295 B.C.), 204
Papirius Masso, C. (C.f., *pontifex*), 344 (*bis*); Papirius Masso, C. (L.f.), 344
Pedanius, T., 392, 394
Perusini, 68; Perusina cohors, 58
Petelia, 100 (*bis*); Petelini, 68 (*bis*), 70
Pettius, Herius, 148
Phileas, 366
Philemenus, 366, 368 (*bis*), 372 (*ter*)
Philippus, king of Macedonia, 114 (*bis*), 116 (*ter*), 118, 130, 132 (*bis*), 134, 162, 206, 214, 300, 302, 306, 430
Philistio, 448
Philodemus, 436, 440
Picenum, 208, 316, 346; Picenus ager, 42, 112, 206
Pinarius, L., 292, 294
Piscina publica, 110
Piso (*historian*), v. Calpurnius

INDEX OF NAMES

Poeni, 6 (*bis*), 18 (*et passim*); Poenus, 2, 4, 18, 20 (*et passim*); collective. 114, 362, etc.
Polyclitus, 448
Polyaenus, 244, 246
Pomponius Matho, M. (*praetor*, 216 B.C.), 78, 206, 226, 314
Pomponius Veientanus, T., 340, 348
Postumius, M., 348 (*bis*), 350, 352 (*ter*), 354
Postumius Albinus, A. (*consul*, 241 B.C.), 40; Postumius Albinus, L. (*consul*, 234, 229 B.C., *designate*, 216), 80 (*ter*), 82, 86, 106
Praeneste, 56, 66, 68; Praenestini 56, 58, 66, 68
Proserpina, 296, 300
Ptolomaeus IV Philopator, 32, 256
Punicus cultus, 118; exercitus, 166, 444, 474; mos, 24; Punica amicitia, 28; ars, 488; classis, 136, 138, 262, 440, 446 (*bis*); societas, 148; Punicum bellum, 40, 104, 132, 356; foedus, 22, 320; imperium, 192; nomen, 36; praesidium, 20, 216, 312, 326; Punicae naves, 380; Punica arma, 374; castra, 308, 310, 390, 408
Puteoli, 196, 212, 214, 418, 424
Pyrenaeus (mons), 152
Pyrgensis, 348, 352
Pyrrhus, 20, 142, 144, 180, 192, 318, 358

QUINCTIUS CRISPINUS, T. (*consul*, 208 B.C.), 300, 440, 442 (*bis*); Quinctius Crispinus, T., 410 (*bis*), 412 (*quinquies*), 414 (*bis*)
Quinctius Flamininus, L., 344
Quirinalis flamen, 198
Quirites, 346

REATE, 364
Regium, 174, 176 (*bis*), 178 (*bis*); Regini, 100
Roma, 6 (*et passim*); Romani, 2 (*et passim*); Romanus (collective), 114 (*bis*), 120, 220, 226, 310, 362, etc.; Romanus civis, 376; consul, 18; exercitus, 438, 444, 464; imperator, 330, 334, 404 (*bis*), 462, 470; miles, 360; mos, 330; populus, 28, 84, 106, 224 (*et passim*); praefectus, 298; praetor, 44; senatus, 68, 294 328; Romana acies, 96, 98, 146, 152, 414, 418 (*bis*); amicitia, 68, 450, 466; classis, 210, 290, 306, 440; cohors, 488; iustitia, 476; provincia, 266; res, 18, 36, 228, 318, 320, 404, 446; societas, 22, 28, 44, 102, 148, 188, 406; statio, 268; urbs, 96; Romanum agmen, 306; foedus, 24; imperium, 12, 16, 40, 110, 148, 316; nomen, 18, 276, 484; praesidium, 114 (*bis*), 214, 292 (*bis*), 294, 302, 308, 436, 458, 460 (*bis*); Romani di, 494; duces, 464, 466; fines, 18; Romanae legiones, 420; naves, 114, 430, 446; Romana castra, 308, 326, 408, 442, 444; hospitia, 376

SABINI, 206
Saguntum, 60, 312
Salapia, 240, 326
Salinae, 326
Sallentini, 340; Sallentinus ager, 162, 240, 340
Samnites, 34, 146, 204, 236; Samnites Caudini, 142, 236; Samnis, 14, 236; Samnis ager, 146; hostis, 14
Samnium, 2, 142, 360, 388 (*bis*)
Sardinia, 70 (*bis*), 104, 108, 110, 112, 118, 120 (*bis*), 136 (*bis*), 140 (*bis*), 164, 206, 208, 316, 348, 418, 424, 500; Sardi, 110, 120, 136, 138 (*quater*), 140; Sardi Pelliti, 136
Saticula, 14; ager Saticulanus, 46
Scantinius, P. (*pontifex*), 72
Scipiones (Cn. and P.), 100, 166, 480, 484
Scribonius Libo, L. (*tribune*, 216 B.C.), 72
Sempronius Gracchus, Ti. (*consul*, 215 *and* 213 B.C.), 64 (*ter*), 80, 84, 102 (*bis*), 104 (*bis*), 108, 112, 122 (*ter*), 124, 126 (*bis*), 128 (*bis*), 130, 162, 184, 206, 208, 212, 216, 218 (*bis*), 220 (*bis*), 222, 224, 226 (*ter*), 232, 234, 236 (*bis*), 312, 314, 340, 344, 362, 402, 404 (*ter*), 406 (*ter*), 408 (*ter*), 410, 420; Sempronianus exercitus, 414
Sempronius Longus, Ti. (*consul*, 218 B.C.), 130
Sempronius Tuditanus, P. (*censor*, 209 B.C.; *consul*, 204), 314 (*ter*), 326, 348
Servilius Caepio, Cn. (*consul*, 203 B.C.), 344

INDEX OF NAMES

Servilius Casca, C. (*tribune*, 212 B.C.), 350 (*ter*)
Servilius Geminus, C. (*consul*, 203 B.C.), 396
Sicilia, 18, 70, 84, 86, 102 (*ter*), 104 (*quater*), 106, 108 (*bis*), 112 (*bis*), 132, 164, 182, 184, 192 (*ter*), 196, 206, 208 (*bis*), 210, 212, 230, 240, 250, 258, 262, 266, 268, 286, 288 (*bis*), 290, 300 (*ter*), 344, 348, 356 (*bis*), 362, 446, 448, 450, 494, 496, 500 (*bis*); Siculi, 288, 290, 292, 294, 300, 358, 444 (*bis*), 448 (*ter*); Siculus exercitus, 446; Siculae urbes, 12
Sicilinum, 130
Sidicinus hostis, 14
Sinuessa, 108, 112, 122
Sopater, 248, 254
Sosis, 240, 242, 248, 270, 436
Sositheus, 134
Sospita, v. Iuno
Spes, temple of, 364
Spoletium 208
Statius, v. Trebius
Statius Metius, 232
Statorius, Q., 330 (*bis*)
Suessetani, 468
Suessula, 46, 56, 104, 108, 136, 158, 162, 216, 226, 314, 316, 322, 326, 346, 364, 424
Sulpicius, C. (*praetor*, 211 B.C.), 500 (*bis*)
Sulpicius Galba, P. (*consul*, 211 *and* 200 B.C.), 500.
Syphax, 328, 330, 332 (*quinquies*)
Syracusae, 186, 192, 194, 242, 248, 250 (*bis*), 252, 258 (*bis*), 262 (*ter*), 266 (*bis*), 274 (*quater*), 276 (*bis*), 278 (*ter*), 280, 282 (*bis*), 286, 288, 290 (*quinquies*), 300, 348, 362, 428 (*ter*), 430, 444 (*bis*), 446, 448, 450 (*ter*), 452 (*bis*), 458 (*bis*), 460 (*bis*), 462 (*bis*), 494 (*quater*), 500; Syracusani, 188, 240, 244, 262, 264, 268 (*quater*), 270, 272, 274, 280 (*bis*), 286, 436, 440, 446, 450, 452, 454, 458 (*bis*), 460 (*ter*); Syracusanus dux, 496; exercitus, 288; portus, 440; tyrannus; 192; Syracusana res, 280, 440; Syracusanum regnum, 192; Syracusani milites, 274; praetores, 274; transfugae, 428; Syracusana consilia, 196; moenia, 460

TARENTUM, 112 (*bis*), 132 (*ter*), 134, 212, 214 (*ter*), 228, 238 (*bis*), 370 (*quater*), 382, 386, 396 (*bis*), 426, 448; Tarentini, 20, 214, 238, 340, 364, 366, 368, 374, 376 (*quater*), 378, 380, 382; Tarentinus ager, 238, 240; populus, 204; portus; 114, 396; Tarentina arx, 396 (*bis*); iuventus, 212; res, 214; Tarentini duces, 374; iuvenes, 366, 374; obsides, 366; principes, 380
Tarracina, 316, 366
Tartesii, 88 (*bis*)
Tauriani, 340
Teanum, 80, 108
Telesia, 236
Temenitis porta (Tarentum), 372
Terentius Varro, C. (*consul*, 216 B.C.), 76, 84, 86, 112 (*bis*), 206, 208, 316, 346; exercitus Terentianus, 112; milites Varroniani, 132
Themistus, 252 (*ter*), 254, 256, 260
Theodotus, 190 (*ter*), 240, 242, 248
Thraso, 188 (*bis*), 190 (*ter*)
Thurii, 398, Thurini, 366, 396, 398 (*bis*); Thurinus ager, 398; iuventus Thurina, 398
Tiberis, 204
Tifata, 126 (*bis*), 130, 136, 146, 212
Trasumennus, 4, 60, 146, 154, 164, 202, 212, 272, 376
Trebia, 60, 146, 154
Trebianus ager, 46
Trebius, 2 (*ter*)
Trebula, 134
Trogilorum portus, 430
Troiugena, 384
Turdetani, 312
Tusci, 346
Tycha (Syracuse), 242, 438 (*bis*)

UTICA, 462 (*bis*)

VACUNA, 206
Valerius Antias (*historian*), 492; Valerius Antias, L., 118
Valerius Corvus, M. (*consul* VI, 299 B.C.), 198
Valerius Flaccus, 392; Valerius Flaccus, P., 54, 116, 132 (*bis*), 302
Valerius Laevinus, M. (*consul*, 210 B.C.), 80, 104, 108, 112, 114, 118, 130, 132, 162, 206, 208, 238, 302 (*bis*), 306, 316, 348
Veii, 360

INDEX OF NAMES

Venus Erycina, temple of, 102, 106
Venusia, 12, 360
Vercellium, 130
Vescellium, 130
Veteres campi, 408
Vibellius Taurea, Cerrinus, 24, 158 (*bis*), 160 (*ter*), 198
Vibius Accaus, 392, 394
Vibius Virrius, 16 (*bis*)
Victoriae mons, 306
Villius Tappulus, L. (*aedile*, 213 B.C.), 346
Vismarus, 310
Volcanus, 156, 206
Volturnus, 46, 58, 64, 122, 126, 134, 216, 418, 424

XENOPHANES, 114 (*bis*), 116

ZOIPPUS, 186, 188, 256, 258

PRINTED IN GREAT BRITAIN BY
FLETCHER & SON LTD, NORWICH

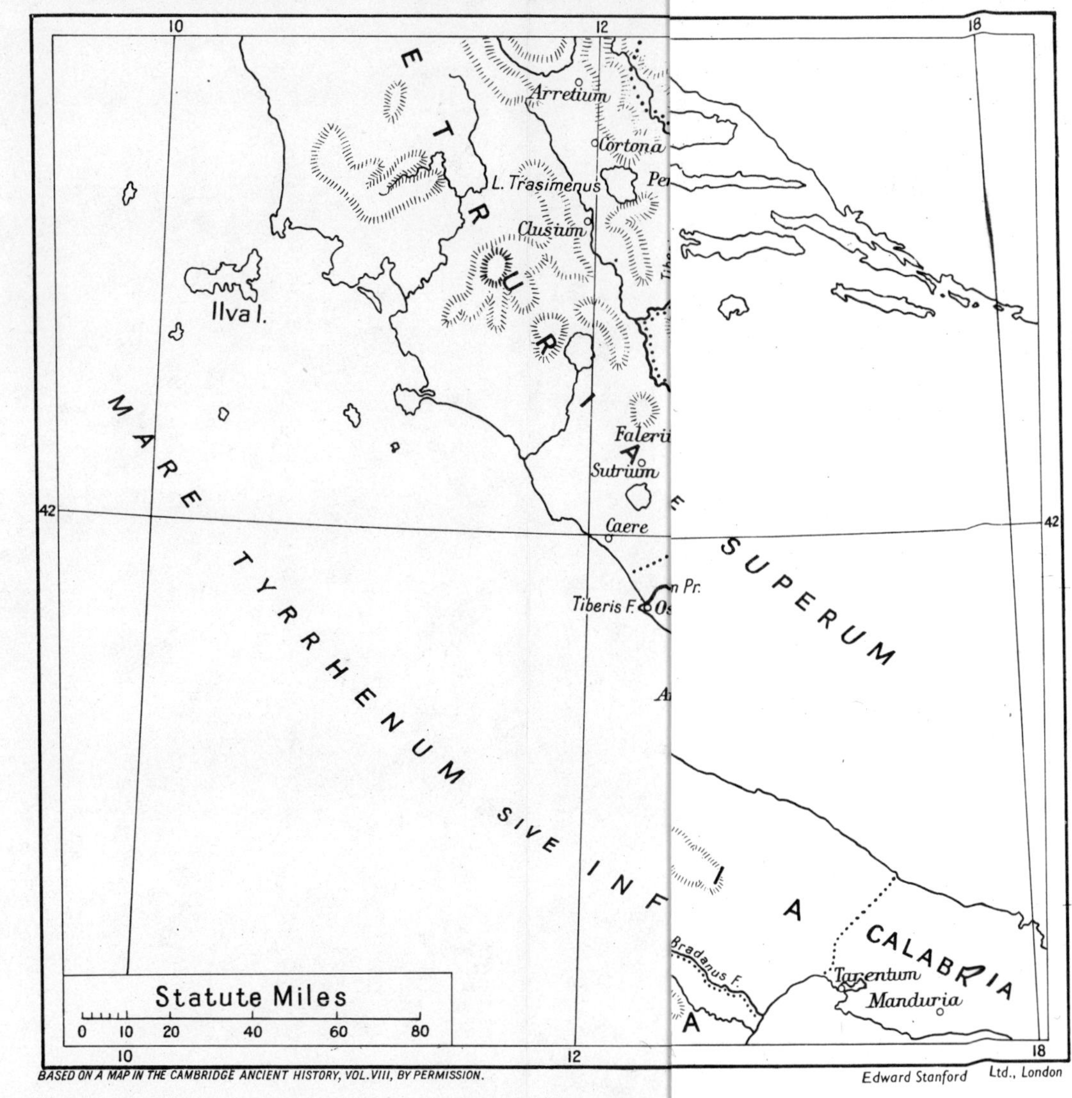
ETRURIA
Arretium
Cortona
L. Trasimenus
Clusium
Ilva I.
Falerii
Sutrium
Caere
Tiberis F.
MARE TYRRHENUM SIVE INF
SUPERUM
CALABRIA
Tarentum
Manduria
Bradanus F.
Statute Miles
0 10 20 40 60 80
10
12
18
42
BASED ON A MAP IN THE CAMBRIDGE ANCIENT HISTORY, VOL. VIII, BY PERMISSION.
Edward Stanford Ltd., London

Minucius Felix. Cf. Tertullian.

Nepos Cornelius. J. C. Rolfe.

Ovid: The Art of Love and Other Poems. J. H. Mosley. Revised by G. P. Goold.

Ovid: Fasti. Sir James G. Frazer

Ovid: Heroides and Amores. Grant Showerman. Revised by G. P. Goold

Ovid: Metamorphoses. F. J. Miller. 2 Vols. Revised by G. P. Goold.

Ovid: Tristia and Ex Ponto. A. L. Wheeler.

Persius. Cf. Juvenal.

Pervigilium Veneris. Cf. Catullus.

Petronius. M. Heseltine. Seneca: Apocolocyntosis. W. H. D. Rouse. Revised by E. H. Warmington.

Phaedrus and Babrius (Greek). B. E. Perry.

Plautus. Paul Nixon. 5 Vols.

Pliny: Letters, Panegyricus. Betty Radice. 2 Vols.

Pliny: Natural History. 10 Vols. Vols. I–V and IX. H. Rackham. VI.–VIII. W. H. S. Jones. X. D. E. Eichholz.

Propertius. H. E. Butler.

Prudentius. H. J. Thomson. 2 Vols.

Quintilian. H. E. Butler. 4 Vols.

Remains of Old Latin. E. H. Warmington. 4 Vols. Vol. I. (Ennius and Caecilius) Vol. II. (Livius, Naevius Pacuvius, Accius) Vol. III. (Lucilius and Laws of XII Tables) Vol. IV. (Archaic Inscriptions)

Res Gestae Divi Augusti. Cf. Velleius Paterculus.

Sallust. J. C. Rolfe.

Scriptores Historiae Augustae. D. Magie. 3 Vols.

Seneca, The Elder: Controversiae, Suasoriae. M. Winterbottom. 2 Vols.

Seneca: Apocolocyntosis. Cf. Petronius.

Seneca: Epistulae Morales. R. M. Gummere. 3 Vols.

Seneca: Moral Essays. J. W. Basore. 3 Vols.

Seneca: Tragedies. F. J. Miller. 2 Vols.

Seneca: Naturales Quaestiones. T. H. Corcoran. 2 Vols.

Sidonius: Poems and Letters. W. B. Anderson. 2 Vols.

Silius Italicus. J. D. Duff. 2 Vols.

Statius. J. H. Mozley. 2 Vols.

Suetonius. J. C. Rolfe. 2 Vols.

Tacitus: Dialogus. Sir Wm. Peterson. Agricola and Germania. Maurice Hutton. Revised by M. Winterbottom, R. M. Ogilvie, E. H. Warmington.

Tacitus: Histories and Annals. C. H. Moore and J. Jackson. 4 Vols.

TERENCE. John Sargeaunt. 2 Vols.

TERTULLIAN: APOLOGIA and DE SPECTACULIS. T. R. Glover. MINUCIUS FELIX. G. H. Rendall.

TIBULLUS. Cf. CATULLUS.

VALERIUS FLACCUS. J. H. Mozley.

VARRO: DE LINGUA LATINA. R. G. Kent. 2 Vols.

VELLEIUS PATERCULUS and RES GESTAE DIVI AUGUSTI. F. W. Shipley.

VIRGIL. H. R. Fairclough. 2 Vols.

VITRUVIUS: DE ARCHITECTURA. F. Granger. 2 Vols.

Greek Authors

ACHILLES TATIUS. S. Gaselee.

AELIAN: ON THE NATURE OF ANIMALS. A. F. Scholfield. 3 Vols.

AENEAS TACTICUS. ASCLEPIODOTUS and ONASANDER. The Illinois Greek Club.

AESCHINES. C. D. Adams.

AESCHYLUS. H. Weir Smyth. 2 Vols.

ALCIPHRON, AELIAN, PHILOSTRATUS: LETTERS. A. R. Benner and F. H. Fobes.

ANDOCIDES, ANTIPHON. Cf. MINOR ATTIC ORATORS.

APOLLODORUS. Sir James G. Frazer. 2 Vols.

APOLLONIUS RHODIUS. R. C. Seaton.

APOSTOLIC FATHERS. Kirsopp Lake. 2 Vols.

APPIAN: ROMAN HISTORY. Horace White. 4 Vols.

ARATUS. Cf. CALLIMACHUS.

ARISTIDES: ORATIONS. C. A. Behr. Vol. I.

ARISTOPHANES. Benjamin Bickley Rogers. 3 Vols. Verse trans.

ARISTOTLE: ART OF RHETORIC. J. H. Freese.

ARISTOTLE: ATHENIAN CONSTITUTION, EUDEMIAN ETHICS, VICES AND VIRTUES. H. Rackham.

ARISTOTLE: GENERATION OF ANIMALS. A. L. Peck.

ARISTOTLE: HISTORIA ANIMALIUM. A. L. Peck. Vols. I.–II.

ARISTOTLE: METAPHYSICS. H. Tredennick. 2 Vols.

ARISTOTLE: METEOROLOGICA. H. D. P. Lee.

ARISTOTLE: MINOR WORKS. W. S. Hett. On Colours, On Things Heard, On Physiognomies, On Plants, On Marvellous Things Heard, Mechanical Problems, On Indivisible Lines, On Situations and Names of Winds, On Melissus, Xenophanes, and Gorgias.

ARISTOTLE: NICOMACHEAN ETHICS. H. Rackham.

Aristotle: Oeconomica and Magna Moralia. G. C. Armstrong (with Metaphysics, Vol. II).

Aristotle: On the Heavens. W. K. C. Guthrie.

Aristotle: On the Soul, Parva Naturalia, On Breath. W. S. Hett.

Aristotle: Categories, On Interpretation, Prior Analytics. H. P. Cooke and H. Tredennick.

Aristotle: Posterior Analytics, Topics. H. Tredennick and E. S. Forster.

Aristotle: On Sophistical Refutations.
On Coming to be and Passing Away, On the Cosmos. E. S. Forster and D. J. Furley.

Aristotle: Parts of Animals. A. L. Peck; Motion and Progression of Animals. E. S. Forster.

Aristotle: Physics. Rev. P. Wicksteed and F. M. Cornford. 2 Vols.

Aristotle: Poetics and Longinus. W. Hamilton Fyfe; Demetrius on Style. W. Rhys Roberts.

Aristotle: Politics. H. Rackham.

Aristotle: Problems. W. S. Hett. 2 Vols.

Aristotle: Rhetorica Ad Alexandrum (with Problems. Vol. II). H. Rackham.

Arrian: History of Alexander and Indica. Rev. E. Iliffe Robson. 2 Vols. New version P. Brunt.

Athenaeus: Deipnosophistae. C. B. Gulick. 7 Vols.

Babrius and Phaedrus (Latin). B. E. Perry.

St. Basil: Letters. R. J. Deferrari. 4 Vols.

Callimachus: Fragments. C. A. Trypanis. Musaeus: Hero and Leander. T. Gelzer and C. Whitman.

Callimachus, Hymns and Epigrams, and Lycophron. A. W. Mair; Aratus. G. R. Mair.

Clement of Alexandria. Rev. G. W. Butterworth.

Colluthus. Cf. Oppian.

Daphnis and Chloe. Thornley's Translation revised by J. M. Edmonds: and Parthenius. S. Gaselee.

Demosthenes I.: Olynthiacs, Philippics and Minor Orations I.–XVII. and XX. J. H. Vince.

Demosthenes II.: De Corona and De Falsa Legatione. C. A. Vince and J. H. Vince.

Demosthenes III.: Meidias, Androtion, Aristocrates, Timocrates and Aristogeiton I. and II. J. H. Vince.

Demosthenes IV.–VI: Private Orations and In Neaeram. A. T. Murray.

Demosthenes VII: Funeral Speech, Erotic Essay, Exordia and Letters. N. W. and N. J. DeWitt.

Dio Cassius: Roman History. E. Cary. 9 Vols.

Dio Chrysostom. J. W. Cohoon and H. Lamar Crosby. 5 Vols.

Diodorus Siculus. 12 Vols. Vols. I.–VI. C. H. Oldfather. Vol. VII. C. L. Sherman. Vol. VIII. C. B. Welles. Vols. IX. and X. R. M. Geer. Vol. XI. F. Walton. Vol. XII. F. Walton. General Index. R. M. Geer.

Diogenes Laertius. R. D. Hicks. 2 Vols. New Introduction by H. S. Long.

Dionysius of Halicarnassus: Roman Antiquities. Spelman's translation revised by E. Cary. 7 Vols.

Dionysius of Halicarnassus: Critical Essays. S. Usher. 2 Vols. Vol. I.

Epictetus. W. A. Oldfather. 2 Vols.

Euripides. A. S. Way. 4 Vols. Verse trans.

Eusebius: Ecclesiastical History. Kirsopp Lake and J. E. L. Oulton. 2 Vols.

Galen: On the Natural Faculties. A. J. Brock.

Greek Anthology. W. R. Paton. 5 Vols.

Greek Bucolic Poets (Theocritus, Bion, Moschus). J. M. Edmonds.

Greek Elegy and Iambus with the Anacreontea. J. M. Edmonds. 2 Vols.

Greek Lyric. D. A. Campbell. 4 Vols. Vol. I.

Greek Mathematical Works. Ivor Thomas. 2 Vols.

Herodes. Cf. Theophrastus: Characters.

Herodian. C. R. Whittaker. 2 Vols.

Herodotus. A. D. Godley. 4 Vols.

Hesiod and The Homeric Hymns. H. G. Evelyn White.

Hippocrates and the Fragments of Heracleitus. W. H. S. Jones and E. T. Withington. 4 Vols.

Homer: Iliad. A. T. Murray. 2 Vols.

Homer: Odyssey. A. T. Murray. 2 Vols.

Isaeus. E. W. Forster.

Isocrates. George Norlin and LaRue Van Hook. 3 Vols.

[St. John Damascene]: Barlaam and Ioasaph. Rev. G. R. Woodward, Harold Mattingly and D. M. Lang.

Josephus. 10 Vols. Vols. I.–IV. H. Thackeray. Vol. V. H. Thackeray and R. Marcus. Vols. VI.–VII. R. Marcus. Vol. VIII. R. Marcus and Allen Wikgren. Vols. IX.–X. L. H. Feldman.

Julian. Wilmer Cave Wright. 3 Vols.

Libanius. A. F. Norman. 3 Vols. Vols. I.–II.

Lucian. 8 Vols. Vols. I.–V. A. M. Harmon. Vol. VI. K. Kilburn. Vols. VII.–VIII. M. D. Macleod.

Lycophron. Cf. Callimachus.

Lyra Graeca, J. M. Edmonds. 2 Vols.

Lysias. W. R. M. Lamb.

Manetho. W. G. Waddell.

Marcus Aurelius. C. R. Haines.

Menander. W. G. Arnott. 3 Vols. Vol. I.

Minor Attic Orators (Antiphon, Andocides, Lycurgus, Demades, Dinarchus, Hyperides). K. J. Maidment and J. O. Burtt. 2 Vols.

Musaeus: Hero and Leander. Cf. Callimachus.

Nonnos: Dionysiaca. W. H. D. Rouse. 3 Vols.

Oppian, Colluthus, Tryphiodorus. A. W. Mair.

Papyri. Non-Literary Selections. A. S. Hunt and C. C. Edgar. 2 Vols. Literary Selections (Poetry). D. L. Page.

Parthenius. Cf. Daphnis and Chloe.

Pausanias: Description of Greece. W. H. S. Jones. 4 Vols. and Companion Vol. arranged by R. E. Wycherley.

Philo. 10 Vols. Vols. I.–V. F. H. Colson and Rev. G. H. Whitaker. Vols. VI.–IX. F. H. Colson. Vol. X. F. H. Colson and the Rev. J. W. Earp.

Philo: two supplementary Vols. (*Translation only.*) Ralph Marcus.

Philostratus: The Life of Apollonius of Tyana. F. C. Conybeare. 2 Vols.

Philostratus: Imagines; Callistratus: Descriptions. A. Fairbanks.

Philostratus and Eunapius: Lives of the Sophists. Wilmer Cave Wright.

Pindar. Sir J. E. Sandys.

Plato: Charmides, Alcibiades, Hipparchus, The Lovers, Theages, Minos and Epinomis. W. R. M. Lamb.

Plato: Cratylus, Parmenides, Greater Hippias, Lesser Hippias. H. N. Fowler.

Plato: Euthyphro, Apology, Crito, Phaedo, Phaedrus, H. N. Fowler.

Plato: Laches, Protagoras, Meno, Euthydemus. W. R. M. Lamb.

Plato: Laws. Rev. R. G. Bury. 2 Vols.

Plato: Lysis, Symposium, Gorgias. W. R. M. Lamb.

Plato: Republic. Paul Shorey. 2 Vols.

Plato: Statesman, Philebus. H. N. Fowler; Ion. W. R. M. Lamb.

Plato: Theaetetus and Sophist. H. N. Fowler.

Plato: Timaeus, Critias, Clitopho, Menexenus, Epistulae. Rev. R. G. Bury.

Plotinus: A. H. Armstrong. 7 Vols. Vols. I.–V.

PLUTARCH: MORALIA. 16 Vols. Vols I.–V. F. C. Babbitt. Vol. VI. W. C. Helmbold. Vols. VII. and XIV. P. H. De Lacy and B. Einarson. Vol. VIII. P. A. Clement and H. B. Hoffleit. Vol. IX. E. L. Minar, Jr., F. H. Sandbach, W. C. Helmbold. Vol. X. H. N. Fowler. Vol. XI. L. Pearson and F. H. Sandbach. Vol. XII. H. Cherniss and W. C. Helmbold. Vol. XIII 1–2. H. Cherniss. Vol. XV. F. H. Sandbach.

PLUTARCH: THE PARALLEL LIVES. B. Perrin. 11 Vols.

POLYBIUS. W. R. Paton. 6 Vols.

PROCOPIUS. H. B. Dewing. 7 Vols.

PTOLEMY: TETRABIBLOS. F. E. Robbins.

QUINTUS SMYRNAEUS. A. S. Way. Verse trans.

SEXTUS EMPIRICUS. Rev. R. G. Bury. 4 Vols.

SOPHOCLES. F. Storr. 2 Vols. Verse trans.

STRABO: GEOGRAPHY. Horace L. Jones. 8 Vols.

THEOCRITUS. Cf. GREEK BUCOLIC POETS.

THEOPHRASTUS: CHARACTERS. J. M. Edmonds. HERODES, etc. A. D. Knox.

THEOPHRASTUS: ENQUIRY INTO PLANTS. Sir Arthur Hort, Bart. 2 Vols.

THEOPHRASTUS: DE CAUSIS PLANTARUM. G. K. K. Link and B. Einarson. 3 Vols. Vol. I.

THUCYDIDES. C. F. Smith. 4 Vols.

TRYPHIODORUS. Cf. OPPIAN.

XENOPHON: CYROPAEDIA. Walter Miller. 2 Vols.

XENOPHON: HELLENCIA. C. L. Brownson. 2 Vols.

XENOPHON: ANABASIS. C. L. Brownson.

XENOPHON: MEMORABILIA AND OECONOMICUS. E. C. Marchant. SYMPOSIUM AND APOLOGY. O. J. Todd.

XENOPHON: SCRIPTA MINORA. E. C. Marchant. CONSTITUTION OF THE ATHENIANS. G. W. Bowersock.